CSWE's Core Competencies and Practice Behavior Examp

D1027557

Competency

Professional Identity

Practice Behavior Examples...

Serve as representatives of the profession, its mission, and its core values	3–11
Know the profession's history	
Commit themselves to the profession's enhancement and to their own professional conduct and growth	1, 4, 5
Advocate for client access to the services of social work	5–11
Practice personal reflection and self-correction to assure continual professional development	4–11
Attend to professional roles and boundaries	6,7,8
Demonstrate professional demeanor in behavior, appearance, and communication	7
Engage in career-long learning	1, 3–11
Use supervision and consultation	3, 6–11

Ethical Practice

Practice Behavior Examples...

Obligation to conduct themselves ethically and engage in ethical decision making	1, 3, 4
Know about the value base of the profession, its ethical standards, and relevant law	1, 3, 4, 6–11
Recognize and manage personal values in a way that allows professional values to guide practice	4, 6–11
Make ethical decisions by applying standards of the National Association of Social Workers Code of Ethics and, as applicable, of the International Federation of Social Workers/International Association of Schools of Social Work Ethics in Social Work, Statement of Principles	1, 3–11
Tolerate ambiguity in resolving ethical conflicts	1–11
Apply strategies of ethical reasoning to arrive at principled decisions	1–11

Critical Thinking

Practice Behavior Examples...

Know about the principles of logic, scientific inquiry, and reasoned discernment	1,2,5
Use critical thinking augmented by creativity and curiosity	2–11
Requires the synthesis and communication of relevant information	1, 3, 5–11
Distinguish, appraise, and integrate multiple sources of knowledge, including research-based knowledge, and practice wisdom	1–11
Analyze models of assessment, prevention, intervention, and evaluation	
Demonstrate effective oral and written communication in working with individuals, families, groups, organizations, communities, and colleagues	1, 5–11

CSWE's Core Competencies and Practice Behavior Examples in this Text

Competency	Chapter
Diversity in Practice	
Practice Behavior Examples...	
Understand how diversity characterizes and shapes the human experience and is critical to the formation of identity	4, 6–11
Understand the dimensions of diversity as the intersectionality of multiple factors including age, class, color, culture, disability, ethnicity, gender, gender identity and expression, immigration status, political ideology, race, religion, sex, and sexual orientation	4–11
Appreciate that, as a consequence of difference, a person's life experiences may include oppression, poverty, marginalization, and alienation as well as privilege, power, and acclaim	4–11
Recognize the extent to which a culture's structures and values may oppress, marginalize, alienate, or create or enhance privilege and power	4–11
Gain sufficient self-awareness to eliminate the influence of personal biases and values in working with diverse groups	4–11
Recognize and communicate their understanding of the importance of difference in shaping life experiences	6, 8
View themselves as learners and engage those with whom they work as informants	4, 6–11
Human Rights & Justice	
Practice Behavior Examples...	
Understand that each person, regardless of position in society, has basic human rights, such as freedom, safety, privacy, an adequate standard of living, health care, and education	2, 3, 4, 6–11
Recognize the global interconnections of oppression and are knowledgeable about theories of justice and strategies to promote human and civil rights	
Incorporates social justice practices in organizations, institutions, and society to ensure that these basic human rights are distributed equitably and without prejudice	2, 3, 5–11
Understand the forms and mechanisms of oppression and discrimination	
Advocate for human rights and social and economic justice	3, 4, 5
Engage in practices that advance social and economic justice	4, 6–11
Research-Based Practice	
Practice Behavior Examples...	
Use practice experience to inform research, employ evidence-based interventions, evaluate their own practice, and use research findings to improve practice, policy, and social service delivery	4, 6–11
Comprehend quantitative and qualitative research and understand scientific and ethical approaches to building knowledge	
Use practice experience to inform scientific inquiry	1, 5–11
Use research evidence to inform practice	1, 4–11

CSWE's Core Competencies and Practice Behavior Examples in this Text

Competency	Chapter
Human Behavior	
Practice Behavior Examples...	
Know about human behavior across the life course; the range of social systems in which people live; and the ways social systems promote or deter people in maintaining or achieving health and well-being	4–11
Apply theories and knowledge from the liberal arts to understand biological, social, cultural, psychological, and spiritual development	5–11
Utilize conceptual frameworks to guide the processes of assessment, intervention, and evaluation	6–11
Critique and apply knowledge to understand person and environment	4–11
Policy Practice	
Practice Behavior Examples...	
Understand that policy affects service delivery and they actively engage in policy practice	5, 6
Know the history and current structures of social policies and services; the role of policy in service delivery; and the role of practice in policy development	
Analyze, formulate, and advocate for policies that advance social well-being	3–11
Collaborate with colleagues and clients for effective policy action	3, 6–11
Practice Contexts	
Practice Behavior Examples...	
Keep informed, resourceful, and proactive in responding to evolving organizational, community, and societal contexts at all levels of practice	6–11
Recognize that the context of practice is dynamic, and use knowledge and skill to respond proactively	4, 6–11
Continuously discover, appraise, and attend to changing locales, populations, scientific and technological developments, and emerging societal trends to provide relevant services	6–11
Provide leadership in promoting sustainable changes in service delivery and practice to improve the quality of social services	

CSWE's Core Competencies and Practice Behavior Examples in this Text

Competency	Chapter
Engage, Assess, Intervene, Evaluate	
Practice Behavior Examples...	
Identify, analyze, and implement evidence-based interventions designed to achieve client goals	1, 6–11
Use research and technological advances	1, 6–11
Evaluate program outcomes and practice effectiveness	
Develop, analyze, advocate, and provide leadership for policies and services	
Promote social and economic justice	5–11
A) ENGAGEMENT	
Substantively and effectively prepare for action with individuals, families, groups, organizations, and communities	6–11
Use empathy and other interpersonal skills	6–11
Develop a mutually agreed-on focus of work and desired outcomes	5–11
B) ASSESSMENT	
Collect, organize, and interpret client data	1, 3, 6–11
Assess client strengths and limitations	6, 8–10
Develop mutually agreed-on intervention goals and objectives	6–11
Select appropriate intervention strategies	6–11
C) INTERVENTION	
Initiate actions to achieve organizational goals	6–11
Implement prevention interventions that enhance client capacities	6–11
Help clients resolve problems	6–11
Negotiate, mediate, and advocate for clients	6–11
Facilitate transitions and endings	
D) EVALUATION	
Critically analyze, monitor, and evaluate interventions	

FOURTH EDITION

From the Front Lines

Student Cases in Social Work Ethics

Juliet C. Rothman
University of California, Berkeley

PEARSON

Boston Columbus Indianapolis New York San Francisco Upper Saddle River
Amsterdam Cape Town Dubai London Madrid Milan Munich Paris Montréal Toronto
Delhi Mexico City São Paulo Sydney Hong Kong Seoul Singapore Taipei Tokyo

Editorial Director: Craig Campanella
Editor in Chief: Ashley Dodge
Editorial Product Manager: Carly Czech
Editorial Assistant: Nicole Suddeth
Vice President/Director of Marketing: Brandy Dawson
Executive Marketing Manager: Kelly May
Marketing Coordinator: Courtney Stewart
Digital Media Editor: Paul DeLuca
Project Manager: Pat Brown

Manufacturing Buyer: Pat Brown
Creative Director: Jayne Conte
Cover Designer: Karen Noferi
Editorial Production and Composition Service: Abinaya Rajendran, Integra Software Services Pvt. Ltd.
Interior Design: Joyce Weston Design
Cover image: Fotolia
Printer/Binder: Edwards Brothers Malloy

Credits and acknowledgments borrowed from other sources and reproduced, with permission, in this textbook appear on the appropriate page within text.

Library of Congress Cataloging-in-Publication Data
Rothman, Juliet Cassuto
   From the front lines: student cases in social work ethics/Juliet C. Rothman, University of California, Berkeley.
      pages cm
   Includes bibliographical references.
   ISBN-13: 978-0-205-86641-0 (alk. paper)
   ISBN-10: 0-205-86641-7 (alk. paper)
   1. Social case work—Moral and ethical aspects. 2. Social workers—Professional ethics. I. Title.
   HV43.R69 2014
   174'.93613—dc23

                                                    2012036329

10 9 8 7 6 5 4 3 2

Student Edition
ISBN-10: 0-205-86641-7
ISBN-13: 978-0-205-86641-0

Instructors Review Copy
ISBN-10: 0-205-87862-8
ISBN-13: 978-0-205-87862-8

Contents

PART TWO: CASE STUDIES: ETHICAL DILEMMAS IN PRACTICE

Contents by Practice Context

III. Adult Mental Health

IV. Gerontology

V. Agency Management, policies, and procedures

VI. Social Justice and Social Policy

VII. Common Themes

Preface

Major ethical issues are inherent in the work of any profession. Yet, as social workers, we often confront problems that are unique and especially difficult, because the work we do has a strong impact on every aspect of the lives of those we serve. We have many obligations—to our clients, their families and communities, and the wider society.

In preparing this 4th edition of *From the Front Lines*, I am struck once again by several thoughts: first of all, I am struck by the persistence of some major ethical issues across the almost 20 years that this book has been in existence. Issues of confidentiality, of informed consent, of client self-determination and the responsibility to protect, of concerns about the application of policies that don't always fit every situation equally well, of value differences, and many others continue to be major ongoing concerns in social work practice.

Although the 20 years have not made an appreciable difference in the special challenges involved in addressing collegial issues, which still seem to create reticence and discomfort in discussion, I am especially grateful to the students who have been willing to share their experiences in their case studies, so that we all may learn and consider these important issues. I am also struck by the range of complex and challenging issues that social workers encounter in host settings, where different values and different ethical codes can create professional conflicts which require both a loyalty to one's own professional code and a willingness to truly understand and consider the code of another profession. I am impressed by the level of awareness of the writers of the effect of national trends and national policies on the day-to-day ethical issues in practice—from very macro to very micro!

Our responsibilities range from care and decision making for those unable to care for themselves, to assisting people to fulfill their hopes and potential, to advocacy and empowerment for vulnerable and oppressed clients and communities, to working for the public interest and the common good of society as a whole, and to supporting social justice in the broader global context. We are the custodians of many of the resources of our society, and we determine how they may be allocated in a just and equitable manner. We administer major social-welfare programs; protect the best interests of children, the elderly, and the disabled; and support families and individuals in developing their optimal potential.

We work in social agencies, schools, the justice system, hospitals, nursing homes, residential treatment centers, clinics, employee-assistance programs, child-welfare programs, governmental and policy-making agencies, NGOs, and a multitude of other settings. In each of these, we work to optimize the "fit" between our client populations and the world they live in. It is our versatility, along with multiple and often conflicting obligations, that creates some of the ethical dilemmas that we all encounter in the course of our work.

We confront our various and conflicting ethical responsibilities armed with our personal values, professional skills, and understanding of the society in which we, as well as our clients, live. For guidance, we turn to the Code of Ethics of the National Association of Social Workers and to ethical principles drawn from theories that support our professional values: respect for the value and dignity of every human being and a concern for the well-being of others. We address our clients' needs in the context of an ever-changing, ever more complex world. We address them with a heightened awareness of the role that our own values, beliefs, and experiences play in our understanding of their problems and needs.

Our understanding of our clients and of our own roles in working with them has evolved with the maturation of the profession. In the early days of the "friendly visitor," it was often believed that the problems people encountered were caused by some personal moral failure. Social workers of this period attempted to lead these unfortunates toward a "better" life by influencing their values and behavior. "If you become like me," the friendly visitor might have said, "you will no longer have problems. You must learn to think like me, act like me, believe like me."

Settlement-house workers lived in the communities they served and developed a different approach—they tried to provide a wide variety of services that were needed by members of the communities. They worked with immigrant groups and with those living in poverty in all of the major cities of the nation.

With time, it became obvious that the problems people faced were often not rooted within the individuals themselves; rather, they were created by the clients' environments or by circumstances beyond their individual control. This led to a proactive stance within the profession, an advocacy for programs and policies to improve the condition of disadvantaged populations.

Mid–twentieth century social workers were profoundly affected by the societal and political movements and issues that were enabling major changes in society. The Civil Rights Movement, so closely aligned with social work values and goals, had a profound effect on the profession, and social workers were strongly involved in protests, advocacy, sit-ins, and voter registration drives, as well as in working directly with individuals and communities to effect much-needed changes. Influenced by the work of Sigmund Freud and others, the profession also focused interest on the development and refinement of clinical skills, and on the application of psychological theories to practice.

Advances in communications and technology also brought global issues to the forefront. From the effects of the Holocaust to the "brainwashing" believed to have occurred in the former Soviet Union, to the war in Vietnam, and the ethnic conflicts in the former Yugoslavia, the former Soviet Union, and Africa, the problems in the Middle East, and global terrorism, social workers became more strongly committed to addressing social justice issues on a broader scale.

In the beginning years of the twenty-first century, several societal issues and concerns have had a strong impact on our profession and our practice. The development and funding of faith-based social services and faith-based institutions have necessitated personal ethical considerations for many social workers. The long years of conflict in Afghanistan and Iraq have created major needs for social services and other supports for veterans and their families. Continuing economic stressors such as the housing crisis, banking and stock market contractions, and the higher rates of unemployment, underemployment, and job displacement have created additional needs for social services at a time when major funding cuts have been enacted by the nationwide economic crisis. Recurrent and unresolved issues around illegal immigration and the "rights" of undocumented immigrants to education, social services, and health care continue as major public issues. Natural disasters such as Hurricanes Katrina and Sandy, the fires in Colorado and California, major heat waves, flooding, and man-made disasters such as the oil spill in the Caribbean have created a more urgent need for prompt, effective, and well-orgnized emergency health as well as social services.

While acceptance of cultural diversity is loudly and publicly espoused, and the first African American president, Barack Obama, has been elected to a second term, stereotyping, discrimination, and limitations on civil rights continue to impact many groups, such as the LGBTQ community, religious minorities, immigrants, people with limited English proficiency, and people with disabilities, as well as ethnic and racial minorities. As our focus expands from local to national to global, we become more aware of, and engaged in, the major humanitarian crises occurring on a worldwide scale, and the need to address social issues beyond our borders becomes a major concern.

Research and literature in the area of ethical issues for social workers appears regularly in books and professional journals, offering us information, data, and a forum for learning. The case studies in this book add to the growing body of knowledge about ethical issues in our profession. They offer a unique perspective: that of student social workers in the field encountering ethical issues on a day-to-day basis, having to face these issues and resolve them in a manner consistent with both their own values and those of the profession.

The title of the book may evoke images of war and thus seem inappropriate to a social-work ethics textbook. Yet, I believe that there are parallels that can be drawn between social work and soldiering that make the title a meaningful one. At times, our work may place us on the front lines of a very real struggle: a struggle for rights, justice, survival, dignity and respect, recognition, peace, and the possibility of a good life.

Like soldiers in battle, we are given training and guidelines. We are given protocols and guidance, supervision and policies. We are sent out into a very different "field" than that of the soldier. But it is a field nonetheless, and upon it, alone, we must encounter difficult situations and make decisions, knowing that the effect of these decisions may go well beyond our immediate time and space and affect the course of many lives. Like the soldier, we do not have the luxury of inaction, for inaction in itself is an action.

Confronting ethical issues may seem daunting to students and practitioners. After all, ethics is its own discipline, with its own body of knowledge and its own methodology. How can we, without years of study, feel that we are qualified and able to make ethical decisions? We are social workers, not ethicists.

Yet, in the course of our work, we can and do make ethical decisions frequently, perhaps more frequently than we realize. It is possible, I believe, for social workers to make reasoned, reflective, and careful ethical decisions without the benefit of years of study. After all, we make ethical decisions in our personal lives all the time. We have a great deal of experience doing this.

What is asked of us, as professionals, is that we carefully consider and define the issues; that we gather the information needed to make an informed decision; that we allow ourselves to be guided by the Code of Ethics to which we all subscribe; that we recognize and consider the effect of our own values and beliefs and our own life experiences upon our decision-making process; that we honor the values and beliefs of those affected by our decisions: our clients, our agencies, our communities, and society at large; that we reason and reflect upon the choices available to us; and that we act with integrity in the manner that we believe will be best for all concerned.

Organization of the Book

The first five chapters of this book take the reader on a focused and intense journey through the process of making an ethical decision. These apply specifically to social-work ethical decision making, but there is much that can be used to reflect on the manner in which the reader and others make ethical decisions in their lives in a variety of contexts and situations. I believe that learning about ethical decision making is of value not just for professional practice, but for the whole person as well. Reading and learning about ethics in a professional context can assist readers to become more conscious and aware of the elements they themselves bring into their decision making, and of the process they use to make decisions.

Chapters 6 through 11 each focus around one of the ethical standards of the NASW Code of Ethics. The order of the Code is preserved in the arrangement of the chapters. Within each chapter, the particular ethical standard is discussed, and examples of cases involving that standard are presented to the reader. After a brief summary, each chapter includes some review questions to assist students to integrate the chapter's materials

The collection includes 26 cases, each unique in terms of the particular combination of setting, issue, worker, and client and/or policy. Cases illustrate both common kinds of dilemmas and more unusual ones; cases where the writer did an extensive and exhaustive research and literature review and cases where less material was used; cases illustrating the use of different theories and methods; cases where the writer carefully examines the impact of his or her own values on his or her decision and cases where this is not accentuated. In some instances, I would have made the same decision as the writer, though perhaps for slightly different reasons. In others, I would have made a very different decision. In still others, I would have framed the ethical problem differently from the way the writer has chosen. Similarly, the reader may find herself or himself agreeing with some writers and disagreeing, slightly or vehemently, with others.

The rationale for this diversity is to illustrate that it is possible to make ethical decisions using a variety of approaches, and in more or less depth, as long as certain elements are always a part of the process: adequate information, reference to the Code of Ethics or to some set of principles and theories, awareness of all of the value systems that impact the decision and are impacted by it, and a process of reason and reflection.

It is my hope that the issues presented in this book will engender good discussion: Ethics flourishes best in an atmosphere of open discussion, respect, and consideration for the views and opinions of others. I also hope that in reflecting on each writer's approach and in considering the questions at the end of the chapter, the reader will feel an increased sense of confidence in his or her own ability to make ethical decisions. References and bibliographies are included with all cases to facilitate further study.

As the classical philosopher Aristotle stated in the *Nichomachean Ethics*, "Ethics is an inexact science." It is not necessary—in fact, it is not possible—for each social worker to make the same decisions for the same reasons as do other social workers. We are each unique; we bring that uniqueness with us to our work. Therefore, we cannot seek absolute consistency among ourselves in ethical decision making. All that can be asked of each of us is that we make the most thoughtful, reflective decision that we can, with sincerity, honesty, and integrity.

Acknowledgments

This project was born on a sunny winter afternoon, early in a new semester, when, once again, I heard the familiar litany, "Why do we have to use ethics cases from other discipline's books? Why can't we have our own casebook?"

"O.K.," I said, tired of this often-repeated complaint, "I'll write one. But you must prepare good cases. I'll use material from them and put a casebook together."

And so, *From the Front Lines* was born.

Over these past 20 years, the students in my ethics classes at the University of California at Berkeley School of Social Welfare and the National Catholic School for Social Service have worked extra hard to prepare cases they thought would be of interest to students everywhere. They helped me classroom-test the book. They read the revised and abstracted versions of their work to ensure that I had preserved the flavor and urgency of their ethical dilemmas. They assisted me always with their enthusiasm, loyalty, and interest. I would like to thank each and every one—those whose cases are included here, and those who, for various reasons, were unable to contribute a case to this endeavor.

It is the sincere hope of each of us that our book will help to stimulate thought and discussion in this essential area of our professional education. I would like to acknowledge the following reviewers who critiqued this book; their comments were very helpful and contributed toward the final version of the textbook: Duane Neff, Boston College; Thomas Watts, University of Texas at Arlington; and Karl Mitchell, Queens College.

Introduction

Ethical issues pervade every aspect of social work. They cross national boundaries, affect all cultures, religions, and ethnic groups, and occur worldwide, for they relate to universal issues that are a part of the human condition, and, in particular, to the issues that are of primary concern to our profession. As we work with these often complex and challenging professional issues, we gain insight into ourselves, our society, and the factors that affect the general well-being of humanity. The six examples below illustrate several kinds of ethical issues social workers may encounter in practice.

Often, the ethical dimension is difficult to identify, for it may be masked deep within clinical issues, funding issues, program development issues, agency policy, and advocacy issues. At times, a sincere consideration and concern for the immediate problem diminishes workers' understanding of the broader professional and societal issues that must also inform ethical decision making. The following examples may help to clarify the problem.

1. A high school student who has been referred by a teacher to a school social worker for service because of classroom behavior and suspected drug abuse sits silently, week after week, refusing to engage with the worker. His parents are aware of the referral, agree that it is needed, and assume that their son is accepting help. However, his problematic behavior is continuing in the classroom, and the question of possible substance abuse is still unresolved. It is easy to label such a client as resistive, or to question the worker's skills or methods. These are clinical issues. Embedded deep within, however, are important ethical dimensions. Should his parents be informed about his refusal to talk with the worker? What if he simply doesn't want service? Should he be coerced, against his will, to engage with the worker? Should active engagement be made a condition of continuing to attend school, or is it enough if he just sits in the worker's office an hour a week? What about his rights—to self-determination, to dignity and respect, to privacy and confidentiality?

2. A resident of a senior citizens' housing project is no longer able to care for himself. His memory is slightly impaired, and he forgets to take vital medications. He recently fell and could not reach a telephone to ask for help, and lay on the floor for 2 days. His meals are nutritionally unbalanced—he tends to open cans of pork and beans or spaghetti daily with little variation, and fresh fruits, vegetables, and dairy products are rarely a part of his diet. He spends long hours alone in his apartment, watching television. The housing manager has referred him to the social worker for nursing home placement, which, she feels, would provide him with the medication monitoring he needs, ensure his physical safety and nutritional health, and offer opportunities for socialization and activities. The worker agrees that the resident would be much better off in a supervised setting, but he adamantly refuses to go. The worker, believing that her obligation is to the client's best interest, feels that she must intervene for his own good. A question of genuine care and concern? Yes, but also a question of self-determination and of the rights of competent individuals. Does his refusal to enter a nursing home make him de facto incompetent? Is the social worker's perception of the client's best interests always the one that must be followed?

3. A 24-year-old woman comes for service to a neighborhood mental health clinic. She and the worker identify the self-esteem issues she would like to work on, and together they develop a contract with goals set within the agency's eight-session framework for treatment. An excellent relationship develops, which enables significant work and an increase in self-confidence. During the seventh session, the client reveals another important related issue, a long-standing problem with a sibling that has also impacted her self-esteem. She asks the worker to extend treatment by enough visits to address this important area. There is little question in the mind of the worker: Of course this client needs continued visits. She just won't mention them to her supervisor. She doesn't agree with the agency's eight-session limit, anyway, and she has to think of her client's needs first. But there are many issues related to deliberately ignoring agency policy. What about her contract with her practice setting? What about her relationship with her supervisor, who is herself being placed at professional risk by the worker's actions? What are some of the repercussions that might occur should the funding source discover that the conditions of funding are not being met? What about the next client, who also has needs, but who can't be served for several more weeks? And, while trying to support her client, what message is the worker sending her about honesty and fidelity, about obligations, about the kind of person that she is?

4. An agency for Latinos with HIV, whose funding is derived from the local Latino community, is designed to serve this specific population only. Its mission, policies, and purpose are clearly stated, and the agency provides bilingual workers to address the needs of this special population. However, the amount of funding, and thus the very existence of the agency, is dependent on the number of persons served annually. This number has been steadily decreasing, and the existence of the agency itself is threatened. If the agency is closed, there will be no services at all for this at-risk minority population. There are many individuals who live in the community, and in neighboring communities, who are HIV positive and in need of service but are not Latinos. Slowly and silently, these people are being accepted for service by the agency. The rationale makes a great deal of sense to the staff: The need for services that the agency can provide is there. It is not being met by any other agency in the community. And, of course, these clients are boosting the number of clients that the agency is serving, thereby ensuring its continued existence and services to the Latino HIV population. The benefits are obvious. But what are the harms? Is the agency engaging in deception by misusing funds designated for one population for services to another? Does the end (keeping the agency in existence) justify the means (abandoning its stated mission and policies)? Are there any other courses of action possible?

5. A public foster care agency social worker finds his caseload nearly doubled as a result of recent across-the-board budget cuts to social services programs. He is required to be in contact with each client monthly and to visit each foster home at least once every 3 months. With the current caseload, this has become impossible. He provides service to the families on his caseload who contact him with a problem, rationalizing that the others must be OK—or they would be calling him too. But his choices have strong ethical implications as well. Program and agency policy state that all clients must be served: Each should have a share of the worker's time and attention. What will he do when he completes the monthly statistics each social worker must provide to the agency? Can a phone call be counted as a "visit"? Can a review of a record, or a note written in a record, be counted as a "contact"? Is there a responsibility to advocate for his clients, for his agency, and for himself to bring attention to the impossibility of serving these numbers of clients?

   6. A social worker is part of a multidisciplinary team in a major medical center that must decide who will be the recipient of a liver that is available for transplant. Each member of the team provides information in his or her area of expertise to the general team meeting, and a decision is made jointly by all members. The pathologist addresses issues of tissue match; the physician, general health; the nurse, potential compliance with medical regimen; and the pastor, spiritual needs. The social worker's area of expertise is the potential recipient's personal and social functioning. She takes a complete psychosocial history, from which she must extract salient pieces of information that impact on the team's decision. Yet clients reveal certain kinds of information in confidence, expecting her to maintain confidentiality, as their previous experiences with social workers have taught them. Should a history of alcohol abuse be included? Should a history of wife battering, which has not been formally charged in a court of law? A criminal record? A potential for mental instability? A history of multiple teen pregnancies and TANF (Temporary Assistance for Needy Families) dependence? A mild mental disability? Where is the line between "necessary information" and the potential recipient's right to privacy? What psychosocial factors should be considered in determining who receives scarce organs? Should any be considered at all? How do HIPAA (Health Insurance Portability and Accountability Act) regulations affect members of professional teams?

   Each of these examples illustrates instances when social workers must make decisions based not only on clinical judgment and expertise, but also on ethical principles and values. Immediately, major problems surface: *Which* principles? *What* values? Drawn from *whose* understanding of human nature and philosophical position?

   To assist workers in considering the ethical dimensions of the work they do, it *is* necessary to consider problems within a basic framework that provides a consistent structure as well as specific guidelines for decision making. The components of ethical decision making can ensure that the ethical position taken is reasoned, clear and theoretically sound, able to be communicated to others and logically supported, reflects the values, goals, and beliefs of those affected by the decision, and lies within the ethics and value base of the social work profession.

   Part One will present a decision-making framework and its components, and discuss various alternative ways of considering each step in the decision-making process. Chapters in this part will address the process for formulating a dilemma, determining and gathering relevant information, selecting an appropriate ethical theory and principles, reviewing the Code of Ethics, exploring values and developing a values hierarchy, considering options, and, finally selecting an option and arriving at a resolution.

   It is important to recognize that, wherever possible, clients should be involved in the ethical decision-making process. Client involvement supports self-determination, validates client values and personal ethics, promotes self-awareness, teaches and models a careful and reflective decision-making process, and greatly increases the potential for success.

All clients can be involved in ethical decision making that pertains to them at some level, from small children to confused elderly people, from monolingual non-English speakers to people who are unable to communicate verbally, from high school sophomores to compliant newcomers, from homeless mentally ill veterans to the prison population.

Because some of the ethical dilemmas with which social workers are confronted do not involve clients directly, and because the Code of Ethics contains many provisions that are not necessarily related to direct client services, there are ethical issues that pertain to the worker alone. However, when the dilemma involves client care and services, it is also assumed that the client will be directly involved in the process.

Part Two provides cases that present ethical problems for discussion and consideration. All of the cases have occurred during students' internship programs, and describe students' work in resolving these ethical issues within the framework suggested in Part One. CSWE (The Council on Social Work Education) Core Competencies will be identified in each chapter, and some questions requiring critical thinking by the social worker will be suggested, to encourage both personal reflection and class discussion.

The cases in this part have been selected and organized around the six standards of the NASW (National Association of Social Workers) Code of Ethics. Where more than one standard is involved, the one which the author believes to be most central to the case discussion has been used to determine placement. Cases reflect the thought processes and ethical issues encountered in two schools of social work to provide a broad perspective in contexts, thinking, and choices of criteria for decision making.

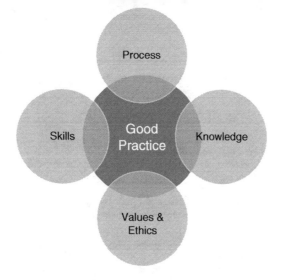

Process

Skills Good Practice Knowledge

Values & Ethics

Kheng Guan Toh/Shutterstock

Framing the Ethical Problem

Competencies Applied with Practice Behavior Examples—in This Chapter				
[x] Professional Identity	[x] Ethical Practice	[x] Critical Thinking	Diversity in Practice	Human Rights & Justice
[x] Research Based Practice	Human Behavior	Policy Practice	Practice Contexts	Engage, Assess, Intervene, Evaluate

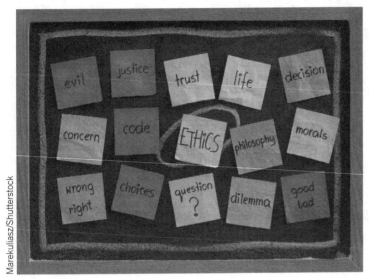

Essential concepts in ethical
social work practice.

INTRODUCTION

Defining the "ethical dilemma" is often one of the most challenging aspects of ethical decision making; yet, it is the essential first step in addressing ethical issues in practice. When the ethical problem has been determined, the worker's sigh of relief is often tempered by the additional challenges of determining what constitutes relevant information, and where and under what circumstances such information may be obtained. This chapter will address these complex issues and provide the reader with a consistent structure for defining an ethical dilemma and determining and gathering the information upon which a sound decision may be based.

DEFINING THE ETHICAL PROBLEM

Because social work ethical issues are usually embedded in complex personal or social issues, one of the most difficult tasks in ethical decision making is focusing on the problem that must be addressed. To do this, ethical discussions generally begin with a brief description of the setting, followed by a presentation of the case. There is often a substantial amount of information that has been gathered about the client, practice setting, policy, community, or other subject matter being considered. The worker's first task is to sort through all the material until the "bare bones" of the ethical issue can be viewed clearly.

This often goes against social workers' training and professional habits of thoroughness and responsibility and, at first, can be a painful exercise. Approaching from a broad person-in-environment framework, where the interplay of multiple elements forms the subject matter of the service, this shift is difficult, but necessary. If the worker is addressing the confidentiality issue described in example one of the Introduction, for example, the occupations of the parents, the relationship among family members, and the kind of school the child is attending, as well as her grades and school performance, her interests, and her after-school activities, are not necessarily part of the *ethical* "presenting problem." That problem is more likely to involve the rights of minor children, the rights of parents, the worker's professional obligations, the policies of the agency providing the service, and the worker's service contract with parents and the child.

Clearly, there may be more than one ethical issue involved in a case. Each must be separated out and addressed individually. Attempting to address more than one issue at a time blurs the lines of process, confusing the issues and creating unclear and at times unreasonable conclusions. While it is important to recognize that there may be more than one issue, it is best to determine the central issue and to begin with that. In that process, the other issues may resolve themselves. If they continue as problems after the central issue has been resolved, they can be addressed separately.

Once an issue has been clearly identified, it should be phrased as an *ethical dilemma* for purposes of consideration and potential resolution. The word *dilemma*, of Greek origin, literally means two (*di*) horns (*lemma*). Each side, or each horn, of the di lemma is as important as the other—the horns are similar in size. If one horn were to be much larger than the other, it would not be a dilemma: The larger one would predominate. An ethical dilemma presents a choice that must be made between two mutually exclusive courses of action. These may be two goods, or benefits, or the avoidance of two harms. The choices that the worker, client, agency, or policymaker have to consider (the two sides of the dilemma) must be evenly balanced and of equal worth. If one side of the dilemma is more valuable, right, good, or desirable than the other side, then there is no dilemma, for the choice would obviously lean toward the more desirable side.

Dilemma formulations are always tied to the overall goals and objectives of the service to be provided by the agency or the program, which must be identified first. Examples might include enhanced self-esteem, optimal opportunities for growth and development, maximization of mental and physical health, well-being of the client, optimal resource allocation, requirements of funding sources, and so on. Goals tend to be fairly general: that's why dilemmas arise in determining the "best" way to meet them. For clarity, dilemmas take the form of _____ v. _____. *Self-determination* v. *Worker's Perception of Best Interest of Client, Confidentiality* v. *Duty to Warn,* and *Agency Policy* v. *Primacy of Client* are examples of dilemma statements.

At times, it may appear that there are more than two sides to a dilemma. It will not be possible to work with the problem under those conditions, and further deliberation will enable the worker to restate the problem so that it is presented in an accessible form.

The sixth example given in the Introduction of the worker whose role is to provide psychosocial assessments in a medical setting, and who is unsure about what information should ethically be included can serve to illustrate some of the complexities of dilemma formulation. Certain kinds of information have been revealed to the worker in confidence. Should that confidence be violated? Under what circumstances? For example, should negative information that results from *actions* of the potential organ recipient be treated differently than negative information for which the client is not responsible? Mental retardation is not the "fault" of the client. Alcoholism may or may not be the client's responsibility, while wife battering tends to be.

Should a certain standard of behavior be considered in determining eligibility for donor organs? Is it the worker's obligation to share all available information or to respect the client's right to privacy? How do HIPAA regulations, which provide legal protections for client privacy, function within this hospital setting? Must the worker *always* adhere to them? Is the worker's primary responsibility to the potential recipient (her client for purposes of assessment and evaluation), her interdisciplinary team, the hospital, or society in the sense of social justice? The overarching issue to be considered is the allocation of resources, which in this case are livers.

Apply strategies of ethical reasoning to arrive at principled decisions.

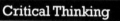
Critical Thinking

Practice Behavior Example: HIPAA, the Health Insurance Portability and Accountability Act, passed in 1996, provides federal protections for personal health information in order to maintain privacy and confidentiality, which also applies to social workers in healthcare contexts of practice. See www.hhs.gov/ocr/privacy/hipaa/

Critical Thinking Question: Client information revealed in social work contexts may be equally personal and private. Yet, there are no uniform regulations that protect such information. Should the profession address this issue?

Practice Behavior Example: In ethical decision making, it is important to be both consistent and appropriate to the individual circumstances and situation.

Critical Thinking Question: When more than one possibility exists and a choice of ethical dilemmas to address must be made, as in the case of the organ recipient discussed earlier, what criteria or priorities should be used?

Distributive justice principles which are often used by social workers include: to each an equal share, to each on the basis of need, to each according to individual effort, to each what is merited, and to each what the law requires.

Possible dilemma formulations might include the following:

Primacy of Client Interests v. Obligation to Social Justice
Distribution by Merit v. Distribution by Equal Share
Privacy and Confidentiality v. Obligation to Colleagues
Social Justice v. Adherence to HIPAA Laws
Primacy of Client Interests v. Obligation to Practice Setting
Distribution by Contribution to Society v. Distribution by Equal Share

It is easy to see where potential problems lie. Primacy of client interests appears in two formulations, with different balanced positions on the opposite side. The worker might be tempted to formulate the dilemma as *Primacy of Client Interests v. Responsibility to Practice Setting or Responsibility to Social Justice.* After all, both of these alternatives fit comfortably opposite *Primacy of Client Interests.*

Social Justice also appears twice: once in relation to the client's interests and once in relation to the law. In formulating the dilemma as *Social Justice v. Primacy of Client Interests or Adherence to HIPAA Laws*, it is easy to assume that these are two completely separate issues and that a choice must be made between them. However, HIPAA is meant to protect the interests of each member of the society in terms of privacy and confidentiality—to protect the client's interest through law. The way the dilemma is ultimately phrased if social justice is one of the "horns" of the dilemma will depend on the social worker's own concept of what is most salient.

When considering which principles of distributive justice to use, similar problems could occur. *Equal Share* can form one side of the dilemma. However, one can state the dilemma as *Equal Share v. Merit or Contribution to Society or Need or Individual Effort.* Such a complex dilemma statement is impossible to address, for each of the four positions on the right side of the dilemma needs to be considered both separately from the others and against each of the others. The dilemma can be formulated in a resolvable way, however, by stating *Allocation by Equal Share v. Allocation using Specific Criteria.*

Once the problem has been stated as a dilemma, it is possible to undertake the next element in the decision-making process—the gathering of relevant information.

GATHERING INFORMATION

It is not possible to make a good ethical decision without some research, discussion, and exploration. The particulars of the case will determine the kind of information that will be needed. Information should be relevant to the dilemma as defined in the dilemma statement, and various sources of information, such as policy manuals, laws, interviews, book, and web research should be considered.

Relevance of Information

To consider relevance of information, let us return to the second case presented in the Introduction as an example of underlying ethical issues—that of the elderly gentleman who refuses to enter a nursing home. The central ethical dilemma may be stated thus: *Self-determination* v. *Worker's Perception of Best Interest of Client.*

Information gathering related to this particular problem might include research about clients who remain at home in precarious conditions, exploration of resources or services available in the home for elderly clients, statistics on injuries to elderly clients who live alone and on nursing home admissions, laws about personal freedoms, research on adjustment of patients to nursing home settings, studies about life satisfaction at home and in an institutional setting, information about the client's medical conditions and any limitations that these might cause, an exploration of the client's family and support network, an examination of policies and relevant laws for residents of senior citizens' housing, and so on.

> **Gather information that explores and supports both sides of the ethical dilemma.**

It may be more difficult to find the necessary information for one side than for the other; however, obtaining balanced amounts of information will ensure the best possible deliberation.

In addition to the information gathered specific to the client's situation, it is also helpful to explore the broader principles, rights, obligations, and needs that define the dilemma. In this instance, learning about self-determination—what it means, the conditions under which it may be limited, and the values and laws that support it—will help the worker gain a deeper level of understanding. The same process should be undertaken in exploring the client's best interest. This might include professional obligations, an understanding of the pros and cons of paternalism, and the importance of addressing "point-of-view" issues in conceptualizing best interest, among others.

In the fourth example discussed in the Introduction that of the agency serving the HIV-positive Latino population, there are various dilemma statements possible, for there are a number of dilemmas present. One dilemma statement might be *Agency Mission* v. *Community Need.*

The specific issues and the dilemma statement, again, determine what information will be useful for resolving the dilemma. It might be helpful to:

1. Explore the agency's mission statement.
2. Gain a historical perspective on the agency.
3. Understand the intent of the funding sources and the auspices that direct how the funds are used.
4. Discover the extent of HIV in the Latino population within the community.
5. Determine whether other resources exist within the community for addressing the problems of HIV clients.
6. Understand completely the unique resources provided by this particular agency.
7. Learn about individuals with HIV who are non-Latino and in need of services in the community.
8. Determine the extent to which Latinos utilize agencies.
9. Explore the reasons that services are requested at this particular agency (presenting problem).
10. Understand the cultural differences between Latinos and non-Latinos that impact on their utilization of the agency's services.

In terms of broader concepts and principles, it might be helpful to learn about resource-allocation issues, advocacy and policy change processes, the obligation of employees to agency mission and purpose, and the relationship between agency and community.

These examples illustrate how the problem definition, the dilemma statement, the setting, and the client or client population will determine the kind of information the worker will need.

Information that can be helpful is often accessible within the agency itself: Colleagues, supervisors, program directors, and agency administrators often have experience and insight to offer regarding the resolution of ethical dilemmas involving clients and policies of their agency. Agencies similar in purpose, population, or philosophical orientation can also provide a basis of comparison and another kind of experience. Government agencies that serve the population or address the problem can provide insight as well. The Office on Aging, for example, may have useful information to assist the worker addressing the dilemma of the elderly gentleman who is refusing nursing home placement.

Research can be an excellent source of information as well: research related to the problem, the population, the culture within which the problem has occurred, and approaches to the problem. Research can provide invaluable insights, avoid duplication of effort, and provide evidence-based information to guide the ethical decision-making process.

Research-Based Practice

Practice Behavior Example: Use research evidence to inform practice.

Critical Thinking Question: Current research can provide invaluable knowledge and insights in addressing ethical dilemmas. However, exploring research might delay the resolution of the ethical dilemma. How might an agency address the research needs of social workers?

Sources of Information

It is important to consider the sources of information that will be utilized in making the ethical decision. Each source offers a different perspective and can broaden the worker's understanding of the nature of the problem. After the problem has been defined, it is helpful to prepare a list of potential sources of information. Sources should be reliable, accessible to the worker, and relevant to the ethical problem statement. They may provide a personal perspective, concrete and specific information about the context, resources, and attitudes and opinions of those affected, theoretical information about concepts and principles, information about relevant laws and policies, and other kinds of information.

In the second case, of the elderly gentleman who refuses to enter a nursing home, some sources of information might include:

It is essential to obtain informed consent from the client before interviewing family members or others, and before obtaining records from outside sources. Preferably, consent should be obtained in writing.

1. Client, family members, client's support network.
2. Client records and charts from other agencies.
3. Research on attitudes of elderly persons toward NH care.
4. Research and statistics of elderly people in the community and in institutions.
5. Available community resources such as adult day care, senior centers, group homes, life care centers, and so on. Interviews with staff members where feasible and appropriate.
6. Applicable laws, and relevant agency policies and procedures.
7. Research on characteristics of successful NH placements.
8. Agency director.
9. Gerontological social workers.

10. Ethical theories and principles relevant to case, such as self-determination, client rights, responsibility to prevent injury, and so on.
11. NASW Code of Ethics.

An example of some of the potential sources of information for the fourth case, the agency serving Latino HIV clients might include:

1. Direct interviews with affected populations.
2. Agency client records and charts.
3. The agency's policy manual and procedure manual, brochures, and other written material.
4. Grants, contracts, and information from funding sources.
5. Community surveys to determine ethnic and cultural characteristics of HIV population, and existing resources for HIV clients, such as agencies, hospitals, clinics, support groups, and other services, and the location of such services relative to the worker's agency. A map of the community may be helpful in this regard.
6. Research regarding the community's utilization of services for HIV.
7. General research regarding Latino populations and HIV.
8. Articles, books, or other resources on culturally appropriate decision-making frameworks for work with Latino clients.
9. Agency director.
10. Social workers at agency and other agencies serving this population.
11. NASW Code of Ethics.

With "facts" in hand, the ethical decision-making process focuses on the determination of an ethical theory that is relevant to the problem, consonant with laws and agency policies, and which offers a process that will be helpful to the specific problem under consideration.

CHAPTER SUMMARY

This chapter has introduced the first steps in the development of an ethical decision-making process. It has suggested that a *process* can be applied to a wide variety of context, issues, problems, and client populations, and that its consistent use is essential to professional practice.

Perhaps the most challenging step in the process is the first one: defining the ethical dilemma. The two sides of the dilemma must be about equal in value and importance: the choice between two goods, or the choice between the avoidance of two harms. It is necessary that there be only one statement on each side of the dilemma; having more than one obscures and confuses the decision-making process. Dilemma formulations should be phrased as _____ vs _____.

The manner in which the dilemma is phrased will serve as the guide to the next process: gathering information which is relevant and necessary to decision making, and identifying the potential sources of information. This information may include exploring the client's beliefs and feelings about the problem, understanding agency policy and procedures, exploring community attitudes and resources for addressing the problem, consulting the NASW Code of Ethics, clarifying relevant laws, and studying and selecting an ethical theory framework and principles.

To begin the process of ethical decision making as described in this chapter, describe what is felt to be the essential ethical problem, or problems, and determine the most pressing issue to be addressed. List potential dilemma statements, using the _____ vs _____ format. From this list, select the one that you believe to be most salient to the ethical context. Then, using both sides of the dilemma statement, develop a list of information that will be helpful in finding a resolution to the dilemma. The information should support both sides of the dilemma, and also provide general information about the problem, populations, context, and agency setting. In examining this list, determine appropriate sources that will be utilized to gather this information.

In the next chapter, ethical theories and principles that may be helpful in further framing and considering the ethical dilemma will be presented.

The following questions will test your knowledge of the content found within this chapter. For questions 1-6, please select the phrase that best completes each sentence. Question 7 is a brief essay question. For additional assessment, including licensing-exam type questions on applying chapter content to practice behaviors, visit **MySearchLab**.

1. In formulating dilemma statements, the two sides of the dilemma should always:
   a. be about equal in importance and value
   b. be opposites
   c. have the prior agreement of the client
   d. be determined by agency policy

2. Ethical dilemma statements should be phrased:
   a. describing all of the ethical issues involved
   b. using the client's wording and associations
   c. clearly and in broad ethical language
   d. related to agency policy

3. Dilemma statements should always encompass:
   a. the social worker's values
   b. the agency's values
   c. the objectives and goals of service
   d. community standards

4. In gathering sources of information, social workers should:
   a. focus on accessible and available information
   b. focus on the specifics of the client's situation rather than general research on the issue
   c. try to obtain information that is balanced in support of both sides of the dilemma
   d. gather information focused on areas of interest to the client

5. Before beginning the information-gathering process, it is helpful to have all except:
   a. informed consent of clients and other involved parties
   b. a list of the possible information needed
   c. a good idea of how the dilemma will resolve
   d. access to current research

6. It is necessary to obtain the client's consent before:
   a. researching the issue
   b. consulting agency policy
   c. reviewing the client's record
   d. discussing the issue with the client's family

7. The Introduction included this case description of the 5th example of an ethical issue: "A public foster care agency social worker finds his caseload nearly doubled as a result of recent across-the-board budget cuts to social services programs. He is required to be in contact with each client monthly and to visit each foster home at least once every 3 months. With his current caseload, this has become impossible." Assuming his supervisor is unable to resolve the problem, develop an ethical dilemma statement that addresses this issue, and explain the reasons for your choices of terms.

2

Theoretical Concepts and Ethical Principles

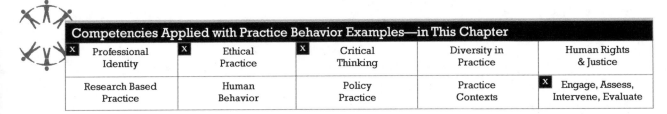

Competencies Applied with Practice Behavior Examples—in This Chapter				
x Professional Identity	x Ethical Practice	x Critical Thinking	Diversity in Practice	Human Rights & Justice
Research Based Practice	Human Behavior	Policy Practice	Practice Contexts	x Engage, Assess, Intervene, Evaluate

INTRODUCTION

In order to work effectively with the ethical problems encountered in social work, it is necessary to become familiar with some of the concepts and theories frequently utilized in the field of ethics. This chapter is not intended as an exhaustive or definitive presentation of ethics; however, it will provide the reader with some of the basic theories and principles used in ethical decision making. The theories, constructs, and systems presented have been selected as particularly applicable to social work, and are most frequently used by social workers in the field. Readers may find that they may be more comfortable with a particular theory; this is frequently the case, and is often a reflection of personal values and experiences. However, it is important to be familiar with several systems for decision making: choices of decision-making systems are often determined by agencies, programs, government policies, and clients, rather than by individual professionals.

THEORETICAL CONCEPTS

Examining Ethical Theories

Ethics is a branch of philosophy, generally drawing from broader philosophical theories in order to formulate concepts. These comprehensive theories address the nature of humankind, the meaning of life, the nature of the universe, and other wide, overarching concerns. While concepts differ in the way in which the answers to these broad questions are determined and how they relate to each other within the theory, all tend to consider the value and worth of human beings, the dignity of life, the central role of "happiness," however that is defined, and the relationship between members of a society.

Ethical theories, more narrowly focused, are generally grounded in these broader concepts. When exploring an ethical theory, it is necessary to consider three important questions:

1. *The authoritative question*: Where does the theory turn for validation of its basic premises? Some possibilities include the Bible, the government and its laws, a knowledgeable person, a philosophical construct, and so on.

2. *The distributive question*: Whose interests does the theory address? Again, there are several possible answers to this question as well, such as every person's, every living thing's, every citizen's, every community member's, and so on.

3. *The substantive question*: What goals or actions are desirable ends within this theory? We often think of "happiness," individually defined, as the overarching end toward which all other ends are directed. In considering these other ends, it is necessary to attempt to define the conditions for "happiness." These may include concepts such as personal freedom, meaningful activity, health and safety, and human relatedness.

Theories that may be helpful in considering the kinds of problems social workers address fall into two general categories: those that place the "good" and "right" in the motive, or starting premise, called *deontological* theories, and those that place the "good" and "right" in the ends achieved, called *teleological* or *consequentialist* theories.

Some well-known deontological theories include those based on religious texts and directions; those based on natural laws (such as Immanuel Kant's); those based on common sense, intuition, and duties (such as W. D. Ross's); and those based on the social contract (such as John Rawls'). Consequentialist theories are often grounded in some form of utilitarianism and consider "the greatest (resultant) good for the greatest number" (such as J. S. Mill's) or costs and benefits as their foundational principle. Other important theories include value-based ethics, including the modern variations of Aristotelian ethics (such as R. Nozick's), and the ethics of care, as described in the work of Carol Gilligan (1982) and Nell Noddings (2003).

The Role of Free Will and Choice

It is also important to recognize that there is a precondition vital to all ethical decision making: free will, or the ability to make choices. If individuals are unable to choose between meaningful alternatives, ethical decisions are not possible.

There are four components that are necessary to the exercise of choice, or free will. These include (1) having the information needed to make a decision, (2) having the ability to understand, reason, and reflect clearly and logically about the problem, (3) having choices of courses of action, and (4) having the ability to put one's selected choice into action—to operationalize it.

In order to fulfill the third necessary factor, there must be *real* choices available. In the first example presented in the Introduction, that of the high school student who refuses to engage with the worker, "making" him talk may not be a choice (unless the worker is willing to use force or very strong coercion). The choice of sharing or not sharing information with the client's parents may be a "real" choice, or it may be constrained by school policy, which mandates a specific position. Of course, the worker has the *choice* of whether to follow the school policy, but that becomes a different dilemma entirely. In the 5th example, of the foster care agency with severe budget cuts, the *choice* of providing truly equal services to every client as required by the agency's policies may be beyond the capacity of a single social worker. Also, the worker may choose to advocate for change rather than to provide services on the basis of need, as he is doing. But advocating for change is a lengthy process: It is not a real choice in this urgent situation.

Having choices is a necessary, but not sufficient condition of ethical decisions. One must be able to put the choice into effect, to operationalize it. In the fourth case in the Introduction, that of the agency that serves HIV-positive Latinos, the staff may *choose* to serve the broader community. They may appeal to the funding source to broaden the mission and amend the policies. However, the agency's strong identity with the Latino community may deter non-Latinos from coming for service. Simply *choosing* to serve everyone in the community may not be sufficient. It may be necessary to change the image of the agency, to engage in public presentations, and to approach community leaders in order to broaden the client base. The ability to put choices and goals into action is a vital part of ethical considerations.

No one has total free will. Constraints on free will may be physical, psychological, emotional, social, cultural, financial, educational, legal, environmental, and others. Constraints vary among individuals, even in situations that may appear outwardly similar.

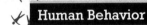

Human Behavior

Practice Behavior Example: Critique and apply knowledge to understand person and environment.

Critical Thinking Question: Expanding meaningful choices for clients is often an important component of professional practice. However, workers must be very careful to consider possible choices within the client's context and the client's "free will" possibilities, and not her or his own. How can social workers attempt to minimize this problem in practice?

FROM THEORIES TO PRINCIPLES

Ethical theories provide a conceptual structure for examining problems. As has been noted, these are grounded in a philosophical consideration of broader issues relating to the nature of humankind, the meaning of life, and so on. However, these theories often remain too broad to provide a clear direction for decision making. It is necessary to draw principles from these theories to provide guidance for the worker.

Principles ensure consistency and justice in the application of theory to specific ethical problems in practice. They decrease the worker's dependence on personal values and biases by providing objective criteria that may be applied in many different circumstances.

Principles may vary, depending upon the theory from which they are drawn. This variation may engender differences in the final decision that is reached. How principles are stated and, more importantly, how they are prioritized strongly affect the final position that emerges.

Social workers' needs in terms of ethical decision making require a set of principles that lend themselves well to the kinds of ethical problems encountered in practice. Five frameworks that are often used in ethical decision making by social workers will be presented here. They are by no means exclusive—there are many other sets of principles that can guide ethical decisions also. It is suggested that more detailed descriptions of these guidelines be consulted prior to applying them in practice contexts. Discussion of each of the frameworks presented in this chapter also includes some special cautions to help raise awareness of the possible limitations of each framework in the context of social work practice.

Selecting a framework is a challenging task, and there are five areas which must be carefully considered prior to determining the appropriate framework to guide decisionmaking the worker should be aware.

a. There is often a tendency to select a framework based on one's personal values, which can result in inconsistent ethical decision making among workers in an agency or organization.

b. A worker may select a framework based upon its ability to provide the "guidance" that she/he prefers.

c. An agency or organization may require the use of a particular framework with which the worker's personal values and/or understanding of the situation involved may conflict.

Critical Thinking

Practice Behavior Example: Critical Thinking

Critical Thinking Question: Of these five potential challenges in the selection of an ethical theory, which present the greatest "constraints" on the worker's "free will" and ability to make a choice of framework?

d. Different frameworks can be selected by workers trying to respond to different client value orientations; this has both positive and negative aspects.

e. As an agent of society, the social worker must consider the framework that "society" (however defined) would select in addressing a particular ethical issue.

Reamer's Application of Gewirth's Principles Hierarchy

Frederic Reamer (2009), one of the earliest social workers to define and describe ethical problems specifically in the context of the social work profession, uses a framework for ethical decision making drawn from the philosophy

of Alan Gewirth, which, he feels, will interface well with the core values of the profession. Gewirth bases his hierarchy of principles on the fundamental right of all humans to freedom and well-being (Gewirth, 1978, pp. 59–65). He proposes three categories of *core goods* that enable or enhance these rights. *Basic goods*, which are necessary to well-being, include food, shelter, life, health, and, interestingly, mental equilibrium; *nonsubtractive goods*, the loss of which would seriously compromise fundamental rights, such as honesty and fidelity in individual relationships, reasonable labor, and comfortable living conditions; and *additive goods*, which increase or enhance well-being, such as education, self-esteem, and material wealth.

Reamer uses Gewirth's guidelines in *Reason and Morality* (1978) to provide a hierarchy that may be used to resolve ethical dilemmas in social work:

> ***Principle 1*** Rules against basic harms to the necessary preconditions of action (the core goods, food, health, shelter, etc.) take precedence over rules against harms such as lying, revealing confidential information (nonsubtractive goods), or threats to additive goods such as education, recreation, and wealth.
>
> ***Principle 2*** An individual's right to basic well-being (core goods) takes precedence over another's individual's right to freedom.
>
> ***Principle 3*** An individual's right to freedom takes precedence over his or her own right to basic well-being.
>
> ***Principle 4*** The obligation to obey laws, rules, and regulations to which one has voluntarily and freely consented ordinarily overrides one's right to engage voluntarily in a manner that conflicts with these laws, rules, and regulations.
>
> ***Principle 5*** Individuals' rights to basic well-being may override laws, rules, regulations, and arrangements of voluntary associations in cases of conflict.
>
> ***Principle 6*** The obligation to prevent basic harms such as starvation and to promote basic public goods such as housing, education, and public assistance overrides the right to retain one's own property.

Reamer provides an easy-to-use set of principles to follow in making ethical decisions. Although he provides rich examples to assist us, and the principles he utilizes are clearly consonant with the NASW Code of Ethics, he does not clearly define the relationship between this framework and the Code.

Dolgoff, Harrington, & Loewenberg's Ethical Principles Screen

Dolgoff, Harrington, & Loewenberg (2012) develop a decision-making model for social workers that gives primacy to the NASW Code of Ethics. The process includes identifying the problem, and the people, organizations, and agencies involved; determining the values, goals, and objectives relevant to the issue held by all who are involved; developing and assessing alternative courses of action; selecting the most appropriate; and implementing it (p. 73).

The essential ethical components of their system provide clear directions for addressing the values and ethical principles that will impact decision making. As a first step, guidance should be sought from the NASW Code of Ethics. If there are relevant sections of the Code that can provide direction, these must be used. If there are no relevant sections, or if different sections of the Code give conflicting directions, social workers should apply the Ethical Principles Screen, which prioritizes seven principles to guide decisions (p. 73). These are as follows:

Principle 1: Principle of the Protection of Life. Biological life must always take precedence over any other principles, because it is in the context of life that ethical decisions are made.

Principle 2: Principle of Equality and Inequality. Similar circumstances and situations should be treated the same. However, if there are relevant significant differences, these should be taken into consideration, and unequal treatment may be accorded where it would lead to greater equality.

Principle 3: Principle of Autonomy and Freedom. Clients' autonomy and self-determination should always be considered, unless their autonomous actions and choices would threaten the life of self or other. The right to freedom, however, is less compelling than the prevention of harm or death.

Principle 4: Principle of Least Harm. Social workers should avoid causing harm and prevent harm from occurring to clients or others. Where harm is unavoidable, social workers should choose the course of least harm, or most easily reversible harm.

Principle 5: Principle of Quality of Life. Enhancing quality of life for clients and others in society should be a goal of social work interventions.

Principle 6: Principle of Privacy and Confidentiality. The right to privacy of clients and others should be enhanced wherever possible and in accordance with laws. However, it may be necessary to break confidentiality when serious harm or death to clients or others may result from maintaining such confidentiality.

Principle 7: Principle of Truthfulness and Full Disclosure. Social workers should be honest and provide full and truthful information to clients and others in order to support a relationship grounded in trust and honesty (Dolgoff et al., 2012).

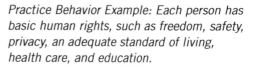

Human Rights & Justice

Practice Behavior Example: Each person has basic human rights, such as freedom, safety, privacy, an adequate standard of living, health care, and education.

Critical Thinking Question: Dolgoff, Harrington, & Loewenberg's first principle, The Protection of Life, defines "life" as "biological life." In so doing, it raises the question of when "life" begins, but does not refer to abortion specifically in the Ethical Principles Screen, perhaps choosing to leave this open to the discretion of the individual worker or agency seeking to apply this theory to ethical decisions. How might the consideration of when "life" begins impact decision making utilizing this theory?

While these principles provide a clear framework, it must be recognized that each abstract terms, such as *life, equality, freedom, harm, quality of life, privacy*, etc. may be defined differently by every social worker, every client, every supervisor, and every agency, and that these differences in definition seriously impact the decision-making process.

A Bioethics Perspective: The Medical Model

Beauchamp and Childress's decision-making framework is included here for two reasons: (1) Their guidelines, which are the core values of medicine, and those of the social work profession seem generally similar, and (2) many social workers provide services within the healthcare system, where this framework is frequently applied to ethical concerns.

Their perspective, developed in *Principles of Biomedical Ethics* (2009), appears easy to use at first glance because of its seeming simplicity, which involves the application of four principles with which most professionals of any discipline are familiar. However, because the principles are not prioritized by the authors, conscientious use requires an understanding not only of the principles themselves, but also of the rules that may be drawn from them to ultimately guide action. The four principles include the following:

> ***Principle 1: The Principle of Respect for Autonomy.*** Autonomy is often referred to by social workers as *self-determination.* In concert with our own profession, Beauchamp and Childress suggested that respect for autonomy means not only acknowledging individual rights in decision making, but also acknowledging the responsibility of the professional in helping people toward the capacity and ability to make such a decision (Beauchamp & Childress, 2009, p. 103). Helping clients toward self-determination involves providing information in a way that is usable and comprehensible, exploring values and options for action, and helping to put clients' choices into effect.
>
> ***Principle 2: The Principle of Nonmaleficence.*** The principle of nonmaleficence, or "do no harm," has an old and distinguished history, and seems especially relevant to social workers, who often work with vulnerable populations.
>
> ***Principle 3: The Principle of Beneficence.*** This principle states that doing no harm is not sufficient—there is an additional obligation to actively pursue the welfare of others. This obligation can include protecting and defending their rights, preventing harm, and helping and rescuing people in need (Beauchamp & Childress, 2009, pp. 197–199).
>
> ***Principle 4: The Principle of Justice.*** Justice is often understood in terms of fairness and is most commonly related to distributive issues of allocation. The principles often used to arrive at determinations of justice are equal share, need, effort, contribution to society, merit, and free-market exchange (Beauchamp & Childress, 2009, p. 243).

There are many similarities across disciplines in ethical codes and standards.

A.S. Zain/Shutterstock

Aftermath of tsunami in Aceh, Indonesia. Disaster relief and assistance is supported by theories of justice.

From these four principles, the authors draw rules, which include (1) the rule of veracity (truth), (2) the rule of privacy, (3) the rule of confidentiality, and (4) the rule of fidelity (Beauchamp & Childress, 2009, pp. 288–316).

The application of these rules to the specific ethical dilemma that is being addressed enables the professional to determine particular actions appropriate to patients and clients. However, the way in which the principles are prioritized might allow for differences based on personal values of the decision maker, or institutional values, which may create an inconsistency in application. In addition, because this system is developed in a healthcare context, it does not always connect with the NASW Code of Ethics or relate easily to some of the social-work-specific issues the practitioner may encounter with clients.

Social Justice: John Rawls's Framework for Decision Making

Rawls is not a social worker; he is a philosopher. However, his theory has been very influential and has informed and guided the development of many social programs in the United States. Professional social workers in both private and public agencies have found this framework helpful in understanding the principles that undergird the particulars of the programs their agencies administer.

Rawls characterizes a "well-ordered society" as one "designed to advance the good of its members and effectively regulated by a public conception of justice" (Rawls, 1999). This society, he states, should be guided by two principles:

1. Equal maximization of liberty principle: Each person has the right to the greatest possible liberty. This liberty must be of the same degree as that available to every person in the society and includes the right to vote, the right to run for office, freedom of speech and assembly, freedom of conscience and thought, personal freedom, the right to own property, and freedom from arbitrary arrest.

2. Distribution principle: Social and economic inequalities cannot be eliminated completely. However, the society should be arranged in such a way that they are
   a. To the advantage of everyone in the society.
   b. Available to everyone in the society (equal and fair opportunity).

This second principle addresses the distribution of income and wealth, and the way that power and authority are assigned. Everyone in the society must benefit from the inequalities that exist (Rawls, 1999, pp. 60–61). Rawls's principles are not tied directly to social work and the NASW Code of Ethics. Therefore, social workers may interpret these principles not only to guide their own actions and decisions but also to design, administer, and evaluate social programs. However, they clearly relate both to the Constitution and to the ways in which social programs are designed and developed through the political process.

Rawls's Theory of Justice has been utilized in the development of social welfare programs and policies.

Ethics of Care

The Ethics of Care has been a fairly recent, but very valuable, addition to the traditional ethical theories most used by social workers. Care, as a moral sentiment and also as an emotion, can be used as a grounding for ethical theory. The Ethics of Care by its very nature appears very appropriate to the social work endeavor, with its focus clearly on individuals.

The Ethics of Care was first developed as a theory by Carol Gilligan. Although she has been associated with feminist ethics and women's issues, Gilligan is careful to state that she does not consider Ethics of Care to be a gender position, but, rather, a distinction between two modes of thought, one based on rights, rules and justice, and the other based on care and concern (Gilligan, p. 2). Nel Noddings suggests that true care of another lies not in assuming one knows what is best for the person, but in being open to understanding the person's own reality. Especially relevant for social workers is her discussion of "unequal relationships" and the responsibilities of the care-giver toward the care-recipient (Noddings, pp. 65–74).

Care is envisioned as a sincere concern for the well-being of another: a concern which then creates a context for action on the part of the person who cares toward to person who is the object of care. Effective caring, however, involves more than an emotional feeling. Care also involves a knowledge of the person who is the object of care's circumstances, concerns, needs, feeling and attitudes, priorities and goals, and the application of reason to the process of understanding. Thus, as it applies to social work, the Ethics of Care requires the worker's full engagement in the client's life, and an openness to understanding the client from his or her perspective. Consonant with social work practice, the Ethics of Care asks that one place one's client's needs above one's own, one's concern with the client before self-interest, and that one use reason and knowledge in developing sensitive ways of assessing and meeting client needs.

The Ethics of Care does not have a clear list of "rules" as do the other ethical theories included in this chapter. Rather, the process is much more loosely defined, and, as applied to social workers, can include:

1. A general concern with the well-being of others, especially those who are suffering or in need.

2. Relationships with clients characterized by open communication and sincere care and interest in the person.

3. Openness and receptivity to understanding and sharing in the client's life situation.

4. The development of an understanding of the client grounded in knowledge of human behavior and potential, societal issues, and context.

5. A desire to assist the client toward well-being, grounded in reason and in knowledge of the client and client needs, client and community resources, and agency.

Different Systems Engender Different Results

The framework selected for application to a specific case is vital, because different results may be obtained with different frameworks. When an individual worker selects the framework, the choice often reflects the worker's personal value system or preferences, and/or the worker's understanding of the clients and situation. Practice settings sometimes specify the framework. This fosters consistency and fairness—all ethical dilemmas in that setting or program follow the same path toward resolution (an element of formal justice, which is used by the court system, called *procedural* justice). Frameworks for deliberation may also be specified by policies, funding sources, and laws. In an optimal situation, where the ethical dilemma involves the client directly, she or he may become involved in the choice of ethical frameworks, such that her or his own values and belief system become an important consideration in decision making.

To illustrate the possible resolutions that can be drawn using the five systems (Reamer's; Dolgoff, Harrington & Loewenberg's; Beauchamp and Childress's; Rawls's, and the Ethics of Care), it is helpful to return to the

---

Critical Thinking

Practice Behavior Example: Empathy and Sympathy

Critical Thinking Question: Consideration of the Ethics of Care requires an understanding of the differences between empathy and sympathy. Words, gestures, and posture can all be used as tools of empathic communication. What are some of the words, gestures, and posture that communicate empathy rather than sympathy?

second case in the Introduction discussed in the Introduction: the elderly gentleman who refuses nursing home placement (see p. 1).

Using the framework preferred by Reamer, one could say that basic goods can be met in either setting—home or nursing facility. Probably, physical health is better provided for in the nursing home; mental equilibrium in his apartment. Nonsubtractive goods and additive goods may vary somewhat with the setting but can probably be met in either setting as well. This leaves us with the system's ordered principles. Reviewing these, the applicable principle appears to be Principle 3. This states that an individual's right to freedom takes precedence over his or her own right to well-being. In other words, the resident has the right to self-determine and to place his well-being at risk if he chooses to do so. Following these principles, then, the worker would leave the resident in his senior citizen's apartment, perhaps building in safeguards if he will accept them.

Using the Dolgoff, Harrington, & Loewenberg hierarchy leads to a different resolution. As the Code of Ethics does not give clear direction in this instance, supporting both self-determination and best interests, one would move on to apply the Ethical Principles Screen. There, the worker finds that the Principle of the Protection of Life, the first in the hierarchy, takes precedence over the Principle of Autonomy and Freedom, Principle 3, and the Principle of the Quality of Life, Principle 5. Thus, a worker might feel obligated to ensure the protection and care of the resident's life by placing him in a nursing home against his wishes.

Application of Beauchamp and Childress's model seems to place Principle 1, Respect for Autonomy, in the dominant position. This is supported by Rule 2, Privacy, which asks that the worker respect the right to privacy for this resident. Privacy of person, and self-determination, would seem to support continued residence in the senior citizens' housing project.

Rawlsian principles suggest that the principle of equal liberty must be applied first and specifically include personal freedom, an essential component of equal liberty that every rational person would indeed choose. This basic liberty may be constrained if everyone in the society chooses to constrain it. If everyone agrees, for example, that at a certain age no one may continue to live independently, then it would be possible to place the gentleman, along with every other elder, in some form of supervised congregate placement.

The Ethics of Care suggests that an essential ingredient in decision making is the worker's openness and receptivity toward understanding the client and the client's own perception of needs, desires, and constraints. Perhaps, by better understanding the client's objections to nursing home placement and perceptions of his present condition, worker and client would be able to develop a resolution that includes both the worker's concerns about medication, nutrition, and socialization and the client's desire for maintaining his present independence and living conditions. The worker's communication of genuine care for the client may assist the client in considering some of the worker's concerns for his welfare, enabling him to consider other options.

As the above case and discussion illustrate, the theoretical framework and principles selected to guide decision making have a strong impact. While it is essential to utilize such frameworks in reasoning about ethical decisions, it is also important to acknowledge that other factors, such as professional codes, personal and societal values, and the availability and feasibility of options, will be an essential consideration in ethical decision making.

CHAPTER SUMMARY

Five ethical frameworks frequently used to guide decision making in social work were presented. These include Reamer's application of Gewirth's *ethical decision making system*, which grounds ethical decisions in fundamental rights to freedom and well-being; Dolgoff, Harrington, & Loewenberg's Ethical Principles Screen, which begins with an examination of the NASW Code of Ethics and develops seven principles to be applied if the Code alone cannot resolve the dilemma; Beauchamp and Childress's medical model, with its principles of autonomy, nonmaleficence, beneficence, and justice, which are, however, not prioritized; John Rawls's method of social justice, which is focused on maximization of liberty and fairness in distribution; and the Ethics of Care, which suggests care grounded in knowledge and reason as a basis for ethical decision making, and focuses on the development of a mutual relationship in which the client is able to accept the worker's genuine care and concern, and enables client and worker to engage together in the process of resolving problems.

In addition to ethical theories and principles, the NASW Code of Ethics provides principles and standards that are accepted by the profession. The Code defines professional values, determines principles, and provides standards to guide practice. Familiarity with the provisions of the Code is essential to ethical professional practice, and these will be addressed in the next chapter.

References

Beauchamp, T. L., & Childress, J. F. (2009). *Principles of biomedical ethics* (6th ed.). New York: Oxford University Press.

Dolgoff, R., Harrington D., & Loewenberg, F. M. (2012). *Ethical decisions for social work practice* (8th ed.). Itasca, IL: F. E. Peacock.

Gewirth, A. (1978). *Reason and morality*. Chicago: University of Chicago Press.

Gilligan, C. (1982). *In a different voice*. Cambridge, MA: Harvard University Press.

Noddings, N. (2003). *Caring: A feminine approach to ethics and moral education* (2nd ed.). Berkeley: University of California Press.

Rawls, J. (1999). *A theory of justice*. Cambridge, MA: Harvard University Press.

Reamer, F. (1994). *Ethical dilemmas in social service*. New York: Columbia University Press.

The following questions will test your knowledge of the content found within this chapter. For questions 1-6, please select the phrase that best completes each sentence. Question 7 is a brief essay question. For additional assessment, including licensing-exam type questions on applying chapter content to practice behaviors, visit **MySearchLab**.

1. In selecting an ethical theory, consideration of the substantive question involves:
   a. understanding to whom the theory applies
   b. considering the goals that are desireable
   c. knowing the areas in which the theory can be applied
   d. identifying the decision-making hierarchy

2. Justice is the defining characteristic of _____'s ethical theory
   a. Beauchamp and Childress
   b. Reamer and Gewirth
   c. Dolgoff, Harrington, & Loewenberg
   d. Rawls

3. In utilizing the Ethics of Care framework, it is essential to consider:
   a. the client's emotional behavior
   b. one's personal feelings about the client
   c. how to communicate empathically
   d. the reaction of colleagues

4. In Beauchamp and Childress's ethical decision-making model, the term *autonomy* most closely approximates the social work term
   a. self-awareness
   b. self-determination
   c. self-control
   d. self-knowledge

5. In selecting an ethical theory, it is important to consider:
   a. the desired outcomes
   b. the history of the theory
   c. different agencies' choices of theory
   d. different theories engender different results

6. Free will and choice are constrained in some way for
   a. all clients
   b. clients from oppressed backgrounds
   c. clients with mental limitations
   d. clients with family responsibilities

7. Using the dilemma statement developed in the essay question in Chapter 1, consider each of the ethical theories presented in this chapter. Which of these appears to be most appropriate for this ethical problem? Why?

3

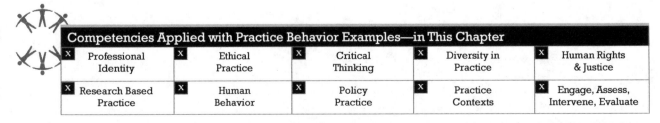

Clearviewstock/Shutterstock

Using the Code of Ethics
of the National Association
# of Social Workers

Competencies Applied with Practice Behavior Examples—in This Chapter				
x Professional Identity	x Ethical Practice	x Critical Thinking	x Diversity in Practice	x Human Rights & Justice
x Research Based Practice	x Human Behavior	x Policy Practice	x Practice Contexts	x Engage, Assess, Intervene, Evaluate

INTRODUCTION

One of the distinguishing marks of a profession is the presence of an ethical code that sets forth and defines the responsibilities of the members of the profession. The first social work Code of Ethics was adopted by the Delegate Conference of the American Association of Social Workers in 1947. After the formation of the NASW, a Code of Ethics was drafted and adopted in 1960. Since then, there have been numerous revisions. A very extensive revision was adopted by the Delegate Assembly in August 1996. The Code of Ethics was revised again by the Delegate Assembly in 2008, expanding and emphasizing the responsibility to cultural competence and diversity in sections 1, 2, 4, and 6 to include "gender identity and expression" and "immigration status." The Code of Ethics in its entirety may be accessed online through the NASW Web site at www.socialworkers.org/pubs/code/default.asp.

Since 1997, the NASW Code of Ethics has been binding upon all students in schools of social work.

It is important to become familiar with the Code, for it should serve as a guide to social work practice at all times. Until the social worker is completely familiar with the contents, it is a good idea to have a copy of the Code easily accessible, so that it may be consulted as needed. In a short time, the worker will become knowledgeable about the tenets of the Code, and practice will easily be guided by its standards.

CODE STRUCTURE AND CONTENT

The Code contains four sections. It is important to be aware of the content and function of each section in making an ethical decision.

Preamble

The Preamble summarizes the mission and core values of the profession, which are as follows:

service
social justice
dignity and worth of the person
importance of human relationships
integrity
competence

The mission of the profession as a whole is "to enhance human well-being and help meet the basic human needs of all people, with particular attention to the needs and empowerment of people who are vulnerable, oppressed, and living in poverty" (National Association of Social Workers (NASW), 2008).

Purpose of the Code

The second section provides an overview of the Code's purpose and functions and presents a guide for addressing ethical issues. The purpose is defined as the determination of the values, principles, and standards that can provide guidance to social workers in practice. The Code is meant to be

Human Behavior

Practice Behavior Example: Both the Code of Ethics' mission statements and CSWE's core competencies address "well-being," although it is not defined in either document. Well-being generally includes health, human rights, access to a reasonable standard of living, social relationships, and opportunities for creativity, growth, and self-fulfillment.

Critical Thinking Question: Because the specific qualities of well-being are fluid and vary by culture, age, context, gender, and other dimensions, it is essential that the social worker explore each client's concept of well-being individually, as well as have a high level of awareness of her or his own concepts of well-being to ensure that personal values do not predominate. Can there be one inclusive definition of well-being for all people?

used by "individuals, agencies, organizations, and bodies (such as licensing and regulatory boards, professional liability insurance providers, courts of law, agency boards of directors, government agencies, and other professional groups) that choose to adopt it as a frame of reference" (NASW, 2008).

Six purposes are to be served by the Code of Ethics: (1) identification of core values; (2) statement of broad ethical principles and establishment of specific ethical standards; (3) assistance to social workers in the identification of professional obligations; (4) provision of ethical standards to which the profession may be held accountable; (5) orientation to mission, values, principles, and standards for new practitioners; and (6) identification of standards which the profession can use to assess its members. "Cooperation" with the Code is required.

Social workers are expected to use the Code as a guide in decision making, but *the values, principles, and standards are* not *prioritized.* It is the social worker's responsibility to consider all relevant parts of the Code in ethical decision making, along with other sources of information.

In determining priorities, values, and principles, it is helpful to consult agency mission and policies for guidance, in order to make ethical decisions that support agency goals.

Ethical Principles

The third section, Ethical Principles, presents the six broad principles that can be drawn from the six core values of the profession. These are as follows:

1. "Social workers' primary goal is to help people in need and to address social problems." This principle is drawn from the value of *service.*
2. "Social workers challenge social injustice." This is drawn from the value of *social justice.*
3. "Social workers respect the inherent dignity and worth of the person." The related core value is *dignity and worth of person.*
4. "Social workers recognize the central importance of human relationships." This is drawn from the core value of the *importance of human relationships.*
5. "Social workers behave in a trustworthy manner." This principle is drawn from the value of *integrity.*
6. "Social workers practice within their areas of competence and develop and enhance their professional expertise." This is drawn from the value of *competence* (NASW, 2008).

Thus, in Section 3, each defined core value from Section 1 relates to a specific principle that can guide professional practice.

Ethical Standards

The fourth and by far the longest and most explicit section, Ethical Standards, provides action guides in six areas of professional functioning. These are also used as a basis for adjudication, both public and self-regulatory, by defining accepted standards of behavior. The case studies in this text is organized around the framework of these six standards, which will be reviewed in full in Part II of this text the relevant chapters. These are:

1. *Ethical Responsibilities to Clients*, which includes commitment to clients, self-determination, informed consent, competence, cultural competence, conflicts of interest, privacy and confidentiality, sexual relationships, termination of services, and others.

Sean Haley/Shutterstock

Ethics in action: LA protest march for immigration reform.

2. *Ethical Responsibilities to Colleagues*, which includes respect, confidentiality, collaboration, consultation, sexual relationships, and impairment, incompetence, and unethical conduct, and others.

3. *Ethical Responsibilities to Practice Settings*, which includes supervision, consultation, education and training, evaluation, commitment to employers, and others.

4. *Ethical Responsibilities as Professionals*, which includes competence, not engaging in discrimination, dishonesty and fraud, impairment, misrepresentation, and others.

5. *Ethical Responsibilities to the Social Work Profession*, which includes maintaining the integrity of the profession, evaluation, and research.

6. *Ethical Responsibilities to the Broader Society*, which includes social welfare, public participation, public emergencies, and social and political action.

As noted in the previous section, it is important to recognize that the Ethical Standards *are not prioritized*. Social workers should not assume, for example, that because the section "Responsibility to Colleagues" is placed before the section "Responsibility to the Broader Society" that one should always consider one's colleagues ahead of community, or society as a whole. Similarly, contents *within* each standard may not be prioritized.

When examining the Code of Ethics for guidance relevant to the client(s), context, or situation in which the ethical problem has occurred, it is easy for the social worker to focus on the people or situations immediately affected

Diversity in Practice

Practice Behavior Example: Standard 1.05 requires that a social worker understand the role of culture and the strengths inherent in all cultures, as well as have knowledge of the cultures of the clients with whom they are working, so that the services provided may be culturally sensitive.

Critical Thinking Question: In addition to reading about the client's culture, what other sources of information may be helpful in understanding the client's culture?

Agency ethics committees are excellent resources, and may be consulted regarding ethical decision making.

Practice Contexts

*Practice Behavior Example: Social workers'
ethical decisions always impact agencies,
and agency goals, mission, context, and
policies should always be consulted.*

Critical Thinking Question: What are some of
the ways that social workers' ethical decisions
can impact agencies?

by the issue or concern. Often, the agency serves merely as background and is not an active player in the consideration of the ethical dimensions of a problem. However, it is essential to include the agency as a factor in the decision-making process. The agency is the context within which services are rendered. The agency has contracts, policies and procedures, and relationships with other agencies.

In addition to guidance provided by the Code of Ethics, the profession, through NASW, has defined its position on many complex current issues. These have been collected and organized in *Social Work Speaks. Social Work Speaks* is available in book form through NASW, and abstracts are available online through the NASW Web site, www.social-worker.org. It is good practice to familiarize oneself with *Social Work Speaks* and to be aware of the profession's position on issues which may occur in individual practitioners' contexts.

The Council on Social Work Education has also defined 10 core competencies essential to professional practice, each of which has a strong ethical, as well as practice component, and provides the structure which underlies this textbook. The core competencies include:

1. identifying oneself as a professional social worker and conducting oneself accordingly.
2. using ethical principles to guide practice.
3. using critical thinking.
4. engaging with diversity and difference.
5. advancing human rights and social and economic justice.
6. engaging with research.
7. utilizing knowledge of human behavior and the social environment.
8. engaging in policy practice to advance social and economic well-being.
9. responding to contexts of practice.
10. engaging, assessing, intervening, and evaluating with clients and client groups and organizations.

A full description of the core competencies may be found online at www.cswe.org, by clicking on Educational Policy and Accreditation Standards (EPAS).

LEGAL CODES AND ETHICAL CODES

There is a delicate balance and relationship between legal codes and ethical codes in a society. In democratic societies, some, or ideally all, members of the society define and ground the ethical principles that will guide behavior and relationships between individual members, groups, communities, and the government of the society. Important and complex ethical standards and expectations are often codified into laws, and laws have been considered as a society's "codified ethics." There is generally a lapse of time between an ethical principle or guideline's development, its acceptance by a society at large, and its formal passage into a code of law. This time lapse can create a tension between legal codes (which are static and consistent), ethical concepts and standards (which are dynamic and evolving to incorporate changes in society), and experiences and occurrences of a more immediate nature. In general, societal ethics change and adapt to new conditions more readily than laws.

Social work professionals may find themselves caught in this tension in practice. For example, laws governing service delivery systems may not account for cultural variations among client groups. The one-size-fits-all program that provides continuity and consistency may not take into account the very special and unique situation of a particular client. Rehabilitation services that require basic changes in client behaviors to meet the requirements of society at large may stifle self-determination. Defined decision-making processes may require one person, rather than a family group, to take ultimate responsibility and sign a "consent" to a treatment or procedure. Agency accountability procedures may require that workers allocate resources and time in a way that does not meet individual clients' needs.

In addition, funding does not always support laws. When laws were passed mandating community-based services for people with mental illness, for example, adequate funding for such services was not allocated. In the Introduction's fifth example, of the foster care agency worker whose caseload was doubled due to budget cuts, preexisting laws that defined the way in which services were to be provided to families were not altered with the current budget cuts, creating the need for difficult choices.

Effecting change in laws—"catching them up" to ethical practice—is a complex and time-consuming task. Social workers specializing in policy and management address these kinds of problems and work with legislators to change laws to enhance ethical professional practice, but, as we will see, all social workers have responsibilities for advocacy where clients' needs are impacted. No matter what immediate specific actions the foster care worker chooses, working to address the imbalance between laws regarding service provision and funding is an important part of ethical responsibility.

LAWS, MALPRACTICE, AND THE NASW CODE OF ETHICS

Laws demand and expect adherence; so do professional ethical codes.

Nonadherence to laws carries legal penalties and is addressed through the justice system. Nonadherence to ethical codes may also carry legal penalties but often is monitored and addressed through the ethical boards of state professional associations or other regulatory bodies. Social workers cannot be sent to jail for nonadherence to the NASW Code of Ethics, unless a provision of the Code is also a formal part of the legal Code. However, once a professional code has been defined and put into place, adherence to the code becomes a standard requirement of membership in the profession.

Social workers can be sued for malpractice in civil court or through a professional association for violation of the NASW Code of Ethics, can be sanctioned, and can be required to make reparations. Sanctions for violations include public sanctioning, suspension of right to practice, monetary penalties, mandated education, and termination of employment. Liability and malpractice suits against social workers have been increasing in recent years, making it especially important for social workers to be familiar with both the Code of Ethics and laws that govern social work practice in the state in which they live.

Careful consideration of ethical dilemmas, with a clear grounding in the Code of Ethics, provides social workers with direction for action that resolves

When making ethical decisions in high-liability risk areas of practice, consultation with a supervisor, agency director, or agency ethics committee can provide additional guidance.

most ethical dilemmas. However, three broad groups of ethical dilemmas carry higher malpractice and liability risks, and extra care should be taken when considering these kinds of ethical dilemmas in practice. The first group is related to interventions used in practice, and include confidentiality, self-determination, paternalism, and truth-telling (Reamer, 1994, p. 238). Ethical guidelines for these issues are addressed primarily in Ethical Standard 1 of the Code.

The second group relates to the way in which social programs and policies are developed and administered. This category includes compliance with laws and regulations, agency-developed rules and policies, and regulations which affect agencies (Reamer, p. 240). Some guidelines for these kinds of ethical dilemmas are found in Ethical Standards 3 and 6, but may also be found in other areas of the Code. The third group includes problems that arise in social workers' relationships with colleagues, particularly impaired or incompetent colleagues (Reamer, p. 241), and are addressed in Ethical Standard 2 of the Code.

LAWS AND PERSONAL ETHICAL STANDARDS

It is essential that all professionals know and understand the personal ethical and moral code that guides them. Students can explore personal values and beliefs, prioritize them, and develop a personal ethical hierarchy, and some suggestions to guide this process will be presented in the following chapter. It is important to recognize that this hierarchy will not only guide personal comportment, but will also affect the way in which ethical dilemmas are formulated and ethical decisions are made in practice.

Adherence to current legal codes is generally a part of an individual's personal ethical system. People generally stop at red lights, don't read other people's mail, respect their neighbor's property, pay taxes, cross at crosswalks, serve on juries, accept the directions of law enforcement officers, call 911 in emergencies, and don't cheat on examinations. They also follow the social ethical codes that guide relationship with others in society, such as treating people courteously, with respect and consideration, having goodwill, and not lying to them.

Ethical Practice

Practice Behavior Example: Laws of professional conduct include veracity, fidelity, loyalty to employing organization, to colleagues, to funding sources, and to those with whom we have a legal contract. Awareness of the specific laws and policies that govern our professional functioning is an essential professional responsibility.

Critical Thinking Question: Following the law is a part of the social contract between individuals and societies. However, it is possible for personal ethical considerations to supercede laws in a person's value system. What are some examples where this might occur?

ETHICAL BUT ILLEGAL PRACTICE

Most of the time, the laws of society correspond to individual personal ethical standards, and there is a comfortable fit between them. However, there may be times when an individual's personal ethical system and the law differ. In that case, he or she must make difficult ethical decisions: Should "adherence to the law" be one's highest personal ethical value? For many of us, it is, and we would never consider breaking the law. For others of us, there may be an imperative higher than law, such as a responsibility to follow religious principles, a sense of primary responsibility to the good of the client, or a responsibility to protect one's individual safety and integrity or that of others. These kinds of ethical professional dilemmas can be among the most difficult to address. Abortion, euthanasia, the rights of undocumented immigrants, and personal privacy are four examples of current issues where ethics and law can collide.

USING THE CODE TO INFORM LEGAL/ETHICAL DECISIONS

The NASW Code of Ethics can assist social workers encountering ethical issues in practice, because it clearly defines professional behavior and expectations in many areas. In others, however, the Code appears purposefully ambiguous, and the play of professional standards, laws, and personal ethical standards can be a fascinating, though often challenging, part of the professional social worker's decision-making process.

CHAPTER SUMMARY

This chapter has introduced the reader to the NASW Code of Ethics. The Code is subdivided into four sections, which focus on core values, purpose, principles, and standards. The standards section provides guidelines for practice and addresses specific circumstances and concerns, as well as defining the six major areas of ethical responsibility: to clients, to colleagues, to practice settings, as professional social workers, to the social work profession, and to the broader society. Standards are not prioritized and may conflict with each other in certain situations; therefore, clear reasoning and judgment of the social worker is an essential ingredient in ethical social work practice.

The laws of society may be regarded as a system of "codified ethics." Ethical considerations, and ethical assumption of certain behaviors and responsibilities generally occur before these are formally passed by the governing bodies of a society into law. Laws are static, codified; ethical positions are dynamic, changing with circumstance, experience, and deliberation. Ethical standards change more quickly and easily than laws. This creates a tension between law and ethics, within which the worker may at times find herself or himself.

In addition to the Code of Ethics, two other resources can be helpful to the social worker. *Social Work Speaks*, available online, presents the official NASW position on a wide variety of issues. The Council on Social Work Education's *Educational Policy and Accreditation Standards* may be found online at CSWE.org.

Both ethical theories and the NASW Code of Ethics are grounded in value systems. As has been discussed in the previous chapter, ethical theories are grounded in the value systems of those who formulate them, and are influenced by culture, context, and historical period. The Code of Ethics clearly states the six values upon which the Code rests. In the next chapter, we shall consider four other value systems that strongly impact ethical decision making in social work practice: values of the client system, agency, "society," and the personal values of the social worker providing services.

References

National Association of Social Workers. (2008). *NASW code of ethics.* Washington, DC: Author.

Reamer, F. (1994). *Social work malpractice and liability: Strategies for prevention.* New York: Columbia University Press.

The following questions will test your knowledge of the content found within this chapter. For questions 1-6, please select the phrase that best completes each sentence. Question 7 is a brief essay question. For additional assessment, including licensing-exam type questions on applying chapter content to practice behaviors, visit **MySearchLab**.

1. The most recent additions to the Code of Ethics address:
   a. age discrimination
   b. dual relationships
   c. national and global social justice issues
   d. gender and immigration discrimination

2. To use the Code of Ethics effectively, one should:
   a. follow the order in which it is written
   b. always consult with a supervisor when using the Code
   c. use information and reasoning to determine applicable sections of the Code
   d. use the Code in its entirety in each situation

3. As stated in the "Purpose" section of the Code, the primary purpose of the Code of Ethics is to:
   a. work for social justice
   b. help people in need and address social problems
   c. address poverty and discrimination in society
   d. support human dignity

4. Three areas which tend to have a higher incidence of malpractice suits are:
   a. relationship with colleagues, client interventions, and administrative policies
   b. client interventions, social justice, and discrimination
   c. social justice, the social worker's professionalism, and relationship with colleagues
   d. agency policy, adherence to public laws, and sexual misconduct

5. Revisions of the Code are enacted by:
   a. mailed ballot to all NASW members
   b. a committee appointed for this purpose
   c. the Delegate Assembly
   d. a poll on the NASW Web site

6. The NASW's position papers on a wide range of ethical issues may be found in:
   a. most practice textbooks
   b. CSWE's core competencies
   c. NASW's Code of Ethics
   d. Social Work Speaks

7. Using the ethical dilemma you have defined and the theoretical framework you have chosen in the previous two chapters' essay questions, examine the Code of Ethics and determine which sections, if any, apply to the dilemma you are considering. (It is understood that there has been no actual information-gathering—your analysis will be based on your best assumptions of the facts that might be the case.)

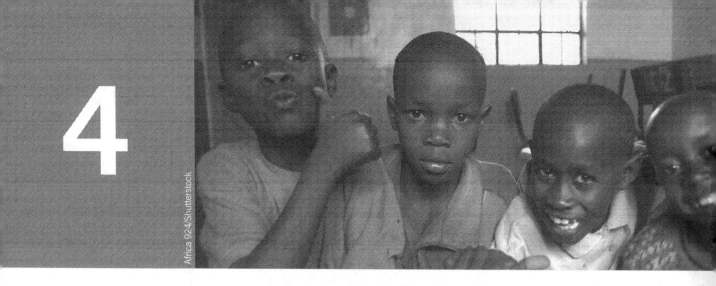

Africa 924/Shutterstock

Exploring Value Systems

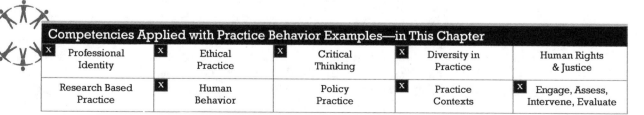

Competencies Applied with Practice Behavior Examples—in This Chapter				
x Professional Identity	x Ethical Practice	x Critical Thinking	x Diversity in Practice	Human Rights & Justice
Research Based Practice	x Human Behavior	Policy Practice	x Practice Contexts	x Engage, Assess, Intervene, Evaluate

INTRODUCTION

No matter how carefully and thoughtfully the social worker defines the ethical dilemma, how thoroughly each ethical theory is considered and information is gathered, and how carefully the Code of Ethics is reviewed, an ethical dilemma cannot be successfully resolved, and the resolution operationalized, if it is not integral to the personal values of those touched by the dilemma, and the broader societal values. Clients cannot be asked to act against their personal system of ethics, their religious beliefs, or their cultural traditions. The resolution of the dilemma will not function successfully in a societal milieu whose ideas and beliefs are contrary to those espoused by the resolution. In addition to these, the social worker's own value system, that of colleagues and supervisor, and the general values that guide and determine agency structure and function can affect every aspect of ethical decision making. Values shape and guide behavior, and play a major role in understanding oneself, relating to others, and functioning in society.

IDEAL VALUES AND REAL VALUES

"Ideal" values are expressed in the Constitution and the Bill of Rights.

During classroom values exercises, students invariably encounter a problem when a discussion of values is initiated. It manifests itself most clearly in relation to societal values, which can serve here as an example. We tend to think of societal values in terms of grandiose concepts such as "freedom," "democracy," and "equality," but it is clear that these do not operate throughout society as we might wish. We are all poignantly aware that democracy is not always the only value at work in Congress and in our political system, fairness is not always the primary concern in our economy and the distribution of goods, justice is not always served under our system of laws, and true equality remains an ideal in many areas of people's lives.

This creates a kind of a "double standard" in values: There are the *ideal* values, which define the image individuals, groups, organizations, and societies would like to have of themselves, and which are often carefully considered and followed. And there are more covert, often *real*, unspoken and unacknowledged values, which may be less "ideal" and, at times, more self-interested, and which also guide a part of our daily lives. Most people function using a combination of both real and ideal values.

Both "ideal" and "real" values have important roles to play in society.

At every level, it is important for the social worker to be aware of this distinction, and the manner in which it is understood, and lived, by individuals, groups, and society. The greater the overlap between "real" and "ideal" values, the better will be the "fit," and the more consistently and effectively the holder of the values can function.

VALUE TERMINOLOGY

Most people are able to use the language of values comfortably. However, there are two issues around the use of words which must be considered by the social worker. The first of these concerns the specificity that is absent in general, abstract, global terms. Most people in the United States would agree that "justice" is an important value. It is easy, then, to believe that everyone is in agreement. And everyone *is*; however, if one asked ten people to define "justice"—specifically what *they understood it to mean*—one would elicit ten very different responses. There is a tendency to relate the specificity of a global term to one's own beliefs, experiences, and cultural context. Thus, social worker, client, colleague, supervisor might all be using the same term—but mean very different things! In general, the more abstract the value ("justice," "relationships") the greater the potential for differences in meaning; the more specific the value ("having children," "getting my master's degree") the less the ambiguity.

The second important issue for social workers concerns similarities and differences in values between worker and clients. When there are many social, cultural, religious, or other differences between the social worker and the client or community, and when everyone is aware of these differences, extra care and consideration is often given to ethical discussions by all participants, especially in determining the specificity of abstract, global terms. It is helpful for the social worker to develop a trusting relationship prior to discussing values issues, and ask for clarification when there is the possibility of differences in meanings and in priorities.

Social workers may feel more comfortable with a client or client group whose values appear to be similar to their own—they might share a religion, or membership in an organization, or a life experience, or concern about a similar issue. Where there is apparent similarity, it is easy to make assumptions: to assume that there is more correspondence between the social worker's values and those of clients than might really be the case. It is important to be *very* careful in making assumptions about value congruity with such clients, and to always be aware that the power differential between workers and clients may make it difficult for clients to distance themselves from the social workers' assumptions about shared values. Clients may seem to espouse the social worker's values to gain the social worker's approval, or to appear to be in agreement with the social worker's decisions.

> **It is important for the social worker to recognize and communicate understanding of the importance of difference in shaping life experiences.**

VALUE SYSTEMS

Personal Values

Often, the values that impact most strongly on the resolution of any ethical dilemma are the values of the social worker. These generally are consonant with the values of the profession as expressed in the Code of Ethics, presented in the previous chapter, and also include personal values that come out of the worker's unique life experiences, training, and belief system. Personal values affect the way in which a dilemma is phrased, the theories and principles utilized in arriving at a resolution, and the ranking of guidelines in the Code of Ethics. This impact is unavoidable: It is a given of the human condition that each person views the world from a unique point of view. However, awareness of one's own values, beliefs, and biases can help workers to understand the role of their personal values in resolving the ethical problem.

Awareness of personal values, both real and ideal, requires observation and reflection. As one ethicist has said, you understand your own values best if you *self-observe*—observe

Critical Thinking

Practice Behavior Example: Congruity between the social worker's professional values and personal values will affect professional functioning.

Critical Thinking Question: The greater the overlap between value systems, the more compatible will be the relationships between the two systems. In thinking about personal values and the NASW Code of Ethics, do you find much overlap between values? Do you see some differences?

your own behavior, your actions, and the feelings they engender. These will point to your deepest, most personal values.

Agency Values

Social workers need to be aware of both "ideal" and "real" values in the practice setting.

Agencies also have values. Ideal, formal values may be most easily accessed in an agency's mission statement and its goals. Policy and procedure manuals can give the reader an understanding of the agency's history and the way that its goals and ideas have developed, and provide some insight into values related to services, clients, communities, and employees. Observation and awareness of an agency's problems and concerns will assist the social worker to understand "real" values as well. As an example: A "real" value generally held by all organizations is a desire to continue to function and to exist.

It is important for the social worker to recognize and communicate understanding of the role of difference in shaping life experiences.

The ethical position of individual supervisors, colleagues, and agency directors can impact strongly as well. For example, the client presented in the fifth case in the Introduction, who is asking for sessions beyond the agency's 8 session limit to address her relationship with her sibling, is relating her request to her own personal values of self-esteem, independence, optimal functioning, and human relationships. The worker, who desires to extend services, might value human relationships, service, and the dignity and worth of the individual, as well as independence in decision making, successful work, and fidelity. If she has "truth" high on her personal values hierarchy, however, she will probably discuss the client's request and her proposed action with her supervisor. As soon as she does this, the supervisor's values also impact on the problem. The supervisor may decide to allow the service to be extended, placing client service above her own obligation to her practice setting, freedom and independence above loyalty to her employer. Or, she may decide that service cannot be rendered, because her understanding of service means providing help to all who are in need, thus requiring the worker's time for other clients. She may also have "justice" and "fairness" high on her list of ethical values and believe that these would not be served if she permitted the worker to continue with the client and beyond the extent of services available to all clients.

Professional Identity

Practice Behavior Example: Supervision and consultation are important elements of professional practice.

Critical Thinking Question: Under the doctrine of *respondeat superior*, supervisors and agency directors may be held legally responsible for the actions of the social workers they supervise. Is it preferable to share all ethical decision making with a supervisor?

Sharing an ethical dilemma with a colleague or supervisor makes her or his personal values, and her or his understanding of agency policies and practice that sharing an ethical dilemma with a colleague or supervisor will engender his or her personal values as an important factor in the equation. While this should not deter the worker from seeking appropriate consultation from a supervisor or from colleagues, it is important to be aware of how the person's values will affect the suggestion or resolution she or he might offer.

Values of the Client System

The resolution of an ethical dilemma which involves a client must be compatible with the client's values, worldview, cultural outlook, and religious beliefs. It is the responsibility of the worker to reach for an understanding of client values, so that these may be integrated into the decision-making process. They will play an important role in the ability of the worker to be of service to the client. This approach is supported by the core values of *dignity and worth of the person* and of both *service* and *competence*. While the values of the client

are of central concern, it is also important to consider values of others who
will be affected by the ethical decision.
These may include the client's significant others, family members, friends
and support networks, as well as the
client's community. Where all of the
clients of an agency may potentially be
affected by an ethical decision, their
values also require consideration.

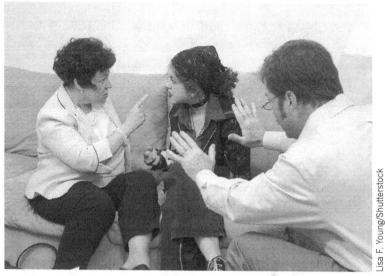

Therapy with a mother and
teenager: The values of each
must be considered.

Returning to the fourth case examples presented in the Introduction—
that of the agency serving HIV-positive
Latinos and considering expanding
its service to include non-Latinos—it
appears obvious that an understanding of the culture and values of the
agency's Latino population as well as
those of the population that might be added to the agency's client base be
considered. Latinos value both the nuclear and extended family, and decisions are often made by the family as a whole, rather than by the individual.
Often, religion plays an important part in family life, as do cultural traditions
that may be tied to the country of origin. The ambiance of the agency, the specific services provided, and the unit of attention support the cultural beliefs,
values, and identity of the Latino client. How will these be impacted by the
inclusion of another population, whose values, culture, and family structure
may be quite different? And how can, or should, services be adapted to meet
the cultural and value needs of the new population? How
would the impact of "outsiders" affect Latino utilization of
services? All of these factors, too, need to be a part of the
ethical consideration.

A discussion of values requires a level of trust on the part
of the client, as well as familiarity with the client's value terminology on the part of the worker. It is important to clarify
meanings, for often, as has been noted earlier, general value
terms have different meanings for different people. An exercise which explores both client values and priorities can
be invaluable in exploring the client's value system and in
clarifying them.

Engage, Assess, Intervene, Evaluate

*Practice Behavior Example: Social workers
sometimes believe that "change client's
values" is an appropriate intervention, based
on their assessment of client's functioning.*

Critical Thinking Question: Is it ethical, and/or
possible, to change another person's values?
Under what circumstances?

Societal Values

All social workers function within the context of the broader society and have
clear responsibilities to this society as defined in Ethical Standard Six of the
Code. In general, workers must uphold societal values, though at times they
may need to advocate for changes. Upholding them requires a clear understanding of what they are. Merely defining "society" can become a very complex task. Yet, because all social workers function within the context of society and are often its agents, it is important to find some way to address and
integrate the values of the broader society into the decision-making process.
These might include, but should not be limited to, the ideal values of equality, freedom, justice, achievement and success, and self-actualization, among

Practice Behavior Example: It is important to recognize that not all groups and societies are equal, and that some groups are oppressed, marginalized, and often disenfranchised in the public discourse, including the discourse on values.

Critical Thinking Question: A discussion of values may be affected by the client's membership in an oppressed and marginalized group. How might such membership affect a client's understanding and expression of personal values?

many others. At times, these values may conflict with those of the client and create an ethical dilemma of their own. At other times, the impact of societal values on the client, and the client's self-image, becomes an important element in the consideration of dilemmas.

As previously discussed, "society,"—however one defines it—has both ideal and real values. In addition, "society" is not one homogeneous whole in the United States, but is made up of many social groups which differ in culture and ethnicity, race, religion, gender, age, section of country, political affiliation, immigration status, length of time in the United States—to name just a few. Each of these "societies" has values which are shared among members, but which differ from the other groups in content and/or priority. In considering "societal" values, the social worker may need to consider the client's affiliations in addition to the values of broader society.

DEVELOPING A VALUES HIERARCHY

In addition to clarifying and describing personal, client/client system, agency, and societal values, ordering these in terms of priorities can be invaluable in ethical decision making. However, this can also be a very challenging task!

It is generally best to hierarchize one's own values before attempting to assist a client to establish value priorities. Completing a personal values hierarchy can accomplish at least two goals: (1) It will help the social worker to develop self-awareness and insights regarding the role of personal values in ethical decision making in practice, in assessment of clients and client problems, in understanding agency mission and policies, and in viewing herself or himself in the context of group, community, and society; (2) it will be helpful in understanding some of the challenges clients will face in completing a similar project.

It is easier to build a values hierarchy in written form. Begin with a list of values. This will engender careful thought and reflection, self-observation, self-awareness, and may include values that range from the very abstract to the very specific. As the process begins, it will become clear that some values can be subsumed under others. "My best friend Paul" and "Socializing with my friends," for example, can both be subsumed under the value "Friendship"; "My MSW" and "Learning about people" might be subsumed under "Education", or "Professionalism"; "Equality" and "Fairness" might be subsumed under "Justice." Generally, the more concrete, specific values will tend to be subsumed under broader, more abstract values. Not all specific values may fit comfortably under an abstract value, however, and can be retained as described. While abstract values can be helpful in providing an overall picture of a values hierarchy, it is important *not* to subsume specific values that are unique and especially important.

The next task will be to order the values. This requires time and reflection; however, the result is a deeper understanding of self and of the things that give life personal meaning.

This process of self-exploration may be utilized with clients, with client systems, and with groups, and is helpful in setting goals for service and determining appropriate interventions.

CHAPTER SUMMARY

A consideration of the values of all parties affected by an ethical dilemma and its potential resolution is an essential component of the decision-making process. Meaningful discussions of values and priorities are essential to professional practice. Several considerations that impact an understanding of values should be included in the worker's reasoning about the dilemma. These include the existence and role of both "ideal" and "real" values, and the defining value characteristics both cultures and populations, as well as an understanding of the role of the worker's own personal values in the ethical decision-making process.

Awareness of one's personal values is the essential first step in considering values of affected parties to ethical decisions. Self-reflection, self-awareness, and self-observation are important tools for the social worker in developing a deeper understanding of personal values. It is important to also consider agency values, values of the client system, and the values of the broader society in which the ethical dilemma is embedded.

The formulation of the ethical dilemma, gathering of information, consideration of the NASW Code of Ethics, and an awareness of values of the system that is affected by the ethical dilemma provide the social worker with the elements needed for resolving the dilemma. The next step, addressed in the following chapter, involves the development of choices: choices which support one side of the dilemma, support the other side, or, optimally, collapse the dilemma. The choices will enable the social worker to make a decision among them, and thus to resolve the dilemma.

The following questions will test your knowledge of the content found within this chapter. For questions 1-6, please select the phrase that best completes each sentence. Question 7 is a brief essay question. For additional assessment, including licensing-exam type questions on applying chapter content to practice behaviors, visit **MySearchLab**.

1. "Real" and "ideal" values:
   a. are always different from each other
   b. may overlap to a greater or lesser extent
   c. really mean the same thing
   d. cannot be held by a person at the same time

2. Abstract values such as "justice" and "freedom" have all of these characteristics except:
   a. clearly defined
   b. generally comfortable to use in conversation
   c. often shared by client and worker
   d. easiest for everyone to agree with

3. In discussing values with clients, it's easier if:
   a. worker and client seem to have the same values
   b. a third party is present
   c. worker and client have obvious value differences
   d. the worker suggests values to a client

4. Clients' values may differ from those of the worker, based on:
   a. the values of their friends
   b. the worker's definitions of abstract values
   c. the client's life experiences
   d. the client's perception of the worker's expectations

5. The development of a personal values hierarchy:
   a. is almost impossible to achieve
   b. is an option in the process of professional development
   c. is best accomplished through group discussion
   d. is essential to competent professional practice

6. In developing a values hierarchy:
   a. specific, concrete values will tend to be subsumed under abstract values
   b. it is possible to find that all values are equally important
   c. it is best to consult a client's family as well as the client
   d. life experiences should not be considered

7. Values tend to be very personal, and not always easy to discuss or to share. How would you initiate a value discussion with a client? What rationale would you offer? How would you clarify to be certain that you are understanding what the client is saying?

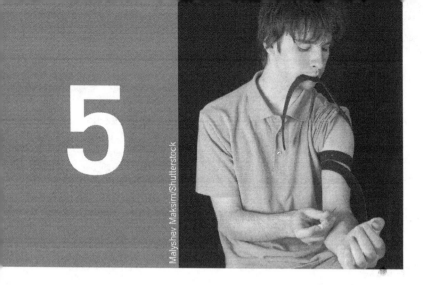

5

Malyshev Maksim/Shutterstock

Considering Options and Resolving the Dilemma

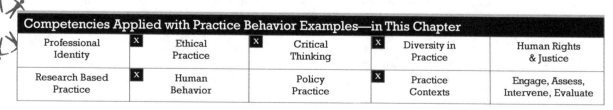

Competencies Applied with Practice Behavior Examples—in This Chapter								
Professional Identity	x	Ethical Practice	x	Critical Thinking	x	Diversity in Practice		Human Rights & Justice
Research Based Practice	x	Human Behavior		Policy Practice	x	Practice Contexts		Engage, Assess, Intervene, Evaluate

INTRODUCTION

When all of the elements needed to make a sound ethical decision are gathered, the worker must consider options for action. Like the four preconditions for choices presented in the earlier discussion of free will, there must be appropriate information available, the options must be well reasoned and considered, they must reflect real possible courses of action, and it must be possible for the worker to implement them or to set them in motion. The final decision will be determined from these options: well-reasoned, researched, and developed options will enable an appropriate final resolution.

DEFINING OPTIONS

Expanding Choices

The development of choices is an exercise in creativity as well as logic. The reason that the dilemma has occurred is generally due to a lack of acceptable or viable options. During this part of the decision-making process, the social worker and the parties affected by the dilemma engage in a period of brainstorming. Considering the greatest number of possible ideas, even if some of them are not feasible, expands thinking, sharpens concepts of goals and methods, and clarifies reasoning. This step in the decision making begins to move the process forward from information gathering and relates to a more practical and definite consideration of courses of action.

With awareness of resources, knowledge of human behavior, relevant research, and familiarity with the practice context and the community, and with a commitment to service, the social worker will be able to develop options which are accessible, achievable, and creative—options which may not have been considered prior to the discussions generated by the ethical dilemma. However, it is essential to recognize that the discussion may have also opened new ideas and possibilities for clients, and that clients themselves may expand the possible options in new and previously unconsidered directions. Options offered by clients will generally be consonant with the clients' personal values, culture, and belief system—an important dimension in considering choices.

Options for action may be derived from either side of the dilemma equation or, as a third alternative, may collapse the dilemma by either finding a way of combining the two sides or finding a solution that is appropriate but does not support either.

Three separate lists may be generated: two for options in support of the two sides of the dilemma as stated, and one for those that do not fit in either category, or fit into both sides of the dilemma. In a well-defined dilemma, at least two of the generated lists, those that support either side of the dilemma, will have a number of options for action listed. If the options are all on one side of the dilemma, it may be necessary to reconsider whether this is, in fact, a true ethical dilemma. What may at first appear to have been a true ethical dilemma may not be one if there are no options which can be put into action, if there are no

Diversity in Practice

Practice Behavior Example: In some cultures, the social worker is considered the "expert," and the social worker's suggestions are generally accepted.

Critical Thinking Question: When working with clients from these cultures, there are (at least) two considerations: If the client prefers to be guided by the social worker, is this preference to be respected and not challenged? If the worker believes it is in the client's interest to be actively involved, how might he or she elicit client ideas and choices for resolving ethical dilemmas?

In ethical decision making, an option which is not considered does not exist.

reasonable options, if there are no options within the client's culture or value system, or if only one side of the dilemma formulation yields options.

Returning to the third case in the Introduction, of the client who asks for service beyond the eight-interview limit, one dilemma formulation might be stated as *Primacy of Client Interests v. Obligation to Agency Policy.*

Several options can be suggested for either side. In support of *Primacy of Client Interests*, the worker can decide to see the client at her agency for additional service as requested, without telling anyone; she can make arrangements to continue to see her client outside of the agency setting; she can tell her supervisor that she plans to offer this

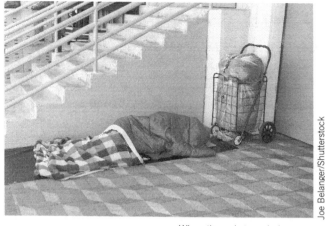

When the only two choices appear to be the street or a shelter, some clients choose the street.

additional service despite agency policy; she can tell her supervisor and ask that an exception be made for compelling reasons; or she can advocate for a change in policy, knowing that this will take time.

In support of *Obligation to Agency Policy*, she can refuse service to the client and terminate as required; she can consult with the supervisor and follow recommendations; she can refer the client to an agency offering similar services without the eight-session limit; or she can terminate with the client and suggest that the client reapply for services with one of the worker's colleagues.

She can also consider other options entirely, options that do not clearly support either side of the dilemma: She can refer the client to the agency's group program, she can refer the client to an outside peer-support group in her area, she can avoid confrontation with the client over this issue by not returning telephone calls and being unavailable to her, and so on. Obviously, however, each of these options is not equally desirable.

Considering Choices

With all of the possible choices defined, it is necessary to consider the feasibility of each. If an option cannot be put into action because there is an insurmountable barrier limiting it as a true option, that option will need to be discarded. If an option will not lead to the expected goal, it also may be discarded. If an option involves actions on the parts of others which cannot be assured, it may not be a feasible one. If an option is contrary to the NASW Code of Ethics, or will result in illegal actions, it must also be discarded. In most cases, a number of the choices listed will be eliminated simply through a consideration of these factors. If the social worker and client are working together on developing choices, exploring the reasons for eliminating some of them can provide many helpful insights, and can often be a moment for levity and humor in an otherwise serious undertaking.

A simple cost-benefit analysis framework can be used to assist social workers and affected parties in thinking about the possible options for action. Using a separate system for each possible resolution, the worker and client, if a client is involved can list all of the potential benefits and harms or costs of a particular course of action in two separate columns. A system can then be developed to weigh each cost and benefit. Social workers and clients will find that some costs are so high that they eliminate the option completely. Other costs impact unfairly and unevenly on others and so affect the desirability of a particular option.

Enabling clients to actually write the list themselves during discussion can be empowering, and increase the sense of some control over decision making.

Cost-benefit analysis provides a consistent structure for evaluating options.

Costs and benefits may vary unexpectedly through developments not wholly within the workers' or clients' control; in some instances, such an option must be discarded, while in others, reasoned reflection can suggest that the cost-benefit proportions would not vary in such a way as to preclude the choice of that option.

Thus, the process of deliberation, consideration, reflection upon each choice will eliminate some choices, while retaining others. When the process is complete, the remaining, fewer, choices will be in harmony with existing resources, client preferences, agency mission, values, and professional guidelines.

Engage, Assess, Intervene, Evaluate

Practice Behavior Example: One of the major components in selecting a course of action is its achievability. Courses of action may embody the best of ideals, the most significant values, and have the support of the client. But, if the action that will resolve the dilemma is not achievable, only frustration and disappointment will result. For this reason, it is very important that each option be assessed for achievability.

Critical Thinking Question: It is often difficult to eliminate an option that sounds perfect to all—but is clearly not achievable. How might the social worker address achievability in the practice context?

While there is a tendency to think in terms of "benefits" in resolving an ethical dilemma, minimization of harms may also be a valid resolution.

SELECTING A RESOLUTION

By the end of the "options" process, several will remain to be considered. The final choice needs to be:

1. Achievable, hopefully within a reasonable period of time
2. Reasonable and agreeable for all parties
3. Ethical and legal
4. Consonant with the NASW Code of Ethics
5. Consonant with agency policies and procedures
6. Grounded in research and appropriate information
7. The best cost-benefit choice
8. Within the value base of all affected parties, or, at least, within the value base of the primary affected parties.

Often, there is no resolution which will have the full support of all affected parties, will benefit everyone, and harm no one. In such circumstances, it is important to consider the client's interests as primary. Negative effects upon others should be mitigated to the greatest extent possible.

As options are carefully discarded, the worker, and the client or client system will determine the best course of action and implement it. If unforeseen problems and obstacles arise that render that option unworkable, it may be necessary to fall back on another option or to begin the option-formulation process over again, adding and subtracting options based on previous experiences.

CHAPTER SUMMARY

Potential choices for resolving ethical dilemmas are grounded in options. In order to best resolve an ethical dilemma, it is important to consider a wide range of options. The process of discarding the most implausible and impractical options can contribute greatly to consideration, as defining the reason for abandoning an option sharpens the general focus and the thinking process. When a good list of options has been developed, a cost-benefit analysis may be used to eliminate some of the options.

The options remaining, all generally feasible, must be carefully considered using reason, and carefully basing the discussion on the information gathered in the process from various sources including research. The selection of a course of action, a resolution to the dilemma, will be grounded in the best of the remaining options available.

The following questions will test your knowledge of the content found within this chapter. For questions 1-6, please select the phrase that best completes each sentence. Question 7 is a brief essay question. For additional assessment, including licensing-exam type questions on applying chapter content to practice behaviors, visit **MySearchLab**.

1. The exercise of expanding available choices and options for resolving an ethical dilemma:
   a. has no consistently valid purpose
   b. can confuse the situation further
   c. should always involve agency colleagues
   d. sharpens focus and clarifies reasoning

2. Cost-benefit analysis:
   a. is a valid way to consider options
   b. is a concept from economics which cannot be applied to social work
   c. is always simple
   d. always involves research

3. Resolutions are often not the optimal choice for all parties involved. When choices must be made:
   a. the family unit as a whole must be considered first
   b. the client's interests are primary
   c. it is best for the social worker to determine the resolution
   d. all parties involved must participate in discussion and determine the resolution

4. If the selected resolution is not effective, all are valid approaches except:
   a. another option may be selected
   b. the process of resolving the ethical dilemma may be reinitiated
   c. the irresolvability of the dilemma is therefore determined
   d. alternatives may be discussed

5. The options developed by the social worker should be:
   a. representative of societal values at all times
   b. easy to achieve
   c. as simple as possible
   d. in accord with the Code of Ethics

6. The options developed by the client should be:
   a. reflective of the client's values and goals
   b. chosen with the support of family members
   c. always agreeable to the client's community
   d. achievable in a short period of time

7. In selecting an option to resolve an ethical dilemma, what are the important considerations?

Part One has provided a guide for a method of ethical decision making that can be used by social workers with all populations, in all contexts, and at all levels (macro to micro) of practice. The process involves a number of clear and easily achievable steps:

After a general description of client, problem, and practice context,

1. Define the ethical problem as a dilemma with two equally weighted sides in the form of _____ v. _____

2. Gather context-specific information to support each side, and general information about theories, populations, problems, and policies. Resources for information include: the client and client system; the community; agency policy and procedures, colleagues, supervisors, agency directors; research; consultation with other agencies or resources; assessment of community and community resources, and others.

3. Consult the NASW Code of Ethics for guidance, as well as laws, legal codes and any other relevant ethical codes.

4. Explore values of the affected system. This can include the client and family, support network and community, the agency, and the community. The social worker should also engage in self-reflection to consider personal values and their effect on the dilemma. These values should be hierarchized as possible.

5. Develop a list of options for resolution. Expand the number and kinds of options possible, and consider each carefully using the available information from #2, #3, and #4. Using a cost-benefit analysis, develop a "short list" of reasonable, achievable options.

6. Consider each option carefully and select the option that best resolves the dilemma.

Part Two will present a series of actual ethical dilemmas encountered by students in field placements. Each student will utilize the method described in Part One to consider and resolve the dilemma presented, and will describe the reasoning process that was utilized.

Cases will also enable the reader to develop a greater familiarity with the NASW Code of Ethics and the ways in which it may be applied in practice.

Lisa F. Young/Shutterstock

6

NASW Ethical Standard One

Social Workers' Ethical Responsibilities to Clients

Competencies Applied with Practice Behavior Examples—in This Chapter									
Professional Identity		Ethical Practice	X	Critical Thinking		Diversity in Practice	X	Human Rights & Justice	X
Research Based Practice		Human Behavior		Policy Practice		Practice Contexts		Engage, Assess, Intervene, Evaluate	X

INTRODUCTION

While the Code of Ethics does not prioritize its standards, it seems appropriate that the first standard addresses the social workers' commitment to clients. Providing services to clients is generally considered to be at the heart of the social work profession—its very reason for existence. This first ethical standard provides direction for professionals engaged in the provision of services to clients in often complex and difficult circumstances, and at times offers guidelines which appear to conflict with each other. In the case studies relating to this standard, the challenges faced by each author both support the need for standards and illustrate the complexities in applying them.

Provisions of the Code

Standard 1 of the Code of Ethics is the longest of the standards, contains many complex provisions, and requires careful review and discussion.

The first section of the Code of Ethics relating to Ethical Standards presents the social worker's ethical responsibilities to clients. It defines and clarifies various professional responsibilities for the welfare and well-being of each client.

The first subsection (1.01) addresses commitment to clients, stating that, in general, clients' interests are primary; however, there may be circumstances in which the legal obligations of workers or the obligation to the larger society may supersede client loyalty. Workers are made aware that clients should be advised about these limitations.

This is immediately followed by the subsection addressing client self-determination (1.02), and then informed consent (1.03). Client self-determination is supported by informed consent, and the Code specifies that services should be provided only when clients have given such consent. Problems that may be encountered related to informed consent, such as language difficulties, lack of decisional capacity, involuntary clients, services rendered through electronic mediums, and audio- or videotaping, may impact self-determination. The obligation of workers who act on behalf of clients who are not competent to consent is addressed in subsection 1.14.

The responsibility to cultural competence requires that social workers be aware of federal and state laws regarding immigration, and their potential effects on clients who are immigrants.

Clients often assume that workers are competent to render services. Subsection 1.04 addresses the responsibility of social workers to represent themselves as competent only within their education, training, license, certification, and so on. Competent professionals also are knowledgeable about human behavior, cultural diversity, and oppression, as addressed in subsection 1.05. In 2008, the National Association of Social Workers (NASW) Delegate Assembly revised subsection 1.5c to include *gender identity or expression* and *immigration status* in the list of cultural and social differences that social workers should seek to understand in order to provide effective service to clients (NASW, 2008).

Subsection 1.06 addresses the difficult area of conflicts of interest, proscribing dual relationships with clients or former clients and the exploitation of these clients for personal interest, and obligating workers to inform clients in cases where there may be any potential conflicts of interest.

The right to privacy and confidentiality has always been a very basic and vital part of rendering professional service. Both the obligation to observe these, and the circumstances under which workers may disclose information are presented in subsection 1.07, which also includes the worker's obligation to inform clients of confidentiality limits. Although clients have the right of access to their records, workers must protect the confidentiality of other individuals identified within them (1.08).

Subsection 1.09 limits sexual relationships with clients, former clients, and persons who have close relationships with clients, and the provision of services to former sexual partners due to the potential for harm to the client that exists in such relationships. Physical contact is limited (1.10) where there is a possibility of harm to the client and, where used appropriately, must be both culturally sensitive and within clear boundaries. Sexual harassment is proscribed (1.11), as is the use of derogatory language (1.12).

Professional guidelines regarding payment for services are addressed in subsection 1.13, the importance of continuity of services in 1.15, and termination of services in 1.16.

THE CASES

The majority of the approximately 200 students whose cases were considered for this collection were aware of strong ethical dilemmas relating to Standard 1 of the Code of Ethics. However, they were also aware that it is often difficult to separate ethical issues from clinical ones. As in the first example discussed in the Introduction, if a client is not relating to a worker or is not sharing personal information, this may easily be perceived as a clinical issue. Does the worker not have adequate skills to work with this client? Is this client being "resistive"? Is it an issue of "control"? It may be necessary to take a step back from the immediate situation to consider a different perspective: Does the client have a "right" to refuse to participate in therapy? The worker, concerned for the client's "best interests," may believe that these can best be served by therapy. The client may disagree and insist on the right to self-determination. This moves, then, from a clinical issue to an ethical one.

The opposite problem can also occur. A worker in a child welfare agency, concerned about ethical dimensions, is unsure of whether his primary responsibility is to the young individual with whom he is working or to the family system. Whose needs, whose interests, should be considered as primary? This may look like an ethical dilemma, but it may in fact not be one. Determining who is the client is often an issue of agency policy, source of referral, clinical need, client preference, or worker preference. Once this determination has been made, the ethical dilemma collapses as the worker's primary responsibility is clarified.

The cases presented in this section demonstrate some of the major ethical issues for social workers relating to clients. Cases where a worker's obligation to clients is in conflict with other obligations, such as to the welfare of society, to the employing agency, to colleagues, and to the social work profession, are presented in succeeding chapters.

In the first case presented, a 2-year-old child is placed in a long-term foster home/adoptive home. A mentally disabled adult male foster sibling states that he has sexually abused her. Although no evidence of abuse is found, the child is immediately removed and placed in another foster home. In the ensuing argument between the foster parents and their son, plans are made for him to move out of the home. The parents want to adopt their foster child, and she wants to return to them. However, there will be limits, the worker knows, to the safety that this home can potentially provide, and, once the adoption is final, the agency will no longer be involved. The worker must decide whether the risk to physical safety outweighs the advantages of a loving, permanent home for this little girl.

The second case is also from the child welfare field. The social worker's client, a young girl, is placed in foster care with her younger sibling. Both girls will shortly be available for adoption. The worker is asked to recommend whether the girls should be placed together or separately in an adoptive home. The older sister, the worker's client, is very attached to the younger and wants to remain with her sister. The younger, in foster care with many other children longer than she can remember, is not personally attached to her sister at this time. If a joint adoptive placement is recommended, the younger child's chances for a permanent placement will be affected by the need for finding a family willing to take two children, one of whom, being older, is less "desirable." If separate placements are recommended, the worker's client will suffer another loss in a life already filled with many losses and traumas. Should the worker recommend what she feels to be in the best interest of her client, when this recommendation might not be in the best interests of her client's sister?

The third case presents a renal dialysis patient who has requested that treatment be terminated and that she be allowed to die. She is very ill and depressed but appears competent, and she states that her poor quality of life and the certainty of her death in the not-too-distant future make it impossible for her to continue with dialysis treatments. Her mother, whom the client has named as surrogate decision maker should she no longer be able to make her own decisions, objects, and asks the social worker to help her to stop her daughter from "committing suicide." The social worker finds that she must either support the patient's request and help her to achieve her goals or attempt to convince her to continue in treatment and extend her life. The dilemma is suggested as one between the prolongation of biological life and the acceptance of the client's ultimate right to self-determination.

The rights of biological parents form one side of the fourth case presented. A father, currently incarcerated, requests reunification with his 2-year-old daughter, placed almost immediately after birth in a nurturing foster home due to maternal abandonment. The foster family has expressed interest in adoption. The worker must determine appropriate planning for the child (i.e., the child's "best interest"). However, the uncertainty and unpredictability of events as far as 20 years in the future make this decision a particularly difficult one.

In the fifth case, an 18-year-old immigrant, homeless and mentally disabled, is referred by another agency to a community-based agency that specializes in services to the immigrant population. Although her parents live in a neighboring county, the client refuses to live with them, preferring to remain on the street. She is placed in a home but runs away within a week.

The worker learns that she has been both physically and sexually abused while out on the streets. His genuine concern for her safety is heightened by her mental status, and he feels that she will be unable to protect herself and may face serious harm. The client wants her freedom to live as she has chosen; the worker is concerned about her safety. What should he do? Should her self-determination take precedence over his obligation to prevent harm? What role does her limited command of the language, her immigrant status, and her mental disability play in the way in which this dilemma must be resolved?

The sixth case explores the social worker's responsibility when a vulnerable client plans to leave the hospital and return to a living situation which she, as well as the hospital staff caring for the patient, feels places the client at risk of harm. While there is some concern about his competence, he has not been judged incompetent, would most likely not agree to a competency examination, and is making a decision clearly grounded in his own knowledge and life experiences. Alternative planning would offer both immediate support and assistance with needed long-term planning.

The last case in this chapter is meant to be studied with its companion case, which may be found in Chapter 11. Both cases address permanency planning for young children currently removed from biological parents. The case discussed in Chapter 11 considers policy in the abstract, while the case included here addresses the policy in terms of a very specific mother and infant, and includes the complex nature of life circumstances, family relationships, and parental history and behavior. This case presents a concrete example of the issues involved in the application of the policy for rapid permanency planning.

Case Study A Protecting The Best Interests of a Minor

Abstracted from an unpublished paper by Elena B. Glekas, MSW

Practice Context and Case Presentation

The mission of the sectarian agency where the social worker is placed is to enable people to strengthen and transform their lives by empowering those most in need, by supporting families, and by engaging the broader community in its work. Although the agency believes in the resilience, strength, and healing power of families, it is also fully aware that under stress the family support system can break down, endangering children's welfare. In such cases, children are often placed in the agency's Foster Care Program.

Kendra is a 2-year-old female whose crack cocaine-addicted mother abandoned her with a caretaker at 1 month of age, with no interest in further contacts. The caretaker refused to continue to care for her and was unable to locate the mother. After Child Protective Services (CPS) intervention, Kendra was placed in the home of Mr. and Mrs. Doe. The foster family and Kendra are supervised by the caseworker through the agency's Foster Care Program.

Kendra has adjusted well to the Does' home and the Does love her very much. They would like to adopt her, and this is being planned, although parental rights have not yet been terminated. Kendra's mother has not been located, and the agency is initiating termination of parental rights through the court system.

The Does have a 24-year-old son, Tony, residing in their home as well. Tony is suffering from schizophrenia. He desperately wants to leave the Does and live independently, but they feel that he does not have the mental ability to do this successfully and that he continues to need their protection.

Tony recently confessed to the worker that he has sexually abused Kendra. The Does claims that Tony is doing this only because he wants to live independently, hoping that they will ask him to leave their home. However, an investigation by CPS, the Youth Squad, and the police department was immediately begun, and Kendra was taken to a local hospital for examination, where no evidence of abuse was found. She was removed from the Does and placed in a temporary foster home.

Since the sexual abuse issue was revealed, the Does have abandoned their opposition to Tony's leaving. They have participated in planning sessions with Tony and his worker, and Tony has located an appropriate living facility, where some supervision will be provided. He is eager to move and plans to leave in a few days.

The Does would like to continue their plans for adoption, offering Kendra a permanent placement. With them, she would be able to establish secure lifetime relationships with nurturing caregivers. Separation from the only parents she has ever known could have a serious impact. However, placement in a foster home would offer protection from possible physical harm to this little 2-year-old girl. It is difficult, if not impossible, to foresee events in regard to Tony and his future. Should he fail at independent living, would the Does take him in, thus possibly placing Kendra at further risk?

The worker must recommend a plan for Kendra. There are several ways in which her dilemma might be phrased. However, she has determined that the most important considerations in making a permanent plan for Kendra are as follows:

PERMANENCY V. PHYSICAL SAFETY

Research and Related Literature

The family has an enduring impact on the development of the person. The family shapes the child's personality, attitudes, behaviors, and beliefs (Thorman, 1982). There is recognition that children can suffer severe emotional trauma when they are removed from their parents. Research indicates that children usually do better if they can remain with their own families (Ames & Springen, 1992).

General agreement supports the view that all children need a stable and continuous relationship with a nurturing person or persons in order to develop physically, socially, emotionally, intellectually, and morally (Hess, 1982). Foster children, therefore, are especially vulnerable individuals, prone to become victims unless special care is taken to protect them. Stone and Stone (1983) emphasize that every child needs security in the home environment and that "security" involves both the physical and emotional well-being of the child.

Children entering foster care placement inevitably experience the pain of separation from their family setting, no matter how inadequate that setting has been. Grisby (1994) cites that the loss of an attachment figure arouses anxiety, and actual loss causes sorrow, which, in turn, is likely to arouse anger. Conversely, the maintenance of the bond is experienced as a source of security, and the renewal of a bond is often the source of joy.

It is very important that foster children, already damaged by past experiences, not be further damaged by abrupt procedures (Carbino, 1991). Abrupt removals of children can be damaging to the well-being of both children and foster families. Grisby (1994) adds that the interruption of the attachment relationship may be, in and of itself, detrimental to the child.

Abrupt removal from all persons to whom the child is relating as family, particularly if carried out by persons with whom the child does not have a solid relationship, may well be experienced from the young child's point of view more as kidnapping than protection. Carbino (1991) states that in all instances, abrupt, unplanned removal severely interferes with any sense of permanency and stability.

Whatever the reason for placement, foster children have not had a normal upbringing. By definition, the bonds to a foster child's permanent family have been disrupted. Foster children suffer disproportionately from serious emotional, medical, and psychological disabilities. To compound matters, Ryan (1981) cites that it is well established that foster children are at high risk of further maltreatment while in foster care.

No one knows how many children are abused or neglected while in foster care, but the problem is more widespread than is currently acknowledged. Much mistreatment of foster children goes unreported (Mushlin, 1988). These children may not report the abuse, or, if they do, they may not be believed. Ryan (1981) states that foster children seem particularly vulnerable to sexual abuse.

Human Rights & Justice

Practice Behavior Example: "Incest" is proscribed in all 50 states, and is defined by degree of blood relationship, although in some states nonblood relationships, such as stepparents, are included in the prohibition.

Critical Thinking Question: In this case, the relationship between Kendra and Tony may or may not qualify as "incest" in all states, as it is not biological, not legal, and not permanent. Research the incest laws for your state, and consider whether these would apply to Kendra and Tony.

This is a special problem because, by definition, there is no permanent kinship bond in foster care. As a result, the traditional incest taboo does not operate.

Several studies have found that the rate of abuse is much higher for foster children than for children in the general public (Mushlin, 1988). Mushlin further contends that the failure of the foster care programs to follow appropriate minimum standards that would ensure the care and protection of children has led to increased rates of foster care abuse and neglect.

One study reported that the rate of substantiated abuse and neglect in New York City foster family care was more than one-and-a-half times that of children in the general population (Ryan, 1981). There were 49 abused children per 1,000 in the general population, and there were 77 abused children per 1,000 for children in foster family care.

Kaucher and Leon's study of the reasons for child foster care placement (1994) revealed that sexual abuse is a more frequent occurrence in the lives of foster children than is generally indicated. The courts identified sexual abuse in only 5 percent of the cases. Three months later, social workers determined that sexual abuse had been a factor in twice as many cases.

Carbino (1991) cites that the well-being of children is inseparable from the well-being of families of which they are members: Foster family stress resulting from agency responses to an abuse or neglect allegation will be felt by everyone in the family and is harmful to family interactions.

It is a policy of the agency that has placed Kendra that the safety of children who reside in their programs be assured. Consequently, if children state that they have been abused by their foster parent(s), they are immediately removed from the home and placed in another foster home, even if no physical evidence is found. In addition, if prospective foster parents state that they use corporal punishment to discipline their children and will continue to do so with potential foster children, they will not be eligible to be foster parents through the agency.

Author's Reflections, Reasoning Process, and Resolution

Welfare of children, family values, safety, and autonomy are societal values that directly impact on this case. Traditionally, society has placed a high value on the welfare of children and the integrity of families. However, it wasn't until recently that the idea of children's "rights" was generally accepted.

Society has mobilized opinion and developed social institutions to support both children and their families. However, when faced with the abuse and neglect of children by their parents and caregivers, society has been reluctant to address the problems. There is, this worker feels, a paramount need for child protection through legislation, family rehabilitation, and awareness in the community at large of the need to report such incidences.

The value of family as a unit (in this case composed of Mr. and Mrs. Doe, Tony, and Kendra) is also strongly supported by society. The Does' behavior exemplifies this: Although there have been severe problems and tensions between the Does and Tony, they have allowed him to remain in the home until he has been able to make permanent plans for himself.

Within the structure of the agency, Kendra is clearly identified as the worker's primary client. The Code of Ethics (Section 1.01) stresses the importance of the worker's obligation to serve the best interests of the client. Therefore, the primacy of Kendra's interests must guide the worker in decision making.

Inherent in the social work profession is the need to respect the rights and dignity of everyone. For Kendra, the worker translates this mandate into two primary obligations: (1) Kendra, as does every other child, has the right to a permanent and stable home; (2) Kendra, as do all children, has the right to safety.

Kendra is very attached to the Does and has been secure and happy in their home. Although the Does are not the primary clients, their values also play a role in the worker's understanding of Kendra's dilemma. They are devout in their practice of religion and value family togetherness and responsibility, having demonstrated this over the years by caring for Tony in their home. They love Kendra and have taken her into their home and hearts fully and completely. They demonstrate this by maintaining their desire to adopt Kendra.

The worker has always been a strong advocate of child welfare. She feels that it is very important that children grow up in a loving, nurturing, and safe environment. This is predicated on personal values that include close family relationships, friends, religious values, sincerity, and equality. In terms of the current dilemma, the worker takes a strong protectionist position, firmly believing that children are in need of special protection and that society has an obligation to ensure that protection. She believes that the welfare of all children should be of utmost concern to society.

The ethical dilemma illustrated by this case focuses on the avoidance of two harms: the family's disintegration (notion of permanency) and the potential for Kendra's abuse (notion of safety).

The Does feel obligation to both Tony's and Kendra's best interests. For them, these would be served by maintaining the status quo: having both Tony and Kendra in their home, since they do not believe Tony's allegations of sexual abuse. As this is not possible, they have had to examine the situation for a more consequentialist position. This has led them to accept a "least harm" position that allows Tony to move to an independent living situation while adopting Kendra and keeping her at home with them. In advocating for Tony's independence, the worker has also supported this position.

If the worker focuses on a "greatest value" position, she must first determine whom she must consider in her equation. If she includes the Does, she might find the greatest value in the return of Kendra to their home; certainly, this would provide immediate happiness for both the Does and Kendra. If, ultimately, she determines that she must consider only Kendra's good, the dilemma resolution is less clear from a theoretical standpoint.

Ethics of Care theory (Caring, 2003) is also relevant to this issue. Both Mr. and Mrs. Doe faced conflicts among their care-giving responsibilities: They had to confront Tony about his allegations, deal with the issue between themselves, watch Kendra be removed from their home, adjust to her loss, continue to live in the home with Tony after Kendra's removal, and struggle with the definition of their family.

Although Tony is not the worker's client, the definition of his "best interest" has an impact on the case. The Does define Tony's best interest as remaining with them, where he can be supervised and not be a disturbance to others. Tony defines his best interest as living independently of the Does. The worker is in agreement with Tony's definition, and the impact of her position can affect the family's attempt to address the problem. The Ethics of Care theory stresses the importance of promoting positive relationships, a difficult task for the worker in these circumstances. To support this ethic, the worker has arranged for the Does to visit Kendra at school weekly until a permanent plan can be made.

Two primary options present themselves as possibilities to the worker: (1) Kendra can remain at her present (new) placement. The family seems to be providing a safe and nurturing environment. This would maximize safety (potentially) and provide permanency (potentially); (2) Kendra can be returned to live with the Does, with the goal of adoption. This option would provide continuity of care as well as permanency, but leaves open the possibility of abuse by Tony at a later date, when the agency no longer has control over Kendra.

After much deliberation, the worker has determined that Kendra's best interests are served by permanency, stability, and security in the only home she has ever known, with the parents who have cared for her and nurtured her thus far. The worker is familiar with the Does and has had a strong, positive relationship with them. It is felt that the values of the Does will support their ensuring the safety of Kendra during future visits with Tony and that the benefits of this placement far outweigh the uncertainties, the potential abuse and neglect, the possible changes in placements, and the lack of identity with parents, which are inherent in the present foster care system.

Case Study A (*Glekas*)

Ames, K., & Springen, K. (1992, June). Fostering the family. *Newsweek*, pp. 64–65.

Carbino, R. (1991). Advocacy for foster families in the United States facing child abuse and neglect allegations: How social agencies and foster families are responding to the problem. *Child Welfare, 70*(2), 131–149.

Grisby, R. K. (1994, May). Maintaining attachment relationships among children in foster care. *Families in Society: The Journal of Contemporary Human Services, 75*(5), 269–276.

Hess, P. (1982, January). Parent–child attachment concept: Critical for permanency planning. *Social Casework: The Journal of Contemporary Social Work, 63*(1), 46–53.

Kaucher, C., & Leon, R. (Eds.). (1994, September). Why are so many kids in foster care? Available from the Metropolitan Washington Council of Governments, Washington, DC.

Mushlin, C. (1988). Unsafe havens: The case for constitutional protection of foster children from abuse and neglect. *Harvard Civil Rights and Civil Liberties Law Review, 23*, 205–207.

Caring (2003). *Ethics of care.* Berkeley, CA: University of California Press.

Ryan, P. (1981, February). *Foster home child protection* (pp. 31–32). New York: Vera Institute of Justice.

Stone, N. M., & Stone, S. F. (1983). The prediction of successful foster placement. *Social Casework, 64*, 11–17.

Thorman, G. (1982). *Helping troubled families.* New York: Aldine Publishing Co.

Case Study B   When "Best Interests of Client" Harm a Third Party

Abstracted from an unpublished paper by Karen Altenberg Libman, MSW, MBA

Practice Context and Case Presentation

This ethical dilemma takes place in a special education treatment center for emotionally disturbed children, ages 6 through 12 years. Part of the treatment involves individual psychotherapy, and Suzanne, aged 7, diagnosed with attachment disorder, has been seeing the caseworker twice weekly since entering the agency program, eight months previously. She lives in a group home with her 3-year-old sister, Cindy, and three other children. The sisters have been in the group home for two years, and parental rights are in the process of being terminated. Alternatives for long-term placement are being explored. Each child has her own worker, and the dilemma presented here is discussed from the perspective of Suzanne's worker.

Both Suzanne's and Cindy's workers have been asked to make an independent recommendation regarding priorities: Should the sisters be placed together, or should each sibling be planned for separately? Both workers are aware that a recommendation to maintain the sibling relationship is likely to greatly reduce the adoption chances of the younger sibling: Cindy is a more desirable candidate if she is alone.

The worker faces a primary responsibility to Suzanne, as well as a responsibility to avoid harm to a relevant third party, Cindy. Suzanne's best interest is clearly to have the support of her sibling in the face of multiple family losses, plus an improved chance of adoption because of her connection with a younger; and therefore more desirable (in terms of adoption), sibling. This "best interest" could, however, harm Cindy, who could find an adoptive home more easily independent of Suzanne.

Thus, the dilemma may be specified as:

BEST INTERESTS OF CLIENT V. OBLIGATION TO NONMALEFICENCE

Research and Related Literature

Empirical research on the question of preserving the sibling relationship among children in foster care and adoption is limited. Although there is agreement in the literature that sibling relationships are an important part of child development, there is little concrete evidence about the impact of maintaining or separating the sibling subsystem (Hegar, 1988; Staff & Fein, 1992; Timberlake & Hamlin, 1982). Of the research that does exist, most investigators agree that most siblings should be placed together (Staff & Fein, 1992). The Child Welfare League of America's (CWLA) standard for out-of-home care for neglected and abused children clearly states that "siblings should remain together," but acknowledges that in some cases separation is indicated (1989, in Staff & Fein, 1992). The following discussion first presents support for keeping siblings together, then outlines some reasons why separation might be preferable.

According to Ward (1984), sibling bonds may be stronger than parental attachments in families where the parental system is dysfunctional. Siblings provide support to each other in the absence of appropriate parenting. When children are removed from the home, and have been separated from their parents for an extended period, as in this case, the sibling attachment becomes primary because the siblings have been with each other longer than they have been with the parents. In such instances, separation from siblings may be even more stressful than separation from parents.

The sibling relationship provides mutual satisfaction for children in foster care and adoption (Ward, 1984). For the older sibling, the relationship provides an opportunity to "undo" the neglect and abuse from parents through caring for and controlling the younger child. This role can give the older child a sense of purpose and power. Meanwhile, the younger sibling gains a sense of protection and safety from the older sibling (Ward, 1984). Given the reciprocal nature of sibling relationships, children often feel that they have lost a part of themselves when separated from siblings, compounding separation and loss issues associated with foster care (Timberlake & Hamlin, 1982). Maintaining the intact sibling group affords children a natural support network for working through grief and developing a sense of identity (Timberlake & Hamlin, 1982). In the crisis of transitioning from one environment to another, the presence of a sibling provides continuity and predictability in a frightening situation (Ward, 1984). The sibling tie provides an important link to the past and preserves a sense of familial and individual identity (M. Owen, personal communication, February 23, 1995; Ward, 1984).

Research suggests that maintaining the sibling relationship reduces the rate of placement disruption (Barth, Berry, Yoshikami, Goodfield, & Carson, 1988; M. Owen, personal communication, February 23, 1995; Staff & Fein, 1992). Minimizing disruption of foster care or adoption placements is important for two reasons. First, according to Barth et al. (1988), previous disruptions increase the likelihood of future disruptions, creating a cycle of multiple placements. Second, multiple placements exacerbate and perpetuate the emotional problems of abused and neglected children.

A final point in support of maintaining the sibling relationship, supported by research noted above, indicates that older children have an increased chance of being adopted when they are paired with a younger, more desirable-age sibling (M. Owen, personal communication, February 23, 1995).

There is some research that supports separating siblings to further the best interest of each. First, despite the CWLA's strong support for keeping siblings together, the organization acknowledges that in some situations siblings should be separated. Unfortunately, there is disagreement about which circumstances indicate separation (Staff & Fein, 1992). Hegar suggests that "if the relationship is stressful for both (siblings), and if one is the consistent loser in competition for adult affection and approval, then a separate placement for that child may develop self-esteem" (Hegar, 1988; Staff & Fein, 1992, p. 258).

In the interest of Suzanne, some research indicates that children with attachment difficulties fare better when placed separately from their siblings. The director of the agency shares this view. In his experience, children with attachment problems are better able to attach to new families when only one child is in the home, because of reduced competition for parental affection. According to new evidence coming out of Evergreen, Colorado, a leading treatment center for attachment disordered children, the likelihood of placement disruption is so great among children with attachment difficulties that siblings of these children should be placed separately to protect them from unnecessary multiple placements (M. Owen, personal communication, March 2, 1995). These findings have not yet been published, however.

There are a number of reasons why Cindy, the younger sister, would be more "adoptable" if she were alone. First, her age—3 years—makes her more desirable to prospective adoptive parents. Second, she is likely to have fewer emotional problems than her older sister because she has lived in a stable and safe environment for two of her three years. The extent of emotional and developmental damage that was done in the first year of life is unclear, but the two years of stability would likely have mended some wounds. Finally, having lived in a group home for the past two years with three other children besides her sister, the younger child's cognitive awareness and emotional bond to Suzanne as her sister may be only nominal. This is in contrast to Suzanne's more developed understanding of the sibling bond. On the other hand, the younger sister will eventually understand that she has a natural sister, and, at that time, might develop feelings of anger toward "the system" that denied her the opportunity and the right to know her sister. Guilt feelings are also likely to emerge from the knowledge that she was the "chosen" sister, the one selected for adoption while her sister was "rejected" (C. Littman, LCSW-C, personal communication, March 25, 1995).

Concern for personal and individual freedom is reflected legally in the increased emphasis on safeguarding the rights of children in juvenile and family court practice (Hegar, 1988). In the legal literature, Reddick (in Hegar, 1988) argues for recognition of a "right of association" for siblings. In divorce and separation cases, where custody is disputed, the courts have shown a preference for keeping siblings together in the same parental home (Hegar, 1988). Generally, the focus is on the best interests of the child, rather than on the interests of the parents.

The value of relationship in the field of social work is reflected in the CWLA standard for adoption services, which states, "When there are several children in a family, it is necessary to obtain information about their relationship to one another, in order to decide whether they should be placed together or separately" (CWLA, 1978, in Hegar, 1988, p. 118). Hegar points out that this is the only policy statement concerning sibling placement from a social work standard-setting body. Hegar (1988) summarizes the differences in emphasis between the social work and legal perspectives on sibling placement as needs-focused versus rights-focused, respectively.

While the NASW Code of Ethics is explicit in stating that the social worker's primary responsibility is to the client (Sect. 1.01), it is silent on providing guidance on the worker's responsibility to third parties who are affected by decisions made in the interests of the client. Section 1.01 discusses "responsibility to the larger society" and "specific legal obligations" (to report) as situations where the primacy of a client's interest *may* need to be subject to other circumstances but does not address the issue under consideration. Section 1.06d discusses workers who provide services to "two or more persons who have a relationship with each other," but, in this instance, two clients are served by different workers in the same agency.

Author's Reflections, Reasoning Process, and Resolution

Our society values the preservation of families and the right to maintain the family system, without undue intrusion from outside sources. While "family values" are loudly espoused, supporting families is a low priority in the allocation of resources.

The worker's personal values may be hierarchized as friendship, love, family, justice, individual freedom, equality, concern for others, knowledge, truth, and honesty. She has a strong responsibility to consider Suzanne's wishes in this regard and notes that Suzanne consistently expresses her strong tie to her sister and her desire to have a family.

The worker's ethical stance includes a tendency toward applying fundamental principles in a flexible manner based on the unique circumstances of a particular case, thus a preference for evaluating situations on a case-by-case basis rather than adhering to specific rules. Motivation is leaned on as a guiding principle, although outcome is also factored into the decision-making process. Reason is strongly valued as the best method for arriving at a decision.

The worker's values bias her views in this case in at least two ways. First, the orientation toward goodness and rightness of motivation determines the best possible plan. Second, the worker is willing to focus on Suzanne as her primary obligation because there is also a worker advocating for the best interests of Cindy.

One possible approach would apply a deontological theory of "shoulds" or "oughts." Under this type of theory, the focus is on motivation, rather than outcome, in determining "right." Ross (1930) presents a deontological theory based on common sense and intuition. He outlines seven obligations that should guide our motives and actions in order for decisions to be moral: nonmaleficence, beneficence, fidelity, reparation, gratitude, self-improvement, and justice. These basic and irreducible moral principles express prima facie obligations, reflecting society's collective knowledge (Beauchamp & Childress, 2009, pp. 14–16). Decisions and actions are considered moral when both the action is "right" and the motive is "good," according to the principles. When two obligations, or principles, are in conflict, we need to use judgment to evaluate the specific circumstances of a case. In the case at hand, the relevant principles in Ross's theory are nonmaleficence and beneficence (Beauchamp & Childress, 2009), which are in conflict. On one side of the dilemma is the beneficence toward the client, Suzanne, while on the other is the nonmaleficence obligation toward her sister, Cindy. Using Ross's theory, it might seem that the worker's obligation not to harm Cindy outweighs her obligation to the best interests of Suzanne. However, this would place the worker's responsibility to both as equal, which it is not, as Suzanne is the primary client.

Another theoretical approach for evaluating the ethical dilemma in this case is consequentialism, which holds that actions are right or wrong according to the balance of their good and bad consequences (Beauchamp & Childress, 2009, pp. 336–337). The right act is the one that maximizes good, or minimizes bad, thereby producing the best overall result. Utilitarianism follows one universal overarching principle of pursuing the greatest good for the greatest number (Beauchamp & Childress, 2009, pp. 336–337).

In evaluating this case using a utilitarian model, one needs to weigh the goods and harms of each side of the dilemma for each party. Tables presenting the goods and harms of two decision options follow. As can be seen, the cumulative goods of keeping the siblings together outweigh the cumulative goods of separating them. In addition, the cumulative harms of separating them outweigh those of keeping them together. Therefore, the utilitarian model points toward keeping the children together. In this case, act utilitarianism is applied. Rule utilitarianism in the case of foster care and adoption decisions seems less valid, considering the lack of concrete, clear evidence supporting the potential outcome on one side or the other. In addition, complicating circumstances that are unique to individual cases seem to demand a case-by-case analysis for placement decision making.

Evaluation of Good and Harm Using a Utilitarian Approach

Client (Suzanne)	Third Party (Cindy)
Siblings Remain Together—Good	
1. maintains familial bond and identity	1. maintains familial bond and identity
2. enhances sense of personal identity	
3. avoids another loss in a life filled with losses	
4. increases chances for adoption	
5. may reduce likelihood of placement disruption	
6. may reduce likelihood of multiple placements	
Siblings Remain Together—Harm	
1. may increase likelihood of placement disruption	1. reduces chances for adoption into a permanent home
Siblings Are Separated—Good	
1. increases administrative expediency	1. increases potential adoptive families
2. may improve the attachment process with new family	2. increases likelihood of permanent placement
3. may reduce likelihood of placement disruption	3. adoption may occur more quickly
Siblings Are Separated—Harm	
1. creates loss of familial bond	1. creates loss of familial bond
2. reduces sense of identity	2. creates guilt for being the "chosen" sister
3. may increase the likelihood of placement disruption	3. generates anger toward "the system" for being denied the opportunity to know her sister
4. creates another loss in a life filled with losses	
5. reduces chances for adoption	
6. may inhibit the attachment process	
7. increases feelings of rejection and low self-esteem	

Although the final decision is not the worker's, there are three possible recommendations she can make:

1. Actively pursue separate adoptions for the sisters.
2. Keep the siblings together unless or until an adoptive home becomes available for only one sister, and then separate the children.
3. Keep the siblings together until a single adoptive home is available for both sisters.

The first alternative enables workers to assist the siblings to address the emotional and psychological issues. The worker's personal value of honesty supports this position. If both girls are considered equally the responsibility of the worker, then a deontological position could support this option as avoiding harm to Cindy.

The second alternative appears to be a nondecision—a postponement of resolution of the ethical dilemma. The illusion of the goal of maintaining the siblings together is preserved, but, in reality, one must acknowledge that an adoptive family will be found more easily for Cindy, and that, therefore, the girls are likely to be separated under this alternative. This alternative assumes that greater harm is done if placement is delayed until a home can be found for both: The younger sister is entitled to a stable, permanent home, despite the implications of this for Suzanne.

Upon reflection, the worker feels that the third alternative, keeping the sisters together, is the preferred choice. It is supported strongly by the utilitarian model, while the application of Ross's theory is affected by the need to determine whether Suzanne and her sister should be considered equally the worker's responsibility. Many of the values explored earlier support keeping the siblings together. Societal and legal values reflect family unity, kinship, and preservation. Social work considers relationship and primacy of client interests as the most important values guiding ethical behavior. The client's own value system supports maintaining the sibling bond. The worker's personal values, which stress the importance of family ties, and her emotional bond with Suzanne also lead toward the support of this option. The uncertainty of the outcome that is inherent in this kind of decision making, however, must still be considered.

Although not unambiguous, the research supports the importance of the sibling bond for healthy child development, especially in cases where other family relationships are dysfunctional. In the face of all the losses that the girls have encountered, preserving the sibling tie as a source of continuity, identity, and security seems very important. The worker's motivation has been to benefit both girls, and it is felt that keeping them together would be the best way to do this.

Case Study B (*Libman*)

Barth, R. P., Berry, M., Yoshikami, R., Goodfield, R. K., & Carson, M. L. (1988). Predicting adoption disruption. *Social Work, 33*(3), 227–233.

Beauchamp, T. L., & Childress, J. F. (2009). *Principles of biomedical ethics* (6th ed.). New York: Oxford University Press.

Dolgoff, R., Loewenberg, F. M., & Harrington, D. (2009). *Ethical decisions for social work practice* (8th ed.). Itasca, IL: F. E. Peacock.

Hegar, R. L. (1988). Legal and social work approaches to sibling separation in foster care. *Child Welfare, 67*(2), 113–121.

National Association of Social Workers. (2008). *NASW code of ethics*. Washington, DC: Author.

Ross, W. D. (1930). *The right and the good*. Oxford: Oxford University Press.

Staff, I., & Fein, E. (1992). Together or separate: A study of siblings in foster care. *Child Welfare, 71*(3), 257–270.

Timberlake, E. M., & Hamlin, E. R. (1982). The sibling group: A neglected dimension of placement. *Child Welfare, 61*(8), 545–552.

Ward, M. (1984). Sibling ties in foster care and adoption planning. *Child Welfare, 63*(4), 321–332.

Case Study C When Living Feels Like Dying: Ethical Decision Making With A Depressed Dialysis Patient

Abstracted from an unpublished paper by Mary A. Kardauskas, SHCJ, MSW

Practice Context and Case Presentation

Renal dialysis social workers encounter a variety of ethical issues in their professional practice. Ethical dilemmas frequently center around client self-determination, prolongation of life, confidentiality, resource availability, and hospital/insurance company policies and practices, which may conflict with social work values. The following "composite" case illustrates several of these issues.

The Department of Social Work Services and Utilization Case Management at a major medical center employs two full-time renal dialysis social workers to address the biopsychosocial needs of patients in the inpatient and outpatient dialysis units. Renal social workers provide emotional and concrete support services to patients and families on a long-term basis, addressing patients' adjustment to illness, rights, financial/resource concerns, and social support needs. Renal workers also discuss the issue of advance directives with patients and are occasionally called on to interpret patients' wishes when surrogates cannot be reached during a medical crisis.

Mrs. B., a divorced 38-year-old, was diagnosed with end-stage renal disease (ESRD) and juvenile-onset diabetes. She had been a hemodialysis patient since 1996. Forced to leave her job in 2001 due to rapidly declining health, Mrs. B. was soon after faced with desertion by her husband. Her mother, sensing her need and vulnerability, moved in to provide stability and support to her daughter and 8-year-old grandson. Her mother and her son have turned to religion for support.

Over the past year, Mrs. B. has been repeatedly hospitalized, and her intermittent depression has been noted by family and staff. One day during her treatment, she announced to her physician and social worker, "I'm tired of fighting. Living on this machine is worse than dying." She stated she wanted to terminate treatment. Her mother long ago agreed to act as her son's guardian, and she knew he would be well cared for. Mrs. B. had an advance directive that named her mother as her decision maker should she be unable to make decisions herself.

Mrs. B.'s mother was appalled by her daughter's request. She stated that her daughter is "too young to die," and considered her daughter's request suicidal. She stated that Mrs. B.'s giving up like this would set a bad example of coping for her son. Their church holds that all life is sacred, that taking life is a sin, and that "God never gives you more than you can bear." She insisted that the hospital deny Mrs. B.'s request because her depression rendered her incompetent to make medical decisions. She invoked her power as the decision maker named in her daughter's advance directive.

In considering Mrs. B.'s request to terminate dialysis, the principal ethical dilemma seems to center on *quality* of life versus prolongation of *biological* life. Related ethical issues include client self-determination, competency, determining who is the client, welfare of the child, advance directives (surrogate's unwillingness to uphold patient wishes), conflicting religious beliefs and values, and physical and psychological definitions of life and death.

The dilemma is specified as follows:

QUALITY OF LIFE V. PROLONGATION OF (BIOLOGICAL) LIFE

Research and Related Literature

Over the past quarter of a century, dialysis treatment (and near-universal health coverage under the 1972 End-Stage Renal Program of Medicare) has saved and extended the lives of literally hundreds of thousands of renal patients. Dialysis prolongs, but does not necessarily ensure quality of, life.

ESRD affects body function, self-perception, self-image, lifestyle, relationships, vocational function, and financial security and requires ongoing adaptation to illness (Frazier, 1981; Wolcott, 1990). Patients with long-term renal failure and uremia may eventually experience dysfunction in nearly any organ or part of the body. Concurrent illness, such as diabetes or AIDS, may exacerbate the problem (Wolcott, 1990). Depression, the most common psychiatric problem among such patients (Hodroff, 1994; Kimmel, 1994) and an important predictor of mortality (Kimmel, 1994), has been associated with lower quality of life, impaired immunologic function, treatment noncompliance, withdrawal from treatment, and higher suicide rates (Levy, 1991; Sensky, 1993; Wolcott, 1990). Children whose parents are chronically ill may experience fear of abandonment, anger, resentment, guilt, and worry about what will happen to them upon their parent's death.

Requests to terminate dialysis are not unusual, and poor quality of life is a frequently cited reason. Withdrawal from dialysis is now the third most common cause of death among dialysis patients in the United States (Kjellstrand, 1992) and accounted for 8.4 percent of all ESRD deaths in the United States in 1990 (U.S. Renal Data System, 1993). Once dialysis is terminated, death is painless, gradual, but inevitable. Neu and Kjellstrand's (1986) study of 155 renal patients who stopped dialysis found that death occurred in 1 to 28 days, with an average of 8.1 days.

While the concept of the *quality of life* can be traced back to such ancient philosophers as Aristotle (Ferrans, 1987) and is today often cited as a reason to refuse or withdraw life-sustaining medical treatment, there exists no one standard definition of the term (Ferrans, 1987; Walter & Shannon, 1990). Some common definitions focus on an individual's "social utility," ability to live a normal life, and happiness or satisfaction. Perlman and Jonsen (1990, p. 100) note that many authors use the term to reflect an individual's "subjective satisfaction...with his or her own personal life (physical, mental, and social situation)," but that it may alternately refer to an onlooker's (e.g., physician, surrogate) evaluation of another's life situation. An onlooker's view might not match that of the patient, as is evident in the present case.

The sanctity-of-life principle, central to Jewish and Christian religions as well as to secular humanism, maintains that all life is sacred and that the value of physical life is not conditional on an individual's property or characteristics. In doing so, it stands as an important reminder that quality-of-life judgments based on life satisfaction and social utility risk are heading down the "slippery slope."

"Sanctity of life," however, has been argued from different perspectives. Absolutists (such as Immanuel Kant) vehemently protest humans' propensity to "play God." Lammers and Verhey (1987, p. 439, emphasis added) illustrate this view: "If withdrawing care results in death, is this really different from more actively aiming at the death of the patient?...Death *cannot* be chosen in preference to some lesser evil...." Similarly, Smedes (1987, p. 147) writes:

> (God) gives us the right to stave death off, if we can, with medicine and machines....God alone has the right to take away life, because he is the one who authors it in the first place....If there is a right time for any person to die, God alone may decide what it is.

Meanwhile, others (including Roman Catholic ethicists) distinguish between ordinary and extraordinary treatment. Keyserlingk (1990, p. 43) maintains that preserving a life where there is "excruciating, intractable, and prolonged pain and suffering," or where there is "minimal capacity to experience, to relate to other human beings," could be a "dishonouring of the sanctity of life itself," and further suggests that allowing death might be "a demonstration of respect for the individual and for human life in general."

While theologians and others denounce subjective judgments of one's "relative worth" or "social utility," they acknowledge a person's legal/ethical right to make medical decisions. Personalistic quality-of-life judgments involve assessing the benefits and burdens of medical treatment: one's experience of joy, satisfaction, burdens, and suffering; the kind of life possible, given one's prognosis; and the degree to which a condition allows one to live a life that he or she views as worth living (Hastings Center, 1987). Consequentialists also consider the impact on others.

Client self-determination is closely linked to quality-of-life decisions, but serious ethical dilemmas abound. As evidenced by the 1990 U.S. Supreme Court decision in *Cruzan* v. *Director, Missouri Dept. of Health* (Cranford, 1992), the legal system recognizes a competent patient's right to refuse treatment. Similarly, the Patient Self-Determination Act of 1990, enacted to "enhance an individual's control over medical treatment decisions" at hospitals and healthcare institutions (Sabatino, 1993, p. 12), has resulted in guidelines for forgoing life-sustaining treatment. Kidney machines are included among such treatments. If competency is an issue, guidelines specify a psychiatric consultation to determine capacity.

Renal social work colleagues note the intensely personal decision-making process followed by patients who consider terminating dialysis. Issues of competency, however, raise special dilemmas. Patients' abilities to make rational choices may be severely compromised by depression or by other psychiatric conditions. Many chronically ill patients experience bouts of depression and confusion (Beauchamp & Childress, 2009). Since termination of treatment inevitably results in death, renal patients' competence to make such decisions must be carefully assessed. Unfortunately, patients whose request is not supported by the wider medical community may be subjected to a psychiatric consultation, deemed "incompetent," and their care decisions rendered by surrogates. Thus, a process designed to empower patients may leave some patients feeling depressed and powerless to free themselves from unwanted life-sustaining measures.

While appearing to avoid quality- and sanctity-of-life issues, the NASW Code of Ethics (2008) states that workers "respect and promote the rights of clients to self-determination and assist clients in their efforts to identify and clarify their goals." One might well question how to foster "the rights of clients to self-determination" with a depressed, terminal patient. The position of Mrs. B.'s mother, who is "legally authorized to act on behalf of a client...with the client's best interest in mind" must also be considered. "Best interest" tends to be a subjective judgment, relative to the person making it. In this instance, the client's self-determined judgment of her own "best interest" is quite different from that of her mother.

The values set forth by Compton and Galaway (2004) as the bases for social work may also be perceived to be in conflict here. Belief in "client self-determination" could be seen as grounds to support Mrs. B., while supporting the "uniqueness and inherent dignity of the individual" could be read as grounds for upholding her unique, sacred, valuable life.

Author's Reflections, Reasoning Process, and Resolution

Mrs. B.'s request to forgo dialysis is supported by laws and popular opinion concerning quality of life, self-determination and respect for autonomy, personal freedom of choice, and human/legal rights. Her mother's position highlights other societal values: religious belief of sanctity of life, safety ("protecting" her daughter from suicide, shielding her grandson from "poor coping skills"), youth (an obligation to "protect" her daughter), human/legal rights (to legally contest her daughter's competence to make her own decisions), and child welfare (her grandson's needs).

The worker's values (sanctity of life, freedom/autonomy, relationships, safety, and justice) flow from her religious beliefs, which reverence the life and dignity of each person, but she does not subscribe to the preservation of biological life at all costs. Her personal value of freedom and her respect for autonomy enable her to resonate with Mrs. B.'s desire to balance the benefits and burdens of extraordinary treatment, but conflicts with her concern about Mrs. B.'s ability to make such a decision while depressed. The worker values relationships and the commitments they entail, but views Mrs. B.'s decision about treatment as a personal one that she must make in the light of her own situation. The worker's value of safety could potentially spark paternalistic responses to this depressed, terminally ill patient who requests to end her life, but the patient's grim prognosis suggests an advanced disease process where aggressive treatment might stretch the psychosocial reserves of patient and family beyond their limits. The worker's concern for justice causes her to feel committed to advocate for patient self-determination, yet also to understand Mrs. B.'s mother's desire to act justly by preventing a hastened death.

The four key and sometimes conflicting biomedical ethics principles described by Beauchamp and Childress (2009) are in evidence in this case: beneficence (balancing benefits against risks and costs), nonmaleficence (avoiding harm), respect for autonomy, and justice (norms for distributing benefits, risks, and costs). Mrs. B. balances the risks and costs of treatment and seeks relief via termination of dialysis; her mother sees no way to balance death against life and wants to prolong her daughter's life, keep the family together, and "follow God's will." Mrs. B. seeks to avoid the harm of a poor quality of life with death; her mother desires to block the "suicide request" as the greater harm. Mrs. B.'s autonomous decision sets her against her mother's equally autonomous decision. And Mrs. B. sees justice in being able to control her medical care, while her mother sees it in the prevention of a "tragic" suicide.

In support of Mrs. B.'s "poor-quality-of-life" position, several options might be considered. The social worker could call a patient care conference with the patient, renal physician, primary nurse, dietitian, social worker, and members of the family present in order to better identify and address Mrs. B.'s concerns. Options could be explored that might improve her quality of life while preserving her biological life, such as pain management, diabetes and/or renal treatment, and addressing uremia if present. A psychiatric consult might recommend appropriate therapeutic intervention to treat her depression and enhance her coping skills. A support group might assist Mrs. B. in working through some of her feelings about her condition and situation.

It would also be possible to hold the patient care conference but to respect Mrs. B.'s decision to terminate treatment if she still chooses to do so after being informed of all the risks and benefits. The care conference could then be used to address the family's issues, offer support, and provide them with information as well as appropriate referrals. This option respects self-determination and quality-of-life issues, but by not providing a means to assess Mrs. B.'s "competence," nonmaleficence and sanctity of life might be violated. It would also be possible to accept Mrs. B.'s request for the termination of treatment at face value, without subjecting her to the patient care conference. The worker's role would be to serve both as patient advocate (working with the medical staff, supporting her through her final days, asking her to state her request in writing, helping her to name an alternative surrogate, for example) and as a mediator between patient and family, supporting the family's needs with referrals, legal assistance (for grandson), and so on. This option would also support the values of quality of life and self-determination, but possibly violate nonmaleficence, sanctity of life, and safety by failing to address the competence issue.

In support of the prolongation of biological life, one approach might be to assume that *all* requests to terminate life support warrant a psychiatric evaluation to determine competence. When patients are declared incompetent, surrogates may then override the patients' requests. While this absolutist position upholds the sanctity of life on one level, it also equates patient requests to terminate treatment with "incompetence," invalidates patients' experiences, and thus violates the values of dignity and sanctity it seeks to uphold. It may also violate the principle of nonmaleficence, promote paternalism, and undermine self-determination and justice.

Another possible plan might be to treat Mrs. B. pharmacologically for depression, provide cognitive-behavioral treatment, or logotherapy. As in the first option, the central concern here is who decides incompetence and upon what criteria. If Mrs. B. is judged incompetent only because her choice conflicts with her physician's moral and ethical position, it might be more appropriate to refer her to another physician rather than subjecting her to interventions against her will. Treatment upholds the values of sanctity of life, nonmaleficence, safety, youth, and quality of life, but potentially can violate self-determination and autonomy, quality of life, and human/legal rights.

Another possible approach might be to refer the case to the hospital ethics committee for review. Competence issues might be discussed more objectively in such an environment. However, recommendations of the ethics committee can still be disregarded, by either Mrs. B. or her mother.

The ethical position chosen by the worker combines elements of both quality-of-life and prolongation-of-life approaches. It is consequentialist in nature and utilitarian in approach, focusing on the greatest good for the greatest number. It involves several steps: validation, evaluation, collaboration, short-term contracting, and intervention (if agreed on). Preparation, information, and referral for both Mrs. B. and the family would be provided.

Mrs. B.'s request and right to refuse treatment should be immediately validated, and she should be informed that her request is taken seriously. She also should be informed of any standardized procedures for handling such requests, as well as the reasons for such procedures. A psychiatric evaluation to measure her depression, using measures that have proven reliable and valid with the renal population, should be provided immediately. A patient care conference should follow soon after, spelling out her prognosis, the costs and benefits of her options, and what occurs once dialysis is discontinued. Together, the care team and the patient can address the options and alternatives available to her, such as pain management, therapy, and planning to reduce stresses induced by financial condition, strained relationships, or other problems. If Mrs. B. is agreeable, specified services can be contracted for a brief (three or four weeks) period of time. At the end of the contract period, Mrs. B.'s request could be reviewed again, and changes in her perceptions and decisions could be discussed.

If Mrs. B. continues to request the termination of treatment, this request should be honored. She should be allowed to choose the date she wishes to discontinue treatment, as well as the place she wishes to spend her final days. Clergy, legal counsel, and changes in designated surrogate could be offered.

The social worker should meet with the family to provide information and support, and referrals to the ethics committee and/or outside resources can be offered. They should be assisted in saying their good-byes and be supported upon Mrs. B.'s death.

The resolution suggested here is absolutist (in suggesting a protocol) as well as relativist (in its sensitivity to Mrs. B.'s particular case). The sense of duty to protect life is deontological, while its efforts to offer "the greatest good" are teleological. It upholds the

Human Rights & Justice

Practice Behavior Example: POLST (Physician Orders for Life-Sustaining Treatment) are designed to support self-determination and clarify a person's wishes regarding end-of-life care. However, people may choose to forego making any decisions regarding these issues even when health conditions suggest that such decision making would ensure that wishes would be respected.

Critical Thinking Question: There are two levels of "self-determination" here: self-determination regarding end-of-life decisions and care and "self-determination" regarding the choice to make, or not to make, these decisions. Which of these would you believe should be primary? Is the "greater good" ensuring the person's right to end-of-life care as desired, or the right to make, or not make, any decision? How might this be carried over into other instances involving self-determination issues?

biomedical ethical principles of nonmaleficence in preventing passive, voluntary euthanasia chosen because of depression; of beneficence, by clearly spelling out risks
and benefits; of autonomy in upholding Mrs. B.'s right to self-determination; and of
justice in proposing the development and use of a protocol. It upholds societal, professional, client and worker values of quality of life, as well as sanctity of life, religious
belief, self-determination, family relationships, safety, and justice. It passes Dolgoff,
Loewenberg, and Harrington's (2009) Ethical Principles Screen (EPS): protecting life,
yet also balancing risks and benefits; evidencing equality; reverencing autonomy and
independence; causing least harm; attending to quality-of-life issues; and incorporating
truthfulness and full disclosure.

In facilitating communication between the patient/family unit and the healthcare
team, providing information and support to patient and family, advocating for patient
rights, and providing comfort and support to the family, social workers who work with
cases such as this one can enable individuals and families to face difficult and final
decisions with sensitivity and dignity.

Case Study C (*Kardauskas*)

Beauchamp, T. L., & Childress, J. F. (2009). *Principles of biomedical ethics* (6th ed.).
    New York: Oxford University Press.

Bishops' Committee of the Confraternity of Christian Doctrine. (Eds.). (1970). *New
    American Bible.* New York: Catholic Book Pub. Co.

Bowles, A. L., sr. (1992). Commentary. *Hastings Center Report, 22*(6), 28.

Compton, B. R., & Galaway, B. (2004). *Social work processes* (4th ed.). Belmont, CA:
    Wadsworth.

Cranford, R. (1992). Legal aspects of stopping dialysis. In C. M. Kjellstrand & J. B.
    Dossetor (Eds.), *Ethical problems in dialysis and transplantation* (pp. 127–142).
    Boston: Kluwer Academic.

Dolgoff, R., Loewenberg, F. M., & Harrington, D. (2009). *Ethical decisions for social work
    practice* (8th ed.). Itasca, IL: F. E. Peacock.

Ferrans, C. E. (1987). Quality of life as a criterion for allocation of life-sustaining treat-
    ment: The case of hemodialysis. In V. A. Glesnes-Anderson & G. R. Anderson (Eds.),
    Health care ethics: A guide for decision makers (pp. 109–124). Rockville, MD:
    Aspen.

Frazier, C. L. (1981). Renal disease. *Health and social work, 6* (Suppl. 4), 75S–82S.

Hastings Center. (1987). *Guidelines on the termination of life-sustaining treatment and
    the care of the dying.* Bloomington, IN: Indiana University Press.

Hodroff, K. (1994). Depression and the kidney patient: A nursing perspective. *Clinical
    Strategies: The AKF Newsletter for Nephrology Professionals, 1*(1), 1–4.

Kaye, M. (1992). Religious aspects of stopping treatment. In C. M. Kjellstrand & J. B.
    Dossetor (Eds.), *Ethical problems in dialysis and transplantation* (pp. 117–125).
    Boston: Kluwer Academic.

Keyserlingk, E. W. (1990). The quality of life and death. In J. J. Walter & T. A. Shannon
    (Eds.), *Quality of life: The new medical dilemma* (pp. 35–53). New York: Paulist.

Kimmel, P. L. (1994). Depression and mortality in ESRD patients. *Clinical Strategies:
    The AKF Newsletter of Nephrology Professionals, 1*(1), 1–3.

Kjellstrand, C. M. (1992). Practical aspects of stopping dialysis and cultural differences.
    In C. M. Kjellstrand & J. B. Dossetor (Eds.), *Ethical problems in dialysis and trans-
    plantation* (pp. 103–116). Boston: Kluwer Academic.

Lammers, S. E., & Verhey, A. (Eds.). (1987). *On moral medicine: Theological perspec-
    tives in medical ethics.* Grand Rapids, MI: William B. Eerdmans.

Levy, N. B. (1991). Psychiatric aspects of renal care. In D. Z. Levine (Ed.), *Care of the
    renal patient* (2nd ed., pp. 181–186). Philadelphia: W. B. Saunders.

Medical Center. (1993). Unpublished manual (name withheld).

National Association of Social Workers. (2008). *NASW code of ethics.* Washington, DC:
    Author.

Neu, S., & Kjellstrand, C. M. (1986). Stopping long-term dialysis: An empirical study of life-support treatment. *New England Journal of Medicine, 314*, 14–20.

Perlman, R. A., & Jonsen, A. (1990). The use of quality of life considerations in medical decision making. In J. J. Walter & T. A. Shannon (Eds.), *Quality of life: The new medical dilemma* (pp. 93–103). New York: Paulist Press.

Sabatino, C. P. (1993). Surely the wizard will help us, Toto? Implementing the patient self-determination act. *Hastings Center Report, 23*(1), 12–16.

Sensky, T. (1993). Psychosomatic aspects of end-stage renal failure. *Psychotherapy and Psychosomatics, 59*, 56–68.

Smedes, L. B. (1987). Respect for human life: "Thou shalt not kill." In S. E. Lammers & A. Verhey (Eds.), *On moral medicine: Theological perspectives in medical ethics* (pp. 143–149). Grand Rapids, MI: William B. Eerdmans.

Starck, P. L. (Ed.). (1992). *The hidden dimension of illness: Human suffering* (pp. 25–42). New York: National League for Nursing Press.

U.S. Renal Data System. (1993). *1993 annual report.* Washington, DC: U.S. Government Printing Office.

U.S. Supreme Court. (1990). *Cruzan v. Director, Missouri Department of Health*, 110 C. Ct. 2841. Washington, DC: Author.

Valdez, R., & Rosenblum, A. (1994). Voluntary termination of dialysis: When your patient says, "Enough is enough!" *Dialysis and Transplantation, 23*(10), 566–570.

Walter, J. J., & Shannon, T. A. (Eds.). (1990). Introduction. In J. J. Walter & T. A. Shannon (Eds.), *Quality of life: The new medical dilemma* (pp. 7–8). New York: Paulist Press.

Wight, J. (1993). On discontinuing dialysis. *Journal of Medical Ethics, 19*(2), 77–81.

Wolcott, D. L. (1990). Psychosocial adaptation of chronic dialysis patients. In A. R. Nisserson, R. N. Fine, & D. E. Gentile (Eds.), *Clinical dialysis* (2nd ed., pp. 735–746). Norwalk, CT: Appleton & Lange.

Case Study D   Reading The Future: When "Best Interest" Must Last 20 Years

Abstracted from an unpublished paper by Amy Craig-Van Grack, MSW

Practice Context and Case Presentation

The Out-of-Home Unit provides services to families with children who have been removed from their homes, usually due to substantiated abuse or neglect. Services are provided to the family and child by the assigned social worker on a loosely defined case management basis; that is, the worker (a) assesses the needs of the family; (b) develops a case plan and service contract; (c) delivers or refers, coordinates, and monitors service provision (i.e., drug treatment, therapy, job training); and (d) works with the family and child until case plan goals are achieved. Permanency plans for these children range from reunification with biological parent(s), custodial placement with extended family, adoption, long-term foster care, and/or preparation for independent living. Oversight of the caseworker's activities is provided routinely through supervision, administrative review, and court review of each case.

Tonya Morris was born 15 days after her father, Terence Calvert, was incarcerated due to his conviction on drug possession and distribution charges. The next day, her mother, Paula Morris, left Tonya with an "unwilling caregiver" and never returned to reclaim her. Tonya was placed in foster care with Beverly Becker where she remains today—nearly 19 months later. Tonya's mother is a long-time drug user, and Tonya apparently suffered exposure to drugs *in utero*. Since Tonya's placement in foster care, the agency has been unable to locate her. Mr. Calvert would like to care for Tonya. However, she would likely be 2 years old before reunification could feasibly be initiated.

Tonya is obviously very bonded to and well loved by her foster mother and foster sister. Her foster mother has expressed a desire to adopt Tonya on several occasions. Hers is the only home Tonya has known, and she is happy and secure in this placement.

The worker faces the dilemma of the following:

WORKER'S PERCEPTION OF BEST INTERESTS OF CHILD V. PARENTAL RIGHTS

Research and Related Literature

What Do Children Need? Abraham Maslow delineated a pyramid of "needs and values which are related to one another in order of their strength and priority, in a manner which is both hierarchical and developmental" (Longres, 2000). These needs, in descending order of significance, are (1) basic physiological need, (2) personal safety needs, (3) belongingness and love needs, (4) esteem needs (self and others), and (5) self-actualization needs (Longres, 2000). Similarly, Erik Erikson advanced a theory of psychosocial development "derived from the...principle of epigenesis, or the idea that each stage depends on resolutions of the experiences of prior stages" (Greene & Ephross, 1991). Erikson used the concept of an expanding "radius of significant relationships" to describe the child's experience of human relationships throughout the life cycle. Thus, the child's needs must be assessed on a number of levels—physical, cognitive, emotional, and social. Moreover, these needs must be considered on a vertical axis (signifying priority) and on a horizontal axis (signifying time).

Most developmental theorists identify interpersonal difficulties in adulthood as reverberations of childhood relationship and attachment issues. For children in foster care, the issue of attachment is particularly germane as it may circumscribe development and adult functioning: "[F]oster children in clinical settings have been characterized as lacking the ability to form relationships, having inadequate parental images (either glorified or denigrated) to serve as a basis for socialization, and being confused about their identities...." (Fein, 1991b, pp. 578–579). In addition, there is "evidence that many foster children have serious educational deficits, are in poorer health, and are more likely than other children to suffer developmental and emotional problems and to have limited access to appropriate health and mental health care" (Allen, 1991, p. 613).

Goldstein, Freud, and Solnit substantiate "the need of every child for unbroken continuity of affection and stimulating relationships with an adult" (Goldstein, Freud, & Solnit, 1973, p. 6). They define and differentiate the concepts of the "wanted child," the "psychological parent," and the "biological parent." They advance a number of principles regarding child development—namely, that the child's development unfolds in response to environmental influence; that children have innate characteristics that influence their interaction; that during childhood, children change constantly, whereas adults are more or less psychically fixed; that the child's needs are not stable; that children have a different sense of time than adults; that children lack reason to interpret events; and that "children have no psychological conception of relationship by blood tie until quite late in their development" (Goldstein et al., 1973, p. 12). The integration of these principles led the authors to conclude that "[c]ontinuity of relationships, surroundings, and environmental influence are essential for a child's normal development" (Goldstein et al., 1973, p. 31).

What Are Parents' Rights with Respect to Their Children? Children have historically been viewed as chattel, the property of the father,

Human Behavior

Practice Behavior Example: Tonya's father, currently incarcerated, wishes to care for his daughter when he is released from prison in about two years.

Critical Thinking Question: Different from most parents whose children are placed out of the home, there has been no contact at all between Tonya and her father, but simply a biological link. Placement with her father is less a question of "reunification" than of "unification." Is this a significant factor to consider in planning for Tonya? Why, or why not?

who retained complete control over their well-being, care, and all other aspects of their lives. However, in the late 1800s, "there was a dramatic shift away from fathers' common law rights to custody and control of their children toward a modern emphasis on the best interests of the child..." (Mason, 1994, p. xiii). Currently, when the family breaks down, due to death, divorce, parental abuse or neglect, the state asserts itself as the arbiter of the child's best interests. At this point, issues of child custody and best interests become considerably more complicated. Nonetheless, "[t]he basic right of biological parents to the custody of their children has not appreciably diminished" (Derdeyn, 1977a, p. 377).

Freedom and privacy are first-order principles in the United States, espoused in the Constitution and the Bill of Rights. Rights apply to families as well as to individuals. "Family privacy, freedom from government interference, and the right to raise children according to individual beliefs are among the fundamental rights secured by the Constitution" (Huxtable, 1994, p. 60). Thus, parents have a right to privacy and to freedom to maintain their families as they choose insofar as their actions do not compromise their children's physical safety and general well-being.

When a report of abuse or neglect (or, in this case, abandonment) is made, family freedom and privacy are necessarily reduced as the state exercises its duty to protect the child from harm (Stein, 1991). If a report is substantiated, the family (parent and child) has a statutory right to "reasonable efforts" to preserve the family and prevent placement of the child in alternative care. In fact, state agencies are required to demonstrate reasonable efforts to the courts prior to removing a child. If a child is removed, the family has a right to "reasonable efforts" to reunify the family. Thus, if a report is made and substantiated, the parents and child have a right to services designed to mitigate the conditions deemed harmful to the child. It can be further argued that the right to services includes a presumption of timeliness and efficacy of those services.

The parent has a right to visitation unless visitation is deemed to be harmful to the child. Furthermore, the agency is required to promote and facilitate visitation, including transporting participants and supervising visits, if necessary. Finally, a parent is guaranteed due process prior to the removal of his or her children and prior to the termination of his or her parental rights.

Where Does the Law Stand? Child welfare and the law in the United States have become more deeply and inextricably linked during the latter half of the twentieth century. Moreover, "[i]n the legal arena, superimposed upon the essentially immutable tradition of a biological parent's proprietary interest in his children, there is a growing awareness of the emotional needs of children" (Derdeyn, 1977b, p. 611). Hence, the legislative and judicial domains are increasingly prescriptive and proscriptive regarding service delivery to families and children. Federal policy concerning children in out-of-home placement is primarily contained in Public Law 96-272, the Adoption Assistance and Child Welfare Act of 1980.

That legislation was designed to end the drift of children in foster care by encouraging planning for permanency for each child within a hierarchy of desirable options, ranging from returning the child to his or her biological parents, through adoption, to long-term foster care. It was also meant to provide for oversight to move cases through the child welfare system and to develop preventive services to avert the family breakdown that the removal of children from the home entails (Fein, 1991a, p. 576). States, including the District of Columbia, enact legislation that complies, for the most part, with federal legislation in order to secure funds to deliver services to families with children in out-of-home placements.

In the child welfare arena, children have the right to protection from harm and to reasonable efforts to preserve and/or reunify their families. However, in cases involving conflict over custody, children do not necessarily have the right to choose. Nonetheless, they do have a right to the representation of a *guardian ad litem* who has no conflict of interest or obligation and advises the decision-making body regarding the child's best interest. Also, while professionals across the spectrum concur that a child needs permanence and stability, these cannot be legislated as rights. It is apparent from the often vague or undefined terms in legislation (i.e., "reasonable efforts" and "best interests") that legislators have similarly struggled to strike a balance between the best interests of children and the rights of parents.

Furthermore, with regard to visitation, "[s]tates and federal statutes recognize the importance of parental visiting. Some states require agency staff to promote visiting. Others allow failure to visit to be used as a basis for termination of parental rights..." (Proch & Howard, 1984, p. 140). In addition to legislation, court rulings impact parent–child relationships. With regard to this particular case, "incarcerated parents have a constitutionally protected right to visits with their children" and "efforts of an incarcerated parent to continue contact with her or his children must be considered in relation to the limits that imprisonment places on parents" (Stein, 1991, p. 74).

Finally, however, if reunification with the biological parent is deemed contrary to the child's best interest, the parent has the right to due process prior to termination of his or her parental rights. Nonetheless, "[t]he conditions that serve to justify removing a child from an unsafe environment are not necessarily sufficient to justify severing parental ties.... [T]he state must show that the consequences of allowing the parent–child relationship to continue are more severe than the consequences of termination" (Stein, 1991, p. 71). Again, with respect to the facts of this specific case, "imprisonment alone is not sufficient grounds to terminate parental rights" (Stein, 1991, p. 74). However, a New York court ruled that "an imprisoned parent's consent to adoption was not necessary and that termination without his consent did not violate his due process rights if there was clear and convincing evidence that adoption was in the child's best interests" (Stein, 1991, p. 74).

Where Does Agency Policy Stand?   Legislation and judicial decisions often dictate agency policy. Agency regulations are written and implemented to comply with the law. In child welfare, this can be an onerous task. Nonetheless, the agency attempts to conform with the bulk of the law reviewed above.

In terms of the value-base of the agency, its mission statement makes these clear: "The mission...is to support the development of healthy families; to assist families and children in need; to protect abused and neglected children; and to provide a permanent home for all children. This mission is accomplished...through a service delivery system which recognizes the value of cultural diversity and family strengths..." (Family Services Administration, 1995). Seven principles are delineated to provide guidance for the agency worker: (1) Children need families; (2) safety is the first concern; (3) a crisis is an opportunity for change; (4) not all problems need to be addressed; (5) most families do care about each other; (6) everyone is doing the best he or she can at the time; and (7) power for change resides within the family. In order of preference, the agency supports (1) reunification with biological parents, (2) return to a relative, (3) adoption, (4) independent living, and (5) long-term foster care.

NASW Code of Ethics.   Among the ethical principles that apply to this dilemma, under the value of social justice, is the statement that social workers "strive to ensure equality of opportunity...." As a parent, Mr. Calvert is entitled to be able to maintain a relationship with his daughter. Under the value of dignity and worth of the person, it is noted that workers should treat each client in a "caring and respectful manner" and "promote client's socially responsible self-determination." In addition, under the value of the importance of human relationships, it states, "Social workers seek to strengthen relationships among people in a purposeful effort to promote, restore, maintain, and enhance the well-being of individuals, families, social groups..." (NASW Code of Ethics, 2008).

Certainly, these sections of the Code support the consideration of the rights of Mr. Calvert and the value and importance of family relationships.

In addition, in the Ethical Standards section of the Code (6.04b), it is stated, "Social workers should act to expand choice and opportunity for all people, with special regard for vulnerable, disadvantaged, oppressed and exploited people and groups." In his state of incarceration, Mr. Calvert is certainly vulnerable and disadvantaged. It is uncertain whether the reasons for his incarceration, drug possession and distribution, are related to oppression. Section 6.04d states, "Social workers should act to prevent and eliminate domination, exploitation, and discrimination." To impede the exercise of Mr. Calvert's parental rights would seem to violate this obligation by denying him parental rights due to his incarceration. He is following the laws, accepting punishment, and wants to be a parent to Tonya.

However, Tonya is the worker's primary client, and her obligation, clearly, is to her (Sect. 1.01). As a minor, Tonya lacks full decision-making capacity, and the social worker must act on her behalf. Section 1.14 states, "When social workers act on behalf of clients who lack the capacity to make informed decisions, social workers should take reasonable steps to safeguard the interests and rights of those clients." It is the worker's responsibility to ensure that Tonya's interests are protected. This might support her remaining with her secure and nurturing foster family.

Author's Reflections, Reasoning Process, and Resolution

The worker believes in the determinative nature of childhood experience and values responsible, loving parenting. This position is confirmed by societal values, which, however, place biological ties above other concerns. Translated into agency policy and child welfare laws, the hierarchy supports (1) the primacy of biological ties, (2) the child's well-being, (3) freedom and self-determination, (4) privacy, and (5) the importance of family. It may be assumed that this case remains open at the agency due to society's stronger emphasis on biological ties. (Otherwise, it would have been moved to adoption.) Tonya's age at the time of her placement (20 days old) and the duration of her placement (possibly as long as two years) distinguish this case, for the worker, from similar cases.

Two possible courses of action include (1) continuing efforts for and ultimately reunifying Tonya with her biological father or (2) seeking administrative and court approval of a change in goal from reunification to adoption or long-term foster care. The first option would preserve Mr. Calvert's rights as Tonya's biological father to regain custody. The second option would enhance Tonya's chances for permanence and stability, as it is fairly certain that a change in goals would ensure Tonya's continuing long-term care by Ms. Becker. However, a goal of adoption would require that the agency seek to terminate Mr. Calvert's parental rights. Considering the circumstances of this case and the research elaborated above, it seems plausible that a court would allow a termination in the "best interests of the child." A goal of long-term foster care would not require a termination of parental rights.

Research cites foster care reentry rates of close to 33 percent for children following reunification (Fein & Staff, 1993; Hess & Folaron, 1991). Furthermore, "the most frequent contributor to placement reentry [is] the fact that the problems of the parents that precipitated placement [are] not resolved. The number and severity of the parents' problems also contribute to reentry..." (Hess & Folaron, 1991, p. 408). Other factors that contribute to a poor prognosis for successful reunification in this case include Mr. Calvert's history with drugs, his criminal record, lack of a high school degree or GED, apparent lack of an informal support system, lack of a home or prospective employment, and lack of knowledge and experience in child-rearing.

Reunification with Mr. Calvert would, therefore, be considered very "high risk." In addition, none of these factors address a lack of strong relationship between Tonya and Mr. Calvert.

On the other hand, a change in goal to adoption or long-term foster care would almost certainly ensure that Tonya would remain with her psychological family, maintain her affective ties, and give her the best chance for optimal personal development—all of which are advocated by Goldstein et al. (1973). Her placement with Ms. Becker, who has demonstrated her care to be very loving and comprehensive and is extremely unlikely to withdraw from her current charge as Tonya's primary caregiver, can be considered "low risk." Moreover, remaining with Ms. Becker would not preclude Tonya from establishing and maintaining a relationship with her biological father, regardless of whether his parental rights are terminated.

There are a number of principles to be found in ethical theory that direct the decision-making process. These principles include "nonmaleficence," the "greatest good for the greatest number," "least harm," "substituted judgment," "best interests," and "quality of life." The concept of nonmaleficence might lead one to avoid abrogating the biological relationship. However, it might also discourage interrupting the psychological relationship. All of the other ethical principles weigh heavily in favor of the second option of changing Tonya's goal from reunification to adoption or long-term foster care. For example, in attempting to allow Tonya self-determination regarding her living situation and by recognizing a child's limited understanding of blood ties (Goldstein et al., 1973), one might "substitute" a judgment that she would prefer to remain in Ms. Becker's care until such time as she was old enough to understand her incontrovertible relationship with Mr. Calvert and choose otherwise.

The values hierarchy pits the importance of biological ties vis-à-vis the child's well-being. The practice issues cited above, however, require that one evaluate the high risk to Tonya's well-being of preservation of Mr. Calvert's biological ties to the full extent (i.e., through reunification). Nevertheless, it must be recognized that *custody is not the categorical imperative of an intact biological relationship,* nor even of a psychological relationship, between a parent and child. Thus, the decision for action and its justification take into account all of the social values deemed relevant to Tonya's case and contemplate their maximal fulfillment. Thus, the worker would choose to change Tonya's goal from reunification to adoption under the assumption that Ms. Becker would seek and be approved for her adoption.

Case Study D (*Craig-Van Grack*)

Allen, M. (1991). Crafting a federal legislative framework for child welfare reform. *American Journal of Orthopsychiatry, 61*(4), 610–623.

Derdeyn, A. P. (1977a, July). Child abuse and neglect: The rights of parents and the needs of their children. *American Journal of Orthopsychiatry, 47*(3), 377–387.

Derdeyn, A. P. (1977b, October). A case for permanent foster placement of dependent, neglected, and abused children. *American Journal of Orthopsychiatry, 47*(4), 604–614.

Dolgoff, R., Loewenberg, F. M., & Harrington, D. (2009). *Ethical decisions for social work practice* (8th ed.). Itasca, IL: F. E. Peacock.

Family Services Administration Child and Family Services Division. (1995, March 3). *Policy handbook.* Washington, DC: Author.

Fein, E. (1991a). The elusive search for certainty in child welfare: Introduction. *American Journal of Orthopsychiatry, 61*(4), 576–577.

Fein, E. (1991b). Issues in foster family care: Where do we stand? *American Journal of Orthopsychiatry, 61*(4), 578–583.

Fein, E., & Staff, I. (1993). Last best chance: Findings from a reunification services program. *Child Welfare, 72*(1), 25–40.

Goldstein, J., Freud, A., & Solnit, A. J. (1973). *Beyond the best interests of the child.* New York: The Free Press.

Greene, R. R., & Ephross, P. H. (1991). *Human behavior theory and social work practice.* New York: Aldine de Gruyter.

Hess, P. M., & Folaron, G. (1991). Ambivalences: A challenge to permanency for children. *Child Welfare, 70*(4), 403–424.

The Holy Bible, Revised Standard Version (2nd ed.). Nashville: Thomas Nelson.

Huxtable, M. (1994). Child protection: With liberty and justice for all. *Social Work, 39*(1), 60–66.

Janis, I. J., & Mann, L. (1977). *Decision making: A psychological analysis of conflict, choice, and commitment.* New York: The Free Press.

Kadushin, A. (1977). Myths and dilemmas in child welfare. *Child Welfare, 56*(3), 141–153.

Longres, J. F. (2000). *Human behavior in the social environment.* Itasca, IL: F. E. Peacock.

Mason, M. A. (1994). *From father's property to children's rights: The history of child custody in the United States.* New York: Columbia University Press.

Murray, C. (1993, October 29). The coming white underclass. *Wall Street Journal*, p. A31.

National Association of Social Workers. (2008). *NASW code of ethics.* Washington, DC: Author.

Proch, K., & Howard, J. (1984). Parental visiting in foster care: Law and practice. *Child Welfare, 58*(2), 139–147.

Reamer, F. G. (1990). *Ethical dilemmas in social service* (2nd ed.). New York: Columbia University Press.

Stein, T. J. (1991). *Child welfare and the law.* New York: Longman.

Williams, C. C. (1991). Expanding the options in the quest for permanence. In J. E. Everett, S. S. Chipungu, & B. R. Leashore (Eds.), *Child welfare: An Africentric perspective* (pp. 266–289). New Brunswick, NJ: Rutgers University Press.

Case Study E   In The Client's Interest: Self-Determination and Mental Disability

Abstracted from an unpublished paper by Jose Carlos Vera, MSW

Practice Context And Case Presentation

An urban, community-based organization provides services specifically targeted toward an immigrant minority population. These services include case management, team parenting, alcohol and drug treatment, advocacy, and housing.

Another client of the agency refers Luisa for services, and she is assigned to this caseworker. She is 18 years old, homeless, and mentally disabled. Although her family resides in a nearby county, she refuses contact with them, preferring to live independently on the city streets. Luisa is placed in a home, but she runs away, presumably returning to the unsafe neighborhood where she had been living. The worker loses contact with her.

A week later, through the client who originally referred her, the worker learns that Luisa has been sexually and physically abused. The worker is concerned about her safety, fearing further rape, murder, and violence if this young woman continues to live on the streets. He feels that Luisa does not have the mental capacity to look out for herself and take even elementary precautions to prevent harm.

When he contacts her on the street, Luisa is adamant. She desires to remain in the neighborhood, which she has come to know. She does not desire agency involvement, housing, or other services.

Ethical Practice

Practice Behavior Example: NASW's Ethical Principle 3 states that "Social workers respect the inherent dignity and worth of the person."

Critical Thinking Question: Luisa did not initiate a request for service, and has, in fact, repeatedly let the worker know that she does not desire assistance. Can respecting the dignity and worth of person be utilized to support both self-determination and prevention of harm?

All that she asks is that she be left alone to live as she wishes. She is not harming or disturbing anyone and wishes to live as she chooses.

The worker respects Luisa's right of self-determination—her right to determine what is best for her. Her mental status in terms of her disability has not been legally determined, so the presumption must be that she is competent. However, her mental limitations are immediately apparent, and Luisa is at risk of harm if she continues to live on the street. It would seem to be in her best interest to offer her protection from harm.

The worker finds himself caught in a dilemma that may be defined as follows:

CLIENT SELF-DETERMINATION V. OBLIGATION TO PREVENT HARM

Research and Related Literature

Self-Determination. The Supreme Court upholds self-determination as a fundamental right that is protected by the Ninth and Fourteenth Amendments. The NASW Code of Ethics strongly supports client self-determination (NASW Code of Ethics, 2008). In the United States, people are presumed competent, and thus able to self-determine, unless incompetence has been proven.

Often, however, this fundamental right is divested from mentally disabled citizens and assigned to persons appointed as their guardians. Mentally disabled citizens are often regarded as incompetent to make decisions or to manage their affairs. To protect the rights of these citizens, legal resources are available. Although the agency strongly supports self-determination, experience with mentally disabled clients in this inner-city community has demonstrated that they are often unable to make decisions that are in their best interests in terms of safety and protection.

Beauchamp and Childress (2009) state, "Persons incompetent by virtue of dementia, alcoholism, immaturity, and mental retardation present radically different types and problems of incompetence" (p. 113). One may also be incompetent to make certain kinds of decisions, but not others. The capacity to understand the choices and issues, to reason and reflect, to communicate the choice and explain the reasoning may vary according to circumstance. Thus, Luisa may be competent to make some choices about her life, but not others.

Legally, Luisa is competent. Assessing her in order to establish incompetence is difficult due to communication problems and to her homeless lifestyle. She also demonstrates a reluctance to develop a relationship with the worker. She is not harming anyone (except for exposing herself to risk), and it would be difficult to force a competency evaluation upon her. Thus, from a legal perspective, she remains competent and able to make her own decisions.

Obligation to Prevent Harm. According to Frankena (1988), individuals have a responsibility to do good and to prevent harm. Beneficence, doing good, and nonmaleficence, the prevention of harm, often are considered together as obligations. John Stuart Mill considered beneficence praiseworthy and virtuous, and the "greatest happiness" principle supports always producing the greatest good for the greatest number, or a net balance of good over bad consequences. Immanuel Kant considered beneficence an imperfect duty, for, he states, one has some choice about the occasions in which to do good. However, he states that it is certainly wrong to ever inflict harm on someone. Thus, it would seem justifiable to intervene if an individual's activities present serious harm to another or to that individual (Frankena, 1988).

The debate concerning obligation to prevent an individual from harming himself or herself is an ancient one. On one side, arguments that support self-determination would give the individual the right to choose activities that might result in harm to that individual. On the other side, one can argue that members of a society have the obligation to protect one another from self-destructive behavior, and that it is sometimes necessary to interfere with an individual's self-determination to prevent harm.

Not enough is currently known about Luisa's level of mental disability to enable a clear determination of competence. Inaccessibility, lack of cooperation, and communication difficulties render such a determination difficult. Thus, she continues to have the legal rights of competency.

Section 1.14 of the NASW Code of Ethics (2008) addresses clients who lack decision-making capacity, stating that in these cases "social workers should take reasonable steps to safeguard the interests and rights of those clients."

The Code also supports the social worker's responsibility for promoting the general welfare of the society (Sect. 6.01), which may be interpreted as the obligation to support the welfare of each of the members of the society as well.

Research. Luisa appears to be a homeless person at high risk: She has already been raped and abused, she does not speak English, she is mentally disabled, and she is a woman. A study of this population found that programs must be tailored specifically to women (Hagen & Ivanoff, 1988). Padgett and Struening (1992) found that risk is a constant in the lives of homeless women, particularly risks of physical assault and abuse. They noted a correlation between mental and substance abuse problems and violence encountered by women on the streets. For this population, the struggle is not only for survival, but also for safety. It is unclear due to Luisa's language difficulties and mental disability whether she is even aware enough to "struggle" for her own safety.

Dunn-Strohecker (1987) noted that the population of homeless mentally disabled persons is growing and that there is a lack of success in using traditional methods of treatment and services to this population. This population is in need of innovative services that will include outreach and a variety of possible resources to meet individual needs. It is possible that the current resources in the community are not meeting Luisa's needs.

A descriptive study by Mercier and Racine (1995) of case management with homeless women found that a high frequency of contacts (four a week) and the provision of concrete services were the primary activities. They emphasize the amount of worker time and effort that is required in order to develop a relationship with the women. In Luisa's case, this would be made more difficult by the language barrier.

Author's Reflections, Reasoning Process, and Resolution

The worker must consider various obligations and responsibilities in arriving at a decision regarding whether or not intervention to protect Luisa's well-being is justified. Some of the issues that need to be balanced are

1. The profession's responsibility to the general welfare of the society.
2. The importance of treating all persons with dignity and respect, acceptance, and a nonjudgmental attitude.
3. The worker's obligation to ensure that "all persons have access to the resources, employment, services, and opportunities they require in order to meet their basic human needs and to develop fully" (NASW Code of Ethics, 2008, Sect. 6.04a). Services were provided to Luisa, but she refused them. She does not "require" services—can they be imposed on her?
4. The obligation to protect life, an obligation that can be interpreted as protecting her safety and security, or as not obstructing her right to make life choices despite her retardation.
5. The professional commitment to self-determination, autonomy, and freedom, which may come second to the obligation to protect Luisa from harm.
6. A consideration of Luisa's values: her desire to live independently of her family and/ or others and her desire for an education, which she has expressed to the worker.

The worker's personal values strongly support freedom and the right to make personal choices and decisions—pursuing our own good in our own way, as stated by Varga (1978). However, this population challenges the worker to consider other important issues as well. In particular, the worker perceives a moral obligation as Luisa's social worker to prevent potential harm to her and risks that he is able to assess, and she is not.

In determining a course of action, the worker recognizes that the obligation to prevent harm must be primary, and thus supersedes Luisa's right to self-determination in this instance. The Code of Ethics supports serving the client with maximum professional skills and competence. Thus, the worker will assist Luisa to obtain the services that are needed, being careful to maximize opportunities for self-determination within these. For example, Luisa can be encouraged to pursue an education in a field that is meaningful to her, at a school she selects. She can be given choices regarding living arrangements, so that she can select those that are most comfortable to her. Employment and training can also be explored. Luisa's English skills can be enhanced through instruction as well. From a legal perspective, the worker can also refer Luisa to specialized resources for people with mental retardation to ensure that her rights are protected, and/or initiate guardianship proceedings on her behalf so that she will have someone "looking out" for her best interests.

The worker believes that Luisa's desire for self-determination, and the form in which this has manifested itself thus far, may also be influenced by her status as a recent immigrant with a limited command of the English language. Thus, Luisa may see homelessness as an optimal choice because it provides her with maximum immediate freedom. It is the responsibility of the worker to expand Luisa's choices by providing her with services that will enable her to "take charge" of her own life more meaningfully. This enables the worker to support both sides of the original dilemma statement: Luisa's self-determination and the worker's obligation to prevent harm to her.

Case Study E (Vera)

Abramson, M. (1989). Autonomy vs. paternalistic beneficence: Practice strategies. *The Journal of Contemporary Social Work, 70*(2), 101–105.

Beauchamp, T. L., & Childress, J. F. (2009). *Principles of biomedical ethics* (6th ed.). New York: Oxford University Press.

Burgdorf, R., Jr. (1980). *The legal rights of handicapped persons: Cases, materials, and text.* Baltimore: Paul D. Brookes.

Dolgoff, R., Loewenberg, F. M., & Harrington, D. (2009). *Ethical decisions for social work practice* (8th ed.). Itasca, IL: F. E. Peacock.

Dunn-Strohecker, M. (1987). *From street to treatment: An examination of five demonstration programs for persons who are homeless and mentally disabled.* Unpublished Ph.D. dissertation, Brandeis University.

Frankena, W. K. (1988). *Ethics.* Englewood Cliffs, NJ: Prentice-Hall.

Hagen, J. L., & Ivanoff, A. M. (1988). Homeless women: A high-risk population. *Journal of Women and Social Work, 3*(1), 19–33.

Mercier, C., & Racine, G. (1995). Case management with homeless women: A descriptive study. *Community Mental Health Journal, 31*(1), 25–37.

National Association of Social Workers. (2008). *NASW code of ethics.* Washington, DC: Author.

Padgett, D. K., & Struening, E. L. (1992, October). Victimization and traumatic injuries among the homeless: Associations with alcohol, drug, and mental problems. *American Journal of Orthopsychiatry, 62*(4), 525–534.

Reamer, F. (1990). *Ethical dilemmas in social service* (2nd ed.). New York: Columbia University Press.

Saltzman, A., & Proch, K. (1990). *Law in social work practice.* Chicago: Nelson Hall.

Varga, A. C. (1978). *On being human: Principles of ethics.* New York: Paulist Press.

Case Study F	Determining an Acceptable Risk for a Vulnerable Client: Where Protection Impacts Self-Determination

Abstracted from an unpublished paper by Mira Underwood, MSW

Practice Context and Case Presentation

A large urban county hospital provides ambulatory care and hospital services to the surrounding area through its emergency department, and three intensive care units provide extensive Level 1 Trauma services to its critical care patients.

Marco Madrera, a 20-year-old male who is in a wheelchair due to paraplegia from a gunshot accident at 16, underwent a hip disarticulation—a surgical removal of the entire lower limb at the hip level—due to large necrotizing fasciitis on his buttocks and severe sepsis. He remained in the ICU for 3 weeks, and was then transferred to a step-down ward where he received daily wound care to ensure that the infection in his body finally subsided. During the second month of his hospital stay, Marco has started refusing lab work and treatments, saying that he "just wants to get out." After many life-saving medical procedures, medications, and two months of acute care, he is ready for discharge, with temporary wound care services provided by an out-of-hospital health provider.

The patient's medical team, including the social worker, are recommending a temporary stay at a skilled nursing facility (SNF) for wound care, physical rehabilitation, and assistance in adjusting to his amputation before returning to the community. The SNF would then connect Marco to an intensive case management service, available only to SNF residents, for community follow-up after discharge, to assist him in locating accessible and adaptable housing to maximize independence, and to provide on-site support services. Marco is adamant in refusing to go to another "medical facility," and demands to be discharged home, although he has expressed some interest in finding new housing.

Currently, Marco lives in a large public housing complex, sharing an apartment with three other young men, and does not have a room for himself. He has "only partial use" of the bathroom, as it is not wheelchair accessible. Additionally, the apartment is on top of a steep hill: He must climb stairs to reach it, and he relies on people walking by to carry him up. He shops at a local corner store for food and drink, and smokes marijuana "whenever I feel like it." Marco is also malnourished.

Marco's six siblings, his grandmother, and his mother currently live in the area. When Marco was 16, while his mother was in prison, he and his father were shot while driving in a car. Upon discharge from this first hospitalization as a paraplegic, Marco lived first with his grandmother and later with a sister. Currently, the quality of family relationships is uncertain, and there is no possibility of Marco's living with family members upon discharge. There is no contact with his father.

Marco's healthcare team, which includes the social worker, believes that if he returns to his pre-admission living conditions, he will continue to make poor decisions, and that his physical condition, given his current additional difficulties, will deteriorate. This would create additional health issues, as well as increase the possibilities of death resulting from neglect.

While the social worker wants to respect Marco's right to self-determination, which he expresses by saying that he "knows what is best" for him, she believes that discharge to a temporary SNF could connect him to intensive case management and appropriate and safe housing. His self-determined plan to return to his pre-hospitalization circumstances have made Marco's team question his competence to make a plan for himself, leaving the social worker to question her responsibility to protect him from harm. No competency examination has been administered, and it is highly unlikely that Marco would accede to one.

The worker's dilemma may be stated as:

SELF-DETERMINATION/AUTONOMY v. PROTECTION OF LIFE

Research and Related Literature

Self-Determination. is greatly valued in the United States, both in medical settings and in social work practice. According to Dolgoff, Loewenberg, and Harrington, the U.S. Supreme Court "has developed the rule . . . through a series of cases . . . that self-determination is a fundamental right that is protected by the Ninth and Fourteenth Amendments" in the U.S. Constitution (Dolgoff, Loewenberg, & Harrington, 2009, p. 96).

Self-determination is also one of the most highly valued ethical standards in Section I, 1.2, of the NASW Code of Ethics, immediately after social workers' primary obligations to clients (NASW). At Marco's hospital, the physicians, nurses, medical social workers, and members of the Ethics Committee highly value patients' and families' right to self-determination with regard to consent and refusal of treatment, services, or planning.

> It is important to consider whether a diagnosis of incompetence occurs simply because the client does not agree with the social worker or other staff members' plans, and to evaluate the disagreement through knowledge of the client's world, values, and experiences.

According to the hospital's "Medical Social Services Department Policy & Procedure—Discharge Planning," it is stipulated that ". . . with other members of the multidisciplinary team, the social worker evaluates the type of aftercare needed and begins to develop a plan most appropriate to the patients' (needs and wishes)" _____ Policies 12.1, 2007). The guidelines for an "appropriate discharge" is one that is in agreement with patient's wishes, is safe, and includes "referrals to appropriate agencies or source for support or care following discharge [as well as] placement in a care setting other than the patient's home when necessary" (_____ Policies 4.04, 2007). According to members of the hospital's social work team to whom this case was presented, if a patient disagrees with a suggested discharge plan, and insists on a plan that would not be considered safe, the patient's multidisciplinary team would evaluate patient competence either through an "official" competency test (if the patient agrees) or by asking the patient questions that would allow them to evaluate decisional capacity. If the patient is found to be competent, he or she would be discharged according to the patient's wishes and against medical advice.

Marco's competency to make his own decisions is being questioned by the healthcare team. It is important to recognize that different standards and tests of competence are utilized in determining competence, related to the type of competence required in a particular situation. In Marco's situation, Beauchamp and Childress' range of competence standards four through seven, which "look for the ability to reason through a consequential life decision" appear to be appropriate. These include: 4. Inability to give a reason; 5. Inability to give a rational reason; 6. Inability to give risk/benefit-related reasons; and 7. Inability to reach a reasonable decision (Beauchamp & Childress, 2009, pp. 114–115).

Marco appears to be in Erikson's life stage of Identity Formation versus Role Confusion (About.Psychology.com, 2012). During this stage, which occurs during adolescence and can last into the early twenties, young adults develop a sense of self and personal identity and a sense of direction in life independently (About.Psychology.com, 2012). Teenagers who receive encouragement and reinforcement, and are allowed to explore their independence will emerge from this stage with a strong sense of self, identity, and control (About.Psychology.com, 2012). Teenagers who do not receive encouragement can remain insecure and confused about their future (About.Psychology.com, 2012). Marco appears to be in this stage and, given the difficult experiences he had in adolescence, may be trying to assert himself in the hospital to determine his own future. Though his judgment may seem poor, his decision is made in the context of his personal life experiences and he seems unable, and possibly unwilling, to venture beyond the relative safety and security of these experiences.

Marco's sense of frustration and "acting out" behavior has been discussed at length by the psychiatric nurse, the trauma recovery social worker, medical social workers, his primary care physician, and the violence and gang prevention service, all of whom meet with him regularly, and who advocate for Marco on the ward, deflecting the frustrations of staff due to his unwillingness to become engaged in discharge planning. The social worker has been attempting to maximize Marco's opportunities for making choices and exercising self-determination on the ward. However, long-range planning for Marco is a challenge to her!

Protection of Life is the other side of the social worker's dilemma. According to Dolgoff, Loewenberg, and Harrington's Ethical Principles Screen, the "protection of human life" principle is primary to all others and supersedes all other obligations a social worker has to her clients (Dolgoff, Loewenberg, & Harrington, pp. 80–81).

The principles of nonmaleficence and beneficence are considered core values in medical settings, and undergird hospital policies. The principle of beneficence states that one ought to prevent harm, one ought to remove harm, and ought to do or promote good. In contrast, the principle of nonmaleficence requires an action (Beauchamp & Childress, 2009, pp. 150–153). Beauchamp and Childress continue by distinguishing between specific — unique circumstances that do not apply broadly, and where the "right action" is not well defined — and general beneficence — which is applicable more broadly to situations and with the clear understanding of the "right action" (2009, pp. 150–153). Finally, Beauchamp and Childress suggest that certain circumstances eliminate the aspect of choice of action toward a beneficiary all together, such as the obligation to rescue someone (pp. 153–154). The conditions that need to be satisfied for the obligation to rescue are: (1) there is a significant loss of, or damage to, life, health, or some other major interest; (2) action is necessary to prevent such loss or damage; (3) action has a very high probability of preventing it; and (4) the benefit that can be expected to gain outweighs any harms, costs, or burdens that are likely to occur (Beauchamp & Childress, 2009, pp. 153–154). In order to weigh the risk of harm, one can also take into consideration an analysis of *probability of harm* versus a *magnitude of harm* which is a tool often used in medicine and medical procedures (2009, p. 307).

Research on Amputee Rehabilitation Outcomes and Quality of Life. In addition to Marco's higher risk for future medical complications and premature death due to his episode of necrotizing fasciitis, he will need to adjust to being an amputee as well as a paraplegic. A German study that investigated medical, reeducational, and psychological factors in rehabilitation outcomes of 178 lower limb amputees found several variables to predict the probability of unsatisfactory rehabilitation (Gerhards, Florin, & Knapp, 1984, pp. 379–388). Those that could potentially affect Marco's rehabilitation outcome are: poor social integration, introverted and withdrawn personality traits, amputee's view of why the trauma/amputation occurred, and insight into the necessity of the amputation (1984, pp. 379–388). In addition, in a study on quality of life of amputees in India, the result showed that the quality of life of amputees is significantly affected by coping strategies, social support, and adjustment (Kumar & Srivastava, 2010, pp. 137–151).

Marco became a paraplegic at 16, and he has not seen a physician for medical follow-up appointments for many years. He has been "couch-surfing" with friends, and has not been taking care of himself medically. He lives in a poor, neglected, crime-ridden substandard public housing complex in the community in which he was raised, which has no pharmacies or supermarkets, and whose physical location is inaccessible for wheelchairs. In order to navigate the area, he has to rely on others to assist him with activities of daily living (ADLs and IADLs). His family lives nearby, but do not assist him. Prior to his current hospitalization, he suffered three weeks with fever, before a friend drove him to the ER to seek medical care. At that time, he was also again extremely malnourished.

During his current hospitalization, he remained in the ICU for close to a month after hip disarticulation because his body was "shutting down" due to septic shock, and the social worker's impression is that Marco does not have a good social support system, does not seem well adjusted to his physical disabilities, and has poor coping strategies. According to the pediatrician who has known Marco since he has become a paraplegic, he tends to downplay his condition, and does not ask for needed assistance. His primary coping strategy is smoking marijuana. The social worker is concerned that the recent amputation will require Marco to make additional adjustments in his life.

Studies on Necrotizing Fasciitis. Research has shown that the overall mortality rate of patients who develop necrotizing fasciitis is about 25 to 30 percent of cases, though in individuals with spinal cord injuries, the percentage is often higher (Elliott, Kufera, & Myers, 1996; McHenry, Piotrowski, Petrinic, & Malangoni, 1995, pp. 558–563). Another study, which followed patients who had developed an episode of necrotizing fasciitis over a period of 15 years, found that patients who survived the episode of necrotizing fasciitis remained at a continued higher risk for premature death compared to population-based mortality data (Light et al., 2010, pp. 93–99). The authors also suggested that "patients should be counseled, followed, and immunized to minimize chances of death" (pp. 93–99).

In light of these studies, there is a risk of serious harm from Marco's condition. As he has not sought out medical treatment in the past, the chances of his not doing so again are high. Temporary placement in a SNF and long-term case management may mitigate this risk.

Author's Reflection, Reasoning Process, and Resolution

In arriving at a resolution to this dilemma, it is essential to consider all of the above information and also the way in which professional and personal values, and those of the setting, influence the perception of the dilemma and the way that it is addressed.

Hospital and Staff Values. The hospital's mission is "to provide quality healthcare and trauma services with compassion and respect" (_____ Hospital website, downloaded 9/2012). According to the hospital's "Discharge Planning Policy," "[the hospital] provides discharge planning services…ensuring quality patient care, enhancing medical outcome, and making appropriate use of hospital resources" (_____ Policy 4.04, 2010, downloaded 3/2012). Furthermore, "effective discharge planning requires a team approach. It incorporates the skills and knowledge of the physician, medical social workers, utilization review case managers, eligibility workers, nursing staff, rehabilitation therapists, pharmacists, other hospital staff, the patient, and the patient's family" (_____ Policy 4.04, 2010, downloaded 9/2012). Lastly, "factors to be considered in the discharge plan include: patient and family education about the diagnosis and its implications, the disease process, the importance of effective assessment and management of pain, and requirements for care in the home setting…[or] in a care setting other than the patients home when necessary" (_____ Policy 4.04, 2010, downloaded 9/2012).

The medical team and care team members all respect Marco's right to self-determination, and uphold the medical ethics model, particularly "the principle of respect for autonomy and the principle of beneficence" (Beauchamp & Childress, 2009, pp. 99, 197).

Interestingly, according to a research study conducted on physicians' views on adolescent autonomy, 421 American pediatricians showed that when treatment outcome is expected to be good, only 28 percent of pediatricians would allow a 16-year-old to refuse treatment, yet when treatment outcome is expected to be poor, 65 percent of pediatricians would allow a 16-year-old to refuse treatment, even when the parents accept treatment (Talati, Walsh Lang, & Friedman Ross, 2010, pp. 126–132).

In light of these findings and research on Marco's potential treatment outcomes, much time and energy by staff has been dedicated to consultation in order to ensure research on potential treatment outcomes optimal treatment until he is healed, given that he did not want to go the SNF, have case management, or move from his present living arrangements. All staff members, including social workers, appear to lean strongly toward protection of life for Marco, rather than supporting his self-determined wishes.

Professional Values. NASW Code of Ethics, Section 1.01, states that "Social workers' primary responsibility is to promote the well-being of clients" (NASW Code of Ethics, 2008). As stated earlier, the NASW Code of Ethics also obligates social workers to support client self-determination, although the worker "may limit clients' right to self-determination when, in [her or his] professional judgment, clients' actions...might pose a serious, foreseeable, and imminent risk to themselves or others" (NASW Code of Ethics, Section 1.02). The Code also protects client privacy and confidentiality (NASW Code of Ethics, Section 1.07), and the provision of informed consent prior to sharing information or making decisions (NASW Code of Ethics, Section 1.03, 2008). The Code of Ethics does not prescribe a hierarchy of values and standards; rather, these are meant to serve as a decision-making guide. When NASW Codes conflict with each other, or do not provide specific guidance, social workers can apply Dolgoff, Loewenberg, and Harrington's Ethical Principles Screen to determine which action they should follow (Dolgoff et al., 2009, p. 82). According to the EPS, the "Principle of Protection of Life" supersedes all others (Dolgoff et al., 2009, pp. 260–61). In declining order, the following principles are also applicable in this case: "Principle of Autonomy and Freedom," "Principle of Least Harm," "Principle of Privacy and Confidentiality," and lastly "Principle of Truthfulness and Full Disclosure" (Dolgoff et al., 2009, p. 80, Figure 4.4).

Personal Values. The social worker's personal values are clearly influenced by her upbringing in two very different cultures and countries, as well as by her present community in the U.S.A. Given her collectivist cultural background, she tends to place more value on the group and the community rather than individual autonomy. Her behavior toward others is more informed by duties and obligations than by her own volitions. The social worker also values freedom and independence. Her most important values are freedom, respect, love, honesty, peace, family, duty, harmony, generosity, and courage. She is also sensitive to, and respectful of, values drawn from cultural and racial/ethnic differences, as well as individual and family differences.

In considering ethical theories, the social worker has a high regard for duty and obligation, very much like Kant, in that she concurs that "one must act not only in accordance with, but for the sake of, obligation" (Beauchamp & Childress, 2009, p. 344). In contrast, utilitarians focus on the consequences of an action: If the consequences of actions are good, they are deemed moral. The principle of utility serves as a benchmark which is described by Mill as "happiness and pleasure" (2009, p. 337). Modern utilitarian philosophers describe utility in terms of "knowledge, health, success, understanding, enjoyment, and deep personal relationships," and hence helping to define the principle of beneficence (p. 337). While these theories cannot prescribe a specific course of action in addressing a dilemma, taken together with a model approach of justification of actions as Beauchamp and Childress suggest, they can help the professional in determining the specific action to be taken (2009, p. 334). The model of "reflective equilibrium," developed by John Rawls as "a reflective testing of our moral beliefs, moral principles, and prior judgments," a case-based reasoning in which a decision is made through a thorough process of case comparisons (2009, pp. 381–387), appeals to the social worker the most.

Client and Family Values. Marco's current critical health situation, his developmental phase, and his relational style make it very challenging to determine his personal values, which appear to include self-determination, living in the moment, freedom, the familiarity of his home and neighborhood, independence from family, and smoking marijuana. His values appear circumscribed by his neighborhood, his childhood and adolescent experiences, and his abusive and neglectful parenting, where his grandmother may have been his only positive influence. He appears uninterested in any relationships at present, including interactions with his friends, who have not visited during his lengthy hospitalization.

Options for Action. Based on the information above, five options may be considered to resolve the social worker's dilemma.

1. In support of Marco's right to self-determination, he can be discharged to his home independently with no follow-up, against medical advice. Referral to APS would be made by the social worker.

2. Respecting Marco's wishes and his right to self-determination, he can be discharged to his previous home if he is able to demonstrate to his care team that he can take care of himself.

3. If Marco cannot demonstrate that he can take care of himself, his right to self-determination regarding living arrangements can be respected, but he would also be referred to Home Health to provide wound care management, In-Home Support Services (IHSS) to provide caretaking, and an APS referral would be made to try to ensure that the follow-up care will be provided.

4. The social worker can try to convince Marco that going to the SNF is in his best interest in the long run, if necessary delaying his discharge until he is convinced, and a bed is found for him in a SNF.

5. If Marco refused options 2, 3, and 4, a competency test could be requested. If he passed the test, he would be discharged to where he lived prior to hospitalization against medical advice (AMA). If he was declared incompetent, then a legal conservatorship of person could be pursued. In respect of Marco's wishes, a neutral conservator who is not a family member would be requested.

Costs and Benefits of Each Option. Option (1) requires that Marco sign out of the hospital "AMA" (against medical advice). Under Option (2), Marco would have to demonstrate his ability to care for himself prior to independent discharge. However, because of the physical impediments in his living arrangement, it is not possible for him to take care of himself independently at home. Option (3) also does not appear to support Marco's safety; he has not taken care of himself medically in the past, and it is highly likely that he would not comply with Home Health or the IHSS worker, or that he would terminate services. Also, Home Health and IHSS may refuse to treat him at his current home given all of the safety and sanitary concerns.

Option (4) has the highest likelihood of ensuring that Marco would get the appropriate wound care he needs for as long as it takes for his pressure sores and wounds to heal. An intensive care management team would begin working with him at the SNF, would follow him into the community, provide an IHSS worker as needed, assist him with follow-up care and doctor appointments, and work on locating more appropriate and safe housing, which, ultimately, would best support his value of independence.

Option (5) is the option of last resort. Marco would probably not agree to a competency test, thus precluding formal testing. If Marco did agree to testing and was found competent, he would set his own criteria for discharge. Because Marco would probably view a request for competency testing very negatively, this would also set up an adversarial relationship with the current staff and thus minimize any potential for optimal discharge planning.

Dilemma Resolution. To arrive at a dilemma resolution, potential options are explored considering the *probability of harm* and the *magnitude of harm*, as suggested by Beauchamp and Childress (2009, p. 307). The worker believes that the probability and magnitude of harm are very high if Marco does not receive optimal wound care and rehabilitation, based on both research on his medical condition, and her understanding of Marco and his life experiences and values. Option (4) promises the most optimal outcome for Marco, a decision with which her supervisor concurs. The social worker and supervisor also plan to convene a care team meeting, comprised of Marco's pediatrician, the attending physician, his nurse, the psychiatric nurse, the medical social worker, and social work supervisor to determine how to best ensure a discharge to a SNF to support Marco's post-discharge needs. Thus, in this case, the social worker has decided in favor of the "Protection of Life" principle over the principle of "Self-determination."

Case Study F (*Underwood*)

About.Psychology.com. Erikson's Stages of Psychosocial Development. 2012. Retrieved from http://psychology.about.com/od/psychosocialtheories/a/identity-versus-confusion.htm

Affordable and Low-Income Housing Wait List Opportunities San Francisco and Bay Area—March 2012. Retrieved from http://www.selfhelpelderly.org/services/social_services/housing_list.pdf

Beauchamp, T. L., & Childress, J. F. (2009). *Principles of biomedical ethics* (6th ed.). New York: University Press.

Dolgoff, R., Loewenberg, F.M., & Harrington, D. (2005). *Ethical decisions for social work practice* (8th ed.). Belmont, CA: Brooks/Cole.

Elloit, C., Kufera J. A., & Myers, R. A. M. (1996). Necrotizing soft tissue infections. Risk factors for mortality and strategies for management. *Annals of Surgery, 224*, 672–683.

Gerhards, F., Florin, I., & Knapp, T. (1984). The impact of medical, reeducational, and psychological variables on rehabilitation outcome in amputees. *International Journal of Rehabilitation Research, 7*(4), 379–388.

Kumar, V., & Srivastava, S. K. (2010). Assessment of quality of life in amputees. *Social Science International, 26*(2), 137–151.

Light, T. D., Choi, K. C., Thomsen, T. A., Skeete, D. A., Latenser, B. A., Born, J. M.,... Kealey, J. P. (2010). Long-term outcomes of patients with necrotizing fasciitis. *Journal of Burn Care & Research, 31*(1), 93–99.

McHenry, C. R., Piotrowski, J. J., Petrinic, D., & Malangoni, M. A. (1995). Determinants of mortality for necrotizing soft-tissue infections. *Annals of Surgery, 221*, 558–563.

National Association of Social Workers. (2008). *NASW code of ethics.* Retrieved from http://www.naswdc.org/pubs/code/code.asp

_____ Policies & Procedure Manual (2012).

Talati, E. D., Walsh Lang, C., & Friedman Ross, L. (2010). Reaction of pediatricians to refusals of medical treatment for minors. *Journal of Adolescent Health, 47*, 126–132.

Case Study G   Permanency Placement for Very Young Children:
What Happens to Family Preservation?

Abstracted from an unpublished paper by Amone Bounkhoun, MSW

Note: This case study is a client-specific companion to the case study in Chapter 11, entitled "Permanency Planning for Young Children: Are Brief Time Frames Always in the Child's Best Interest?" In this study, specific clients with specific personal characteristics are presented in contrast to the policy-focused discussion of the issue in Chapter 11. It is recommended that these two cases be read together to enable a consideration of the difference between abstract and concrete policy considerations.

Practice Context and Case Presentation

The Family & Children Services Department is responsible for intervening in the lives of families in order to ensure the safety of abused and neglected children, to assist parents in meeting minimum parenting standards, and to plan alternative permanent care when parents are incapable of or unwilling to meet those standards.

The agency utilizes the "concurrency model," in which two different case goals are developed at the same time, the primary goal being reunification of the child and parent. Should the primary goal not succeed, there is an immediate backup plan already in place for a permanent home for the child. The goal of concurrent planning is to more quickly move children from the uncertainty of foster care to a secure, safe, and stable permanent family.

> The goal of concurrent planning is early permanent placement for young children, providing stability and continuity in their lives. However, concurrent planning can be very challenging for the child, the biological parent(s), foster and adoptive parents, and others, and requires care and consideration from the social worker.

Jane is a 31-year-old mother of three children, all of whom are placed out of the home. The two oldest children, age 8 and 6, are currently living with their grandmother in Texas, and will be legally adopted by her. Jane's youngest child, Baby John, is only 6 months old, and routine hospital tests showed that he was exposed to cocaine *in utero*. A referral to CPS found that Jane has a long history of drug addiction, and had entered and left drug treatment programs four times in the past three years. The infant was placed in a foster home, and Jane entered an inpatient treatment program. She visits with the baby twice a week and the interactions are described as positive and nurturing, and she has said that she couldn't take having another child permanently taken away and would like to reunite with her baby.

Jane was supposed to complete the program in six months, but she had a relapse while in treatment, and shortly thereafter left the facility. She returned after a week and a half, but successful completion of her program is delayed. Previous documentation has noted that Jane reached this plateau several times, but then relapses and begins to use again. The foster family has expressed a desire to adopt the baby.

Reunification is the primary goal and adoption is the concurrent goal if the child is unable to return home. In California, if the child is an infant (0–3 y/o), the parent has six months to comply with the terms of the reunification plan, and failure to do so can trigger a hearing to terminate parental rights so that, babies may have a permanent and stable home that meets the developmental needs.

The implementation of concurrent planning for Baby John is very challenging. On the one hand, it can be an emotional and confusing process for the foster parents, asked to plan for the child to return home, but also to consider being the permanent placement if the child is unable to do so. On the other hand, to recommend adoptions and the termination of parental rights might weaken Jane's already fragile self-esteem and push her to continue to rely on substances.

The state statutes allow a six-month time frame for the exploration and selection of permanency options. Yet, it is a struggle to implement this practice. Is it reasonable to expect troubled parents, especially those like Jane with long-term substance abuse problems, to safely parent in such a brief amount of time? On the other hand, is it fair to the child to be left in limbo for a longer period? The social worker is asked to make a recommendation, and her dilemma may be stated as:

MOTHER'S RIGHT TO FAMILY PRESERVATION V. CHILD'S RIGHT TO PERMANENCY PLACEMENT

Research and Related Literature

Literature Review. In the United States, parents are given primary authority over their children, and thereby accept responsibility for their well-being and development. However, these parental rights are conditional on parents' ability to ensure that children are educated, healthy and safe, and have their basic needs met. When parents become incapacitated and endanger their children, responsibility devolves to the state, guided by federal and state laws, law enforcement and child welfare agency actions, and judicial decisions (Child Welfare Information Gateway, 2012).

The most recent legislation affecting child welfare services is the Adoption and Safe Families Act (ASFA) of 1997. Prior to the passage of ASFA, critics of child welfare policies argued parents were allowed too many chances, and too much time to meet reunification requirements, resulting in children lingering in foster care, deprived of permanency (Christian, 1999). ASFA instituted shorter deadlines for establishing return home, and also developed specific timelines to insure that children achieved permanent and stable living situations. A foster care time limit was established, after which the agency could initiate efforts to terminate biological parental rights. California currently has 15 conditions that allow the agency to deny reunification services to families (California's Welfare & Institutions Code section 361.5 (b) (13)).

Couple in the process of adoption of an infant

Dmitriy Shironosov/Shutterstock

Child welfare agencies have a mandate to make reasonable efforts to support families. The nature and scope of "reasonable efforts" was never specified by Congress. Recent legislative efforts have concentrated on ensuring that children are reunified with their birth families or adopted, if reunification is not feasible. According to California law, under condition #13, which addresses the situation of substance addicted parents, reunification services are not to be offered to substance abusing parents when they have "resisted treatment" in the last three years, or failed to meet case plan requirements twice. Some county courts have interpreted "resisting treatment" to mean a parent has refused to participate in ordered or recommended treatment, while others ruled that merely failing to seek and obtain treatment can be considered "resisting" (D'Andrade and Berrick, 2006, p. 41).

An exhaustive 1999 report on child welfare and drug abuse found that, again contrary to the stereotype, "national treatment outcome studies...clearly show that treatment can be effective" (DHHS, 1999, p. 14). A federal report concluded that one-third of addicts recover on their first attempt, and another third recover "after brief periods" of relapse (Brady & Ashley, 2005).

The complexities of family dynamics and situation make it difficult for the courts to establish standard conditions for the return of children to their parents. A judge usually returns children to parents with substance abuse problems when a combination of objective and subjective criteria for reunifying families have been met: the parent completes treatment, appears to be ready, and remains abstinent for some period of time, but specific conditions are discretionary.

Based on child developmental research, stability and predictability should be held as paramount in children's lives (Frame, Berrick, & Brodowski, 2000, p. 340). If the child is removed from the home, he or she may experience the trauma of multiple moves. Studies have found that there is a relationship between delay in permanency and instability. The longer very young children wait for decisions to be made, the more likely they are to experience changes in homes and caregivers. In addition, the longer a child waits, the older they become, and therefore the more difficult to place (Wulczyn, Hislop, & Harden, 2002, pp. 456–457). Simply put, delaying decision making can have adverse consequences.

Consequently, instead of the standard provision of court-ordered reunification services to families of 12 months for children under the age of 3, California laws state "court order services shall not exceed a period of six months" (AB 1524 Chapter 1083, Statues of 1996). Substantial leeway for extending services if some progress has been made by the parent on the case plan may be extended. However, a study that specifically examined reentry to foster care rates for cases involving parental substance abuse found that cases moving quickly to reunification, and disallowing sufficient time for ongoing services and monitoring, had especially high reentry rates (Terling, 1999, p. 1366).

Even more disconcerting, however, are the difficulties in achieving permanency planning for children from substance-abusing families as evidenced by multiple placements, low rates of reunification with biological parents, and low rates of adoption. Several reports have documented that once children from substance-abusing families enter foster care, they tend to remain in care, are less likely to reunified with their biological parents, and are less likely to be adopted when compared with children who enter foster care with issues unrelated to substance abuse (Maluccio & Ainsworth, 2003, pp. 511–533).

NASW Code of Ethics. The success of concurrent planning relies on the concept of informed consent; thus, transparency between all the parties involved in an open dependency case is essential. At the beginning of agency service, Jane was informed of the concurrent plan for her baby, the consequences of failing to progress with reunification objectives, and the effects of out-of-home care on children.

NASW's principles support consideration of the good for others, and requires social workers to refrain from behaviors and actions that risk harming clients. For Baby John, a delay in pursuing adoption may mean the loss of his current placement, and could prove very harmful if he moves from foster home to foster home over the years, waiting for Jane to recover from her substance abuse so that they can be reunited.

Moreover, the social worker's primary goal to help people in need to address social problems is very challenging in working with Jane. In adhering to justice, the social worker can validate the importance of following the law, and ensure equal consideration for all parents regardless of their personal challenges. The process, and the time frames, may also help Jane to consider the seriousness of her actions and situation more clearly. On the other hand, compassion and care would support giving Jane extra time as may be warranted by her personal situation, may encourage her to remain drug free, and may enable reunification to occur.

The NASW does not appear to have a clear guideline for Baby John and Jane's situation; giving Jane a longer period of time to succeed at remaining drug-free and keeping her child can be seen as an opportunity—or as an inequitable exception.

Theories and Principles. An examination of the dilemma through ethical theories and principles can be very helpful in determining the best recommendation. Based on the deontological perspective, it would be inherently wrong to violate a law regardless of the consequences; therefore, a recommendation of adoption could be rationalized. Deontologists would argue that duty and justice are the underlying and unchanging moral principles to follow in making the decision regarding this case. A person who becomes a child welfare worker accepts the obligations and duties of that role. Denying reunification services and terminating parental rights is one of those responsibilities, as dictated by state laws and policies. Therefore, a child welfare worker's refusal would be a violation of this duty. The recommendation of adoption is also supported by the classic utilitarian perspective because adoption also provides the greater, and more certain, good. An adoption would ensure that the infant has a stable and permanent home for life, while even if Jane succeeded in her rehabilitation, the risk of recidivism would be great given her history.

Child welfare cases are often complex, and Jane's case is an example of a family experiencing many layers of disadvantage including poverty, lack of social resources, and discrimination. The effects of multiple disadvantage may not be easy to address within a six-month time period. Consequently, a relativistic perspective would prevent a strict application of the law and allow for decision making based on the individual circumstances of the family, thus avoiding a potentially broad, unfair, and arbitrary application of the law. In this view, the social worker may recommend to the courts that Jane be granted additional time to help her resolve her current issues.

Author's Reflections, Reasoning Process, and Resolution

Personal Value Base

A Sense of Love and Belonging Is Very High on My Personal Value System. As a refugee family adjusting to a new American community, my family sought support and motivation within our community, and also in our immediate family. In trying to cope with all the changes in our lives, my parents instilled the importance of family: the closeness of our family provided a safety net when life didn't go according to plan. Having a strong family helps me feel that I am loved, that I belong, and that I matter. This sense of belonging is also important in building trust and confidence in other interpersonal relationships of great importance to me.

For this reason, I find one of the most difficult decisions I must make as a child welfare social worker is to decide whether to leave children with birth parents who are finding it difficult to meet their needs, or to separate them and place them with substitute caregivers, temporarily or permanently. I recognize that separating children by placing them in care can cause permanent harm, which can only be justified if such a decision is shown to promote the child's long-term well-being. Furthermore, I also acknowledge that leaving children with parents whose parenting capacity is diminished by multiple long-term difficulties can potentially be more damaging to the child.

It is also my personal belief that every event and every phenomenon is causally dependent upon numerous other events and phenomena. Therefore, a moral reflection on action must not only focus on motivation or on the action itself, or even on its consequences for others. It is my belief that all intentional actions are understood to have unforeseen potential consequences, and these actions may cause harm. I try not to condemn people merely for making bad choices, and I think it's beneficial for people to learn from their mistakes, and to make an effort to understand and change their behavior to achieve long-term happiness. This is especially true in Jane's case because at the beginning I found it difficult to understand how Jane, as a mother, could care so little for her children that she would rather get high than care for them.

On the other hand, I consider each individual responsible for their own fortunes and misfortunes, and that people are born with the potential for both improvement and growth. The goal of life is true happiness, the result of one's own development, and this cannot be imposed, nor granted by some external force. I believe human beings capable of self-evaluating. Furthermore, I whole heartedly believe that everyone has the capacity to change their process, and each individual can give purpose to their own lives. I would like to hold out hope that Jane has the capacity to change her life if she wishes to do so.

Values of the Affected System. Jane is a relatively young mother who came from a challenging socio-economic background, and can be viewed as a victim of extremely difficult circumstances. It is difficult to take harsh action against Jane who is trying, albeit unsuccessfully, to improve her life.

Jane's mother, currently caring for Jane's other two children out of state, was contacted regarding the infant. Although the grandmother voiced interest in providing support to her daughter, and also her grandchild, she stated that she could not become the primary caretaker for a third child. She is a single caretaker, on a fixed income, and does not have the resources and support to adequately raise such a young child. Additionally, she is also aging and does not believe that she is physically fit to provide for this child's everyday needs.

The agency itself is subject to federal and state policies to promote reunification. Furthermore, the agency also receives financial incentives to reduce the number of children in care, and to restrict their length of stay. Although this financial bonus is appreciated, the supervisors within the agency do not believe that this drives the agency's social workers: They would strive for permanency options regardless of any incentive because it is what children need and deserve.

Societal Values. There is significant value placed on family in American society and there is also a reluctance to intrude on family privacy. A parent has a legally protected right to the care and custody of her or his child. This core principle has deep historical roots and it has helped to shape federal and state legislation and laws. In deference to parental rights, the state cannot remove a child from the custody of a parent absent a showing of imminent danger to the child. However, society recognizes that children have rights too, grounded firmly and pragmatically in the basic human needs for life, growth, and development. When a parent's care falls beneath minimally adequate standards or jeopardizes the well-being of the child, the state must intervene to help protect a member of its most fragile citizen group.

A fundamental political and economic goal of our society is to help low-income or otherwise disadvantaged families. The agency tries to intervene with families during times of crisis, and to provide much needed support. Society also recognizes that children have an interest in maintaining a bond with their biological parents and other family members and can be very traumatized when this bond is disrupted. This recognition that children suffer when separated from their parents and family also helps to rationalize resource allocation to help mend broken families.

Options for Action. Decision making in child welfare is filled with risk and uncertainty and options are frequently complicated by incomplete or disputed facts, time deadlines, and the unpredictability of future events. For this particular case, there appear to be two viable recommendations that could be made. The first is a request that Jane be granted an additional six months of reunification services to allow her to return to her residential in-treatment program, successfully complete the service, and eventually reunify with Baby John.

The second option is to initiate the process of termination of parental rights and adoption of Baby John by the foster family. Jane appears too overwhelmed by her addiction, and perhaps by the thought of complete responsibility for the child, to give Baby John the order and stability he needs. This option is especially attractive in the case of Baby John, because there is a loving family with a stable home, with whom he is already familiar and comfortable, ready to adopt him. He has already endured much as a drug-exposed infant; he should be given every opportunity to reach his full potential. In this case, the optimal situation to foster the maximum development for Baby John could be continue care for by the foster-adoptive family.

Course of Action. Given the compelling reasons supporting each of the two options, it appears to this social worker that a recommendation of adoption would be in the best interest of Baby John. The agency had attempted diligently but unsuccessfully to work with the Jane. She had come to the attention of the agency for the same reason that her previous two children had been removed from her care: long-term drug addiction for which past treatment efforts have been unsuccessful. Therefore, it may be valid to conclude that this parent would most likely not be able to benefit from further rehabilitative efforts. Baby John could be forced to spend a long time in foster care waiting for his mother to meet the requirements of the child protection agency. Within the first six months of services, Jane was unable to adequately prepare to care for Baby John, and the question remains: Why should he continue be punished for Jane's failure? He has already suffered enough and should be entitled to a loving home.

If Baby John were placed in Jane's care, he may find himself in a marginal home environment, and would not have the developmental capacity to protect himself. Jane's past history of substance abuse, and her involvement with the child welfare system indicates a history of inadequate social, occupational, and personal functioning even before the onset of her drug use. More importantly, while Jane does have a nurturing relationship with Baby John in foster care, she has had little history of successful parenting prior to the onset of drug use, and has a limited identity as a parent.

The science of early childhood development has concluded that a child's first three years of life are the most formative for cognitive and emotional development. This particular period of life is when an infant's brain "hard wires" for speech, self-esteem, motor skills, and social relationships (Trickett and McBride-Chang, 1995, p. 318). Therefore, researchers recommend that it is imperative that babies have at least one parent or caregiver who provides consistent love and care (Johnson and Fein, 1991, p. 406). Baby John has formed a strong attachment to his foster family while he has been in their care. He has foster parents who are willing to adopt him, and able to provide for all of his basic needs as well as a safe home.

Jane was informed that she had every right to refute the adoption recommendation and could request that her legal counsel appeal on her behalf. The foster-adoptive family has been strongly encouraged to allow Jane to have contact with Baby John after the adoption is finalized. The costs and benefits of allowing such contact was discussed with both Jane and the adoptive family, and possible options on ways in which Jane could maintain a relationship with John were considered.

Case Study G (*Bounkhoun*)

Brady T. M., & Ashley, O. S. (2005). Women in substance abuse treatment: results from the alcohol and drug services study (ADSS). Retrieved from http://www.drugabusestatistics.samhsa.gov/womenTX/womenTX.htm

Child Welfare Information Gateway. (2012). *Laws and policies.* Retrieved from http://www.childwelfare.gov/systemwide/laws_policies/

Choi, S., & Ryan, J. P. (2007). Co-occurring problems for substance abusing mothers in child welfare: Matching services to improve family reunification. *Children and Youth Services Review, 29*(11), 1395–1410.

Christian, S. (1999). *1998 state legislative responses to the Adoption and Safe Families Act of 1997.* Denver, CO: National Conference of State Legislatures.

Clark, H. W. (2001). Residential substance abuse treatment for pregnant and postpartum women and their children: Treatment and policy implications. *Child Welfare, 80*(2), 179–198.

D'Andrade, A., & Berrick, J. D. (2006). When policy meets practice: The untested effects of permanency reforms in child welfare. *Journal of Sociology & Social Welfare, 33*(1), 31–52.

Department of Health and Human Services. (1999, April). *Blending Perspectives and Building Common Ground: A Report to Congress on Substance Abuse and Child Protection.* Washington, DC USHHS.

Dore, M., & Doris, J. M. (1998). Preventing child placement in substance-abusing families: Research-informed practice. *Child Welfare, 77*(4), 407–426.

Dozier, M., Peloso, E., Lewis, E., Laurenceau, J., & Levine, S. (2012). Effects of an attachment based intervention on the cortisol production of infants and toddlers in foster care. *Development and Psychopathology, 20,* 845–859.

Famularo, R., Kinscherff, R., Bunshaft, D., Spivak, G., & Fenton, T. (1989). Parental compliance to court-ordered treatment interventions in cases of child maltreatment. *Child Abuse and Neglect, 13,* 507–514.

Frame, L., Berrick, J. D., & Brodowski, M. L. (2000). Understanding reentry to foster care for reunified infants. *Child Welfare, 74*(4), 339–369.

Greenfield, S. F., Brooks, A. J., Gordon, S. M., Green, C. A., Kropp, F., McHugh, R. K., et al. (2007). Substance abuse treatment entry, retention, and outcome in women: A review of the literature. *Drug and Alcohol Dependence, 86*(5), 1–21.

Humphrey, K. R., Turnbull, A. P., & Turnbull, H. R. (2006). Impact of the Adoption and Safe Families Act on youth and their families. *Children and Youth Services Review, 28,* 113–132.

Johnson, D., & Fein, E. (1991). The concept of attachment: Applications to adoption. *Children and Youth Services Review, 13*(5/6), 397–412.

Kim, C. H. (1999). Putting reason back into the reasonable efforts requirements in child abuse and neglect cases. *University of Illinois Law Review,* no. 1, 287–326.

Maluccio, A. N., & Ainsworth, F. (2003). Drug use by parents: A challenge for family reunification practice. *Children and Youth Services Review, 25*(7), 511–533.

Osterling, K. L., & Austin, M. J. (2008). Substance abuse interventions for parents involved in the child welfare system: Evidence and implications. *Journal of Evidence-Based Social Work, 5*(1/2), 157–189.

Terling, T. (1999). The efficacy of family reunification practices: Reentry rates and correlates of reentry for abused and neglected children reunited with their families. *Child Abuse & Neglect, 23*(12), 1359–1370.

Trickett, P. K., & McBride-Chang, C. (1995). The developmental impact of different forms of child abuse and neglect. *Developmental Review, 15,* 311–337.

Wulczyn, F., Hislop, K. B., & Harden, B. J. (2002). The placement of infants in foster care. *Infant Mental Health Journal, 23,* 454–475.

CHAPTER SUMMARY

Ethical Standard 1, which focuses on relationships with clients, addresses ongoing and frequently recurring issues in social work practice. One can assume that all social workers have at some point struggled with client self-determination when they have been concerned about potential harm from decisions clients have made, have considered the ethical issues that encircle the responsibility to informed consent, have had to address client requests for social, as well as professional contacts, have been challenged by competency issues and wondered about the relationship between "competence" and a client's making decisions that the professionals working with him or her do not support, have been careful about considering cultural and ethnic perspectives, and have made often painful and difficult decisions about maintaining or violating client confidentiality.

It is important to review this section of the Code carefully and to consider each nuance. However, in spite of this, social workers often find themselves needing to make "judgment calls" around some of these challenging issues, and the cases presented here certainly suggest the challenges a social worker encounters.

In the first case, where there is a concern about potential sexual abuse of a young foster child removed from the foster home she knows and loves for her protection, consideration must be given to the risk of ongoing abuse. The self-proclaimed perpetrator, the son of her foster parents, has left the home, and the foster parents state that they love and will care for the child and not allow their son to return home. No evidence of abuse has been found. The social worker determines that the child's best interests are served by returning to her loving foster home.

Always complex, sibling adoption presents several challenges, not the least of which is that each sibling may have a separate worker. The responsibility of each is to ensure the best interests of "their" child—which can create conflict of priorities when age, appearance, health, behavior, and other factors in the children are considered in terms of adoption placement. Waiting for an adoptive home for siblings may conflict with the right to an early placement in a stable home for one of the siblings. In this case, the worker determines that the maintenance of the sibling relationship must be primary.

The young, depressed, renal dialysis patient in the third case wishes to terminate treatments, and the social worker finds herself immersed in a profound consideration of religious, ethical, and policy considerations, as well as reflections on quality of life. What role does her depression play in her request to terminate dialysis? Referral to psychiatric evaluation, care conferences, patient meets all help to assess and explore the patient's life situation. Ultimately, when the options and information and conferences have all been presented, the worker understands the need to accept the validity of the patient's choices.

Parent's rights are central to the fourth case study, where an incarcerated parent who has had no contact with his daughter for all her 19 months of life is requesting reunification. The child is placed with a foster family who desires to adopt her. Although there is a strong legal recognition of the rights of biological parents, there is increasing societal awareness of the needs of young children for stability and permanency as well. Out of concern for her young client, the social worker determines that adoption best ensures her well-being.

In the following case, a homeless, mentally disabled 18-year-old referred to the agency by another client is choosing to remain "on the street," despite the clear potential for violent harm. While the social worker clearly values freedom and self-determination highly, he chooses to limit the client's self-determination, and to offer choices and expand possibilities for her within the service network.

The next case also addresses the importance of protecting a vulnerable client, in this case a paraplegic amputee who wishes to leave the hospital after his leg amputation and return to living quarters that are inaccessible to him, and to a substance-abusing lifestyle with no social supports, employment, or possibilities for a future. He refuses rehabilitation and follow-up case management, which can also assist him toward accessible and viable living arrangement. Believing that the client is not aware of the possible options and resources available to him, the worker determines, with the support of her supervisor and healthcare team, to insist he accept rehabilitation for a period of time, and work toward long-term arrangements which would maximize his independence—his own stated highest goal.

The last case in this chapter, as noted, is meant to be a companion to a similar case which has been placed in Chapter 11. Both cases address issues relating to time frames in permanency planning for young children. This case presents a concrete case, while the case in Chapter 11 considers policy in a more abstract manner. In the case presented here, the social worker determines that permanency planning and placement in a foster/adoptive home is in the best interest of the child, despite the mother's desire to reunify. While the fourth case addressed parental rights where there has been no contact, in this case the mother has had contact with her child. However, the strong possibility of future harm and disruption in living conditions for the child if reunified with the mother is of concern to the worker, who determines that adoption best ensures the child's well-being.

Standard 1 is focused on social workers' responsibilities to clients, a responsibility that is primary for most professionals. It addresses the foundational issue of self-determination, and the worker's responsibility to the client's best interest and well-being.

It is essential, however, to be aware that "best interest" is always subjective: It is determined by the worker, by agency staff, by an ethics committee, by interdisciplinary team, and so on. It is vital, in considering this standard, to be aware that the client's "self-determination" is *the client's own* perception of "best interest." Even when it appears to others that the client's decision is contrary to his or her own well-being, one must consider the subjective nature of the "best interests" judgment—and recognize that clients' subjectivity may be ultimately as valid *for them* as one's own.

The self-determined choices of clients in this section may also be reconsidered in this perspective, which involves a clearer understanding of the client's world and values, and an appreciation for the special conditions that have impacted their lives. The next chapter, Standard Two—responsibility to colleagues—will address several challenging situations, and will consider the essential fact that in social work, colleagues are always present, and that relationships with colleagues is basic to professional practice.

The following questions will test your knowledge of the content found within this chapter. For questions 1-6, please select the phrase that best completes each sentence. Question 7 is a brief essay question. For additional assessment, including licensing-exam type questions on applying chapter content to practice behaviors, visit **MySearchLab**.

1. In cases of suspected child abuse, mandated reporters include:
   a. childcare providers, physicians, nurses
   b. teachers, school bus drivers, healthcare personnel
   c. daycare program managers, aides, social workers
   d. all of the above

2. "Best interest" is:
   a. always determined by policies
   b. always subjective to the person making the judgment
   c. always professionally determined
   d. always the opposite of self-determination

3. POLST stands for:
   a. Physicians' Orders for Life-Sustaining Treatment
   b. Preventive Orders for Life-Support Termination
   c. Patient Orders for Lowering Stress Triggers
   d. Practical Orientation for Long-term Services Teams

4. Client self-determination is supported by:
   a. family members
   b. confidentiality
   c. informed consent
   d. social worker intervention

5. Effective interventions must:
   a. occur rapidly
   b. include family members
   c. be culturally sensitive
   d. involve the client directly

6. A client's ability to give informed consent may be limited by all except
   a. capacity to comprehend
   b. difficulty with language
   c. insufficient or erroneous information
   d. agency policy

7. Some social workers believe that clients always self-determine based on their perception of their best interests, while others believe that other factors may influence client choices. Your personal ethical stance on this issue will affect your professional attitudes and decisions around client self-determination, and speaks to your understanding of human nature and character. Consider some of your ideas about best interests and self-determination, and arrive at a reasoned position on this important issue.

7

NASW Ethical Standard Two

Social Workers' Ethical Responsibilities to Colleagues

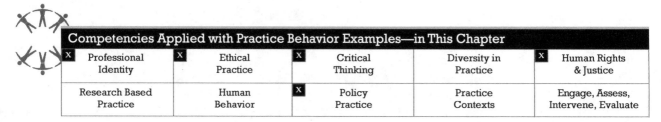

Competencies Applied with Practice Behavior Examples—in This Chapter				
X Professional Identity	X Ethical Practice	X Critical Thinking	Diversity in Practice	X Human Rights & Justice
Research Based Practice	Human Behavior	X Policy Practice	Practice Contexts	Engage, Assess, Intervene, Evaluate

INTRODUCTION

As colleagues and coworkers, supervisors and supervisees, students and field instructors, employers and employees, most social workers interact with their fellow professionals on a daily basis. Standard 2 of the Code of Ethics addresses ethical standards that should be observed by all parties regarding such relationships.

Provisions of the Code

The very first statement (2.01a) obligates social workers to treat colleagues with respect and to represent qualifications, views, and obligations of colleagues in a fair manner by avoiding "unwarranted negative criticism," particularly in reference to competence or individual attributes (2.01b). In 2008, the National Association of Social Workers (NASW) Delegate Assembly revised this section to include *gender identity or expression* and *immigration status* as issues covered in the proscribed "unwarranted negative criticism" (NASW, 2008, www.socialworkers.org/pubs/code/code.asp). This section also asks that social workers cooperate with colleagues in their own and other disciplines on behalf of client well-being (2.01c).

Specific guidelines follow this broad statement. Social workers are obligated to respect confidential information shared by colleagues in the context of professional relationships (2.02). They also are obligated to participate in the work of interdisciplinary teams of which they are members (2.03a). When ethical issues for the worker arise from the actions or decisions of an interdisciplinary team, workers should use appropriate channels to try to revise them (2.03a). If this is not possible, other avenues should be pursued consistent with the well-being of the client (2.03b). Where a worker is aware of a dispute between colleagues or colleague and employer, the worker should be careful not to exploit the situation (2.04).

Social workers use consultation with colleagues on a frequent basis, and guidelines for such consultation are included in Section 2 of the Code. They are encouraged to seek the advice of knowledgeable and competent colleagues for the benefit of their clients but should disclose "the least amount of information necessary" (2.05) to obtain such advice. In addition to consultation, social workers should utilize referral to other professionals when this is beneficial to the client's interests. They are prohibited from "giving or receiving payment" for such a referral (2.06).

The major problematic areas addressed include sexual relationships, which are proscribed in the relationship between supervisors and educators and their supervisees, students, trainees, and others over whom they may hold authority, and should also be avoided between colleagues (2.07); the proscription against sexual harassment (2.08); the obligation to address the impairment of a colleague, first with the colleague and then, if unsuccessful, with appropriate channels (2.09); and the very similar guidelines in the case of the incompetence of a colleague (2.10).

An important subsection addresses the unethical conduct of colleagues, obligating social workers to "take adequate measures" to discourage, prevent, and/or expose such behavior (2.11a), and to be knowledgeable about policies and procedures for handling ethical complaints (2.11b). Where a social worker believes that a colleague has acted unethically, the worker should follow

"Appropriate channels" and "other avenues" might include a supervisor, the head of the social work department, the head of the department most affected by the decision, the chair of the committee, a grievance committee, NASW, the state's licensure board, and so on. The policy manual should be consulted to determine "appropriate channels" and "other avenues" in individual settings.

procedures similar to those developed for incompetent and impaired social workers. He or she should first discuss the concern with the colleague, and, if such concern is legitimate and cannot be rectified by the colleague, action through formal channels is required (2.11c, d).

Social workers also have a clear obligation to assist colleagues who are being unjustly accused of unethical conduct (2.11e).

Professional Identity

Practice Behavior Example: It is especially difficult to address collegial issues when they involve a supervisor, or colleague whose position holds status and authority. Addressing the problem directly may be quite challenging, and the worker may be concerned about differing values and standards of behavior, differing process and practice methodologies, as well as the possible effects on his or her position.

Critical Thinking Question: What procedures are defined in your agency's policy manual for addressing these kinds of issues? How might the agency raise awareness of this section of the Code of Ethics among its professionals?

THE CASES

There is surely no dearth of issues surrounding colleagues, but while students were aware of these, the particular vulnerability that attaches to student status prevented most from choosing to address these concerns. There seem to be several reasons for this: Students were uncomfortable about addressing ethical issues relating to presumably much more experienced colleagues; they were unwilling to place their grades and education at risk by openly attempting to address an ethical issue regarding a colleague; they were afraid that they would offend a colleague; they were concerned that addressing collegial issues in so public a forum would cause loss of anonymity to both student and colleague; and they were unsure of where their personal and professional responsibilities lay.

It is hoped that the three cases included in this chapter and the specific guidelines in the Code of Ethics will encourage both students and social work practitioners to feel more comfortable in expressing ethical concerns related to colleagues.

In the first case, a worker is presented with an all-too-familiar challenge: While policy at all levels requires the availability of services in languages other than English when a client is not proficient in English, this policy is often violated. Expedience, cost efficiency, worker and/or client preference, and "understood" agency policy often create major misunderstandings and compromise the health and well-being of clients. Placed in a dialysis center, the worker is often called upon by a colleague to assist her in working with Spanish-speaking clients. The colleague is barely fluent, and the social worker does not consider herself fluent either. No fluent staff or interpreters are available, and the use of the Language Line is discouraged. As a result, possible harm to a client with whom the colleague has been working may occur. While the student has observed the lack of adequate communication on other occasions, indirectly participating in this clear, direct, and unnecessary harm to an unaware client forces her to confront this difficult issue.

She considers several options for addressing her dilemma, but is aware that, for her, determining how to address this apparent unprofessional conduct by a colleague that she otherwise highly respects as a caring and competent social worker is the central issue. Should she remain silent, out of loyalty and respect to her colleague, or do her professional responsibilities require her to act? And, if so, what actions are required?

The second case was transferred to an intern from her supervisor, after she had attended an ethics committee meeting as an observer while the client was still her supervisor's case, and heard a decision taken at the meeting which presented her with a serious ethical dilemma. The client was a patient in a locked dementia ward in a hospital. However, in addition to dementia, he also required the administration of oxygen treatments to improve breathing and therefore reduce pain and discomfort. His dementia caused agitation and aggressiveness, making administration of his treatments difficult, which, on several occasions, resulted in injury to staff. The ethics committee had determined that the patient be left without treatments unless he was cooperative in order to prevent injury to staff, a decision which the student felt was harmful to him.

The patient has no family or friends to support his interests, and has no legally appointed conservator to advocate for him. In exploring options, the intern is very aware of her own responsibility to the patient, and also of her own vulnerability as an intern in addressing actions taken on a case which had been her own supervisor's and which had been addressed formally by an interdisciplinary ethics committee. How could she advocate for the patient, respect her supervisor's actions, and prevent injury to the staff?

Colleague misconduct and how it may be defined poses a challenge for the intern in the third case presented here. A clinician approaches her with a problem, and asks her to keep it private, a condition to which she agrees. He then reveals that during an agency review of charts, it was discovered that he was writing identical notes for every one of his clients. He had decided to do this to save time, reasoning that the therapeutic process was the same for all of his clients. Now, however, he has been asked to rewrite his notes, individualizing clients and therapies, and to complete this task prior to the agency's outside review.

He then asks the intern to rewrite these notes for him, creating both therapeutic interventions and client responses to them, in order to correct his documentation. He offers to pay the intern for her services. The intern tactfully refuses to become involved, the clinician accepts her decision, and no further contact occurs. However, the intern is left with a persistent ethical question: If no actual harm and no actual misconduct occurred, to her knowledge, was any further action required of her by professional standards and by the Code of Ethics? How could she address her concerns, when she had agreed to maintain his confidentiality?

Case Study H   Interpreting for Limited English Proficiency Clients: Is "Some" Really Enough?

Abstracted from an unpublished paper by Sarah Thibault, MSW

Practice Context and Case Presentation

A major urban dialysis center serves patients for both peritoneal (at-home) and hemodialysis (in-center) through both private and public healthcare providers. Patients are referred when they have a diagnosis of end-stage renal disease, in which their kidneys are functioning at 15 percent or less. Dialysis removes wastes and excess fluid from the blood, and most patients receiving hemodialysis treatment come to the dialysis center three times weekly for about three-and-a-half hours per visit.

The social worker's role in a dialysis setting is to assist patients and their families in coping with kidney disease by talking with patients about their emotional needs; working to enhance coping skills; providing education about kidney disease; referring to community resources for kidney transplant; and assisting with advance directives, transportation, home health services, nutrition, benefits, insurance, and end-of-life planning. Social workers also work with other members of the dialysis team to teach them about the emotional aspects of dialysis and offer skills to encourage positive and professional interaction with patients and fellow team members. By presenting a full

Language Line is often utilized by agencies serving non–English speaking clients. Interpretation is available by telephone 24/7 in over 170 languages. Language Line may be accessed at www. languageline.com

picture of all the patient's needs to the dialysis team, social workers help ensure that the best decisions will be made regarding the patients' overall health and well-being.

The dialysis center serves a large number of patients who are limited English proficient (LEP). Although there are many Spanish-speaking clients, there are no translators, or clinicians who are bilingual. And, while clinicians have access to a Language Line, it is accessed infrequently, and is often not ideal due to the level of terminology used in such a specialized medical setting.

I became fully aware of this issue when a monolingual patient from Nicaragua came in to meet with one of the social work supervisors. The supervisor attempted to understand what the client was saying and also asked me to assist with translation, as I had done on other occasions. Neither of us was fully fluent in Spanish. The patient seemed to be saying that he was returning to Nicaragua the very next day, and that he had a plan for receiving dialysis there, but we couldn't understand the details due to the language barrier. He received some printouts of his history and treatment regimen, and left. Had there been clinicians who spoke Spanish or easy access to a translator on a regular basis, it is possible that my colleague would have found out about the patient's plan to return to Nicaragua ahead of time and would have been able to provide needed assistance and referrals. In the absence of Spanish-speaking clinicians or translators, accessing the Language Line, available nationally for translation services, would have been effective in assessing the situation and informing the patient of options and special considerations.

While I had observed numerous ethical issues in terms of language services and access in addition to the above-mentioned incident, I chose the following as my focus because it was the most frustrating, and also the one in which I thought I could most likely make a difference. This was the conflict between what seemed an obvious ethical breach and the respect I have for this supervisor, my colleague.

I defined my dilemmas as follows:

RESPECT FOR COLLEAGUE V. RESPONSIBILITY TO PROFESSION

Research and Related Literature

Cultural competence is of utmost importance to social workers, who encounter people from many different backgrounds and cultures in every context of practice. There is a multiplicity of languages spoken in the United States, and issues relating to language are an essential part of cultural competence. In the context of service provision, these include whether translators are available, whether written materials are provided in clients' primary languages, and whether efforts are made to ensure that information is exchanged in an accessible and respectful manner. There are many laws and regulations regarding this, both for social workers and for services provided in a health setting.

The most general and far-reaching laws governing access to interpreter services are Title VI of the Civil Rights Act of 1964 and the U.S. Department of Health and Services Guidelines, which require all health organizations that receive federal funds, including Medicare, Medicaid, and Schip payments, to take reasonable steps to ensure meaningful access to their programs and activities by persons with LEP. For instance, the U.S. Department of Health and Human Services states, in Section 4 of the National Standards for Culturally and Linguistically Appropriate Services in Health Care, that "health care organizations must offer and provide language assistance services, including bilingual staff and interpreter services, at no cost to each patient/consumer with limited English proficiency at all points of contact, in a timely manner during all hours of operation" (U.S. Department of Health and Human Services, 2001). This is a very clear statement of expectations for best practices, which include high availability of interpreter services. While the Civil Rights Act extends to all settings, medical settings have a particular duty due to their funding base.

The dialysis center's policies, procedures, and guidelines manual reflect the requirements of the National Standards for Culturally and Linguistically Appropriate Services in Health Care. In fact, the dialysis center's code is a restatement of the government's policies to ensure that public guidelines correlate with the dialysis center's written policies.

The NASW Standards for Cultural Competence in Social Work Practice addresses this issue in Section 9, which states that "social workers shall seek to provide and advocate for the provision of information, referrals, and services in the language appropriate to the client, which may include the use of interpreters" (2001). While this seems vague as to the obligation to secure language interpretation, the standard further explains social workers' ethical responsibility regarding language accessibility by stating:

> Agencies and providers of services are expected to take reasonable steps to provide services and information in appropriate language other than English to ensure that people with limited English proficiency are effectively informed and can effectively participate in and benefit from its programs. It is the responsibility of social services agencies and social workers to provide clients services in the language of their choice or to seek the assistance of qualified language interpreters.... The use of language translation should be done by trained professional interpreters (for example, certified or registered sign language interpreters). (NASW, *Standards for Cultural Competence*, 2001)

Thus, not only must we be sure that social work services are available in a patient's primary language, we must also seek the assistance of qualified interpreters. My colleague's provision of services using both of our limited fluency in Spanish is in violation of this code.

In addition, Section 2.06 of the NASW Code of Ethics states that social workers should refer clients to other professionals when the other professionals' specialized knowledge or expertise is needed to serve clients fully or when social workers believe that they are not being effective or making reasonable progress with clients and that additional service is required. My colleague and I are not trained interpreters, and we lack the specialized knowledge that is necessary to provide culturally accessible services to LEP patients. The Code states that it is our obligation to refer patients who are LEP to fully qualified interpreters in order to serve them fully.

Perkins points out:

> Translation needs often go unmet or are handled inappropriately in health care settings. Many hospitals and clinics do not have qualified interpreters on hand. Rather, they rely on family, friends, or untrained staff, or they allow providers to deliver services without any verbal communication with the patient. (Perkins, 1999)

Ethical Practice

Practice Behavior Example: Healthcare settings and social agencies often rely on family and friends to serve as translators for clients.

Critical Thinking Question: What are some of the issues that might occur when family and friends provide translation? Conversely, what are some of the issues that might affect communication when professional interpreters are utilized?

Perkins explains that "the lack of appropriate translation services also affects the cost of care. Non-English-speaking patients may be reluctant to deal with providers who cannot communicate with them, seeking care only when their conditions become acute and more costly" (Perkins, 1999). When information is not conveyed appropriately by either patient and family members or healthcare professionals, negative health outcomes may result, causing stress for patients and families, and increasing the cost of health care.

In addition, Perkins states that "translation of a medical visit by unqualified interpreters is prone to omissions, additions, substitutions, volunteered opinions, and semantic errors that can seriously distort care" (Perkins, 1999). This lack of culturally competent practice puts particular individuals and groups at a disadvantage, affecting their access to best practices in both health care and psychosocial care.

Because I respected my colleague, believed her to be a generally competent and efficient social worker, and had seen evidence on many occasions of culturally competent practice and excellent therapeutic and case management work, it was difficult for me to determine how to address what I perceived as unethical practice. An important aspect of professional social work addresses supporting our colleagues, coworkers, teammates, and agency. I turned to the NASW Code of Ethics to find clarity on what our relationship with colleagues should be and what is considered respectful.

> Section 2.01 of the Code states: (a) Social workers should treat colleagues with respect and should represent accurately and fairly the qualifications, views, and obligations of colleagues. (b) Social workers should avoid unwarranted negative criticism of colleagues in communications with clients or with other professionals. Unwarranted negative criticism may include demeaning comments that refer to colleagues' level of competence....(NASW, *Code of Ethics*, 2008)

The Code, then, supported my thoughts about my colleague. I knew that I did have respect for her, and had no desire to defame her, or to presume from this issue that she was less than fully competent. I wanted to accurately examine and remedy the situation, rather than assuming a critical stance, staying focused on the ethical issue, on the realities of the practice setting, on how these affected her decisions about the use of interpreters, and on how to find a way to address this in a constructive manner.

In addition to respect for my colleague, there were other ramifications to the problem that needed to be considered. One was the way in which taking action would affect my standing as a student. While my role as a student intern might protect me from employment and professional risk, my experience with this internship during the remainder of the semester might be affected. Also, the site's view of my MSW program and their likelihood of accepting future interns could be affected.

Author's Reflection, Reasoning Process, and Resolution

Gewirth's Principles Hierarchy (1978) was helpful in analyzing this ethical issue and the potential harms to clients and to my colleague. One of the major issues was the harm being done to clients by poorly translated interactions with social workers, which could impact the sharing of information to make appropriate decisions. Another was the potential for harms that might occur by addressing or reporting that interpretation services weren't always used at the dialysis center. If a report was made to the dialysis center administration or to a licensing body specific to my colleague, she might be at risk of losing her license or her job.

In examining ethical issues, Gewirth defines three kinds of "goods": core goods necessary for freedom and well-being. The most basic, and thus most essential, include life, food, shelter, health, and mental equilibrium. Without Gewirth's nonsubtractive goods, which include not being stolen from, cheated, or lied to, as well as reasonable living conditions and labor, basic goods are compromised. Additive goods such as knowledge, education, self-esteem, and material comforts enhance people's ability to achieve well-being (Gewirth, 1978).

In decision making, Gewirth's First Principle states: Rules against basic harms to the necessary preconditions of action (core goods) take precedence over rules against harms such as lying or revealing confidential information (nonsubtractive goods) or threats to additive goods such as education or wealth. (Basic goods must be met first.) (Gewirth, 1978)

Thus, the potential harm to patients at the clinic superseded the potential harm to my colleague's job or to my own educational status, because the patients were at risk of negative impacts to their basic core goods. In addition, Principle Four of the Hierarchy states: "The obligation to obey laws, roles, and regulations to which one has voluntarily and freely consented ordinarily overrides one's right to engage voluntarily in a manner that conflicts with these laws, rules, and regulations" (Gewirth, 1978). I understood this as saying that because I had agreed to abide by the rules of my profession, my field placement's written policies, and state and national laws and codes, I must follow them, even if a part of me wanted to do otherwise and protect my colleague and, possibly, my internship. As these codes directly mandated interpreter services for LEP clients, I had an ethical duty to act.

My personal value base affects my perspective of, and reaction to, both sides of the ethical dilemma. I am very social justice oriented and strive to provide egalitarian services to all. I believe that it is our duty to pay special attention to individuals who are disadvantaged due to barriers in accessing services, which include language. At the same time, I possess a strong sense of loyalty to coworkers, especially those I believe to be generally competent and working toward the best interests of their clients. It is difficult for me to overstep this bond of loyalty. However, I view equitable access to information as an issue of social justice. Providing language interpretation is both a basic right and best practice in healthcare settings, supporting health, self-care, and informed consent.

The values of the dialysis center expressed in the Mission Statement seem to support federal guidelines, stating the goal of improving patient outcomes, which seems to necessitate culturally competent services. However, cost efficiency and utility are also values that affect operation and services. The dialysis center's manual states that "every effort should be made to utilize internal resources for language assistance before Language Line is accessed" (2008). Because there were no paid interpreters and few staff members were available to interpret, family members or dialysis team members who weren't fully fluent were providing language services. While the rest of the language section of the manual highlights the need for language services to be qualified and competent, the above statement points to the monetary bottom line, as Language Line is an expensive service.

There are many societal values involved in this issue. I think one reason that social workers at the dialysis center take the expedient route in relation to interpreter services is the rationing and funding of health care. While in some cases it is the lack of attention to cultural competence, more often, especially in busy healthcare settings like this one, where social workers have caseloads of over a hundred and seemingly endless documentation duties, there is a pressure to produce more with limited resources. A utilitarian perspective such as that of John Stuart Mill (Beauchamp & Childress, 2009), which advocates for the greatest good for the greatest number, might ask, "When resources such as time and money are limited, is it fair to all or indeed necessary to expend resources to provide language services to the few, rather than focusing on quality care for the many?"

From an egalitarian perspective, everyone deserves the opportunity equally to access the goods of life (Beauchamp & Childress, 2009). Applied to a medical setting, all patients deserve equal access to appropriate treatments and services, including education about health and treatment options. Inability to communicate in one's primary or sole language is an obvious impediment; and unless addressed, it creates an unequal opportunity to access these resources. Thus, interpreter services and reliable, easy access to them is integral to equal opportunity and egalitarianism.

The potential courses of action included doing nothing, talking to my school field adviser with or without also talking to someone at the placement, confronting this colleague, discussing the problem with my field instructor, talking with the dialysis center's administrator, contacting the NASW, writing to the dialysis center's board of directors, working to organize with other staff to push for the company to employ translators (and thus taking more of an organizational and policy route), among others. Given the stated and unstated policies of the dialysis center governing translation services, I wondered how the administrator or the board of directors might react to my concerns.

I refocused on my stated conflict and attempted to work toward the most effective way to address both my ethical responsibilities to clients and to the dialysis center community as a social worker, and my respect and concern for my colleague.

In deciding which specific course of action to take, I referenced the NASW Code of Ethics.

> Section 2.11, entitled "Unethical Conduct of Colleagues," states: (a) Social workers should take adequate measures to discourage, prevent, expose, and correct the unethical conduct of colleagues. (b) Social workers should be knowledgeable about established policies and procedures for handling concerns about colleagues' unethical behavior. Social workers should be familiar with national, state, and local procedures for handling ethics complaints. These include policies and procedures created by NASW, licensing and regulatory bodies, employers, agencies, and other professional organizations. (c) Social workers who believe that a colleague has acted unethically should seek resolution by discussing their concerns with the colleague when feasible and when such discussion is likely to be productive. (d) When necessary, social workers who believe that a colleague has acted unethically should take action through appropriate formal channels (such as contacting a state licensing board or regulatory body, an NASW committee on inquiry, or other professional ethics committees). (NASW, *Code of Ethics*, 2008)

In considering this section of the Code, it seemed clear to me that once I confirmed that my colleague had acted in an unethical manner, it was my duty to try to prevent and correct future unethical behavior. The first recommended course of action was a relatively simple one: having a conversation one-on-one with the colleague in question. Further steps should be taken if this step is not effective.

Paul Fusco/Magnum Photos

An interdisciplinary team meets in an apartment hallway after visiting clients in the field.

My decision, based on my view of my colleague as a generally competent, receptive professional, was to have a dialogue with her. I intended to explain the reason that I examined the issue so thoroughly, and to let her know my concerns based upon the Code of Ethics and the responsibility to cultural competence. If she did not respond positively and somehow indicate that she would be willing to work to address the issue, I would need to take steps to report the issue to the administrator, her supervisor, and possibly the NASW.

I had the conversation with this colleague during my last week of field placement. I had wished to do it earlier, but two things happened: I was finishing up this paper the last few weeks and decided at the last minute that talking to her was the first and foremost step in addressing this issue, and she was on vacation for two weeks and returned during my last week of field placement. I was very diplomatic in my approach, and explained that the reason I examined this issue so deeply was because it was part of my ethics course. She was very open and receptive to the conversation and told me that she was happy I brought the concern to her. We discussed all aspects of it in detail, with mutual respect, and she told me that one of the benefits of having student interns is to have a fresh set of eyes. I left feeling certain that she took my concern to heart and assured that she would be much more conscientious about utilizing interpreter services, despite the many obstacles to doing so. My hopes, long term, are that the dialysis center will prioritize having well-trained, in-person interpreters and secure and allocate the funding to do so. Perhaps my colleague will take the initiative in advocating for this priority.

Case Study H (*Thibault*)

Beauchamp, T. L., & Childress, J. F. (2009). *Principles of biomedical ethics* (6th ed.). New York: Oxford University Press.

Gewirth, A. (1978). *Reason and morality.* Chicago: University of Chicago Press.

National Association of Social Workers. (2001). *Standards for cultural competence in social work practice.* Washington, DC: Author.

National Association of Social Workers. (2008). *NASW code of ethics.* Washington, DC: Author.

Perkins, J. (1999). Overcoming language barriers to health care. *Popular Government, 65*(1), 38–44. Retrieved from www.sog.unc.edu/pubs/electronicversions/pg/over.htm

U.S. Department of Health and Human Services, OPHS, Office of Minority Health. (2001). *National standards for culturally and linguistically appropriate services in health care: Executive summary.* Washington, DC: Author.

Case Study I   Staff Safety and Patient Care: What Is the Social Worker's Role?

Abstracted from an unpublished paper by Natalie Aragon, MSW

Practice Context and Case Presentation

Scott Spanner, a 65-year-old male, has been a resident in a locked dementia ward of a hospital for two weeks, with a diagnosis of severe vascular dementia, which caused him to become agitated easily, and chronic obstructive pulmonary disease (COPD), which required that he receive several oxygen treatments daily. He bruised and scratched nursing staff on several occasions, becoming combative, agitated, and uncooperative when oxygen treatments were administered. If treatments were not administered, his behavior deteriorated further, he paced the unit until he could no longer walk, and his confusion increased greatly due to the lack of oxygen, making treatments still more difficult to administer. His condition began to worsen markedly around day four.

An ethics committee meeting with the Director of Nursing, medical team, chaplain, and the medical social worker assigned to this patient was held to discuss the physical condition of the patient, the progression of his diseases, his behavior, and possible solutions. The medical team presented the patient's physical condition, which was generally worsening due to the lack of oxygen absorption and advanced stage of vascular dementia. The Director of Nursing described the patient's pacing the unit until he could not breathe any longer and then sitting in the middle of the floor, finally permitting the nursing staff to give him the oxygen treatment, too exhausted to fight them off any longer. The medical social worker presented the psychosocial aspects of the patient's life: He had no known family members or friends and was unable to speak. There was no one to act on his behalf, or offer support. Scott was this MSW intern's first assignment, but her role at this meeting was that of an observer only, shadowing the patient's social worker of record.

It was determined that in order to provide the best possible quality of life for Scott, he should receive around-the-clock morphine for the pain and discomfort caused by his COPD, and that the nursing staff should attempt to administer the oxygen and assist the patient with his activities of daily living (ADLs) *only* if he was noncombative and compliant. These decisions left this intern feeling that the patient's wishes were unknown, and not included in planning. The social worker did not advocate for Scott, and his potential rights were not addressed by the ethics committee. The ethics committee as a whole appeared to be much more concerned about the safety of the staff members than the care of the patient.

On the other hand, the ethics committee and the professional staff also have the responsibility of ensuring safety for direct caregivers. Requiring nursing staff to provide a treatment when there is certain to be injury seems unreasonable and unethical. The hospital itself might also be at risk of legal action should injury result when the predictability of such injury was high.

The dilemma is stated as:

SUPPORT FOR STAFF SAFETY V. ADVOCACY FOR OPTIMAL CARE OF PATIENT

Research and Related Literature

The Illness and Its Symptoms. *Vascular dementia* is a general term describing problems with reasoning, planning, judgment, memory, and other thought processes caused by brain damage from impaired blood flow to the brain (www.mayoclinic.com/health/vascular dementia/DS00934). *Mental capacity* is a functional term that may be defined as the "mental or cognitive ability to understand the nature and effects of one's acts," and "dementia, in its many forms, is a leading cause of functional limitation among older adults worldwide and will continue to ascend in global health importance as populations continue to age and effective cures remain elusive" (www.mayoclinic.com/health/vascular dementia/DS00934). Scott's level of vascular dementia affected his ability to communicate, comprehend, and care for himself.

Beauchamp and Childress note that defining and determining competence is a complex issue, as competence is relative to the situation or function that needs to be completed (p. 112). The authors define competence as the ability to perform a task or range of tasks. Currently, a standardized test to determine competence does not exist; however, a psychologist can perform a neuropsychological evaluation to determine if a mental illness diagnosis exists (pp. 114–117).

The Mini Mental State Examination (MMSE) is the most commonly used test for memory loss, used by clinicians to help diagnose dementias and assess progression and severity (www.mayoclinic.com/health/vascular dementia/DS00934). Competency tests are designed to assess one single or only a few aspects of cognition, and multiple tests must be administered to obtain an overall "picture" or "map" of an individual's cognitive ability (www.mayoclinic.com/health/vascular dementia/DS00934). However, Scott's inability to communicate or focus effectively limits the applicability of these tests.

The dementia rating scale assesses for time and place orientation, memory, understanding, and coherence (www.mayoclinic.com/health/vascular dementia/DS00934). However, Beauchamp and Childress state that "persons who are incompetent by virtue of dementia, alcoholism, immaturity, and mental retardation present radically different types and problems of incompetence" (p. 113). Individuals are competent to make a decision about various topics only if they "have the capacity to understand the material information, to make a judgment about this information in light of their values, to intend a certain outcome, and to communicate freely their wishes to caregivers or investigators" (p. 113). Scott's competence appeared compromised to some degree.

Chronic obstructive pulmonary disease refers to a group of lung diseases that block airflow as one exhales, causing hypoxemia (low blood oxygen) and making it increasingly difficult to breathe. According to the Mayo Clinic, "emphysema and chronic asthmatic bronchitis are the two main conditions that make up COPD" (www.mayoclinic.com/health/vascular dementia/DS00934), and damage to the airways eventually interferes with the exchange of oxygen and carbon dioxide in the lungs. Scott's condition required administration of oxygen treatments to increase the level of oxygen in his blood.

Staff Injuries in Dementia Settings. There have been several research studies on the subject of staff injuries due to aggressive behavior of patients. According to the U.S. Department of Justice National Crime Victimization Survey, mental health workers in general become crime victims at work 5.5 times as often as the general worker population, and more than three times as often as acute hospital workers. Research done at five California mental hospitals found that workers are "dangerously outnumbered and isolated." Workers are suggesting reforms which include factoring in staff safety issues in therapeutic planning (Nurse Alliance, 2011).

Yassi, Cohen, Cvitkovich et al. (2004) have researched staff injuries at intermediate care facilities, which had a large population of patients with dementia and other varying needs. They found that injuries occurred in these facilities 50 percent more frequently than at acute care hospitals. Their study found that facilities where the institutional culture was "people oriented," where workers participated in discussions, where "workplace hazards were promptly addressed to improve working conditions," and where workers were invited to have "meaningful input into care decisions" had lower injury rates (p. 88).

A third study found that the "high frequency of aggression by people with dementia in care homes" also produced a "high level of distress" among staff in these homes (Berry, 2011, p. 9). Specialized dementia units have even higher aggression rates than care homes generally (p. 12), and aggressive behavior seems to occur most often "where care staff must assist with very intimate needs...as a person with dementia may be fearful or view this as an invasion of their privacy" (p. 9).

This research suggests that the nursing staff working with Scott was experiencing a common problem in working with dementia patients, and that staff feelings of stress and concern for possible injury occurs frequently. Meaningful input and a consideration of safety issues as a general staff concern on the part of the hospital may have been helpful in addressing these concerns.

Hospital Policy and Procedures. The hospital's Mission Statement notes the goal "to provide high quality, culturally competent rehabilitation and skilled nursing services to the diverse population of (The city)," and values state that the "patient comes first" (_____ Policy and Procedure Manual, 2010). Hospital policy states that "restorative nursing care is directed toward the conservation of residents' abilities, restoration of maximal levels of function and independence, promotion of quality of life, adaptation to an altered life style, and prevention of deterioration and complications of disability" (_____ Policy and Procedure Manual, 2010). The Policy and Procedure Manual states that nurse and CNA responsibilities include: "Provision of nursing care as normally expected, including feeding, bathing, toileting, repositioning, dressing and skin care," as well as " Close monitoring of assigned residents to prevent residents from injury to self or injury to others" (_____ Policy and Procedure Manual, 2010). Specific policy regarding administration of oxygen treatments is not included in the manual.

Policies and procedures require that nursing staff concerned about rights of a patient who is unable to communicate or advocate for himself or herself should discuss these concerns with their direct supervisor, and develop a collaborative plan of action and/or referral (_____ Policy and Procedure Manual, 2010). The Policy and Procedure Manual also notes that all patients must be screened for history of significant psychiatric and/or behavioral problems prior to admission, and the nursing staff is required to use the hospital's Nursing Behavioral Risk Assessment (MR 340) to aid in identifying residents with behaviors that pose potential risk to themselves or others. If a patient is found to be a behavior risk, the Resident Care Team must assess and monitor patient behaviors with "daily observations, review of the Behavioral Monitoring Record (BMR)

Human Rights & Justice

Practice Behavior Example: "Aggressive behavior" is often defined by the potential for causing injury to self and others, and thus requiring attention from staff and professionals in order to minimize harms.

Critical Thinking Question: "Aggressive behavior" thus defined may vary widely by age, gender, strength, size, and general physical condition, all of which affect staff and professionals' assessment of the potential for harm. Similar behavior by a 7-year-old and by an adult male in good physical condition may present very different risks of harm. However, applying different standards according to these categories risks discrimination. Should issues other than risk of harm be considered in defining "aggressive behavior"?

(MR330 A & B) to identify, track and review the potential risk behaviors, regular review and revision of the resident's plan of care and discussions during Resident Care Conference" (_____ Policy and Procedure Manual, 2010).

In cases of aggressive behavioral crisis without intentional risk of harm, the unit physician determines if the patient's condition is the likely cause of the behavior. If it is likely caused by "a psychiatric condition including mental illness, traumatic brain illness, dementia and other neurological disorders, the unit physician will notify the psychiatric staff, who will assess the patient and determine if the patient can be treated at a SNF level or requires to be placed on a 5150 hold." This temporarily places a patient under involuntary commitment for further evaluation at Psychiatric Emergency Services (PES). If the patient's aggression seems to be caused by a medical condition, the unit physician will assess and attempt appropriate medical intervention (_____ Policy and Procedure Manual, 2010).

If it is determined that the patient who displayed aggressive behavior can continue to be safely cared for at the hospital, the care team will meet by the next business day to develop and write a Behavioral Plan of Care developing goals for the patient. If she or he has adequate cognitive capacity, incentives for behavior change, as well as disincentives for nonadherence to the plan must be clearly communicated and understood by the patient (_____ Policy and Procedure Manual, 2010).

Ethical Theory. Alan Gewirth's Principles Hierarchy develops three kinds of "core goods" which address life quality: *basic goods*, which include food, shelter, life, health, and mental equilibrium; *nonsubtractive goods*, without which fundamental rights are compromised, such as veracity, fidelity, and comfortable living conditions; and *additive goods*, which increase well-being, such as a good education and self-esteem (Gewirth, pp. 59–65). It is very possible that Scott had all three of these core goods at some point in his past. He most likely attended school, worked, lived some place comfortable, had friendships and family. However, at this time he has neither his health nor mental equilibrium, two essential basic goods.

In discussing institutional ethics committees, Beauchamp and Childress note that "surrogate decision makers sometimes refuse treatments that would serve the interests of those they should protect, and physicians sometimes too readily acquiesce in their preferences" (Beauchamp & Childress, p. 189). Thus, the patient's decision maker may not always be the best person to make decisions, and the physicians will most likely agree with whatever they say. If this is the case, it seems preferable to have a public guardian assigned to oversee care. Beauchamp and Childress also discuss "allowing" a patient to die, and state that withholding treatment and/or technology which results in a patient's death is not actually considered to be "killing" the patient (pp. 172–175).

Laws. According to California law, a court-appointed person who addresses financial matters is called a "conservator of the estate," while one who makes medical and personal decisions is a "conservator of the person." An incapacitated person may need one type of representative, or both, and the same person can be appointed to hold both responsibilities. Conservators are accountable to the courts. Conservatorships are time-consuming and expensive; they often require court hearings and the ongoing assistance of a lawyer (http://www.leginfo.ca.gov/). The paperwork can also be daunting, because the conservator must keep detailed records and file court papers on a regular basis (http://www.leginfo.ca.gov/). It may be necessary for the individual to fill out applications for conservatorship several times, and the completed document may be 30 pages long. The majority of conservatorships are established for people who are in coma, suffer from advanced Alzheimer's disease, or have other serious illnesses or injuries (http://www.leginfo.ca.gov/).

Author's Reflection, Reasoning Process, and Resolution

Because this dilemma appears to be very much affected by values differences, a consideration of the values of those involved in, and affected by, the dilemma can assist greatly in informing this author's decision. At least three professions are involved in this dilemma, and reference to the physicians' and nurses' ethical codes will be included in addition to the social worker's.

Nursing Code of Ethics and the Medical Oath. The American Nursing Association (ANA) states that "The nurse, in all professional relationships, practices with compassion and respect for the inherent dignity, worth, and uniqueness of every individual, unrestricted by consideration of social or economic status, personal attributes, or the nature of health problems." Compassion, respect, dignity and worth all support the ANA's position that the primary commitment is to the patient, whether defined as an individual, a family, a group, or a community (http://nursingworld.org/MainMenuCategories/ThePracticeofProfessionalNursing/EthicsStandards/CodeofEthics).

The Hippocratic Oath of doctors includes the statement "I will apply dietetic measures for the benefit of the sick according to my ability and judgment; I will keep them from harm and injustice" (www.nlm.nih.gov/hmd/Greek/GreekOath/html). Physicians' obligation to "benefit the sick" would imply a primary concern for the well-being of patients, and "keep(ing) them from harm and injustice", ensuring that they receive the optimum care.

Social Work Code of Ethics. The section entitled Social Workers' Ethical Responsibilities to Clients, Standard 1.01, Commitment to Clients, states that "Social workers' primary responsibility is to promote the well being of clients. In general, clients' interests are primary" (NASW, 2009). Standard 1.02, Self-Determination, states that "Social workers may limit clients' right to self determination when, in the social workers' professional judgment, clients' actions or potential actions pose a serious, foreseeable, and imminent risk to themselves or others" (NASW, 2009). As Scott was not able to participate in decision making, and the possibility of risk to others existed, the social worker's role was to consider his interests as primary. Dolgoff, Harrington, and Loewenberg state that social workers must be trained in ethical decision making, and develop advocacy skills in order to be successful advocates for their patients and clients who are unable to advocate for themselves (2012, pp. 274–275).

Standard 2.03 of the Code of Ethics, Interdisciplinary Collaboration, states that "Social workers who are members of an interdisciplinary team should participate in and contribute to decisions that affect the well being of clients by drawing on the perspectives, values, and experiences of the social work profession" (NASW, 2009). In support of the Code and specific to interdisciplinary teams, Dolgoff, Harrington, and Loewenberg, recommend that social workers serving on these teams should "attain knowledge and skills that will allow them to contribute effectively in ethical discussions involving social workers and clients or patients, as well as other professionals" (2012, pp. 274–275).

Personal Values. Ranked in the order of importance to this writer, her highest personal values are: spirituality, family/relationships, trust, respect, honesty, self-worth, compassion, and equality. Spirituality is placed first because it is her personal belief that she is who she is thanks to God. The seven other values are the key ingredients to being a "good person." As a Christian, this writer believes that she must attempt to be a model citizen, a good parent, a positive role model, kind to others, trustworthy, and an honest person. These are very similar to Beauchamp and Childress' list of moral values (Beauchamp & Childress, pp. 45–46). The core values of the *NASW Code of Ethics* also fit well into this writer's personal values. The overall themes of the core values—service, social justice, dignity and worth of the person, importance of human relationships, integrity, and competence (NASW Code of Ethics)—are, in general, very similar to the writer's own values.

Values of the Affected System. It is difficult to speak of this patient's values with any certainty, due to his physical state and cognitive deficits. He was not able to communicate with the medical staff, nursing staff, or social worker. He does not have any family or support network involved in his care; therefore, the values of the client's world are largely unknown. However, based on his resistance to care and his frequent pacing, it may be possible to assume that the client values freedom and independence, and being free of restraints, at least on a physical level.

Parens patriae literally means that the state is the parent. In the social contract between the state and the people, the state may step in to protect the interests of its vulnerable members. *Parens patriae* may be used in cases of abuse and neglect, custody, and healthcare decision making, as well as in other circumstances.

The nursing staff is also affected by this ethical dilemma. One can assume that personal safety and the prevention of injury and harm are important personal values for the staff. However, helping their patients, a concern for the well-being of others, a desire to relieve pain and sickness, concern for the care and health of all of their patients are also values that the nursing staff holds. Had there been no risk of harm, nursing staff would have diligently provided all of the oxygen treatment to help Scott to be as comfortable as possible.

Societal Values. Because this dilemma also affects hospital policy and thus broader society, it is also important to consider societal values that impact the resolution. Our society is diverse, and there are a number of possible values that are related to the dilemma. As examples: values could reflect the stance that human life must be protected at all costs, regardless of the individual's quality of life; others may argue that since the patient's quality of life appears very limited, and is irreversible, he should be allowed to die; some people might feel as though a person with minimal cognitive ability to refuse or accept medical intervention requires the state to step in, as *parens patriae*, and take responsibility for decision making; still others might be concerned about the utilization of medical resources for a patient with such severe dementia and inability to interact with his surroundings; and others might conclude that when it is someone's time to die, one must just let it be so, but whether "time to die" includes refusal of treatments is uncertain.

However, it may be possible to say that societal values in general, as reflected in health care and other laws and policies, support Scott's right to have treatments and to be given medication for pain, because his refusals might be due to his mental state rather than personal, rational decisions and, in general, society supports the value of life.

Options for Action. There are several options that can be considered in resolving this dilemma.

1. To accept the decision of the ethics committee in offering this patient comfort care for pain only, which will most likely create conditions that will cause rapid deterioration and death, but will also ensure the safety of the nursing staff.

2. To accept the decision of the ethics committee in principle, but suggest a team meeting to explore and examine options for creating conditions that would enable treatments to be provided with no staff injury. For example, might there be a staff member to whom Scott relates more positively? Is there a time of the day when he is less agitated? Can treatments be given when he is asleep? Can treatments be given after comfort measures, when he might be calmer?

3. To discuss her concerns for Scott with her supervisor and with the Social Work Department at a meeting, and request advice, help, and support from fellow social workers.

4. To request a competency determination, and apply for public guardianship. Applying for conservatorship of the patient is usually done by the social worker, and is a very time-consuming process that requires much paperwork in addition to an extensive search for family members and friends. As soon as the paperwork is generated, a medical probate would go into effect. Having a conservator advocating for the client's best interests, however, does not ensure that either course of action will be supported.

5. To request another ethics committee meeting and present her concerns to the committee, requesting a reconsideration of their recommendation of comfort measures only.

6. To request that hospital policy regarding staff safety and care of patients be reviewed and amended to include more specific recommendations and policies in this regard, as was suggested by the research on staff injuries in caring for dementia patients.

Evaluation of Options. In considering each of these options, the social worker must select the option which most supports the rights and interests of all of the parties, is in accord with laws, policies, and professional codes, is consonant with personal, professional, affected system, and societal values.

Option (1) supports safety for the staff, and respects the decisions made by the ethics committee, recognizing their right to rule in this matter. However, it is contrary to this writer's personal and professional values, which suggest a responsibility to advocacy and to treatment for Scott.

Option (2) also respects the decisions of the ethics committee and the concerns of the staff, but asks that they consider other options. However, staff may have already considered all possible resources, and/or attempted them and found them to be unsuccessful. They might be annoyed that this writer challenges them in this regard, and be more unwilling to address other possible actions on behalf of the client.

Option (3) is difficult because the writer's supervisor is the social worker who attended the ethics committee meeting and supported the positions of the nursing staff and medical team. The supervisor might feel challenged or disrespected, and this might also affect the position of the writer as a student with this supervisor and with this hospital.

Option (4) involves a series of complicated steps for the social worker: arranging for a competency examination and obtaining a definitive result from the physician, applying for conservatorship, possibly appearing in court, and then abiding by the determination of the conservator. This option removes personal responsibility for advocacy from the social worker, but does not ensure that Scott will receive treatments.

Option (5) Requesting another ethics committee meeting and a reconsideration of the decision taken is a very challenging position for an intern! It combines the negative possibilities of Option (2) and Option (3).

Option (6) is a long-term option, but would not address Scott's immediate circumstances, although it might prevent future difficulties similar to this one. During this process, Scott might die.

Course of Action. There is only one option that makes complete sense to this MSW student, and that is Option (4), the competency examination and the application for conservatorship. Although these take some time, hopefully it will be possible to expedite the process because the situation for Scott may be termed an emergency.

This intern initiated the process as she was writing this case study. However, most unfortunately, the supervisor did not support the intern's actions, Scott continued to refuse all medical attention and assistance with his hygiene and care, and the staff continued to provide comfort measures only. Scott died within one week.

Case Study I (*Aragon*)

Beauchamp, T., & Childress, J. (2009). *Principles of biomedical ethics*. New York: Oxford University Press.

Berry, R. (2011). Survey on challenging behaviour in case homes. *The Journal of Quality Research in Dementia*, issue 2. London: Alzheimer's Society.

California Government, www.leginfo.ca.gov

Dolgoff, R., Harrington, D., & Loewenberg, F. (2012). *Ethical decisions for social work practice* (9th ed.). Belmont, CA: Brooks/Cole.

Gewirth, Alan (1980). *Reason and morality*. Chicago: University of Chicago Press.

_____ Policy and Procedure Manual (2010).

Mayo Clinic, www.mayoclinic.com/health/vascular-dementia/DS00934, downloaded March 2012.

National Association of Social Workers (2009). *NASW code of ethics*. Washington, DC: NASW Press.

National Library of Medicine, www.nlm.nih.gov/hmd/Greek/GreekOath/html, downloaded April 2012.

Nurse Alliance (May 2011). Violence in California's Mental Health Hospitals, www.nursealliance.org//SEIU-1000-Research_white-paper_DMH, downloaded April 2012.

Nursing World, NursingCodeofEthics/nursingworld.org/MainMenuCategories/ThePracticeofProfessionalNursing/Ethics Standards/CodeofEthics, downloaded April 2012.

Rothman, J. (2011). *From the front lines: Student cases in social work ethics* (3rd ed.). Boston: Allyn & Bacon.

Yassi, A., Cohen, M., Cvitkovich, Y., et al. (2004, March–April). Factors associated with staff injuries in intermediate care facilities in British Columbia, Canada. *Nursing Research*, 53(2), 1–12.

Case Study J   Colleague Misconduct: If Nothing Harmful Really Happened, Do I Still Have To Report?

Abstracted from an unpublished paper by Rosa Lutrario, MSW

Practice Context and Case Presentation

A community mental health agency, under contract to a county mental health agency, provides language-appropriate and culturally sensitive mental health services at several sites such as outpatient clinics and schools in a large urban center. Clinicians are required to maintain standardized, careful, and thorough documentation of all services provided to their clients on a regular and timely basis. Services are billed to Medical Assistance, state, or county insurance programs.

Quality assurance of record-keeping is an essential ongoing process. Internally, the agency conducts "peer reviews," through which staff members review clinicians' documentation in order to identify missing paperwork in client charts, signatures that need to be obtained by the clinician, and anything else that may be required to meet legal and administrative standards. This internal review process is designed to prepare the agency for external reviews from the county agency, and to ensure compliance with necessary billing requirements. Failure to have adequate documentation for services rendered results in the denial of claims and withholding of funds by insurers.

During the peer-review process, the content of therapeutic notes written by clinicians is also scrutinized, in order to ensure that they are thorough and complete, and utilize a standardized content. For most notes, the standard content includes a statement of the need for a particular treatment intervention, observation of the client's behaviors or presenting problem, a description of the intervention performed on that particular day, observations of the client's response to the intervention, and a plan for future action. The template is designed to ensure accountability to funding sources, to help clinicians track progress in meeting the goals and objectives specified in treatment plans, and to inform future clinicians of the therapeutic work done with a particular client.

The pressure to produce and maintain thorough notes is high, and for some clinicians, the demands of documentation can become overwhelming. This was indeed the case for one experienced clinician, who had been working at a school-based site for many years. During his most recent peer review, a majority of his notes from the previous year were deemed unsatisfactory by the reviewers. The major issue with his documentation was that notes on many charts, belonging to many different clients, were actually identical to one another. Thus, the notes did not track the therapeutic progress of clients, did not meet financial accountability criteria, and did not maintain a record of treatment to inform future clinicians who may inherit the case. The peer-review committee requested that he immediately correct, and accurately document, all of his contacts with clients.

The clinician did not know this second year MSW intern well, as they worked at different sites. Perhaps because of this, he approached her with a proposition that presented a very serious ethical dilemma: He proposed to pay the intern to "fix" his notes. He framed the problem as a personal, as well as a professional, crisis. He explained that he was in danger of losing his job over the results of this peer review. He was given a short amount of time to correct all of his notes, which seemed an impossible task to him. He stated that he had decided to approach the intern because she was familiar with the agency's expectations regarding notes, and as a graduate student, he thought she would likely be interested in making some extra money.

A discussion followed during which the clinician explained his expectations regarding how the intern could make the notes in question satisfactorily meet requirements. Essentially, the intern was asked to fabricate interventions with clients she never met, and then creatively describe the clients' responses. The clinician stated that he was unconcerned about ethical considerations because he held, as his highest professional value, the well-being of his clients, and the quality of his *actual* interventions with them, and not how well that work was reflected in his notes.

> **Generally, the accepted rule in social work settings is, "If it's not documented, it didn't occur."**

The clinician explained that he has a caseload of long-term clients whom he sees on a weekly basis. Often, according to him, the sessions are very similar in content and style, and he practices similar interventions with many different clients repeatedly over time. As an example: He might engage clients in a play therapy approach for several sessions, with the goal of helping each to develop an awareness of his or her internal emotional state; or, he might engage clients in a cognitive-behavioral intervention for several sessions, during which they focus on extinguishing a specified behavior in the classroom. From his perspective, trying to find creative ways of saying the same thing is a waste of time, which was his justification for using the shortcut of recycling the same clinical note.

This intern declined the proposition to help the clinician modify his notes. However, she was left with the difficult ethical dilemma of whether or not to report his request of her as some form of misconduct. The clinician had specifically requested that the intern not mention anything about the proposition to her supervisor, or to anyone at the agency. In an effort to make peace with the clinician over this embarrassing situation, and her refusal of his request, the intern had hastily agreed to keep the matter secret.

The primary issue to resolve in this dilemma seemed to be whether or not there was any misconduct in what had occurred. Was an unethical action averted, or was the clinician's proposition misconduct in itself? By keeping the matter secret, was this intern colluding in an unethical situation? Does the proposal in itself reveal that this clinician is, or might be, unethical in other aspects of his work with clients? How would a manager, or another clinician, have responded to his proposal?

The dilemma can be framed in several ways, but, for the purpose of this analysis, it is framed as:

Responsibility to Agency v. Responsibility to Colleague

Research and Related Literature

The agency's policy on misconduct provides some guidance in addressing this dilemma. According to the agency's Personnel Manual protocol,

> Any person who has knowledge of or, in good faith, suspects any wrongdoing in the documenting, coding, or billing for services, equipment, or supplies, in this agency's financial practices, or violation of the Standards of Conduct should report it internally so that an investigation can be conducted and appropriate action taken. (_____Personnel Manual, 2011)

The policy further elaborates:

> Wrongdoing includes billing for services not performed at all, or not performed as described; submission of claims for unnecessary or undocumented services, equipment, or supplies; double billing. (_____Personnel Manual, 2011)

The agency policy seems clear: If this intern had agreed to help the clinician, wrongdoing would have occurred. According to Frederick Reamer (1990), who draws from moral philosopher Alan Gewirth to propose a guide for ethical decision making, "The obligation to obey laws, rules, and regulations to which one has voluntarily and freely consented ordinarily overrides one's right to engage voluntarily and freely in a manner which conflicts with these laws, rules, and regulations" (Reamer, p. 64). Clearly, had actions been taken, there would have been an obligation to report.

In this case, however, wrongdoing on the part of the intern did not occur. In order to determine if an actual wrong was committed by the clinician which should be reported, it is helpful to consider the differences related to the theoretical standpoint being applied. From a deontological perspective, the motive is most essential in determining the quality of the action, whereas from a teleological point of view, the actual result determines the rightness (Rothman, 2011, p. 8). In this specific situation, therefore, a deontological point of view would suggest that the therapist's motive to commit a wrongdoing warrants attention, whereas a teleological point of view might indicate that no action needs to be taken by this intern because no notes were actually falsified.

One of the challenging issues also involves whether the intern suspects that the clinician's behavior and request might indicate that there may be possible wrongdoing in the future. Might this clinician approach someone else within the agency to help him commit this fraud? Perhaps this clinician would decide to modify his own notes, but with no actual memory of specific events that occurred during each separate client contact, might plan to make up the information in the notes regardless? The potential harm might involve actual client treatment, as well as falsified documentation.

It may also be helpful to consider the degree of violation presented by this situation. The agency policy presented earlier does not dictate how to handle every specific instance of misconduct, from very grave to very minor. Rather, it presents some general guidelines. Reamer (1990) notes the need to "distinguish between actions which appear to have *broken* rules, and those which appear to have *bent* them" (Reamer, p. 220). This distinction is important because it has implications for how to respond. He urges that "Before a practitioner decides to report a colleague for violating a law or policy, he or she should consider carefully whether the wrongdoing might be remedied in a way that would not require disclosure to an agency official" (Reamer, p. 221).

Dolgoff, Loewenberg, and Harrington (2009) suggest an equally cautious approach, noting a variety of courses of action and rationales in addressing colleague misconduct. These include ascertaining that the behavior won't continue, punishing the perpetrator of the behavior, identifying the colleague so that others will not refer to or utilize the clinician, warning others not to engage in a similar behavior, and ensuring that the public is aware that the profession does not sanction the behavior (Dolgoff, Loewenberg, & Harrington, p. 164).

In this instance, reporting might provide the agency with more information regarding the character and professional conduct of this therapist. It is possible that this incident may be just another in a series of incidents that have been problematic with this clinician, of which this intern is unaware. Because the agency is unionized, terminating a clinician involves a process of documenting misconduct. If other instances of misconduct have already been documented, this additional one may support an ongoing investigation.

According to the agency's Personnel Manual, if a report is made that suggests "substantial charges" of misconduct, a proscribed investigation will be launched (Appendix I, p. 2):

> The purpose of the investigation is to identify situations in which applicable Federal or State laws, including the laws, regulations and standards of the Medicare and Medicaid programs, or the requirements of the agency compliance program may not have been followed, to identify individuals who may have knowingly or inadvertently violated the law or the agency's compliance program requirements, to facilitate the correction of any violations or misconduct, to implement procedures necessary to ensure future compliance, to protect the agency in the event of civil or criminal enforcement actions, and to preserve and protect the agency's assets. (_____ Personnel Manual, 2011)

However, as Reamer (1990) suggests, the obligation to obey an agency policy is itself not absolute. He states that "Situations can arise where, because of a threat to an individual's basic well-being, a law, rule or regulation can justifiably be violated" (Reamer, p. 223). In this situation, the possibility exists that reporting the incident may affect the well-being of the clinician's clients. Terminating the clinician due to documentation failures, an administrative matter, may negatively impact the progress of the work with his individual clients, and thus their basic well-being.

In support of this consideration, research on the therapeutic treatment of children suggests the importance of maintaining stable adult relationships in their lives in order to heal disrupted attachments and associated psychopathology (Kobak, Little, Race, & Acosta, 2001, p. 255). The research on attachment and early termination of the therapeutic relationship is significant in this instance because this clinician practices at a middle school, and all of his client population are children who might be adversely affected by premature termination of treatment. A study regarding the treatment of emotionally disturbed children found that the "greatest need of children who have experienced major disruptions in their attachment relationships is to establish a secure relationship with an adult" (Kobak et al., p. 255). A child's clinician is a prime example of such an attachment figure. Howe and Fearnley propose that "Therapy aims to create a 'corrective emotional experience' which approximates to what should have occurred in the child's formative years" (Howe & Fearnley, 2003, p. 381).

Furthermore, in a study that examined the transition of children in foster care from one home to another, it was emphasized that "consistent contact with the therapist and extensive preparation for treatment termination are essential to the successful fostering of a child's sense of safety and control within the context of relationships. When permanency decisions are made without extensive preparation, foster care children are often forced to prematurely terminate treatment. This kind of termination reenacts the child's experience of attachment-based trauma, significantly endangering the capacity to preserve the newly created relational template" (Miller, 2011, p. 65).

In order to understand the impact that terminating the clinician may have on his clients' lives, it is also important to consider the possibility of transfer to another clinician. Agency policy mandates that clients be evaluated for their need to continue to receive services after the departure of a clinician. However, there is an *informal* policy of terminating clients whose clinicians leave the agency, unless there is a significant need to continue therapy. This determination is made through the clinical judgment of the departing clinician and his or her supervisor. Thus, it can be assumed that clients in severe distress will continue to receive ongoing support through another clinician, which may somewhat mitigate the effect of the separation, but a disrupted attachment occurs nonetheless. The assumption here, however, is that the clinician's clients have some level of attachment to him; it is also possible that they do not, but client confidentiality and the inaccurate record-keeping render accurate assessment of this issue impossible.

The selfless consideration of duty to agency and to clients underlies many of the considerations in this matter, but there are also real and personal factors weighing upon this intern that must affect the ultimate decision that is taken. One of these is the personal right to protect oneself from retaliation—a real issue in collegial ethical matters that involve reporting misconduct. The intern would like to maintain a good rapport with the agency, and individual staff members, in the hope of completing her internship with relative harmony, and with the further hope of continuing with the agency as an employee upon graduation. Blowing the whistle on this coworker potentially jeopardizes her present as well as future position with the agency.

Agency policy stipulates that "retaliation or reprisal in any form against anyone who makes a report of wrongdoing, cooperates in an investigation, or participates in the compliance program is strictly prohibited," and that "The Human Resource Director shall maintain a confidential log in a secure place of all reports of compliance concerns and shall update the Board of Directors once a year" (_____ Personnel Manual, Appendix I, p. 2). The policy builds in a measure of protection for the intern; however, should she report the clinician's misconduct, it is also very likely that the individuals responsible addressing it will also be the same individuals involved in the agency's hiring process. The policy does not indicate that individuals conducting an investigation, or participating in the process of a misconduct claim, should recuse themselves from participating in a job interview panel, and the intern is not aware of their feelings regarding this clinician or reporting misconduct.

In support of protecting her own interests, Reamer (1990) suggests that the obligation to report is not absolute. A three-part guideline for determining the limits of obligation is suggested: "First, one must consider both the kind and degree of harm which threatens another person…Second, we must consider the extent to which individuals in need are able to help themselves…Finally, we must consider the extent to which providing assistance to others threatens our own well-being" (Reamer, p. 187). With the evaluation of these factors, it is important to note that choosing not to act may be a valid action in itself.

NASW's Code of Ethics should also be consulted for guidance in considering a colleague's misconduct. Section 2.11 of the Code suggests that social workers take measures to address unethical conduct by colleagues, that they be familiar with policies and procedures for handling such issues, should attempt to resolve the issue by discussing it with the colleague if possible, and then, if necessary, should utilize formal channels to address the concern (NASW, 2012).

Critical Thinking

Practice Behavior Example: "Whistle-blowing" is a difficult action for social workers to take, and presumes a clear understanding of wrongdoing, its repercussions, and also potential personal effects on the whistle-blower.

Critical Thinking Question: What are some of the considerations you would want to address before making a decision to "blow the whistle" on a colleague or on an agency?

The Code defines various options and suggests that different types of misconduct warrant different actions, to be evaluated by the social worker in conjunction with other professional values. Some of these are included in Section 2.01, which includes treating colleagues with respect and representing them fairly to others, as well as avoiding "unwarranted negative criticism" (NASW, 2012, Section 2.01). However, the Code does not provide any specific guidance regarding reporting misconduct that a colleague was planning but that, to this intern's knowledge, did not actually occur.

This option also follows NASW Code Section 2.03, which suggests that "Social workers who are members of an interdisciplinary team should participate in and contribute to decisions that affect the well-being of clients by drawing on the perspectives, values, and experiences of the social work profession" (NASW, Section 2.03).

In consultation, social workers should also provide consultant with the "least amount of information necessary" (NASW, Section 2.05) in order to respect privacy.

Author's Reflection, Reasoning Process, and Resolution

In addition to considerations grounded in ethical theory, agency policy, and professional social work values and standards, other considerations, which include the intern's family, peer group, and cultural heritage, as well as personal and cultural values must also be considered.

One personal value drawn from these sources is that "whistle-blowing" or "snitching" is an option of last resort. It is the mark of an individual who is not loyal to friends, and consequently, may not have many friends. Within the intern's value system, snitching often indicates some weakness of character, such as a manifestation of jealousy, or evidence of little faith in other individuals in the community's ability to assess for themselves the need for action. There is also the idea that if an individual does something wrong, it will become a public issue eventually; therefore, there is no need for any individual to make the matter public: things will take care of themselves.

Another personal value is the intern's real appreciation for collaboration between colleagues. Team values such as working together, utilizing consultation, and turning to others for help when necessary complicate the intern's approach to this particular ethical dilemma, as well as the intern's feelings toward the clinician. These team values were evident in the intern's initial desire to be helpful to the clinician in "fixing" his notes, and more inclined toward understanding his motives. However, his request that she remain quiet about the proposition is contrary to the value of collaboration, giving her a more negative perspective on his request.

Also significant to this discussion is the personal value of empathy. To be critical of this clinician without having empathy for his difficult circumstances would feel wrong. Empathy is also part of the agency's culture, and is valued for healing. The intern is aware that all clinicians at this agency have struggled at one point or another to keep accurate notes; this makes the dilemma more poignant, eliciting empathy from the intern and probably from other clinicians as well.

Finally, this intern values giving people the benefit of the doubt. While the clinician's motives are questionable, and while she is concerned with future wrongdoing, she would like to give him the benefit of the doubt, and assume that the discussion of her ethical concerns would make the clinician reconsider his options. Others at the agency might not agree with her, and may be concerned about the possible negative impact of his behavior on the agency's future.

There are several different options for action to resolve this dilemma. Each of them carefully weighs the various factors and falls to one side or the other depending on the values that take precedence.

Option One: To approach the clinician for discussion without making a formal report. In considering this approach, the intern takes a teleological approach, given the fact that the intern has no evidence of actual wrongdoing. This supports her personal value of giving people the benefit of the doubt, and assumes that the clinician is sufficiently deterred by the intern's rejection of his proposition. Trusting the clinician's statement that he will not engage in future wrongdoing also resolves the intern's obligation to support the agency's policy by reporting the incident, for it eliminates the "suspicion of wrongdoing," which the agency stipulates as a condition that warrants making a formal report.

This position is also consonant with the NASW Code of Ethics' statement that "Social workers who believe that a colleague has acted unethically should seek resolution by discussing their concerns with the colleague when feasible and when such discussion is likely to be productive" (NASW, 2012). This course of action also supports Dolgoff et al.'s suggestions that one must "ensure discontinuance of unethical behavior" (Dolgoff, Loewenberg, & Harrington, p. 164).

The intern judges that choosing not to report does not immediately endanger clients, and actually protects them from the negative impact of the clinician's possible termination for a nonclinical policy violation. The intern's personal value of giving people the benefit of the doubt and assuming that there is no further wrongdoing, or that the therapist conducts himself ethically in clinical matters is supported.

Option Two: Consult with supervisor and follow supervisor's suggestions for action. Consulting with the supervisor is supported by Section 2.03 of the Code, which advises social workers to draw on the "perspectives, values, and experience" of team members to address ethical issues that affect client well-being, as this issue does (NASW, Section 2.03). The supervisor's role is also to support supervisees' decision making, which can best be done through consultation. This approach is consonant with the intern's personal value of working collaboratively as well, and the intern would be able to consult with supervisor without revealing the identity of the social worker involved in order to protect him pending supervisory advice. In this option, the intern does not need to initiate a formal action against the colleague unless this is recommended by the supervisor. Should the supervisor believe that no formal action is necessary, the intern would be supported in following this course of action as well, and be able to avoid "unwarranted negative criticism," as suggested in Section 2.01 of the Code (NASW, Section 2.01).

Option Three: File a formal complaint. In this scenario, the intern takes a deontological position, considering that a wrong has been committed because the therapist intended to commit fraud. This approach considers that the clinician has *broken* a rule rather than *bent* it. The clinician's judgment is called into question, raising the suspicion that he may also be harming clients in some other way. Given the high level of "suspicion of wrongdoing" in this scenario, the intern has a compelling motive to follow agency protocol. The values follow Reamer's concept of the responsibility to obey laws, rules, and regulations to which one has voluntarily and freely consented (1990).

Clients would thus be protected from this unethical clinician and assigned to a more ethical therapist. The clinician would be sanctioned for his transgression. Drawing from the NASW Code of Ethics, this decision assures that the intern is taking adequate measures to "discourage, prevent, expose, and correct the unethical conduct" (2012).

Option Four: Do nothing—no discussion, no contact, no complaint. This option supports a teleological position and dismisses the dilemma because no harm was done. In choosing this option, the intern would support her personal value of "not snitching" on a colleague, and would also relieve her from possibly difficult and unpleasant confrontations and complaint procedures that the other approaches might require.

Course of Action. At the time that this intern formulated the options above, she had not yet resolved her dilemma. She was inclined to choose the first course of action, which involved having a discussion with her colleague. If the suspicions of the intern were not fully allayed by the conversation, then another option would be selected.

In the meantime, the values and ethical considerations that prevailed in her decision-making process were those that considered limits on the need to report. It was unclear from the information available how the clients would be affected, so that this essential factor cannot readily be included in decision making. Ethical theory—deontological and teleological—leads to different courses of action, but the choice between them presents no strong imperative.

However, the social worker's personal values, her tendency to collaborate, empathize, and give the benefit of the doubt, to disdain "snitching," and the concern that reporting would negatively impact her position at the agency suggest a course of action that did not involve reporting.

All of the professional and personal values explored in this decision-making process leave the door open for the intern to choose a more aggressive and public stance in the future if this seems warranted. If someone were ill and requiring a time-sensitive medical treatment, it would be essential to make to resolve the dilemma quickly, but here, expediency did not seem to be essential, so a decision did not appear critical at this moment in time. One limitation to this was the threat that the agency may be audited at any point by the county, and that the therapist's notes may draw attention and cause problems for agency funding, but the likelihood of that happening within the time frame needed by the intern to complete her service is slim. If there is notification of an audit, the intern would have the chance to move quickly on the reporting process. In the meantime, this intern is happy to bide a little more time, and, possibly, to complete her internship without making a final decision. However—no decision *is* a decision, and Option 4, by default, would be the choice that has been made.

In reviewing this material, during her last week of internship, a decision was finally made: Option 2 was selected, and the intern met with her supervisor to share her dilemma, keeping the identity of the clinician confidential. This supported Section 2.05 of the Code by maintaining privacy. Her supervisor felt strongly that she needed to advise the clinician to self-disclose to the mental health manager, telling the manager that the pressure to address necessary revisions was so great that assistance was needed with the project. This course of action would present the reality of the pressure the clinician is feeling, with perhaps the suggestion that more frequent chart reviews would enable any charting issues to be addressed before they became so overwhelmingly daunting. In the remaining days, this intern will consider how best to follow the supervisor's advice.

Case Study J (*Lutrario*)

Dolgoff, R., Loewenberg, F., & Harrington, D. (2009). *Ethical decisions for social work practice* (8th ed.). Belmont, CA: Brooks/Cole.

Howe, D., & Fearnley, S. (2003). Disorders of attachment in adopted and fostered children: Recognition and treatment. *Clinical Child Psychology and Psychiatry. Special Issue: Adoption and Fostering, 8*(3), 369–387.

Kobak, R., Little, M., Race, E., & Acosta, M. C. (2001). Attachment disruptions in seriously emotionally disturbed children: Implications for treatment. *Attachment & Human Development. Special Issue: Attachment in Mental Health Institutions, 3*(3), 243–258.

Miller, S. E. (2011). Fostering attachment in the face of systemic disruption: Clinical treatment with children in foster care and the adoption and safe families act. *Smith College Studies in Social Work, 81*(1), 62–80.

National Association of Social Workers. (2012). Code of Ethics, http://www.naswdc.org/pubs/code/code.asp

Reamer, F. (1990). *Ethical dilemmas in social work practice*. New York, NY: Columbia.

Rothman, J. (2011). *From the front lines: Student cases in social work ethics* (3rd ed.). Boston, MA: Allyn & Bacon.

CHAPTER SUMMARY

Ethical Standard Two addresses professional relationship with colleagues. This is a particularly challenging issue for social work professionals, who must balance collegial relationships, agency function, decision-making hierarchies, client interests, and, often, personal relationships with colleagues as well. In addition to these concerns, social work students also must consider their own positions as students, which create special vulnerabilities in interventions with colleagues. These vulnerabilities, and the concerns that flow from them, are poignantly addressed in each of the three cases presented.

In considering conduct of colleagues, this standard offers clear guidelines: When a worker has determined that a colleague's behavior is unprofessional, incompetent, impaired, or unethical, the first step should be to dialogue with the colleague if at all possible. This in itself may be a daunting project, especially if the colleague is in a hierarchically higher position than the social worker. Confronting a supervisor, a program director, or an agency director may pose special challenges and concerns, but these can be mitigated by a review of the guidance the Code provides and by considering the most viable approach to the problem.

With the burgeoning diversity in our client populations, working with non–English speaking clients is a common professional issue, as the author of the first case notes. Special attention must be given to ensure clear understanding for both client and social worker—of both verbal and nonverbal communication. It is important for social workers to *learn* how to use interpreters in practice: how to communicate directly with the client, how to position oneself and the interpreter, and how to phrase questions and comments that are functional within the client's culture. Social workers can observe the interpretation process, as well as read literature to enhance practice across language.

If a social worker is even somewhat proficient in a language, she or he may be called upon to interpret for clients and social workers. Before engaging in this "helpful" activity, it is important to consider the ethical dimensions: does this violate client privacy; does the worker's level of language familiarity enable her or him to provide the *professional* interpretation which might be necessary to ensure accuracy; is interpreting for other social workers impacting the social worker's own caseload and responsibilities; will the social worker be able to remain completely detached from the events and experiences she or he is translating, and others. In the case presented, the social worker both respects her client's cultural sensitivity and addresses her concerns as a professional.

Vulnerability with a capital "V" is central to the second case presented, where the intern is faced with attempting to determine whose vulnerability she must consider first: her patient's, her own, or her heal are colleagues'. Responsibility to her client, who is unable to communicate and is experiencing both pain and stress, seems at first to be the obvious choice. However, research regarding staff safety in mental health setting reveals that there is indeed a much higher incidence of injury in these settings, and that staff can become stressed from attempting to address the needs of this group of patients. Her own personal concerns are heightened by her awareness that her supervisor has agreed with the ethics committee decision, and thus might view the student's ethical concerns as a criticism of her own actions should she attempt to address them.

The intern determines that the best course of action for all concerned is to have a court-appointed conservator of person work with the patient and determine how best his needs might be met. Though this option appeared reasonable and feasible, and the student initiated the conservatorship process, she did not have the support of her supervisor or of the staff. The patient's untimely demise resolved the immediate situation.

The intern in the third case presented her dilemma to the class during the course of the semester, and it engendered a lively class discussion. If there is the intent to commit misconduct, but it does not actually occur, is there an ethical obligation to act? Ethical theory points clearly in both directions, depending on the theory selected. The Code of Ethics does not address this particular concern. Personal values include not "snitching"—yet there is a concern for the potential harm that may occur to the clinician's young clients should records be falsified in any way. Several sources suggest that it is important to distinguish between types of misconduct, or whether rules have been "broken" or merely "bent."

After considering various options, the intern chooses to consult with her supervisor, keeping the identity of the clinician involved confidential, and thus respecting his request for privacy. The intern reasons that the supervisor's advice would be helpful in supporting her decision, and that consultation is advised by the Code of Ethics. The supervisor provides the intern with guidance without asking for the identity of the clinician involved. However, the advice asks the intern to reopen the discussion with the clinician, and we are left with the open question of whether the intern will follow the supervisor's advice.

This chapter has served to raise some very challenging and difficult issues, and it is hoped that readers will consider this ethical standard carefully: It has much impact on professional functioning!

The following questions will test your knowledge of the content found within this chapter. For questions 1-6, please select the phrase that best completes each sentence. Question 7 is a brief essay question. For additional assessment, including licensing-exam type questions on applying chapter content to practice behaviors, visit **MySearchLab**.

1. When a worker is aware of colleague misconduct, the first action step to consider is:
   a. consulting with a supervisor
   b. talking with the colleague involved
   c. reporting the misconduct to NASW
   d. addressing the misconduct at a staff meeting

2. Sexual harassment includes all except:
   a. sexual advances
   b. requests for sexual favors
   c. discussion of sexual issues in therapy
   d. inappropriate touching

3. Social workers should always consult with colleagues:
   a. when collegial knowledge and expertise might benefit clients
   b. when clients are requesting it
   c. when there is inadequate documentation
   d. when supervisors are unavailable

4. Interpretation services by agency staff:
   a. may be harmful to clients
   b. can be provided if there is no funding available
   c. is common in most agencies
   d. is against the law

5. *Parens patriae* means that:
   a. parents are responsible for their children
   b. the social worker must sometimes act as the parent to protect clients
   c. vulnerable clients need parents to act for them
   d. ultimate responsibility for vulnerable people rests with the state

6. Official agency policies tend to be:
   a. clear, specific, and concisely stated
   b. broad and subject to interpretation
   c. determined by all agency social workers
   d. the responsibility of the agency director

7. Sexual activities with supervisees, students, trainees, and others over whom a supervisor exercises professional authority are prohibited by 2.07 of the Code of Ethics. Why are these proscribed? What are the ethical dimensions of this proscription?

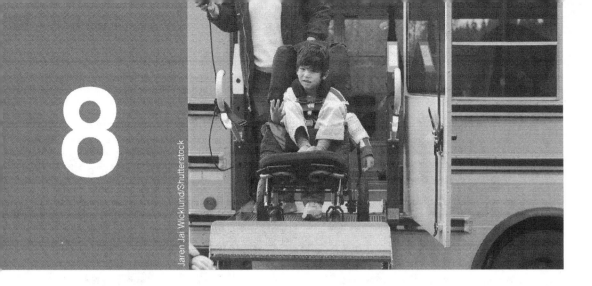
Jaren Jai Wicklund/Shutterstock

8

NASW Ethical Standard Three

Social Workers' Ethical Responsibilities to Practice Settings

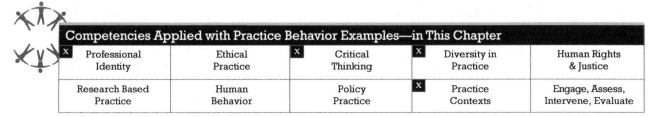

Competencies Applied with Practice Behavior Examples—in This Chapter				
x Professional Identity	Ethical Practice	x Critical Thinking	x Diversity in Practice	Human Rights & Justice
Research Based Practice	Human Behavior	Policy Practice	x Practice Contexts	Engage, Assess, Intervene, Evaluate

INTRODUCTION

When a professional social worker is hired by an organization, there are generally both explicit and implicit terms to which both parties agree. On the part of the worker, these might include loyalty and fidelity to the mission and purposes of the organization; the responsible use of resources, including one's own time and expertise; and adherence to the organization's policies and procedures. The worker should also seek to prevent and eliminate discrimination by the organization in terms of work assignments, policies, procedures, and services.

This section of the NASW Code of Ethics (2008) calls for particularly careful and reflective consideration. Because workers are generally very dedicated to the interests of their clients, there is often an assumption that these interests supersede their obligations to the agency when the two appear to conflict. Some common examples include instances where the client's behavior or actions violate agency policy and thus the terms of the service agreement, such as disregarding curfew at a residential treatment center, missing appointments for mandated services, having an outside, unreported job while receiving TANF (Temporary Assistance for Needy Families) funds, cheating on examinations in a school setting, or continuing to abuse drugs "occasionally" in a substance abuse treatment program that supports abstinence. In each of these cases, the client presents a strong argument in support of his or her action, an argument that the worker finds plausible and with which he or she can empathize. In addition, the client often has confided this information to the worker with the presumption that confidentiality will be observed.

The practice setting is the "big guy," and the client is the "little guy." What harm can a little infraction do to the agency, the worker reasons? Not much. The client's benefit can outweigh it. Besides, there are those sticky issues of trust, confidentiality, and relationship building.

However, the employer has given the worker a position of trust, in the expectation that this trust will not be violated. In addition, such behavior can seriously injure the organization. Nonadherence to policy often violates funding criteria and causes resources to be used inappropriately, thus deflecting the accomplishment of the agency's mission. It may also affect the availability of service to future clients. In addition, policies may reflect years of experience and careful reflection and are usually designed specifically to meet the stated mission and purpose of that particular setting. Do practice settings, as well as individuals, have a right to self-determination within certain parameters?

Siding with the client against the practice setting also affects the client's perception of self, the worker, and the agency. The client sees the worker colluding with him or her against the practice setting; thus, the organization, the source of help to which the client originally came, the very meeting ground that has brought client and worker together, is seen as the enemy. The client observes that the proscribed behavior is condoned by the worker, which can serve to reinforce it, cause the client to lose respect for the worker, or both. In violating agency policy, the worker is also modeling for the client behavior that is contrary to the ideals of honesty and integrity, which are integral to a well-functioning society.

There are other ethical issues in the relationship between a social worker and his or her agency that may create conflicts as well. The problems suggested above involve ethical issues between an agency and a client, with the worker caught in the middle. Other scenarios may relate primarily to the relationship between the worker and the employing agency. Many of these problems between the worker and the employer are related to policies with which the worker may disagree, or question. Out of concern for clients, workers often have difficulty with policies that compromise what may be viewed as the client's rights and interests on behalf of organizational efficiency, funding needs, or expediency.

In such cases, workers have several choices: They may privately disregard agency policies and procedures, thus violating their employment contract; they may publicly disregard them, thus undermining the authority and legitimacy of the agency; they may follow them, thus denying their own personal standards of ethics and justice, and possibly compromising clients' welfare; or they may follow them while advocating for change through the agency's own system, possibly compromising present clients but seeking to prevent the effect of such policies and procedures on future clients.

Where personal values, religious beliefs, cultural norms, or worldviews of individual social workers differ from those embedded in the agency's mission, policies, and programs, social workers may find themselves having to make uncomfortable choices by following agency guidelines out of a sense of responsibility to their employer, while violating personal beliefs and values, or undermining the agency's stance in order to be true to themselves. It is always best to address these potentially painful problems and ensure that this type of ethical conflict is minimized by familiarizing oneself with agency policies and procedures prior to employment. While this will ensure that such problems are at least minimized, even such precautions cannot always ensure that an administrator's, a supervisor's, or a committee's interpretation of policies and procedures will always be the same as the worker's.

Social workers also have the choice of going outside the agency to government bodies, licensing and/or funding sources, or to the general public in attempting to address issues of vital concern. They may also terminate their employment with the agency, thus releasing themselves from a "contract" that conflicts with personal values and worldview.

Provisions of the Code

Section 3 of the Code of Ethics addresses the relationship between the social worker and the practice setting specifically. Because supervision and consultation are an integral part of the functioning of the profession as a whole, the first subsection addresses these. It obligates supervisors and consultants to act only within their areas of expertise (3.01a) and maintain "clear and sensitive boundaries" (3.01b); it proscribes dual or multiple relationships where there is risk of harm to the supervisee (3.01c); and it requires that supervisee evaluations be "fair and respectful" (3.01d), on the basis of "clearly stated criteria" (3.03).

Education and training is a particularly important area within practice settings. Field instruction is a vital part of social work education, enabling students to experience and learn from actual client contact within a practice setting. The Code addresses competence and fairness for educators and field instructors (3.02a and b), proscribes dual or multiple relationships (3.02d), and requires that clients be routinely informed when a student provides services (3.02c).

Subsections 3.04a through 3.04d set guidelines for client records that support accuracy, timeliness, privacy, and storage and promote both the efficiency of the practice setting and a concern for the privacy and dignity of clients. The guidelines for privacy have become an extremely salient ethical issue in practice as electronic record-keeping has become common, creating

Social Workers employed in the criminal justice system have ethical responsibilities to both clients and government agencies.

the possibility of access to client records by others within the agency, and by other agencies or resources within the agency's network as well as funding sources. While electronic record-keeping may be more efficient and effective, issues of privacy and confidentiality must always be considered. How can workers be accurate and thorough in documentation, while knowing that clients' information may be viewed by others? This subsection also notes that billing practices should "accurately reflect the nature and extent of services" (3.05).

Subsection 3.06 addresses transfers of clients, suggesting that workers consider and discuss transfers with clients carefully in advance (3.06a). When a worker finds that a client has previously been served by another organization or colleague, the worker must discuss with the client "whether consultation with the previous service provider is in the client's best interest" (3.06b).

Administrators have the responsibility for (1) advocating for funds adequate to the clients' needs (3.07a) and ensuring that they are distributed within the agency in a nondiscriminatory manner (3.07b), (2) setting aside funds for adequate staff supervision (3.07c), and (3) staff development and continuing education (3.08). Administrators are also responsible for ensuring that their organization is in compliance with the NASW Code of Ethics (3.07d).

Subsection 3.09 addresses the worker's commitment to the agency, stating that workers should generally adhere to commitments (3.09a) and work to improve "policies and procedures" and the "efficiency and effectiveness" of services (3.09b). Social workers must ensure that employers are aware of the NASW Code of Ethics and their ethical obligations (3.09c) and not allow organizational policies to interfere with ethical practice (3.09d). This obligation would support the following one: preventing and eliminating discrimination (3.09e). During labor–management disputes, workers should "be guided by the profession's values, ethical principles, and ethical standards" (3.10b).

Ethical principles in the practice setting should also be explored when employment or field placement is planned (3.09f). Last, but surely not least, workers are obligated to be careful stewards of the resources of their organizations (3.09g).

THE CASES

The first case presented in this chapter addresses the issue of informed consent. The worker, employed by a mental health outpatient center, is confronted by an upset client, who claims that the consent form used by the agency is so broad and so general that she was left unaware of the implications of signing. She states that she would not have signed the form had she known of its potential applications. Initially agreeing with the client, the worker undertakes to examine agency policy in regard to informed consent, relating it to the agency's mission, clientele served, efficiency, and effectiveness. She then assumes a position of advocacy for change using the agency's structure for policy considerations.

Many social agencies work with ethnically and culturally diverse populations, and "sensitive" practice is an obligation of the worker, whose primary concern is the well-being of the client. The agency also purports to be concerned with the well-being of the client. The difficulty occurs when the client's perception of "well-being" is defined by a cultural perspective that differs from that espoused by the agency in defining this same "well-being." With obligations to both agency and client, how can a worker balance the two in order to provide service that both meets the needs of the client and fulfills the mission, policy, and program of the agency?

This ethical dilemma is clearly evident in the second case presented in this chapter. The adults in a Cambodian family, living in public housing, resist obtaining the education and language skills necessary for the achievement of the independence that is the goal of the program, in favor of traditional values of family unity and responsibility of children to parents, which it sees as primary. The family sees its "best interest" and strength as upholding the traditional Cambodian cultural values. The agency sees the family's "best interest" in achieving financial independence, learning the language of the new country, and, eventually, leaving the housing program—all Euro-American, "Western" goals established by the dominant societal system. The agency has structured its services to support and encourage these goals. How can the worker meet the needs of both client and agency?

In the third case, a worker in an employee assistance program (EAP) finds herself with a severe conflict of loyalties. She has been hired specifically to provide services that will enhance employees' work performances. She begins to work with a self-referred employee who is depressed and whose work performance is poor, but who tells her that her job is the only stability in her life, necessary to her support as well as her general functioning. Despite efforts on her part and on the part of the employee, performance does not improve with intervention. The worker realizes that her obligation to her employer demands that if she is unable to assist her client's performance to improve, she should bring the matter to the employee's supervisor to request help. However, she also knows that this action will call attention to the employee's problems and place her job in jeopardy. Whose interests must the worker consider primary?

In the fourth case, the intern's placement is in a host setting—a private hospital which serves an affluent community. Her patient, an alcoholic who was known to the hospital, is admitted to the trauma unit after a pedestrian-vehicular accident in which he was the pedestrian. He determines that this accident is a wake-up call, and wishes to try the hospital's inpatient detoxification program, which he has already failed numerous times. The patient is stabilized in the trauma unit. The physician, with the certain support of the hospital administration, does not feel that the patient will be successful in the program, and is requesting discharge for him, while the social worker is advocating for the patient to remain in the hospital awaiting a bed in the treatment unit. The issue appears to involve his history of failed attempts in the past, the immediate unavailability of a bed in the treatment unit, general resource-allocation issues, and the need to best utilize trauma service beds.

Case Study K   Can Limitation of Informed Consent by an Agency Ever Be Justified?

Abstracted from an unpublished paper by Diane Inselberg Spirer, MSW, M.S.

Practice Context and Case Presentation

A partial hospitalization program provides intensive treatment for adults whose problems do not require full hospitalization. The goal of the program is to assist individuals in attaining their optimal level of functioning in the community through the use of structured, intensive outpatient treatment. The program utilizes treatment modalities offered in inpatient settings, but in an environment that permits patients to interact more fully and effectively with the family and the community. Psycho-education and expressive therapies help patients set goals, practice new behaviors, and learn new skills.

Treatment is provided by a multidisciplinary staff, including psychiatrists, nurses, social workers, and expressive therapists. Goal-specific, individualized treatment plans are approved by a physician and include assessment and diagnosis; individual, group, and family therapy; expressive therapies; pharmacotherapy; psycho-education; and chemical dependency deprogramming.

Agency policy requires that clients have a therapist outside the program who will continue with them at the conclusion of their treatment with the agency. Close collaboration with the patient's outside therapist is an integral part of the program, and it provides a smooth transition to conventional outpatient treatment. Patients are informed prior to admission to the program verbally or in writing that collaboration with community therapists is an integral feature of the program. The staff will refer those patients who do not already have such a relationship to outside practitioners. The patient is requested to sign a consent to the release of information to the outside therapist on the first day of treatment. If the patient refuses to sign the form, or declines contact with an outside therapist, admission to the program is denied.

The consent to release information is a limited-consent form. The purpose of the disclosure to the outside professional, as written on the form, is "to facilitate treatment involvement and communication." The form indicates that the type of information to be disclosed consists of "information on patient progress, treatment and discharge planning, psychological evaluation."

A patient who has been in the program for six months expresses significant distress with the frequency and content of the agency's contact with her outside therapist. She states that the form she signed was not detailed and that she had not realized that the extent and content of the contacts were at the total discretion of the treatment team.

The worker became concerned with considering how the agency should craft its outside therapist consent form so as best to meet its mission of providing successful treatment. Could this best be achieved by providing clients with a comprehensive informed consent form, which details all situations in which an outside therapist will be notified, or by having a limited, briefer informed consent form, which preserves the agency's flexibility in providing treatment?

From the client's perspective, comprehensive informed consent might be viewed as empowering, upholding autonomy, and furthering self-determination. It provides clear guidance and structure to the agency staff members in contacts with outside therapists. However, it limits agency flexibility. Thus, fully comprehensive informed consent forms empower the client, but may impede successful treatment; limited-informed consent empowers the therapist in treatment, but may limit the patient's autonomy. The dilemma may be stated as follows:

> **To be fully valid, informed consent must include information that is complete, specific, and comprehensible; the client must be competent to consent, and consent freely and voluntarily, free of constraints or coercion.**

INFORMED CONSENT V. OPTIMAL FULFILLMENT OF AGENCY'S MISSION

Research And Related Literature

Social work literature regarding informed consent issues may offer little specific guidance (Reamer, 1987). Indeed, confusion over this issue tends to persist both within and among professional groups (Lindenthal & Thomas, 1984).

In the late eighteenth century, Western physicians and scientists began to develop traditions that encouraged professionals to share information and decision making with their clients (Reamer, 1987). In 1914, the first major judicial ruling, *Schloendorff* v. *Society of New York Hospital*, upheld the right to self-determination in regard to one's own body (Reamer, 1987).

However, in support of the agency's limited-consent position, clients' competence affects their capability to give informed consent. Clients must be able to make choices, understand factual issues and their own situation, and manipulate information (Reamer, 1987). These capabilities may be seriously impaired in a severely disturbed individual whose cognitive faculties are influenced by the disturbed emotional state (Sehdev, 1976). Although an advance directive may provide a means for avoiding competency issues, it may be assumed that few such directives specifically deal with mental health treatment and the flexibility of professionals in making disclosures to outside therapists (Spirer, personal communication, 1995).

It is possible to question whether all clients are prepared, or even desirous, to assume full responsibility for self-direction. Individuals may have differing amounts of experience, physical or mental abilities, and ability to cope with frustration and disruption (Rothman, 1989). As mental illness is still a poorly understood phenomenon, one may question whether self-determination should not be superseded by a responsibility to prevent suffering (McGough & Carmichael, 1977).

Exceptions to the obligation of informed consent have centered on duty-to-warn cases, where there was a danger to a third party. Such legal cases include *Tarasoff* v. *Regents of the University of California, Lipari* v. *Sears, Roebuck & Co., Brady* v. *Hopper, Thompson* v. *County of Alameda, Jablonski by Pahls* v. *United States*, and *Shaw* v. *Glickman*, the last of which takes the opposing position and upholds confidentiality. Less clear is the obligation to violate informed consent for the sake of preventing injury to the person whose consent is violated, where the general safety of the public is not an issue. In any case, it is probably unlikely that all violations of comprehensive informed consent in this practice setting involve actual danger to the clients served.

Self-determination connotes free choice or self-direction on the part of the beneficiaries of professional helping services (Rothman, 1989), and it has been related to informed consent. It can be viewed as a basic human right, a vehicle for client improvement, an opportunity for learning coping skills, and a way of keeping public assistance agencies out of inappropriate areas of a client's life (Rothman, 1989). It has been seen as basic to human development, dignity, and freedom (Perlman, 1965).

The Constitution affords protection of self-determination and bodily integrity through judicial interpretation and application. Personal autonomy is seen as the fundamental right of each citizen to select and abide by his or her own values so long as he or she does not infringe on the rights of others (McGough & Carmichael, 1977).

Social workers' orientations to confidentiality management and their likelihood of breaking confidences in particular may relate to the nature of their professional role, which is relatively more vulnerable and probably more ambiguous than that of psychiatrists and psychologists. Thus, they might err in a conservative direction by disclosing information as a defensive strategy in response to an increasing number of legal decisions obligating disclosure. This role ambiguity and lack of legal knowledge regarding this issue possibly contributes to social workers' breaching of confidences in clinical situations (Lindenthal & Thomas, 1984).

The NASW Code of Ethics supports informed consent, based on the values of dignity and worth of the person, the importance of human relationships, and integrity, which further supports the ethical principle of trustworthiness for social workers. Obligations to clients are addressed in the first subsection of the first section of the Code, thereby giving them prominent place in guiding social workers' practice. Subsection 1.01 obligates workers to their clients as their primary responsibilities, while 1.02 defines the obligation "to promote the rights of clients to self-determination."

Although the terms *privacy* and *confidentiality* are often used interchangeably, they connote different things. "Privacy" supports noninterference by others in a person's property, thoughts, knowledge, and acts. "Confidentiality" involves a person's rights when private information is shared, includes the stipulation that such information will be utilized only for vital needs, and will be shared with others only with the individual's knowledge and consent.

There are five parts in the subsection on informed consent, which immediately follow. Subsections 1.03a and 1.03c are applicable to this dilemma and are thus quoted below in their entirety.

Social workers should provide services to clients only in the context of a professional relationship based, when appropriate, on valid informed consent. Social workers should use clear and understandable language to inform clients of the purpose of the service, risks related to the service, limits to services because of the requirements of a third-party payer, relevant costs, reasonable alternatives, clients' right to refuse or withdraw consent, and the time frame covered by the consent. Social workers should provide clients with an opportunity to ask questions. (1.03a)

In instances when clients lack the capacity to provide informed consent, social workers should protect clients' interests by seeking permission from an appropriate third party, informing clients consistent with the clients' level of understanding. In such instances social workers should seek to ensure that the third party acts in a manner consistent with clients' wishes and interests. Social workers should take reasonable steps to enhance such clients' ability to give informed consent. (1.03c)

Additional guidelines for privacy and confidentiality are specified in subsection 1.07 of the Code of Ethics:

Social workers should respect clients' right to privacy. (1.07a)

Social workers may disclose confidential information when appropriate with a valid consent from a client or a person legally authorized to consent on behalf of a client. (1.07b)

Social workers should protect the confidentiality of all information obtained in the course of professional service, except for compelling professional reasons....does not apply when disclosure is necessary to prevent serious, foreseeable, and imminent harm...social workers should disclose the least amount of confidential information necessary. (1.07c)

Social workers should inform clients, to the extent possible, about the disclosure...and the potential consequences, when feasible before the disclosure is made. (1.07d)

These statements appear to strongly support a comprehensive informed consent and/ or the maintenance of confidentiality. The client presented here is not in "clear, foreseeable, imminent danger" of harm in the extreme sense that appears to be alluded to in the Code. She has not been deemed legally incompetent, and thus has a right to act in her own behalf in terms of informed consent. However, a social worker's first ethical obligation is to service and to the client's best interests. These may be better furthered by providing information to her therapist, which will enable the provision of appropriate therapeutic services.

Author's Reflections, Reasoning Process, and Resolution

Professional values emphasize the primacy of the client's interests. However, competency issues also are recognized to affect how a social worker should appropriately respond to a client with mental illness and possible impairment in competence. Although the client signed the consent form that the agency required, she did not fully understand all the implications of what she was signing. Whether this was due to her mental disability or to ambiguity in the form and explanations offered is not clear. "Primacy of client interest" can be seen to support both sides of the dilemma: If getting well is the primary interest, an argument could be made for the looser, more limited form. If self-determination and autonomy is the primary interest, a comprehensive consent form would be required.

It is important to consider the societal values that might impact on this dilemma. These include self-determination and independence, autonomy and self-respect, trust in others and in oneself, and honesty. These would seem to support the "informed consent" side of the dilemma. However, one could say that for the client population served, the societal values could best be achieved by optimal treatment, which includes the flexibility on the part of the agency to maintain appropriate contact with the client's outside therapist.

This client, and probably the majority of the clients treated in the program, does value self-determination and autonomy very highly. She has established her treatment goals. She has, however, also chosen the program, read the information about the program, and signed the release of information consent form.

The worker's personal values also impact on the dilemma. Trust, truthfulness, acceptance, loyalty, sincerity, patience, wisdom, and knowledge as values caused the worker initially to favor a comprehensive informed consent for all agency clients.

The worker found two additional sources of ethical guidance useful in developing a resolution to this dilemma: the Bible and the Declaration of Independence. The Bible tells us to do unto others as we would have others do unto us. This brings the worker into the dilemma in a much more direct fashion: She needs to understand what she would prefer were she in the position of this client. This process of self-reflection can also be helpful in

Critical Thinking

Practice Behavior Example: In considering possible options, the worker has focused on two alternatives: continuing the use of the limited-consent form, or providing a comprehensive consent form, and cites the clients' mental condition as a rationale for choosing the limited form.

Critical Thinking: In considering the validity of any consent form obtained from a mentally impaired client, and in reflecting on all possible choices which might be available to the agency in meeting their clients' needs through the provision or services, what are some additional possible alternatives for resolving this dilemma?

understanding the client more fully. The Declaration of Independence includes this vital and basic statement: "[A]ll men are created equal, and are endowed by their Creator with certain unalienable rights: among these are life, liberty, and the pursuit of happiness." While these seem to support the self-determination and comprehensive informed consent position at first, later reflection on "the pursuit of happiness" might lead one to consider whether optimal mental health would be a great asset in this regard.

Aristotle saw the goal of human life as the achievement of happiness. We achieve happiness, he believed, through the fulfillment of our natural function, living a life with reason and moving always toward self-actualization. Following this line of thought does not provide much guidance either, however, for it is still unclear whether happiness can best be achieved, in this dilemma, by full-informed consent and the opportunity to refuse the help of the program, or by a limited-informed consent and the benefits the program can provide in terms of mental health.

The agency has integrated the use of an outside therapist as a necessary part of its program, and a condition of acceptance into the program is the signing of a consent form that allows the treatment team to share information with the outside therapist. The agency has determined that this is necessary to the fulfillment of its mission and goals: to assist clients to become independent and well-functioning members of society.

The use of a comprehensive consent form, which specifies all of the circumstances under which the agency may contact the outside therapist, supports the client's right to participate in determining when the intervention of the outside therapist would be useful. Comprehensive informed consent supports autonomy and self-determination and helps clarify the client's values, beliefs, and priorities. It assists in the development of a mutually supportive and trusting relationship between the client and the agency based on full knowledge and participation in all aspects of treatment.

The limited form currently in use acknowledges that the client may not be able to evaluate the need for outside intervention for the very reason that the client is seeking treatment: a disturbed emotional state. It can protect the client from harm in some circumstances and provide the information needed by an outside therapist, so that the best service can be rendered after the client's participation in the program is terminated. It preserves some self-determination in that the client has the right to refuse to sign the form as offered and thus refuse treatment with the program.

In trying to balance these competing positions and priorities, the worker would recommend the continuation of the use of a limited-consent form, with an additional statement added that defines the two instances in which the outside therapist may be contacted: for assistance in treatment and to provide notification of a threat to the client or the third party; stipulates that when possible, the client will be informed in advance of the contact; changes program policy to require that a reasonable effort to notify clients in advance of the contact of the outside therapist be made; and stresses the importance of the outside therapist to the treatment process.

This resolution was chosen because it was felt that comprehensive informed consent might be difficult for some clients to comprehend. A limited form would allow greater freedom and flexibility in tailoring the actions taken upon the needs of each individual client. However, the changes incorporated into the form would also serve to maximize self-determination as much as possible.

Case Study K (*Spirer*)

Beauchamp, T. L., & Childress, J. F. (2009). *Principles of biomedical ethics* (8th ed.). New York: Oxford University Press.

Cohen-Mansfield, J., Kerin, P., Pawlson, G., Lipson, S., & Coleman, N. (1988). Advance directives preserve autonomy despite incapacity. *Health and Social Work, 12*(1), 71–72.

Lindenthal, J. J., & Thomas, C. S. (1984). Attitudes toward confidentiality. *Social Work, 33*(2), 151–159.

McGough, L. S., & Carmichael, W. C. (1977). The right to treatment and the right to refuse treatment. *American Journal of Orthopsychiatry, 47*(2), 307–320.

National Association of Social Workers. (2008). *NASW code of ethics.* Washington, DC: Author.

Perlman, H. H. (1965). Self-determination: Reality or illusion? *Social Service Review, 39*, 410–421.

Reamer, F. G. (1987). Informed consent in social work. *Social Work, 32*(5), 425–429.

Reamer, F. G. (1990). *Ethical dilemmas in social service* (2nd ed.). New York: Columbia University Press.

Rothman, J. (1989). Client self-determination: Untangling the knot. *Social Service Review, 63*(4), 598–612.

Sehdev, H. S. (1976). Patients' rights or patients' neglect: The impact of the patients' rights movement on delivery systems. *American Journal of Orthopsychiatry, 46*(4), 660–669.

Case Study L   Meeting the Needs of Immigrants: Must Acculturation Be a Condition of Agency Service?

Abstracted from an unpublished paper by Thomas W. Gray, Ph.D., MSW

Practice Context and Case Presentation

Ms. Li and her five children live in a Section 8 public housing unit, supported primarily through public program funds. Her oldest daughter, Pareth Li, is enrolled in a GED course, but her attendance has been sporadic. She would like to complete high school, but feels strong obligations to her mother and the rest of the family. Her mother wants her at home to help with the children, handle various housekeeping responsibilities, and serve as interpreter as needed.

Ms. Li complains of headaches and difficulty sleeping. She dresses in traditional Cambodian garb. Her mother, father, and seven older brothers and sisters were murdered many years ago, and a Cambodian therapist has stated that she may be continuing to suffer from posttraumatic stress disorder. She has been defined programmatically as displacing child-rearing responsibilities onto her teenagers, particularly to the client, 19-year-old Pareth. But in the Cambodian culture, this is quite normal, even to be expected.

Social services within the housing development are oriented toward economic independence and movement out of low-income housing. Ms. Li has expressed a desire to learn English and has been scheduled for ESL classes, but she does not attend. Agency staff members have labeled her highly resistive: She says she will learn English when the children are grown. Her youngest child is 4 years old.

Pinderhughes (1989), in *Understanding Race, Ethnicity, and Power*, states that a counseling situation that ignores cultural issues is setting the client up for disempowerment and reoppression. Chan's (1992) work "contrasting beliefs, values, and practices," in *Developing Cross-Cultural Competence*, suggests 10 potential impasses in worker–client relationships that may be attributable to cultural differences between the Cambodian culture and the Eurocentric culture of the United States. These are included below, with Cambodian/Asian values listed first.

1. Family is understood as the primary unit versus the individual as the primary unit.
2. Family solidarity, responsibility, and harmony versus individual pursuit of happiness, fulfillment, and self-expression.
3. Continued dependence on family is fostered versus early independence is encouraged.
4. Hierarchical family roles and ascribed status are emphasized versus variable roles and achieved status.
5. Parent–child (parental) bond is stressed versus husband–wife (marital) bond is stressed.
6. Parent provides authority and expects unquestioning obedience and submission to structure versus parent provides guidance, support, explanations, and encourages curiosity and critical/independent thinking.
7. Family makes decisions for the child versus child is given many choices.
8. Children are the extension of parents versus children are individuals.
9. Parents ask: "What can you do to help me?" versus parents ask: "What can I do to help you?"
10. Older children are responsible for the siblings' actions versus each child is responsible for his or her own actions.

Many Eurocentric values are congruent with the values of the agency, such as individualistic focus, independence, and success/performance/achievement orientation. The ethical dilemma then becomes honoring culturally specific family structures and life orientations versus following agency program and policies. It can be stated as follows:

CLIENT SELF-DETERMINATION V. AGENCY POLICY AND VALUES

Research And Related Literature

Honoring Culturally Specific Family Structures and Cambodian Life Orientations. Draine and Hall (1986) state: "Cultural understanding in one's...culture occurs early and is typically established by age 5." We use these groundings to interpret our reality and to think, feel, and behave in a manner that provides safety and adaptiveness. Our culture becomes an integral part of our lives, and we become culturally programmed. As such, it remains outside of our conscious awareness.

When attempting to function within a second culture, we continue to interpret reality with our original, culturally specific cognitive structures, assuming that these interpretations are "right." These orientations may be ineffective for cross-cultural work. Client discomfort may be expressed in such emotional or physical ways as "frustration, anger, depression, withdrawal, lethargy, aggression, and/or illness" (Lynch & Hanson, 1992, p. 24). Both clients and workers may distance themselves from the client–worker relationship as a result of such personal discomfort.

Axelson (1993, pp. 43–44) suggests that cultural minorities may choose one or a combination of four positions in cross-cultural situations: (1) They may accept mainstream conditions to the extent of reducing primary group identity and suppressing various personal psychological needs "in order to gain success." (2) They may compromise with mainstream standards by blending and harmonizing distinctive cultural aspects with demands of the larger society. (3) They may revolt against the dominant cultural conditions, seeking to change the standards of "acceptable behavior." (4) They may withdraw "into the security of familiar cultural ... patterns with which the person most clearly identifies and ... can readily gain self-respect," providing for personal needs for security, status, and social relationships. Each position is espoused at a price: The first can frequently result in ridicule from the primary group. The second can be extremely stressful, demanding constant personal monitoring to bring congruency in many social roles. The third can be fraught with constant anger, hostility, resentment, and explicit "retaliatory hostility" from the dominant culture. The fourth can lead to a sense of imprisonment and suffering, "life apathy," depression, grieving a sense of loss of meaning in life, and to feelings of "nonbeing."

Chan (1992) suggests that cross-cultural competence can be built by workers through (1) self-awareness, (2) knowledge specific to each culture, and (3) skills that enable the worker to engage in successful interactions.

The NASW Code of Ethics requires workers to be culturally sensitive and addresses this issue in several sections. Section 1 states:

> Social workers should understand culture and its function in human behavior and society, recognizing the strengths that exist in all cultures. (1.05a)
>
> Social workers should have a knowledge base of their clients' cultures and be able to demonstrate competence in the provision of services that are sensitive to clients' culture and to differences among people and cultural groups. (1.05b)
>
> Social workers should obtain education about and seek to understand the nature of social diversity and oppression with respect to race, ethnicity, national origin, color, sex, sexual orientation, gender identity or expression, age, marital status, political belief, religion, and mental or physical disability. (1.05c)

In reference to broader responsibilities:

> Social workers should engage in social and political action that seeks to ensure that all people have equal access to the resources, employment, services, and opportunities they require to meet their basic human needs and to develop fully. (6.04a)
>
> Social workers should act to expand choice and opportunity for all people, with special regard for vulnerable, disadvantaged, oppressed, and exploited people and groups. (6.04b)
>
> Social workers should promote conditions that encourage respect for the cultural and social diversity ... promote policies and practices that demonstrate respect for difference. (6.04c)

Social workers should act to prevent and eliminate domination...against any person or group. (6.04d)

Demographic changes are also demanding cultural competency even from the U.S. Census Department, which has revised the wording and methodology used in questions about race and Hispanic origin, and now includes the category "two or more races" along with single race. Statistics for 2010, issued in March 2011, offers the following demographic information: the Hispanic/Latino population 12.5%, people viewing themselves as one race alone 97%, which includes white 75.1%, black or African American 12.3%, American Indian or Alaskan Native 0.9%, Asian 3.6%, Hawaiian or Pacific Islander 0.1%, and other 5.5%, with 2.4% of the populations viewing themselves as two or more races (Census.gov 2010, downloaded 9/12). While traditional Asian and Cambodian orientations espouse philosophical positions of fatalism, tradition and living with the past, and contemplative circular thinking, the dominant cultural orientation in the United States emphasizes one's personal control over environment and fate, values change and a future orientation, and utilizes analytic linear thinking. In addition, traditional Cambodian culture emphasizes a collectivist social orientation and group welfare, collective responsibility and obligation, while U.S. cultural values emphasize autonomy, independence, and self-reliance. Hierarchy, role rigidity, and traditionally ascribed status are generally emphasized in Cambodian culture, while U.S. dominant culture values equality, role flexibility, and assigning status based on achievement.

Diversity in Practice

Practice Behavior Example: Cultural competence involves both knowledge of a client's culture and understanding of the individual client's relationship to that culture.

Critical Thinking Question: Optimal cultural competence requires gathering and assimilating knowledge from a variety of sources. In order to provide services which are both culturally sensitive and client-appropriate what sources of information might be helpful to the practitioner?

Honoring Program Imperatives and Obligations: An Expression of an Anglo-European Life Position. The *stated goals* of the agency program include:

1. Empowering residents to take control of their lives through various self-sufficiency initiatives.
2. Providing a comprehensive and integrated program of social services.
3. Helping families become economically self-sufficient.

The housing project agency utilizes case management to provide services.

> Central to case management is the function of linking clients with essential resources and empowering clients to function as independently as possible in securing the resources they need. (Hepworth, Rooney, Dewberry Rooney, Strom-Gottfried, & Larsen, 2010)
>
> Social work case management is a method of providing services whereby a professional social worker assesses the need of the client and the client's family when appropriate, and arranges, coordinates, monitors, evaluates, and advocates for a package of multiple services to meet the specific client's complex needs. (NASW, 1992)

The effectiveness of case management in providing services to people with multiple needs has been documented in a number of studies, which include "Case Management in Health Care," by Loomis (1988), "A Social Work Practice Model of Case Management," by Moore (1990), and *The Practice of Case Management*, by Moxley (1989).

Implicit and embedded in case management are the stated objectives and values of the social work profession, which include the dignity and worth of the individual and a commitment to social justice and integrity. The case management approach is congruent with Anglo-European values (Hanson, 1992). Relevant to this dilemma are commitment to change, human equality, individualism, self-help, competition, future orientation, an action/goal/work orientation, directness, materialism, and personal control over the environment. As a tendency, teleological and utilitarian ethical positions would be more congruent with this life position.

Section 3 of the NASW Code of Ethics supports the obligation of the worker to the practice setting:

> Social workers generally should adhere to commitments made to employers and employing organizations. (3.09a)
>> Social workers should work to improve employing agencies' policies and procedures. (3.09b)
>> Social workers should...ensure that employers are aware of the social workers' ethical obligation as set forth in the *NASW Code of Ethics.* (3.09c)
>> Social workers should not allow an employing organization's policies, procedures, regulations, or administrative orders to interfere with their ethical practice of social work. (3.09d)

Author's Reflections, Reasoning Process, and Resolution

The worker follows the worldview of the client as able, while recognizing that personal values might conflict with some Cambodian values. The worker values both "accomplishment" (Anglo-European) and "being" (Cambodian). Values include oneness of people, spiritual connection, sharing of power, compassion, perseverance, accomplishment, flexibility, and fairness/justice.

Dolgoff, Loewenberg, and Harrington (2008) state: "To thine own self be true." For purposes here, "To thine own self, be aware" might be more appropriate. From a postmodernist, social constructionist position, values and beliefs are understood as forever with us, shaping our perceptions and actions (Goldstein, 1990; Nelson, Megill, & McCloskey, 1987).

The worker and the client are in a relationship. The shape of that relationship and the response of the client are strongly influenced by the theoretical orientation(s) assumed by the worker. The ethically defined choices available are in some ways prefigured by the orientation chosen.

The Kantian theory of obligations, the utilitarian theory of consequences, and the liberal individualism theory of rights tend to come out of the positivistic science tradition. These theories move epistemologically from several assumptions, among them (1) a separation of subject from object, and by corollary, worker from client, and (2) judgments formulated from "firm universal principles" (Beauchamp & Childress, 2009). Critics of the "obligations/consequences/rights" orientations suggest that they can only provide limited insight into what should be much broader conversations on moral decision making (Baier, 1985).

The Ethics of Care orientation emphasizes relationship, contextually given relationships, compassion, sympathy, discernment, sustenance, and care. Nel Noddings notes that "caring is largely reactive and responsive. Perhaps it is even better characterized as receptive" (2003, p. 19). Beauchamp and Childress (2009) suggest that an ethics of care is especially appropriate in considering roles such as parent, friend, physician, and nurse [and social worker] where the authentic expression of caring for another assumes greater importance than the equal treatment espoused by more traditional theories. Moreover, Pinderhughes suggests that people in power tend to define reality for everyone (Pinderhughes, 1989). We can mitigate this imbalance by selecting an ethical theoretical base that works to minimize hierarchical influence.

Instead of being viewed as resistant, a culturally sensitive ethics of care approach might understand Ms. Li as possibly fearful of authority and involvement in a cultural community that is foreign to her. Pressure may drive her further into her house, possibly into depression, hurting individuals and family structural ties. Compassion from an ethics of care would suggest the worker tread easy and remain aware of imbalances in the worker–client relationship.

> For culturally sensitive practice, it is essential to develop an understanding of one's own as well as the client's cultural context, and to recognize that experiences and events shape the relationship to one's own culture as well as to that of others.

A communitarian theory might be chosen as a supplemental framework. This orientation has grown out of reactions to social and familial fragmentation, understood as due to the individualism espoused by advanced industrial societies (Beauchamp & Childress, 2009). It can serve as criteria for judging actions that do or do not reinforce and promote communal and family values, cooperative virtues, and goals and obligations built up from and within historically constituted groups. Family is understood as communal and includes parents and children involved in complementary roles and responsibilities. These roles, responsibilities, and obligations are understood as historically constituted.

The communitarian ethics approach closely approximates the Asian/Cambodian life orientation presented previously. This framework tilts the worker in the direction of the cultural side of the previously presented dilemma.

One must begin by redefining the client as the family as a whole, rather than Pareth as an individual. This is not altogether in opposition to the program imperative that states: "Helping families become economically self-sufficient"—though family in this context is understood in "American" family terms of performance and achievement. Focus needs to be given to family solidarity and responsibilities, as understood from the Cambodian orientation.

Ms. Li, the hierarchical head of the family, places her responsibility to her children above her desire to learn English. Pareth has also expressed a sense of responsibility to her mother and family ties and a willingness to delay GED studies. Continued dependence and integration within ascribed family roles is expected and fostered.

An appropriate goal perhaps would be to help facilitate better linkage to a Buddhist temple. Ms. Li describes herself as Buddhist, though only visiting the temple on New Year's Day. The Buddhist orientation is consistent with an ethics of care/relationship perspective.

The worker may also advocate that the agency move toward greater cultural competency, a value supported by the NASW Code of Ethics. Cross, Bazron, Dennis, and Isaacs (1989) might perceive the agency as being "culturally blind" in espousing a set of convictions, values, behaviors, and/or policies seen as "unbiased." The consequence of this "universal" philosophy is assimilation of cultural values into the Eurocentric (dominant) melting pot.

A "culturally proficient" agency "improves services . . . actively seeks advice and consultation from a variety of ethnic communities and include such practices into the organization." Communication and mutual support between the agency and Buddhist temple would possibly both assist Ms. Li and establish a valuable link to enhance "cultural proficiency."

"A professional [case management] social worker assesses the need of the client and the client's family when appropriate, and arranges, coordinates, . . . and advocates for a package of multiple services to meet the specific client's complex needs" (NASW, 2008). These approaches would enhance "respect and appreciation for individual and groups differences; willingness to persist in efforts on behalf of clients despite frustrations, and commitment to social justice . . . for all members of society" (NASW, 1981).

Case Study L (Gray)

Axelson, J. (1993). *Counseling and development in a multicultural society.* Baltimore: Paul D. Brookes.

Baier, C. (1985). *Postures of the mind.* Minneapolis: University of Minnesota.

Beauchamp, T. L., & Childress, J. F. (2009). *Principles of biomedical ethics* (6th ed.). New York: Oxford University Press.

Chan, S. (1992). Families with Asian roots. In E. Lynch & M. Hanson (Eds.), *Developing cross-cultural competence.* Baltimore: Paul D. Brookes.

Cross, T. L., Bazron, B. J., Dennis, K. W., & Isaacs, M. R. (1989). *Toward a culturally competent system of care.* Washington, DC: Georgetown University Child Development Center.

Dolgoff, R., Loewenberg, F. M., & Harrington, D. (2008). *Ethical decisions for social work practice* (8th ed.). Itasca, IL: F. E. Peacock.

Draine, C., & Hall, B. (1986). *Culture shock: Indonesia.* Singapore: Times Books.

Goldstein, H. (1990, May). Strength or pathology: Ethical and rhetorical contrasts in approaches to practice. *The Journal of Contemporary Human Services, 71*(5), 267–275.

Hanson, M. (1992). Families with Anglo-European roots. In E. Lynch & M. Hanson (Eds.), *Developing cross-cultural competence.* Baltimore: Paul D. Brookes.

Hepworth, D., Rooney, R., Dewberry Rooney, G., Strom-Gottfried, K., & Larsen, J. (2010). *Direct social work practice* (8th ed.). Pacific Grove, CA: Brooks/Cole.

Herndon, R. (2001, March 31). The nation's new mix. *Los Angeles Times,* p. 4.

Loomis, J. F. (1988). Case management in health care. *Health and Social Work, 13,* 219–225.

Lynch, E., & Hanson, M. (1992). *Developing cross-cultural competence.* Baltimore: Paul D. Brookes.

Moore, S. (1990). A social work practice model of case management. *Social Work, 35*(5), 444–448.

Moxley, D. P. (1989). *The practice of case management.* Newbury Park, CA: Sage Publications.

National Association of Social Workers. (1981). NASW working statement on the purpose of social work. *Social Work, 26*(6).

National Association of Social Workers. (1992). *NASW standards for social work case management.* Washington, DC: Author.

National Association of Social Workers. (2008). *NASW code of ethics.* Washington, DC: Author.

Nelson, J. S., Megill, A., & McCloskey, D. (1987). *The rhetoric of the human sciences.* Madison: University of Wisconsin.

Noddings, N. (2003) Caring. Berkeley: University of California Press.

Pinderhughes, E. (1989). *Understanding race, ethnicity, and power.* New York: The Free Press.

U.S. Census Bureau. Retrieved from www.censusscope.org/us/chart_race.html

Case Study M   An Employee Assistance Counselor's Dilemma

Abstracted from an unpublished paper by Mel Hall-Crawford, MSW

Practice Context and Case Presentation

Employee assistance programs (EAPs) are increasingly being utilized in both the private and public sector, with the general goal of addressing employee problems that impact on work performance and conduct, attendance, reliability, and other issues that affect employees' ability to perform their assigned tasks in an optimal manner. Programs are generally available to employees either through self-referrals or through formal or informal referrals by supervisors. They are, therefore, generally unlimited in terms of the types of problems that may be addressed.

Elena, a Japanese American woman and a self-referred employee in a large corporation, asks for assistance from the EAP due to the level of difficulty she is experiencing in performing her duties as a policy analyst. She recently separated from her husband and describes their relationship as filled with anger and mistrust. However, since he has left, she has become very frightened of being alone, and she feels very isolated, both at work and in her personal life. Her job is her sole source of support and, beyond that, her sole opportunity to interact with others.

Elena feels that she has been assigned an impossible task of creating a database, a project that she has been working on for more than two years. She is frustrated by the lack of clarity from her supervisor regarding expectations and expresses concern that her job is in jeopardy. Elena says she stares at a blank computer screen in her office hour after hour, getting almost nothing done, and has actually curled up on the floor and cried on occasion.

Although Elena repeatedly refuses suggestions of involving her supervisor in these discussions, the worker feels strongly that this is advisable in order to determine (1) if things are as bad as Elena describes them and (2) if perhaps the supervisor could clarify what was expected of Elena so that her job performance could improve. However, the worker is also concerned that bringing this situation out into the open might further jeopardize Elena's job security in that such a meeting would spotlight Elena's performance and force the supervisor to examine the seriousness of the situation. After many discussions, Elena reluctantly consents to involve her supervisor.

Practice Contexts

Practice Behavior Example: The context of practice in this case study is a corporation, rather than a social agency or health care or social welfare service.

Critical Thinking Question: Ethical dilemmas for social workers may occur in all practice contexts. Are there certain specific issues that tend to occur in settings which are for-profit rather than the traditional social service settings?

During the meeting, her supervisor indicates that she wants to be supportive of Elena, but she also acknowledges that Elena's emotional state is indeed affecting her work performance. Elena breaks down in tears, but finally it is agreed that the supervisor will work with her to help her gain a better sense of how to proceed with her assignment, and will also give her other projects that would give Elena a sense of closure and accomplishment in her job. The worker agrees to help Elena deal with the larger issue of her depression and emotional problems by exploring other treatment options and by continuing counseling.

Following this meeting, Elena receives an informal performance appraisal rating her work at "satisfactory," a decline from prior ratings of "excellent," a bad rating by general corporation standards. She believes that her job is in jeopardy and that the bad rating would make it difficult, if not impossible, for her to find another position.

The worker feels an obligation to protect Elena's best interest, but she is unsure whether she should continue to try to resolve Elena's work situation without further involving the supervisor or to urge that the supervisor be brought in as a consultant to the process in an effort to gain needed perspective and clarification. There is also a concern about whether the worker's urging Elena to consent to supervisory involvement infringes upon her self-determination. Because Elena's job appears to be in greater jeopardy since the involvement of her supervisor, the worker feels responsible.

However, the worker is also concerned about the larger ethical dilemma: What is her obligation to her client and to the employer of both herself and Elena? What if her obligation to her employer (to support and maintain optimum job performance for employees, which might in this case mean terminating Elena) and her obligation to her client (to keep her in a stable job situation, through which she is able to support herself) conflict?

The dilemma may be stated as follows:

WORKER'S OBLIGATION TO EMPLOYER V. WORKER'S OBLIGATION TO CLIENT

Research And Related Literature

A definition of occupational social work must be the starting point for an exploration of this issue. Googins and Godfrey (1987) define occupational social work as being "a field of practice in which social workers attend to the human and social needs of the work community by designing and executing appropriate interventions to insure healthier individuals and environments" (p. 38).

EAPs help organizations by reinforcing their basic management principles and goals to employees (Googins & Godfrey, 1987). Assuming that one of an employer's basic principles and goals is employee job productivity, an EAP counselor has a responsibility to help an employee whose job performance is not meeting the employer's expectations.

There has been some discussion in the literature regarding the dilemma that EAPs/ counselors encounter when the interests of the employee and the employer appear to conflict. Dolgoff et al. (2008) suggest that the client was traditionally defined as the person(s) who engaged the practitioner and paid her a fee and/or who is the focus of the worker's and client's interventions. However, applying this definition in an EAP setting, the employee assistance counselor's "client" is both the employing organization who is paying his or her salary and the employee who has come to the counselor for help. Stated in another way, the EAP counselor has an obligation to both the employee and the employer. Factoring in a social worker's ethical responsibility to the employer (Wells, 1986), the dilemma arises when a social worker or EAP counselor experiences difficulty in delivering effective service or affecting positive change in accordance with the employer's mission for the program.

Kurzman (1988) distills the issue in terms of the fundamental conflict between the profession's commitment to people's well-being and industry's dedication to profits. He poses the question "Whose agent are we?" in light of circumstances when "organizational goals—in this situation productivity and profit maximization—are not entirely congruent with client needs" (p. 21).

Briar and Vinet (1985), while not explicitly advocating the employee's needs over those of the employer, point out that this approach or ordering of priorities "infinitely expands opportunities for the professional to address unmet needs of employees" (p. 351).

An interesting theme that has arisen in the literature reviewed is that when such a conflict arises between the best interest of the employee and the employer, a holistic or systems approach may be appropriate. Googins and Godfrey (1987) suggest that a systems approach to problem solving in the workplace is advantageous as problems exist within a specific context and addressing the problem may necessitate micro- and macro-solutions. "The EAP practitioner, joined by others in the workplace with similar humanistic functions, can help to promote new perspectives on corporate investment in employees and their families, consumers, and the wider community" (Briar & Vinet, 1985, p. 357). One caveat to this approach is that the employee must be comfortable with, and must consent to, the course of action that he or she feels is in his or her best interest. Overall, this perspective in the literature suggests that even when the employee's situation is at odds with the employer's expectations, the employee assistance counselor can be creative and endeavor to produce a positive outcome outside of the traditional relationships and ways of operating.

Professional Identity

Practice Behavior Example: Despite clear ethical responsibilities to confidentiality noted in the Code of Ethics, laws regarding the confidentiality of information provided to social workers are often ambiguous and can create uncertainty for practitioners.

Critical Thinking Question: What are some resources that social workers can utilize to gain some clarification in specific instances?

A review of the Code of Professional Conduct for Certified Employee Assistance Professionals (CEAP; Employee Assistance Certification Commission, 1994) touched on the ethical dilemma at hand in Section 1 of the Code of Conduct that deals with the workplace. Subsection c states: "*Human Resources Management:* The CEAP will seek to use all appropriate organizational resources in resolving job performance problems due to employee personal problems. The goal is to seek solutions for returning the employee to acceptable work performance." There is no guidance, though, as to what should be done, what the goal should be if the employee's work performance continues to be unacceptable, or what the obligation is to the employer.

In summing up the research and literature reviewed with regard to this ethical dilemma, it is clear that one of the primary goals of

EAPs is to help employees with problems, personal or job related, so that their work performance will improve. The literature acknowledges that there is a dynamic tension between individual human needs and the needs of the work organization but offers little guidance on how to deal with these needs when they come into conflict. This may be attributable to several factors: (1) Every situation is unique, and therefore it is difficult to speak broadly or in categorical terms; and (2) the field of occupational social work, while not new, is still evolving and has not received mainstream social work attention. Briar and Vinet (1985) point out that "it is often argued that ethical discussions can deter the progress of human services in the workplace, especially if future service developers perceive value dilemmas as hazardous roadblocks" (p. 342).

Author's Reflections, Reasoning Process, and Resolution

Values are concerned with what is good and desirable (Dolgoff et al., 2008). In attempting to frame this issue in terms of general values derived from society, it is clear that the Protestant work ethic is an underlying principle. Our society places great value on hard work and having a job. "Work for economic gain is the way to success, a sign of personal morality, and a moral obligation" (Day, 1989, p. 7). Related to the Protestant work ethic is the societal value that productivity at work is good and desirable, and the converse is also true in that the lack of productivity is viewed as a problem and is not well regarded.

Briar and Vinet (1985) take the position that employee assistance professionals derive their values from "ethical beliefs in the integrity and human potential of each individual, his or her right to self-expression..., and the centrality of human welfare above and beyond other potential overriding organizational goals, such as profitmaking, efficiency, and productivity" (p. 343). This vantage point would suggest that the client's best interest would take primacy over the employer's.

One value that emerged from researching the issue was that employing organizations recognize they have a responsibility to offer help to their employees who may be having personal or job-related problems, because ultimately such help will benefit the organization through improving the employees' performance. It also helps the organization by enhancing its image as being socially responsible. However, the outer limits of the employer's obligation to continue employing a worker whose performance, despite her seeming best efforts, is not easily amenable to improvement are uncertain.

Personal responsibility is another value on which our society places an emphasis. In this case, an individual or employee has a responsibility to take care of himself or herself, to seek help when necessary, and to deal with the consequences of his or her decisions. Elena wants help with her problems and has taken the initiative of seeking help from the EAP.

Ethics deals with what is right or correct (Dolgoff et al., 2008; Joseph, 1983). In this instance, there is a tremendous ethical responsibility for the client's best interest, but there is also an ethical responsibility to the employer. The dilemma is best considered in terms of ethical relativism (Dolgoff et al., 2008). What makes it so difficult is that one cannot always be sure whether the anticipated consequence will occur. However, in this situation of conflict between the obligation to the employee versus the obligation to the employer, one has to prioritize to whom there is primary and secondary responsibility.

Another ethical principle relevant to this situation is the client's right to self-determination. If a client is adamant about not proceeding with the course of action recommended by the practitioner, unless there is a serious threat or harm to the client or another person, it seems that the practitioner is bound to honor the client's position. However, again there can be gray areas in a situation in which a client agrees to a practitioner's recommendation, but both have trepidations about the course of action and are not sure about the outcome or repercussions.

Several of the core values in the NASW Code of Ethics relate to the situation that is the subject of this case. These are Value I—service and my desire to help an employee in need, drawing on my knowledge, values, and skills; Value II—respecting the dignity and worth of the employee; Value IV—understanding the importance of my relationship with the employee and our effort together to deal with her situation at work.

Ethical Standard Section 1, Social Workers' Ethical Responsibilities to Clients, has several subsections that are relevant to the ethical dilemma that is being discussed here. Specifically, subsection 1.01, which deals with commitments to clients, seems pertinent in that this worker believes that the interest and welfare of the individual employee is primary. However, the worker also recognizes a responsibility to the larger organization. Subsection 1.02, which addresses self-determination, must be a consideration as the worker believes that she may have infringed on client self-determination by bringing in the supervisor. Subsection 1.06a, relating to conflict of interest, makes the point that social workers should be alert to and avoid conflicts of interest.

Amplifying the possibility of a conflict of interest, Section 3 of the Code deals with ethical responsibilities in practice settings. Subsection 3.09 speaks to the importance of social workers adhering to their commitments to their employers and of not allowing the policies and procedures of the agency to interfere with their ethical practice of social work.

Based on the above exploration and discussion in this ethical model, I believe appropriate ordering of the values/principles relating to this ethical dilemma are as follows: (1) In general, the employee's best interest is primary over the interest of the employer; (2) the worker needs to honor the client's right to self-determination; (3) the worker should act in the client's best interest and not encourage unnecessary risks that may conflict with the secondary client or, in this case, increase job jeopardy; (4) if a conflict of interest arises between the employee and the employing organization, the worker should try to balance the interests of both parties and find a mutually agreeable accommodation. However, in the absence of that, it still behooves the social worker to work on behalf of the individual as opposed to the organization, as the impact on the individual is greater, and his or her access to resources can be rather limited.

The worker is aware that her personal values impact strongly on ethical decision making. These include compassion and caring, respect, equity, balance, loyalty, honesty, and consistency. Although considering herself mostly a relativist with a touch of absolutist, the worker believes that things need to be taken in context and looked at in terms of the result and that it is important to be open-minded and flexible in judging what is right or wrong.

If the worker determines that her primary obligation is to Elena's best interest, she would choose to continue working with Elena in individual sessions without further supervisory consultations and/or seek outside resources for treatment for Elena, such as a day treatment program or a therapy group. This course of action would be supported by the belief in Elena's integrity and her right to human welfare. She needs the job, and her functioning at work *might* improve, despite little evidence for this thus far. This choice would honor Elena's self-determination as well.

If the worker determines that her obligation to her employer is primary, she would make herself available to the supervisor for consultation. She would exercise caution in protecting the confidentiality of information Elena has shared in sessions, but would be open to assisting with direct interventions to improve Elena's work performance. The worker would of course let Elena know that she would be consulting with her supervisor and be available to Elena should crises occur.

On a different and higher level, addressing the obligation to the employer, the issue of an under-functioning employee could be raised generically with the human resources department and other appropriate personnel in management to explore what options or guidelines might be created. The underlying position here is that it is in the employer's best interest to retain employees rather than to let them go. It is more costly and disruptive to hire and train someone new unless it is clear that the incumbent employee is unable to meet his or her job responsibilities over the long run.

As a resolution, the worker has opted for the ethical stance that supports obligation to the client as primary. This position is a relativist one: If the client/employee were breaking clear-cut rules or harming others in the workplace, the worker's obligation to the employer would probably override the obligation to the employee. The worker believes that Elena is not hurting anyone. She is not breaking any clearly stated work rules. She may be breaking some unspoken rules (by being unproductive in her job), but she needs her job to survive. She has far fewer resources than her employer. This worker feels that she is supported by the NASW Code of Ethics, which states that "in general, clients' interests are primary."

The worker believes Elena's supervisor has her own responsibility in this situation. She is aware of Elena's poor job performance and depression and can take her own steps, independent of the worker's involvement, to deal with the situation. The lines of accountability and obligation appear to this worker to be quite different for herself, as an employee of the EAP, and for Elena's supervisor. Each must therefore follow the path that appears ethical and just from her vantage point and from her own values.

Case Study M (*Hall-Crawford*)

Briar, K. H., & Vinet, M. (1985). Ethical questions concerning an EAP: Who is the client? (Company or individual?). In S. H. Klarreich, J. L. Francek, & C. E. Moore (Eds.), *The human resources management handbook: Principles and practice of employee assistance programs.* New York: Praeger.

Day, P. (1989). *A new history of social welfare.* Englewood Cliffs, NJ: Prentice-Hall.

Dolgoff, R., Loewenberg, F. M., & Harrington, D. (2008). *Ethical decisions for social work practice* (8th ed.). Itasca, IL: F. E. Peacock.

Employee Assistance Certification Commission. (Revised, 1994). *Code of Professional Conduct for Certified Employee Assistance Professionals (CEAP).* Arlington, VA: Employee Assistance Professionals Association.

Googins, B., & Godfrey, J. (1987). *Occupational social work.* Englewood Cliffs, NJ: Prentice-Hall.

Joseph, M. V. (1983). Ethical decision-making in clinical practice: A model for ethical problem solving. In C. B. Germain (Ed.), *Advances in clinical practice* (pp. 207–217). Silver Spring, MD: National Association of Social Workers.

Kurzman, P. A. (1988). The ethical base for social work in the workplace. In G. M. Gould & M. L. Smith (Eds.), *Social work in the workplace.* New York: Springer Publishing.

National Association of Social Workers. (2008). *NASW code of ethics.* Washington, DC: Author.

Wells, C. C. (1986). *Social work ethics day to day: Practice guidelines for professional practice.* New York: Longman.

Case Study N Supporting "Best Interest" In A Host Setting

Abstracted from an unpublished paper by Kylie Pedersen, MSW

Practice Context And Case Presentation

As an intern, my placement is in a medical center's Social Services Department, which serves all of the units in the hospital. As a private hospital, Medi-Cal patients and uninsured patients are not accepted at my hospital, except as trauma patients requiring emergency care. I was assigned work with an uninsured 47-year-old male trauma ICU patient, who had been admitted through the ER requiring acute medical care following an auto versus pedestrian motor vehicle accident where he was the pedestrian. He had sustained multiple injuries, as well as a leg fracture, in the accident. He had been seen by Social Services during several previous ER admissions, and had attended the hospital's inpatient treatment program for alcoholism three times in the past four years, relapsing each time. However, he felt that this accident was a wake-up call and wanted to attend the hospital's inpatient program for the fourth time.

When he was cleared for discharge, a bed in the inpatient program he desired was not available, and his physician stated that medically speaking, it would be in his best interest to be discharged from the hospital to continue to drink before going through delirium tremens because, given his prior history, he would surely relapse again in any case. Discharging him immediately would negate the need to hold him in the hospital medically stable, while awaiting a bed in the inpatient treatment program. It was unclear to me whether this was a financial issue, a resource-allocation issue, or a medical futility issue for this physician. The patient's family is estranged due to his alcoholism and cannot advocate for inpatient treatment for him.

The physician's decision conflicted with my personal values, and also with both the NASW Code of Ethics' principles of service, social justice, and dignity and worth of person, and the American College of Physicians' ethical principles of respect for autonomy, beneficence, and justice. However, I also had a clear obligation to support the decisions of my colleague, the physician, and the hospital as well, as this was a host setting. One side of my dilemma was clearly my responsibility to advocate for my client, while the other side presented a choice: Was the central issue one involving responsibility and relationship to my colleague, or my responsibility to my employing agency, in this case, the hospital? After much reflection, I determined that the employing agency would most certainly support the physician's position, and thus have addressed the dilemma as:

RESPONSIBILITY TO CLIENT ADVOCACY V. RESPONSIBILITY TO SUPPORT DECISIONS OF THE EMPLOYING AGENCY

Research And Related Literature

Literature Review.

Cost-containment, Social Work, and Physician Roles. A review of the literature revealed information on hospital staff roles and responsibilities coupled with the administrative expectation of cost-containment. "Clearly, cost-containment has given rise to ethical dilemmas for the social work practitioner in the hospital setting" (Beckerman, 1991, p. 61). "Cost-containment demands the simultaneous acceleration and sustained efficacy of hospital service, goals often not equally attainable, thus limiting the ability of members of the medical team, such as nurses, physicians, patient accounting representatives, and social workers, to provide detailed and comprehensive care" (1991, p. 61).

Dyer notes how difficult it may be for a physician to carry out the dual roles of patient advocate and societal agent (Beckerman, 1991, p. 62). This dilemma holds true across the medical team, but it is often physicians who receive the most pressure to discharge or expedite patient hospitalizations from administration, thus compromising patient care due to pressures to reduce length of stay. This limits the physician's ability to act as a patient advocate.

In discussing cost-containment efforts and the qualitative effects on patient populations, Walsh stresses the importance of the NASW Code of Ethics and social work values to "ensure that the dignity and individuality of the individual is respected in the provision of social resources and that individuals have access to the resources, services, and opportunities to meet various life tasks, alleviate distress, and realize their aspirations and values" (Beckerman, 1991, p. 63). This highlights the importance of patient advocacy.

Alcohol Withdrawal and Recidivism. Studies of alcoholism have found that up to 85 percent of all patients relapse, independently of whether they have been treated as inpatients until the complete remission of physical withdrawal symptoms (Heinz, Beck, Mir, et al., 2010, p. 137). This high percentage supports the possibility that repeated treatment programs may be necessary prior to successful rehabilitation.

One neurobiological research study using neuroimaging found specific regions of the brain highly associated with alcohol dependency and recidivism rates and concludes that: "It seems plausible that patients experience drug-craving and drug-seeking behavior 'against their own conscious will' and should not be blamed for their behavior, but be treated with the same respect as other patients in the health care system" (Heinz, Beck, Mir, et al., 2010, p. 155). In addition, because of its high mortality, *delirium tremens*, a severe form of alcohol withdrawal, may worsen abruptly, and is a medical emergency (Elliott, Geyer, Lionetti, & Doty, 2012, p. 25).

Stages of Change and Psychosocial Development. The Transtheoretical Model of Stages of Change has been utilized in substance abuse care in order to assess patient readiness to engage in treatment. The Stages of Change Model allows practitioners to assess the client's stage in the process of changing behavior. In this ethical dilemma, the patient is in the Action stage, actively pursuing treatment and attempting to begin changing his behavior (Connors, Donovan, & Diclemente, 2001, p. 7).

According to Erikson's Stages of Psychosocial Development (Erikson, 1968, pp. 138–139), the patient appears to be in the stage of Generativity versus Stagnation, where the primary focus is on parenthood and work. However, this patient did not have an engaged family, was not a parent, and was not currently employed, so may have been experiencing feelings of stagnation and unproductivity. Alcohol may have been a tool to for self-medicating and numbing his feelings around that stagnation. Perhaps with the implementation of social supports this patient would be able to maintain sobriety.

NASW Code of Ethics. An in-depth examination of the Code of Ethics (Code of Ethics, pp. 1–19) reveals conflict in several ethical standards. Standard 1.01, Commitment to Clients, supports both sides of the dilemma: the attending physician is concerned about providing care to patients awaiting further medical attention, whereas the social worker advocates for the current patient's needs. Standard 1.02, Self-Determination, may also be argued from both sides. The physician may argue that the patient may make the decision to attend treatment and do so on his own after discharge. The social worker may argue that the patient requires the additional assistance of being discharged directly to an inpatient treatment program, and that the hospital is obligated to meeting his need. In Standard 1.15, Interruption of Services, it may be argued that the patient's continuity of care is being interrupted by the physician's push to discharge the patient without care in place, thus posing a threat to patient's well-being.

In Standard 2.01, Respect for Colleagues, respect for the physician's skills and evaluation suggest accepting his assessment and plan for the patient, Standard 2.03, Interdisciplinary Collaboration, suggests that the conflict between social worker and physician disrupts necessary collaboration for effective patient care, and Standard 3.07, Administration, states that administrators should take adequate steps to ensure resource-allocation procedures are open and fair, and that adequately meet client needs. In this particular case, the social worker may argue that resources are not being adequately allocated to address the needs of the patient. Conversely, the physician may argue resources are not being adequately allocated for patients in need of more critical medical attention.

Author's Reflection, Reasoning Process, and Resolution

Personal Values Base: Theories, Principles, and Ethics

Personal Values. Most people's personal values are largely shaped from experiences during the formative years of their childhoods. Our early relationships and observed models of behavior during that time impact our values and decision-making processes. In discussing "common morality," Beauchamp and Childress posit that there are no such things as major changes in morality, only "exceptions" in the patterns we have developed over a lifetime (2009, p. 390). I do not entirely agree with this position, because it invalidates individual self-determination, insofar as it suggests that an individual is incapable of altering what they value both in themselves and in the world at large. People are ever changing and have the ability to alter their beliefs at any point in time if they resolve to do so.

My values have been greatly influenced by my family and my various life experiences. My grandmother and mother began to instill a sense of morality in me, enveloped in their own values of kindness, generosity, humility, and altruism. I believe the values they attempted to instill in me as a child, though lost for a time, underlie and support my values today. The Aristotelian goal of aspiring to an admirable life resonates strongly with what my grandmother and mother taught me.

Beauchamp and Childress refer to the five focal virtues in moral character building: (1) compassion, (2) discernment, (3) trustworthiness, (4) integrity, and (5) conscientiousness (2009, pp. 38–45). I believe that these virtues address what it is to be moral, in action as well as in thought. I believe that morally conscious acts, performed not only out of obligation, but, rather, out of a genuine commitment, are most important. These five virtues are reflected throughout my hierarchy of values, which includes: happiness, family/relationships, fidelity, kindness, honesty/integrity, humor, justice, health, optimism, and equality.

Ethical Theory and Principles. The ethical theory which resonates the most for me generally is the Ethics of Care, which seems especially appropriate in healthcare settings, as "many human relationships in health care and research involve persons who are vulnerable, dependent, ill, and frail" (2009, p. 37), but which also guides me in the practice of social work and in my personal life. The motive behind the actions we carry out is very important to me, and I consider myself a deontologist in my thinking. I also see value in the theories of Liberal Individualism, Rights, and Communitarianism, each of which can be related to the Ethics of Care in its own unique manner.

Principles that guide my ethical decision making in my internship include Alan Gewirth's Principles Hierarchy as presented in Reamer (1990, pp. 62–65) and his three types of "core goods" (pp. 59–60) have been helpful in delineating patients' rights and needs. I also use Dolgoff et al.'s Ethical Principles Screen and Beauchamp and Childress' Medical Model, especially as I am placed in a hospital setting. I believe that autonomy, or self-determination, is an essential ingredient in healthcare settings.

Professional Values. My experiences as a social work student and intern, as well as my prior career and personal experiences, have helped me to develop a set of personal and professional values which have in turn shaped my professional ethical perspective. As professionals, social workers assume two often conflicting roles—that of helper or advocate for the client and that of societal control agent—that require balancing principles, values, and responsibilities to individual clients, agencies, and society. In a medical setting, it is also necessary to consider the Code of Ethics of the American College of Physicians and of other healthcare providers. In addition, Beauchamp and Childress discuss the importance of having a threshold of integrity (pp. 41–43) and it has become very important to me to learn to balance my personal values with those of the agencies for whom I have worked, without exceeding my integrity threshold.

When practicing in a setting with professionals from other disciplines, such as physicians, nurses, lawyers, pharmacists, or psychologists, it is very helpful to be familiar with their Codes of Ethics in order to understand the ethical considerations that undergird their decisions and positions.

Values of the Affected System. The patient values his right to services and self-determination regarding health and substance use. His lack of relationship with his family, estranged due to repeated relapses, and the physician's lack of faith in his ability to successfully engage in treatment may have a very negative impact on the his self-image and ability to advocate for himself.

Should he be able to successfully complete treatment and remain sober, he may have the potential to rekindle family relationships. Seeking treatment may resonate with the family's values; however, their absence precludes my ability to judge on this matter. The patient did have a small group of friends, whom he describes as strong and supportive, but admits that they may also have been adversely impacting his drinking habits. He feels that they are the only people he could go to for help, as they still occasionally provide support.

The hospital's Statement of Objectives states: "We are dedicated to improving the health of the communities we serve with quality and compassion." The Vision Statement addresses more systemic goals: "We will exceed our patients' expectations for seamless consistency and we will distinguish ourselves by: providing quality health care services, providing health care services that promote patient safety and the prevention of injury; attracting and retaining quality employees to deliver exceptional care; fostering an organizational culture that respects employees, supports them in developing their skills and talents, and encourages superior performance" (_____Hospital Policy Manual, 2012). However, I do not believe the hospital administrator would become involved in this issue at this time.

The hospital is located in a predominately financially affluent and politically conservative area. It is a private institution and does not contract with Medi-Cal or accept uninsured patients with the exception of trauma patients. A longer and medically unnecessary hospital stay in order to conserve continuity of care for a patient admitted through the ER with trauma seeking inpatient treatment for substance abuse would not have community support. There is a clear distinction between "deserving" and "undeserving" populations, and the community would view alcohol abuse as indicative of life choices which are not a community responsibility.

As this ethical dilemma is taking place in the trauma ICU, new trauma patients in the ER would be affected. The trauma ICU provides a high level of care to trauma patients, and this patient's continued occupation of a bed in this unit could adversely affect a new admission. In addition, the medical team on the unit may feel that patient needs no longer require their care, and that while the patient may have the right inpatient treatment for his substance use, continuing his care in the trauma unit should no longer be their responsibility. As noted earlier, the attending physician described these as the primary reasons for discharging the patient.

Options for Action. There are a number of options available to address both his leg fracture and his expressed need for substance abuse treatment of the dilemma:

Options in Support of Obligation to Client

- Advocate to enable patient to stay in trauma ICU until in-treatment bed becomes available. While this may appear to be a good option, advocacy may not be successful in this case as the physician has made a determination that care on the ICU is no longer necessary.
- Transfer patient to a unit providing a lower level of care until an in-treatment bed becomes available. This would provide continuity of care while releasing the ICU bed for new trauma patients.
- Discharge to a skilled nursing facility with rehabilitation to provide continuity of care for patient's leg fracture and then transfer to an inpatient program. With this option, the patient would be moving from the hospital ICU to a skilled nursing facility, and from there to an as-yet uncertain inpatient alcohol treatment facility.
- Explore other in-patient substance abuse programs accepting new referrals in the general area which might also be able to address his leg fracture. This exploration would take time which may not be available if the physician is requesting prompt discharge.
- Referral to an out-of-area in-treatment program, and provision of taxi vouchers and/or other public transportation tickets for transport. However, it is uncertain that the patient would be able to use public transportation until his leg heals further.

Options in Support of Obligation to Decisions of Employing Agency

- Discharge patient home to await in-patient bed to become available. This would support the physician's request, but heighten the possibility of a return to drinking.
- Suggest the transfer of the patient to a unit providing a lower level of care until in-treatment bed becomes available. This option would free the ICU trauma bed for emergencies, but keep the patient under supervision until a treatment bed became available.
- Explore alternative inpatient treatment programs which might have an available bed.
- Attempt to contact a reliable friend to provide supervision for patient until in-patient bed becomes available. However, the patient has suggested that his friends might not support his desire to stop drinking and even under the best of circumstances, "supervision" would be minimal at best, based on the patient's description of his friends.

Course of Action. In establishing the appropriate plan of care for the patient, careful analysis of all the options was considered. I did not feel it was in the patient's best interest to discharge him to his home with no support services in place, as he was reaching out for assistance and attempting to alter his pattern of behavior. He did not feel he would be able to remain sober at home until he could engage in treatment; therefore, this was not a viable option for the patient. This would also have conflicted with Beauchamp and Childress' principle of respect for autonomy as well as nonmaleficence. It would have conflicted with the NASW Code of Ethics in regards to self-determination and interruption of services.

However, it did not appear ethical to have him remain in the trauma ICU, as there were other patients who were in need of that acute level of care which he no longer required. This would have disregarded the needs of others and the appropriate utilization of resources, and thus not fit in with either my own or the profession's hierarchy of values. The case management team, which collaborates with the social work team in order to organize plans of care and facilitate discharge for patients, also stated that he did not qualify for a skilled nursing rehabilitation stay. Remaining in the trauma ICU would also ignore the physician's recommendations and thus the hospital's decisions.

Other inpatient substance abuse treatment programs options were explored. However, placing the patient in a distant treatment program seemed detrimental to his recovery, as he did not have reliable transportation, or a support network to facilitate his transition back home after the program was completed. Providing him with taxi vouchers to the program was possible, but did not take into account what would occur upon his discharge from the facility. Additionally, when I presented this option to the patient, he stated that he was not comfortable with engaging in treatment out of the area. He also declined my suggestion to reach out to his estranged family, or to other individuals within his support network, thus precluding his returning home under supervised care.

Having thoroughly considered and explored all of these options with the staff and with the patient, and, having found none of them viable, I determined that advocacy on behalf of the patient for an extended hospital stay until a bed in the inpatient treatment unit was available was my only truly viable option. I was successful in this advocacy, and the patient was transferred to a lower level-of-care unit until a bed became available in the alcohol treatment unit. Soon after his transfer, my internship ended, and I can only hope that he was successful in this new effort at sobriety.

Case Study N (Pedersen)

Beauchamp, T., & Childress, J. (2009). *Principles of biomedical ethics.* New York: Oxford University Press.

Beckerman, N. L. (1991). *Ethical dilemmas facing hospital social workers: Implications.* D.S.W. dissertation, Yeshiva University, United States—New York. Retrieved from Dissertations & Theses: Full Text. (Publication No. AAT 9130421).

Connors, G., Donovan, D., & Diclemente, C. (2001). *Substance abuse treatment and the stages of change: Selecting and planning interventions.* New York, NY: A Division of Guilford Publications, Inc.

Dolgoff, R., Harrington, D., & Loewenberg, F. (2012). *Ethical decisions for social work practice* (9th ed.). Belmont, CA: Brooks/Cole.

Elliott, D., Geyer, C., Lionetti, T., & Doty, L. (2012). Managing alcohol withdrawal in hospitalized patients. *Nursing, 42* (4). Retrieved from http://ovidsp.tx.ovid.com/

Erikson, Erik. (1968). *Identity: Youth and crisis.* New York, NY: W. W. Norton & Company, Inc.

Heinz, A., Beck, A., Mir, J., et al. (2010). Alcohol craving and relapse prediction. In C. M. Kuhn & G. F. Koob (Eds.), *Advances in the neuroscience of addiction* (2nd ed.). Boca Raton, FL: CRC Press.

_____Hospital Policy Manual. (2012).

NASW. (2008). *Code of Ethics.* Retrieved from www.socialworkers.org/pubs/code/code.asp

Reamer, F. (1990). *Ethical Dilemmas in Social Service.* New York: Columbia University Press.

Rothman, J. (2011). *From the front lines: Student cases in social work ethics.* Boston: Allyn & Bacon.

Snyder, L. (2012). American colleges of physicians ethics manual: Sixth edition. *Annals of Internal Medicine, 156*, 1.

CHAPTER SUMMARY

Ethical Standard Three is often particularly challenging for social workers. As professionals, the predominant orientation tends to place responsibility to clients as primary, and agency and organization responsibilities may be viewed as secondary. However, when social workers are agency employees, there is a clear responsibility to support agency mission and goals, to function within agency policies and guidelines, and to honor and respect the mutual commitment between themselves and the agency as their employer.

Three major areas of ethical responsibility are defined in this standard: supervisory responsibilities, agency responsibilities toward clients, and responsibilities of workers toward agencies. Because both supervision and education and training are integral to the practice of social work, relationships between supervisors and field instructors and supervisees and interns require fairness, clear boundaries, competence, and professionalism.

Agency responsibilities toward clients include maintaining confidentiality of records and documentation, exercising care when client transfers are necessary, consulting with clients regarding accessing and sharing information, distributing agency funding and resources fairly and equitably. Workers' responsibilities toward their employing agencies include providing agency services efficiently and effectively, and be careful stewards of resources while functioning within the Code of Ethics.

The cases included in this chapter have addressed some of these provisions, including optimal utilization of agency resources, conflicting loyalties and responsibilities to client and agency, addressing agency and client's different values, and the rights of clients in limiting access to personal information to outside resources.

Concern with limitation of informed consent and confidentiality of services has led the social worker in the first case to carefully consider the comprehensiveness of the informed consent form utilized by her agency. Upon reflection and research, the intern determines that clients coming to the agency might be adversely affected by a complete, comprehensive consent form. However, while supporting the use of the limited form, she would provide additional information if the client's wishes or situation would benefit from this, or if the client requests it.

Providing services to immigrants requires cultural sensitivity, which must be balanced with American values, laws, and practices. In the next case, the intern explores the differences between Cambodian and American values and priorities, and determines that services can best meet client needs if there is a careful consideration of the manner in which "clienthood" is perceived culturally, and if efforts are made to link clients with culturally sensitive resources in the community. Self-sufficiency, the value under consideration in this case, is perceived very differently in different cultural systems.

Employee assistance programs confront social workers with serious ethical issues, which are often focused on determining "who is the client," and to whom one owes one's primary loyalty. While many social workers would determine that the employee is the client, strong arguments can be made that the program has been developed with a goal of increasing general functioning and productivity of the employing organization. Issues of privacy and confidentiality point out some important areas of ethical concern. In the case presented here, the intern determines that the client's interest must be primary, as she is not harming others and has not broken any rules. However, she also suggests that the client be assisted in taking more responsibility for her own concerns and self-advocacy.

Social work services are often provided in host setting, such as hospitals, schools, and justice settings. In this case study, the intern has been placed in a hospital, and finds herself wanting to advocate for services for a patient whose physician disagrees with her perception of need. The "host," in a medical setting, is clearly the physician, and the primary mission is just as clearly health. In advocating for inpatient detoxification services for her patient, the intern must consider the physician's evaluation of need and service utilization, along with her own. Ultimately, she determines to advocate for her patient and is successful in accessing the requested services for him.

The following questions will test your knowledge of the content found within this chapter. For questions 1-6, please select the phrase that best completes each sentence. Question 7 is a brief essay question. For additional assessment, including licensing-exam type questions on applying chapter content to practice behaviors, visit **MySearchLab**.

1. In utilizing electronic record-keeping, it is most essential to consider:
   a. ease of access by professionals
   b. staff training in utilizing programs
   c. client privacy
   d. needs of supervisors and field instructors

2. To function effectively in an agency setting, it is essential:
   a. to be knowledgeable about agency policy
   b. to collaborate with other agencies
   c. to serve diverse clients
   d. to advocate for change

3. When students work with agency clients, agencies must:
   a. engage students in all aspects of agency services
   b. ensure that students do not have access to client charts
   c. assign the most recent cases to students
   d. inform clients that students are providing services to them

4. Social workers in host settings should:
   a. give precedence to the guidelines and practices of the "hosts"
   b. always consult with the "hosts" before making decisions with clients
   c. limit interactions with clients
   d. offer services within the context of the NASW Code of Ethics

5. In working with a mentally ill adult:
   a. capacity to consent may be limited
   b. client self-determination is always primary
   c. hospitalization is a preferred intervention
   d. informed consent is not possible to obtain

6. In making ethical decisions in an agency setting, agency mission and policies:
   a. should not be a consideration
   b. should be considered when clients are impacted
   c. should always be considered
   d. mandate supervisory consultation

7. Familiarity with HIPAA regulations is essential to ethical social work practice. Access the regulation through the HHS.gov website and explore under what circumstances HIPAA applies, or does not apply, to you in your current internship.

NASW Ethical Standard Four

Social Workers' Ethical Responsibilities as Professionals

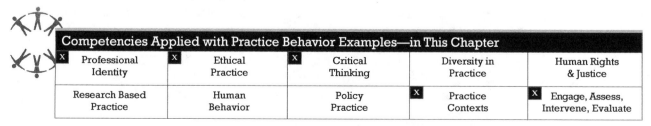

Competencies Applied with Practice Behavior Examples—in This Chapter				
x Professional Identity	x Ethical Practice	x Critical Thinking	Diversity in Practice	Human Rights & Justice
Research Based Practice	Human Behavior	Policy Practice	x Practice Contexts	x Engage, Assess, Intervene, Evaluate

INTRODUCTION

The fourth section of the NASW Code of Ethics addresses expected standards of professional conduct and comportment. Close examination of the tenets of this part of the Code reveals that, while it is phrased specifically for social workers, such standards may be considered to be the norm for professions in general. Standards of competence, nondiscrimination, private conduct, dishonesty, against fraud and deception, impairment, misrepresentation, solicitation, and acknowledging credit appear in many professional codes of ethics and/or ethical standards. Thus, this section may, in part, define what is meant by being a professional—specifically, a social work professional.

Provisions of the Code

The first subsection, 4.01, directs the social worker to "accept responsibility or employment...on the basis of existing competence" (4.01a) and to "become and remain proficient in professional practice" (4.01b). Practice should be based only on recognized professional knowledge and ethics (4.01c).

The following three subsections address the obligation not to practice, condone, facilitate, or collaborate in any form of discrimination (4.02), dishonesty, fraud, or deception (4.04), and to conduct oneself in private in a manner that does not compromise one's professional responsibilities (4.03). Section 4.02 was revised by the NASW Delegate Assembly in 2008 to include discrimination on the basis of *gender identity or expression* and *immigration status* among the proscribed forms of discrimination (NASW, 2008).

Section 2.09 of the Code, which addressed relationships with colleagues, was presented in Chapter 7. While it was noted in that section that it was the obligation of the social worker to address impairments in functioning, the focus was, rather, on the responsibility of colleagues to address such impairment if the worker who is affected does not do so. The subject of impairment is again addressed in Section 4, from the perspective of professionalism, and it is noted that it is the social worker's own obligation to address personal impairments in functioning and not to allow "personal problems, psychosocial distress, legal problems, substance abuse, or mental health difficulties to interfere" with the performance of professional responsibilities. (Section 4a) Workers whose problems do interfere must seek professional help, adjust workload, terminate practice, or take other steps to "protect clients and others" (4.05b).

In terms of misrepresentation, the Code obligates social workers to make a distinction between "statements and actions" made as a private individual and those made as a member of the social work profession (4.06a). When speaking on behalf of professional social work organizations, workers are required to "represent the official and authorized positions" of such organizations (4.06b). Because social workers' personal values may at times conflict with "official" social work positions on a number of issues, this distinction becomes essential, but may also be challenging for some social workers. The professions' positions on many issues may be found in NASW's *Social Work Speaks* (NASW, 2008), and it is important for social workers to be aware of these.

Personal values and behavior have become an emergent major concern in relation to the social media. Posts on Facebook, Twitter, and blogs that reflect personal ideas and conduct may not always reflect the values embodied in the NASW Code of Ethics. The line between personal freedom and professional expectations may be challenging to maintain, and ethical conflicts around these issues may also have legal and professional dimensions.

Returning to the issue of professional credentials, the Code obligates social workers to represent themselves fairly and accurately and to correct any inaccuracies in others' representations of their qualifications (4.06c).

Professional comportment also prohibits social workers from soliciting clients who are potentially vulnerable to exploitation (4.07a) and from soliciting endorsements from persons who are similarly vulnerable (4.07b). Social workers should also take credit only for work actually performed (4.08a) and acknowledge the work and contribution of others (4.08b).

THE CASES

The cases selected for discussion of this ethical standard present some very unique and difficult challenges and invite careful reflection by the reader on the nature of professional roles. In the first case, the author's internship is with a community service agency. In the course of her professional practice, she realizes that she has handled two potentially suicidal clients very differently. Both clients asked that the social worker hold in confidence discussion of their plans for suicide. In one case, the social worker chose to violate confidentiality, and contacted the police to have the client confined and treated. In the other case, she chose to maintain confidentiality. The second client successfully effected her plans and committed suicide.

The social worker understood why she had handled the two cases differently: The differences were related to her evaluation of the potential life quality of each client were she or he to continue to live. However, she questioned whether, as a professional, her reasons were sufficient and also whether she should act consistently in all instances of suicidal threats.

In the second case presented, a physician has asked the hospital social worker to plan for a patient. Because the patient is unable to communicate, the social worker initiates planning with the spouse. The physician has ordered referral for long-term care, while the spouse is adamant in her desire to take the patient home. This appears to be a potential conflict between client's self-determination (as expressed by his wife) and the physician's perception of client's "best interests," addressed in Standards of the Code of Ethics —Standard 1, Obligations to Clients; Standard 2, Obligations to Colleagues; and Standard 3, Obligations to Practice Settings.

However, the author has viewed the conflict in different terms: Empirical knowledge suggests that older people are indeed at high risk of accidents and harm, but meaning-of-life issues are also important to well-being; ethical obligations support not only self-determination but also the worker's obligations to the client's well-being. The worker, in subsection 4.01c, is obligated to practice based on both empirical knowledge and social work ethics. Social work core values support a commitment to "well-being," which generally would seem to include physical, mental, and emotional well-being. How can the worker balance these seemingly conflicting obligations?

The third case presents a fairly common problem: eager to build a relationship and to demonstrate trustworthiness, a social worker promises a client confidentiality early in the relationship. However, information is revealed

Professional Identity

Practice Behavior Example: Social workers should be aware of the line between the personal and the professional. However, social media make the maintenance of this line a serious issue in professional ethics.

Critical Thinking Question: Determining what is posted on social media sites is a personal decision. However, it may impact professional identity and practice as well. What guidelines might help social workers maintain their professional identity while respecting their personal freedom and rights?

Developing and following rules provides consistency and fairness in practice. This must be balanced against using a case-by-case approach which considers individual circumstances and develops a practice plan focused on individual needs and circumstances.

which impacts care and services in a potentially negative manner, undermines interdisciplinary cooperation, and is contrary to the personal and professional values of truth and veracity. Yet—there is the promise:

> An end-stage cancer patient shares both meth use and physical abuse issues with his social worker early in their relationship. As time goes on, more details emerge, and the social worker observes the potential negative physical effects of his meth use. She is unsure of the effects of meth use on chemotherapy. Complicating her difficulties further, both the physician and his assistant's reactions are unpredictable and may further injure this terminal patient. Where does her responsibility lie? In meeting a promise made in haste 6 months earlier? In being a responsible professional, sharing vital information with team members?

Each of the three cases presented relate to a section of the Code which requires the social worker to consider her *professional* responsibilities, not in terms of a group of colleagues, or her agency, or even in terms of an individual client or situation. Rather, what is addressed in this section of the Code is that the social worker arrive at an understanding of the meaning of "professional" in terms of the behavior that is expected in a professional setting. It might be that no one but the social worker herself or himself will ever know of these situations and dilemmas. It might be that the field instructor, colleagues, team members, and others are completely unaware of the difficult issues and decisions that the worker is facing. In each case, the worker is alone, with her or his own concept of professional responsibilities.

Case Study O   When a Client Threatens Suicide: Client Autonomy and Professional Obligation

Abstracted from an unpublished paper by Gigi Stowe, MSW

Practice Context and Case Presentation

An urban community service agency addresses special client issues, such as substance abuse, teenage pregnancy, children with difficulties in school, residential treatment for chronic mental illness, and court-mandated clients. Upon intake, clients are informed of their right to confidentiality and its limitations, including specifically the threat of harm to self and others. An agreement is signed in the record supporting the client's understanding of this agency policy.

Agency policy with suicidal clients requires the utilization of the least restrictive measures possible. These range from verbal guarantees of safety, to a contract not to harm self, to hospitalization and confinement. It is the responsibility of the worker to assess each situation and take the appropriate action to guarantee a client's physical safety.

Two suicidal clients are assigned to the caseworker within a common span of time. Client A is a 19-year-old African American male, with significant recent losses. In particular, the recent breakup of a long-term romantic relationship has been difficult, and he is now threatening suicide. His former girlfriend is with him during this interview. In previous interviews, the client has told the worker of his pride in his employment, his intention of going to college, and the extensive support system in his community.

The worker's assessment of Client A determines that his verbalizations, as well as his gestures during the interview, are designed more to elicit his girlfriend's sympathy and attention than to be actual statements of intent. Nevertheless, as he has made the statement that he plans to commit suicide and refuses to retract it, the worker determines that her course of action must be to notify the police and to detain the client. She proceeds to do so, and Client A is immediately hospitalized and treated.

Client B is a 40-year-old white female, who was found unconscious, lying in a park. Her story is one of extremely severe sexual, physical, emotional, and verbal abuse during the entire course of her life. Her father had, since early childhood, raped, beaten, and cut her, and inflicted invisible scars on her psyche. She is isolated from her family and has no social contacts. Because of her severe depression, she is unable to hold a job. She is unable to make friends due to frequent dissociations, panic attacks, and basic insecurity. She cannot return to school due to her inability to concentrate. She spends her days running, swimming, self-mutilating, and engaging in bulimia. She has a history of multiple suicide attempts, hospitalizations, and treatments and tells the worker that she only wants to be allowed to die. While the worker would like to believe that with time and therapy, she can be helped to find a reason for living, her history seems to render such hope nearly impossible. The worker decides to continue to try to motivate her toward life, but takes no steps to detain her forcibly from committing suicide. Client B commits suicide.

These two side-by-side events, so different, yet so similar, are resolved with striking differences. In each case, the worker used reasoning and reflection, care and concern, and the best of her professional skills in addressing the problem. Yet her courses of action differed markedly, and the implications of these differences were, literally, vital. The differences that the worker perceives as significant could be justifiable, or not, depending on the ethical position taken.

Although the simplest course of action suggests that agency policy be followed in all instances, the worker is conflicted. While the client's personal situations were very different, their statements of ultimate intention were the same. Should the worker, to honor consistency, make the same decision in each case, no matter what the surrounding issues might be? Or should the worker consider each case individually and base her decisions on that evaluation? What role, if any, should the worker's perception of the quality of the client's life have in her assessments and decisions? What role, if any, should the client's own perception have?

In both cases, the issue of client autonomy must be considered. The worker violates Client A's in the service of what she believes to be his excellent future potential for a good quality of life. She supports Client B's autonomy based on both her own and the client's assessment that good quality of life is not possible for this severely disturbed individual. This client's autonomous wish to die appears "rational" to the worker. Client A's does not.

The dilemma is thus stated as follows:

CLIENT AUTONOMY V. PROFESSIONAL OBLIGATION TO PREVENT DISCRIMINATION

> **Supervision and consultation, as well as a review of agency policy guidelines, may be very helpful when addressing challenging issues.**

Research and Related Literature

Neither suicide nor assisted suicide is, at present, a crime under the statutes of any state in the Union. However, a majority of states do make it a crime to *assist* with a suicide (Chase, 1986). It seems to this author, however, that there must be some logical difficulty in punishing someone who assists with an act that is not itself illegal.

Perhaps the most famous advocate and practitioner of assisted suicide Dr. Jack Kevorkian served 8 years of his 10–25 year prison sentence for providing physician-assisted suicide to many patients who requested his assistance as their personal, autonomous, choice He was paroled in June 2007, under a promise not to offer assistance to anyone further (www.wikipedia.org/wiki/Jack_Kevorkian). Dr. Kevorkian died at age 83 in June 2011 from cancer (pbs/org/wgbh/pages/frontline/Kevorkian).

There is some lack of clarity in legal definitions of "autonomy," which range from "self-governance" to "freedom," and these variations can affect the interpretation of professional obligations. In a civilized society, restrictions must necessarily be placed on individual freedoms that trespass on the liberty of others. However, this would not appear to be clearly applicable to suicide, and even the law declines to impede the individual from harming himself or herself.

A number of sources have actually addressed the relationship between autonomy and suicide. For example, the *Encyclopedia of Social Work* states that "practitioners usually see individuals who are experiencing temporary impulses to kill themselves. These impulses occur in response to a loss, to interpersonal conflict, and to other distressing life events, or they may be secondary symptoms of depression or psychosis. Few people who have these impulses appear to be free or autonomous" (Minahan, 1987, p. 744). Beauchamp and Childress (2009) appear to agree with this position by stating that "many persons who commit suicide are either mentally ill, clinically depressed, or destabilized by a crisis, and are therefore not acting autonomously" (p. 386).

In another discussion of the subject, Beauchamp and Childress ask, "Do individuals have a moral right to decide about the acceptability of suicide and to act unimpeded on their convictions? If suicide is a protected moral right, then the state and other individuals such as health professionals have no legitimate grounds for intervention in autonomous suicide attempts" (p. 386).

Further support for the decision not to intervene is provided by John Stuart Mill: "Intervention is justified to ascertain or establish the quality of autonomy in the person; further intervention is unjustified once it is determined that the person's actions are substantially autonomous" (Mill, 1977, p. 76).

Critical Thinking

Practice Behavior Example: "Harm," as well as "best interest" and other professional ethical terms, is a subjective determination. What constitutes "harm" may be understood differently by different people, and in different circumstances.

Critical Thinking Question: NASW Code Standard 2.1 states the social workers' responsibility to prevent harm. How should the social worker determine what constitutes harm? Should a personal definition be used, or that of a group of professionals (there's strength in numbers!), or should a client's determination of what constitutes "harm" be utilized?

Professional values, as addressed in the NASW Code of Ethics, stress the social worker's primary responsibility to clients. However, in the case of a client who expresses an autonomous desire to kill himself or herself, it is unclear whether the obligation is to support the exercise of autonomy, or to prevent harm to the individual. Because both the obligation to self-determination and to the prevention of harm are given similar weight in the Code of Ethics (both are in the same subsection, 1.02), and "harm" is not clearly defined, absolutist and relativist positions would lead the worker to different courses of action.

It is obvious that this problem is not unique to the worker—it has been addressed by many in different times and circumstances. Attempts to work through the issues seem to lead to conclusions that are useful but do not address the specific problem. As the worker's clients have mental problems, does this limit the autonomy of each of them? Where does it place the worker's responsibility? How should "harm" be defined?

There is a professional obligation, clearly, to the primacy of client interests, as supported by Standard 1, subsection 1.01, of the Code of Ethics. Prominent in this section is the client's right to self-determination; however, this may be limited in cases of imminent, foreseeable harm. If one expands the concept of "harm" from the physical to the mental, and includes quality-of-life issues as well, however, the perception of what constitutes "harm" may change markedly. In one case, it would seem, the worker focused on the physical harm that suicide would engender— the harm of death. In the other, the worker gave stronger weight to considerations of quality-of-life issues within the definition of "harm"—including mental harms, which, to the worker, seemed to override the physical ones.

The worker has a professional obligation, as noted in Standard 4, subsection 4.02, of the Code of Ethics, to prevent discrimination: "Social workers should not practice, condone, facilitate, or collaborate with any form of discrimination on the basis of race, ethnicity, national origin, color, age, religion, sex, sexual orientation, gender identity or expression, immigration status, marital status, political belief, or *mental* or physical disability" (NASW, 2008, 4.02; emphasis added). Mental disability was an issue in both of these cases. However, the worker's perception of the mental disability of the first client was that of a transient disability, amenable to treatment. The client could be expected to return to a good quality of life with professional intervention.

Perception of the mental disability of the second client, however, led the worker to believe that this was extreme and unresolvable, and thus precluded any possibility of a quality of life that would be acceptable to the client. Discrimination in the case of the middle-aged client can be based on her mental disability, which, in the worker's perception, would render impossible a reasonable quality of life and thus is included in the worker's definition of "harm."

Author's Reflections, Reasoning Process, and Resolution

This dilemma is clearly embedded in society, and societal values must play a role in influencing the positions of each individual involved. "Society" values human life, yet it allows for the death penalty, abortion, war, and societal values that are often fraught with contradiction and conflict. It values life, liberty, and equal opportunity to pursue wealth, power, education, and happiness. There is a lack of clear definition and many contradictions in societal values.

The lack of clarity about what constitutes "harm" in the Code of Ethics may be a reflection of the lack of clarity in the perception of "harm" in the wider society. Thus, it would seem, the worker's personal values become more central to her decision making. This course of action, however, has led to actions that can be interpreted as discrimination. Discrimination in the case of the young man might be evidenced in the restriction placed on his self-determination by the worker's decision to confine him to prevent physical injury. Discrimination in the case of the middle-aged woman might be evidenced by the worker's evaluation of quality-of-life potential with severe mental illness.

While seeking to avoid discrimination and to arrive at a position of consistency in regard to suicide threats, the worker, on reflection, determines that the appropriate course of action is to evaluate each case on an individual basis, thus taking a relativist position. The concept of free will, and free choice, is a valuable one and applies to the worker as well as to the clients.

However, the ethics of the profession with which the worker has chosen to identify may limit the complete exercise of free will in deciding on actions in individual cases. While the author thinks that intuition is a valuable tool in making professionally sound decisions, there is still the necessity of supporting the intuition with rational arguments and processes in order to provide some structure. It would seem that, while it is important to retain the ability to tailor decisions and actions to the specific needs of each individual circumstance, it might be possible to develop a *procedure* that would be universally applicable and would provide a structure for thought. Procedural justice would uphold the strong social work commitment to social justice.

In conclusion, this writer believes that it is important to professional functioning, and to both professional and personal values, that each case, and each situation, be evaluated and treated as unique. Careful use of intuition as a tool to guide the worker in assessments can assist in this process.

However, in order to provide some of the consistency that may be necessary for professional functioning and to minimize any possible discrimination, the author believes that workers need to develop a structure and a procedure that will ensure adequate evaluation and reasoning and impartial assessments while also maximizing client autonomy and permitting individual treatment.

Case Study O (*Stowe*)

Beauchamp, T. L., & Childress, J. F. (2009). *Principles of biomedical ethics* (6th ed.). New York: Oxford University Press.

Chase, R. N. (1986). Criminal liability for assisting suicide. *Columbia Law Review, 86*, 348–362.

Minahan, A. (Ed.). (1987). *Encyclopedia of social work* (18th ed., Vol. 2.). Silver Spring: NASW Press.

Mill, J. S. (1977). *On liberty: Collected works of John Stuart Mill* (Vol. 18). Toronto: University of Toronto Press.

National Association of Social Workers. (2008). *NASW code of ethics.* Washington, DC: Author.

Ostrom, C. M. (1993, August 29). Law about helping suicide not explicit. *The Seattle Times*, p.A14.

Case Study P   Fidelity to a Client Unable to Communicate

Abstracted from an unpublished paper by Marian D. Kaufman, MSW

Practice Context and Case Presentation

Mr. and Mrs. Smith, a couple in their mid-eighties, have been married for 60 years. In the past five years, Mr. Smith has suffered a series of strokes, leaving him unable to ambulate or to speak clearly. Two months ago, another stroke left him semicomatose. He was placed in a long-term care facility, but, after three weeks, was admitted to the hospital with pneumonia and bedsores. Mrs. Smith feels that these are the result of poor care in the nursing home. Mrs. Smith is legally blind and walks with the aid of a cane. She is mentally acute, handles all the finances, and makes all the decisions for Mr. Smith. She has decided to take Mr. Smith home.

Social work intervention was requested by the physician, who feels that Mr. Smith's quality of care will be severely compromised. He is also concerned that Mrs. Smith may become ill or seriously injure herself trying to care for Mr. Smith. He would like Mr. Smith returned to the long-term care facility to ensure his safety, his quality of care, and Mrs. Smith's well-being. He feels that Mrs. Smith has made a poor decision.

Mrs. Smith is adamant about her decision. She tells the social worker that if Mr. Smith returns to the long-term care facility, it will break his heart, and he will die. He has told her repeatedly that he does not ever wish to be in a long-term care facility, and she considers his statement her personal obligation to fulfill. She also feels that the quality of care at the facility is poor, and that she should not subject her husband to this further. She states that two neighbors, who have been very devoted, will assist her in caring for Mr. Smith. She feels that remaining together is vital to the well-being of both herself and Mr. Smith.

It is clear to the worker that Mrs. Smith has the right to make decisions on her husband's behalf. She is mentally competent and has been responsible for him since his stroke. Thus, his "patient rights" devolve to her, as his representative. She is exercising these

Ethical Practice

Practice Behavior Example: The client in this case, Mr. Smith, is unable to express his wishes or make a decision about care. His wife becomes his surrogate decision maker, and is determined to take Mr. Smith home despite the doctor's recommendation that he be placed in long-term care.

Critical Thinking Question: It is the social worker's responsibility to support client self-determination. Is this responsibility the same whether it is the client or a surrogate making the decision? Is there an additional responsibility to client's "best interest" and the prevention of harms for the social worker when there is a surrogate decision maker?

"rights" as surrogate decision maker by expressing her intention to take her husband home with her. However, the worker's primary obligation to Mr. Smith as her client suggests that she assess his needs separately from Mrs. Smith's understanding of them.

The social worker is caught in an ethical dilemma that places her obligation to support client self-determination, through the surrogate decision maker, against her obligation to safeguard the client's health and safety, which his physician feels may be seriously compromised should Mr. Smith return home with Mrs. Smith.

The worker must consider two competing claims:

CLIENT SELF-DETERMINATION V. PHYSICIAN'S PERCEPTION OF CLIENT'S HEALTH AND SAFETY

These must be placed in the context of the worker's professional obligations, the recognized knowledge base regarding patients in Mr. Smith's condition, and the Code of Ethics.

Research and Related Literature

Much has been written on the issue of long-term care versus independent living for the older people. Thompson, Futterman, Gallagher-Thompson, Rose, and Lovett (1993) assess the amount of social support the caregiver needs as she or he assists an older family member. Social workers have an important role in educating and counseling families before such decisions are made, as well as in continuing to assist families at home as new needs arise. Often, the social worker is the only professional who is involved with the family from the beginning to the end of treatment (Nicholson & Matross, 1989).

The subject of client safety has a central place in the literature. In 1985, there were 6.2 to 6.5 million older persons with one or more dependencies in activities of daily living (ADLs). By the year 2020, this population will increase to 14.4 million, 4.2 million of whom will need nursing home care (Council on Scientific Affairs, AMA, 1993). The problem of how to care for frail elders has become a major social issue.

Ranson (1990) notes that in 1984, the World Health Organization stated that accident injuries ranked fifth among the leading causes of death, and in the older population, the rate is often higher for accidents than for infectious diseases. It has been proven that the effects of accidents in the home greatly increase the likelihood of invalidity, extended periods of medical care, and even death. Over half of all at-home accidents occur to persons above 75 years of age and have serious consequences (Ranson, 1990).

The use of home safety measures has not proven to be particularly successful in reducing the number of in-home accidents. Families often wait until after an accident to install them. Among households where smoke alarms, medic alert bracelets, and "panic buttons" exist, noncompliance is a problem (Devor, Wang, Renvall, Feigal, & Ransdell, 1994).

General public impressions to the contrary, at present long-term care facilities are caring for an ever-shrinking number of the elderly. The total nursing home population in the United States in 2008 numbered just 1,412,540 persons (census.gov/compendia/2008), despite a general rise in the elderly population. In 2011, persons 65 years of age and above constituted 13.3% of the general population (census.gov/quickfacts/2011). Family caregivers are responsible for the vast majority of home health care (Council on Scientific Affairs, AMA, 1993). The demographic trend over the last generation has been for families to become geographically separated, usually due to career demands. The responsibility for at-home care often falls on elderly relatives, many of whom have health issues of their own.

Much attention has been given to the rights of the older persons in terms of autonomy and self-determination. Nicholson and Matross (1989) note that the foundational values of freedom and independence are supported by the President's Commission for the Study of Ethics, Problems in Medicine, and Behavioral Research (1983), which defends a competent person's right to make decisions regarding medical procedures and overall treatment.

In cases where a client lacks decisional capacity, one of two standards of judgment is generally used. The first, substituted judgment, asks that the surrogate decision maker make the choice that the client would have made has she or he been able (Wicclair, 1993, p. 53). Substituted judgments require that the decision maker know the client sufficiently well to be able to determine with some degree of certainty the action she or he would have chosen and be able to lay aside any personal interest in a specific course of action. Generally, family members or close friends fill this function (Wicclair, 1993, pp. 54–55). The second standard of judgment, best interest, considers harms and benefits and asks that the decision selected maximize benefits and minimize harms, *from the point of view of the decision maker*. The person filling this function is presumed to be a reasonable person acting within what she or he believes to be the best interests of the client (Wicclair, 1993, pp. 58–59). Typically, then, social workers' decisions tend to be made from a best-interest judgment perspective. The two decision-making processes can easily lead to potentially different courses of action.

Recent research emphasizes the relationship between a sense of control over one's life and positive outcomes in aging (Kapp, 1989). Although professionals in the field have a tendency to say, "If this patient is refusing the recommended discharge plan, it proves that the patient is incompetent," patients have the right to refuse care plans and also to make risky decisions (Dubler, 1988). Collopy (1988) examines six case studies and describes the loss of freedom and dignity people experience in nursing homes.

The mission of the profession, as stated in the Preamble of the Code of Ethics, includes a commitment to (1) service, which the worker is attempting to provide; (2) social justice, which might support both the right to safety and the right to self-determination; (3) the dignity and worth of the person, also supportable through both sides of the ethical dilemma; (4) the importance of human relationships, which seems to obligate the worker to strengthen and support the marital bond; and (5) integrity and (6) competence, both of which suggest that the worker has an obligation to act in a manner consistent with both the value and knowledge base of the profession.

The worker's obligation to the client is specified in Section 1 of the Ethical Standards of the profession. This stipulates that the worker hold as a primary responsibility the "well-being of clients" (1.01) and supports self-determination, except where there is a "serious, foreseeable, and imminent risk to themselves or others" (NASW, 2008, 1.02). Both of these obligations may be interpreted in a manner that could support either side of the dilemma—well-being will be affected by the worker's definition. Does it include physical well-being only, or also mental and emotional well-being? "Serious, foreseeable, imminent risk" is also open to interpretation. Is it possible to clearly predict the kind of "risk" that says that harm could occur if the client returns home? While such harm can be "foreseeable," many factors can impact on the degree of risk.

The worker also has the obligation to interdisciplinary collaboration defined in Section 2.03. The physician, as head of the multidisciplinary team working with the client, has taken a position in support of client safety and has asked that the social worker implement this. Collaboration would lead the worker to support his determination, although she may disagree. In the event of such disagreement, the Code states that the worker "[s]hould attempt to resolve the disagreement through appropriate channels. If the disagreement cannot be resolved, social workers should pursue other avenues to address their concerns consistent with client well-being" (NASW, 2008, 2.03b).

Section 3.08, which addresses commitments to employers in the practice setting, is also applicable to the dilemma, since the structure of the practice setting establishes clear guidelines that seem to place determination of action on behalf of patients in the hands of physicians. Social workers who operate in a host setting, such as a hospital, accept this structure as part of their commitment to the agency.

Included in this section is the obligation to adhere to commitments to employers and also to ensure that employers are aware of the social workers' ethical obligations to the NASW Code and its practice implications. It also states:

> Social workers should not allow an employing organization's policies, procedures, regulations, or administrative orders to interfere with their ethical practice of social work. Social workers should take reasonable steps to ensure that their employing organizations' practices are consistent with the *NASW Code of Ethics.* (NASW, 2008, 3.09d)

Furthermore, subsection 4.01c asks that social workers "base [their] practice on recognized knowledge, including empirically based knowledge, relevant to social work and social work ethics" (NASW, 2008).

Author's Reflections Reasoning Process, and Resolution

Our society values the dignity and worth of the individual, thus respecting each person's right to make decisions on his or her own behalf. Our society also values the maintenance of the family as a unit whenever possible. However, another strong American value is safety. We tend to think that everyone has a "right" to safety. When the two rights, freedom and safety, conflict, difficult problems can ensue.

It is difficult to assess Mr. Smith's values due to his inability to communicate. However, Mrs. Smith has stated that she believes it would "break his heart and probably kill him" to become institutionalized. She has promised him that this will never happen to him. She feels a duty to fidelity and to the honoring of her promises.

The social worker strongly supports the value of family integrity and feels that the efforts of an elderly couple to remain together should be supported wherever possible. Freedom is also an important value, and the worker might tend to be biased against persons or institutions that might tend to remove freedom from any person.

An ethically absolutist position could support either side of the dilemma. It is possible to reason that safety and health must come before other considerations, as a primary condition of life and quality of life. It is also possible to argue, with Kant, that a person's right to self-determination is unconditional, and that violating it considers someone else's goals above the individual's goals (Beauchamp & Childress, 2009, p. 103). This is in accord with the strong support for self-determination in the Code of Ethics. W. D. Ross, a deontologist, would support Mrs. Smith's position based on the moral duty to fidelity (Frankena, 1973). Her obligation is to honor her promise. Normative relativism might argue that what is good for one individual might not be good for another. Therefore, each situation must be considered individually.

The Code of Ethics advocates the social worker's primary responsibility to the well-being of the client. While "well-being" is not defined, social work's core values would seem to include mental and emotional, as well as physical, well-being within this obligation. While empirical data support the incidence of harm and accidents in the elderly populations, especially the at-risk population, literature also supports the position that self-determination, and a sense of control over one's life, has a strong impact on the desired possibility of positive outcomes for the older people. Thus, the commitment

Professional licensure often requires ongoing professional education.

to use empirically based knowledge supports both sides of the dilemma.

A consideration of social work ethics, however, tends to support a position that would enhance self-determination as a foundational part of "well-being." A commitment to respect the primacy of a client's interests through self-determination, and to respect the client's own definition of "well-being," would support an ethical obligation to base practice on this as well.

In attempting to resolve this dilemma, the worker chooses to examine both of the original options. In addition, a third option is considered: placement in an assisted living complex. This would allow the couple to remain together and retain some of the "comforts of home." While some self-determination might be sacrificed with this option, the increased margin of physical safety would seem to justify this position, combining both sides of the dilemma in a compromise that maximizes the benefits of both positions.

The third alternative would necessitate the sale of the Smiths' home, an action to which Mrs. Smith might object. However, because this position maximizes both safety and self-determination, the worker feels comfortable suggesting and advocating for the third option. Should Mrs. Smith refuse, other potential options might include providing caregivers in the Smith home.

Case Study P (*Kaufman*)

Beauchamp, T. L., & Childress, J. (2009). *Principles of biomedical ethics* (6th ed.). New York: Oxford University Press.

Collopy, B. J. (1988). Autonomy in long-term care: Some crucial distinctions. *The Gerontologist, 28* (Suppl. 1), 10–17.

Council on Scientific Affairs, American Medical Association. (1993). Physicians and family caregivers. *Journal of the American Medical Association, 26*(10), 1282–1284.

Devor, M., Wang, A., Renvall, M., Feigal, D., & Ransdell, J. (1994). Compliance with social and safety recommendations in an outpatient comprehensive geriatric assessment program. *Journal of Gerontology, 49*(4), M168–M172.

Dubler, N. N. (1988). Improving the discharge planning process: Distinguishing between coercion and choice. *The Gerontologist, 28*, 76–81.

Dolgoff, R., Loewenberg, F. M., & Harrington, D. (2008). *Ethical decisions for social work practice* (8th ed.). Itasca, IL: F.E. Peacock.

Frankena, W. (1973). *Ethics*. Englewood Cliffs, NJ: Prentice-Hall.

Kapp, M. B. (1989). Medical empowerment of the elderly. *Hastings Center Report, 19*(4), 5–7.

McCullough, L. B. (1985). Long-term care for the elderly: An ethical analysis. *Social Thought, 11*(2), 40–52.

National Association of Social Workers. (2008). *NASW code of ethics*. Washington, DC: Author.

Nicholson, B. L., & Matross, G. N. (1989). Facing reduced decision-making capacity in health care: Methods for maintaining client self-determination. *Social Work, 34*(3), 234–238.

Ranson, R. (1990). Home safety: The challenge to public health. *Journal of Sociology and Social Welfare, 17*(1), 93–113.

Thompson, E. H., Futterman, A. M., Gallagher-Thompson, D., Rose, J. M., & Lovett, S. B. (1993). Social support and caregiving burden in family caregivers of frail elders. *Journal of Gerontology, 48*(5), S245–S254.

Wicclair, M. R. (1993). *Ethics and the elderly*. New York: Oxford University Press.

Case Study Q Keeping Client Secrets: Where Does Professional Responsibility Lie?

Abstracted from an unpublished paper by Catherine Turnbull, MSW

Practice Context and Case Presentation

Oncology Center social workers are assigned to work closely with specific doctors, and each social worker is assigned a caseload from two oncologists at the Center. The social worker's primary role is to help patients receive optimal care by providing psychosocial support, and assistance with concrete needs. Social workers work directly with the medical oncologist, radiation oncologist, nurses, and all other support staff.

At the start of her internship year, the social worker was assigned to work with Dr. Crowley, the medical director of the Oncology Center, who has the reputation of being one of the best oncologists in all of Northern California, but whose attitude is as infamous as his intelligence is famous. Dr. Crowley always states the facts, does not consider feelings, and does not veer far from the ten minute-time frame he allots to patients. Mary, Dr. Crowley's practice nurse, helps with check-up appointments and provides day-to-day support for his patients.

One of her first patients was Mr. Grantham, a 39-year-old male who is married with two children, who had just started a new regimen of chemotherapy to help combat his stage IV metastatic colorectal cancer. Both Mr. and Mrs. Grantham are college-educated professionals, currently not working due to Mr. Grantham's increasing pain, the stress of the chemotherapy, and childcare responsibilities.

Prior to being diagnosed four years ago, Mr. Grantham was a successful professional with a stable, well-paying job. The social worker's supervisor shared that she had met the Granthams through a pregnancy support groups and, at that time, their life appeared perfect as they awaited the birth of their child. In the support group, Mr. Grantham had shared a history of heavy drug use, with exposure to crystal meth by his parents at an early age, and regular use by the time he was twelve, but had been sober for many years prior to his wife's current pregnancy.

At the Center, Mr. Grantham disclosed to this social worker that while he was going through his first year of chemotherapy and trying to continue to work, he was struggling with a lot of pain. Dr. Crowley had prescribed Dilaudid, an opiate derived from morphine, to help with his pain. Mr. Grantham had become addicted to the Dilaudid, and had shared this with Mary, who had quickly placed him in an inpatient detoxification and rehabilitation center.

The detoxification process had proven to be very difficult, as Mr. Grantham had found it harder to quit Dilaudid than meth. During another round of chemotherapy, again experiencing pain, he had asked Mary for medication. Mary "went into a rage," and began yelling at him, accusing him of being ungrateful for the work she had done in arranging for his rehabilitation, and told him that he was just seeking more drugs.

As trust in the social worker increased in the early weeks, Mr. Grantham disclosed that he had started using meth again about four months prior, and that his wife had begun using meth as well. Their relationship has become physically abusive, with Mrs. Grantham abusing him, and he defending himself by pushing her. The meth use had started to "get out of hand," the abuse from his wife had escalated: they fought, she bit his finger to the bone, he slapped her, she called the police, and he had had to spend a night in jail. At that point, Mrs. Grantham had stopped accompanying him to his appointments, and he had started to miss appointments, including chemotherapy.

At that time, still early in the worker's internship year, Mr. Grantham had asked her not disclose this information to Dr. Crowley or to Mary, and she had agreed. The social worker had not included any information in his chart regarding either his physical abuse or his drug abuse. His healthcare team was unaware of his history, as the social worker felt that if Mary saw that Mr. Grantham was using meth she would berate him, and he would terminate the treatment he needed.

That promise, and that decision, was made six months ago. During that time, Mr. Grantham's drug use has become more severe, and he is starting to display signs classically associated with meth use such as acne, a gaunt disheveled appearance, and strong body odor. However, his current chemo regimen includes Erbitux, which causes, he may be experiencing weight loss from his lack of appetite, and he has a colostomy bag which could explain some of the odor. It would be unlikely that staff would assume his change in appearance was due to meth use.

The Central Ethical Issue. The social worker is now caught in an ethical dilemma. Should she document Mr. Grantham's meth use, or discuss the issue with Dr. Crowley or Mary? What complication might arise with meth use and chemotherapy? Should she keep the promise of confidentiality made six months ago? The ethical dilemma may be stated as:

RESPECT OF CONFIDENTIALITY PROMISE TO PATIENT V. OBLIGATION TO RESPECT PRACTICE
STANDARDS

Research and Related Literature

The Health Insurance Portability and Accountability Act (HIPAA) is often cited within the context of medical records and the patients right to privacy. HIPAA was created to improve portability and continuity of health insurance coverage, to combat waste, fraud, and abuse in health insurance and healthcare delivery, and to simplify the adminis-tration of health insurance (HIPAA, 1996). National standards and guidelines were established to restrict the sharing and accessing of information and provide patients with greater control over their medical records (Richards, 2009, p. 550). However, HIPAA is aimed at protecting patients' information from being shared with unauthorized individuals or institutions; it does not address the sharing of personal health information within the care team.

> It is important for the social worker personally to present and review confidentiality policies directly with clients and to obtain their informed consent during a first or second interview, so that both parties fully understand any limitations which might require that the social worker share information with others.

The Individual Choice Principle was developed as part of a series of companion documents to help simplify and clarify the rules and regulations within HIPAA. The Individual Choice Principle states that "individuals should be provided a reasonable opportunity and capability to make informed decisions about the collection, use, and disclosure of their individually identifiable health information" (Individual Choice). One component within the Individual Choice Principle is the Privacy Rule, which gives the patient more control over health information. Part of the control a patient can exert is the right to have certain information amended; the right to agree, or authorize, cer-tain disclosures; the right to request restrictions of certain uses and disclosures; and provisions allowing a covered entity to obtain consent for certain uses and disclosures (Individual Choice). An individual has the right to decide whether specific sensitive information is disclosed through a Health Information Organization, but policies and consents would have to be developed to handle such requests. Furthermore, the Pri-vacy Rule also allows providers to have optional consent, where each provider can tailor the way in which they would like to handle the consent and release of information (Individual Choice).

When Mr. Grantham began treatment at the Oncology Center, he signed a consent form which outlined the details of his right to privacy. The social worker had never discussed her role in documentation and what she discloses to other staff. Furthermore, she had acceded to Mr. Grantham's request that she not disclose.

According to Gewirth's Principles Hierarchy, the right to the basic goods of well-being, such as food, health, and shelter, is primary; however, a person has the right to choose not to have these if he or she wishes (Rothman, 2009, p. 10). Thus, it would seem that healthcare providers must consider Mr. Grantham's well-being first, but Mr. Grantham *himself* can choose to give up his basic well-being—in this case by using meth while receiving chemotherapy.

Beauchamp and Childress' Medical Model states that professionals should help clients express self-determination, and also recognizes the responsibility of professionals to assist people to make decisions with knowledge (Rothman, 2009, p. 12). However, this would imply an obligation on the part of the healthcare provider to present all of the information needed in a comprehensible manner, so that an informed choice may be made. The Medical Model also establishes rules that value veracity, privacy, confidentiality, and fidelity to strengthen the patient–professional relationship (Beauchamp & Childress, pp. 288–317). Beauchamp and Childress even argue that underdisclosure, nondisclosure, and/or deception in medical records can be justified when veracity conflicts with other obligations (p. 284).

Other ethical models would disagree with placing Mr. Grantham's self-determination over his health. It can be argued that withholding Mr. Grantham's meth use from Dr. Crowley and Mary would place an undue risk on Mr. Grantham's life. Dolgoff, Loewenberg, and Harrington's Ethical Principles Screen places the protection of life as the highest responsibility, above self-determination (Dolgoff, Loewenberg, & Harrington, 2008, p. 66). From the perspective of medical professional clinical ethics, Jonsen, Siegler, and Winslade (2006, p. 2) assert that one should consider, in order, (1) medical indications, (2) patient preferences, (3) quality of life, and (4) contextual features. Therefore, both of these systems support providing the information to the medical team that would support Mr. Grantham's life.

Ethical obligations within the professional setting must also consider the relationship among professional team members, all of whom are working to support the patient's well-being. Veracity, privacy, and fidelity should be considered in the collegial relationship as well as in the patient relationship. As a professional, the social worker should uphold professional standards, which include colleagues and the hospital as employer as well as the patient.

Social Work Code of Ethics. The National Association of Social Workers Code of Ethics is a guide for social workers. Standards, core values, and principles in the Code are not ranked, as these must be applied contextually on a case-by-case basis. Of the six core values of service, social justice, dignity and worth of the person, importance of human relationships, integrity, and competence (NASW, p. 2), there are two that directly apply to this case: the importance of human relationships and integrity.

The value of importance of human relationships translates into the ethical principle that social workers behave in a trustworthy manner (NASW, p. 4). The principle goes on to state that social workers should foster relationships while supporting the well-being of individuals, families, groups, and communities.

The relationship between Mr. Grantham and the social worker is based on mutual respect and trust, and the worker is certain that Mr. Grantham would consider her revealing his meth use to the healthcare team to be a violation of his trust and of confidentiality. This would effectively destroy the relationship between patient and worker. The relationship between the Granthams must also be considered and supported, however, and it is less clear whether this would be better supported by the intern maintaining the privacy, or by the healthcare team as a whole assisting the Granthams to work through their problems.

Integrity is also a core value of the social work profession, stating that social workers must act in a trustworthy manner, honestly, and responsibly to promote ethical practices on behalf of the organizations with which they are affiliated (NASW, p. 4). Practicing with integrity, the social worker should provide information to Dr. Crowley and Mary so that they, and the hospital, can function within the standards of care. It would be considered dishonest to withhold information that is pertinent to Mr. Grantham's health.

Values and principles support ethical standards, which provide guidance on ethical conduct in specific areas. Standard 1.01 states that social workers have a commitment to their clients to consider their interests as primary. That commitment includes providing information to clients in a comprehensible form, and assisting them to explore and consider decisions they might make (NASW, p. 5). Standard 1.02, self-determination, notes that self-determination may be limited in the case of "serious, foreseeable, and imminent risk" (p. 5). Standard 1.03 states that professional services should be provided based on informed consent, and includes patient rights and the sharing of information as part of informed consent issues. The Code of Ethics specifically states that social workers can only disclose information when appropriate with valid consent from the client (NASW, 1.07b, p. 7). Furthermore, medical records should be considered confidential sensitive information and they should provide information that is only directly related to care. Of special relevance to this case is Standard 1.07d, which states that social workers are obligated to inform clients about the disclosure of confidential information and the possible consequences of such disclosure (NASW, 1.07b, p. 7). If the social worker determines that it is her responsibility to disclose the information regarding Mr. Grantham's use of meth to the healthcare team, it is essential that he be informed, in advance if possible, of such a disclosure.

Standard 2 addresses ethical responsibilities to colleagues. It specifically states (NASW, 2.03, p. 10) that social workers who work on interdisciplinary teams should be involved in decisions that affect the well-being of the client, and should bring the social work perspective to team consults. Standard 3 of the Code advises that social workers respect the commitment they have to their employers (NASW, 3.09a, p. 14) but that they should not allow the employers' policies and procedures to interfere with the ethical practice of social work (NASW, 3.09d, p. 15).

Author's Reflections, Reasoning Process, and Resolution

In addition to research and related information, it is important to recognize the major role of values—the social worker's, the patient's, and those of others in the system who may be affected by this dilemma, and to be aware of the process of decision making itself, in order for the social worker to fully understand and commit herself to a dilemma resolution.

Personal and Professional Values. The personal values of the social worker involved in this case are:

1. Quality of life	6. Fidelity
2. Honesty	7. Happiness
3. Autonomy	8. Health
4. Relationships	9. Respect for others
5. Life	10. Privacy

These values may shift over time and with different cases, but are values that generally guide the social worker's life. In regard to this case, it is hard to say if respecting Mr. Grantham's wishes to not disclose his drug use to Dr. Crowley and Mary would really impede his quality of life, the worker's highest value. Would Mr. Grantham have a poorer quality of life if his oncologist knew about his drug use and judged him differently for that? If his current pain medication were decreased or discontinued, he would be in pain, and his quality of life would be negatively affected.

Honesty is the social worker's second highest value, and, by not informing Dr. Crowley of the drug use the social worker would be rejecting that value in favor of autonomy and relationships, the third and fourth highest values. Withholding information would maintain the relationship between the social worker and Mr. Grantham, but violate trust in the professional relationship with Dr. Crowley and Mary.

In Mr. Grantham's case, the value of life and health should be favored over privacy and fidelity, but the worker is unclear whether continued meth use while undergoing chemotherapy has any specific contraindications in addition to its general detriment to overall health. The social worker has not been able to locate any studies that have indicated that continued meth use while undergoing chemotherapy would enhance or inhibit the progression of cancer. It is also of note that Mr. Grantham is in treatment for final-stage colorectal cancer, and the chemotherapy is only being used to extend his life, and not as a curative treatment. In addition, the ethical dilemma in this case is not focused specifically on Mr. Grantham's well-being itself, but on the worker's conflicting responsibilities to both honor her promises and respect confidentiality and to maintain a high professional standard of functioning.

Values of the Affected System. *Mr. Grantham:* Clearly, Mr. Grantham values the privacy and trust that he has with the social worker. He also values his health, but he understands that his time is limited, and he would like to enjoy this time without pain, and with the physical and mental comfort that he prefers. The relationship that he has with his family has always been very important to him, but due to the stress of his relationship and the escalating abuse it has become difficult for him to relate positively to his spouse. Furthermore, he values self-determination, and believes it is his right to use meth, even though he knows that it is impacting all of his other relationships and affecting the quality of his life.

Mrs. Grantham: It is hard to understand Mrs. Grantham's values at this point in time because she has not accompanied her husband to the cancer center, nor contacted the social worker, in many months. Calls made to Mrs. Grantham are rarely returned, and, on the rare occasions that she speaks with the social worker, she appears to be more concerned with herself than the health and well-being of her husband. It may be that Mrs. Grantham is angry, sad, and confused about her husband's impending death and is having a difficult time preparing for this.

Agency: The primary focus of the Oncology Center is to "meet the unique needs of each of our patients and their families by offering comprehensive, integrated cancer care in a friendly, comfortable environment" (_____ Policy Manual, 2012). This general statement implies that the staff should be understanding and accommodating to Mr. Grantham's needs, but Mary's reaction to his request for drugs and Dr. Crowley's general inaccessibility and impatience do not support this policy. Because of this, the social worker is uncertain how they would react to her sharing information about Mr. Grantham's meth use with these primary caregivers. There seems to be little teamwork in the efforts of staff members, and each seems to function independently.

Supervisor: As his previous social worker, the supervisor has a personal interest, but no longer has contact with Mr. Grantham. Although the supervisor had shared the knowledge of Mr. Grantham's early history with meth, the subject of current meth use has not surfaced in supervisory conferences. Thus, the social worker is not aware of any current information the supervisor might have in this regard, nor what she may have done with any information prior to transferring the case. She inquires about Mr. Grantham, but appears detached and uninvolved.

Dr. Crowley: The social worker has not had the opportunity to work closely with Dr. Crowley and to understand his values and concerns. As a physician, he presumably values the life and the health of his patients, but since the social worker has not had much experience with him, she is unsure as to his reaction to illicit drug use. It is also assumed that Dr. Crowley would prefer that patients provide him with a thorough, honest, medical history so he can make informed decisions about their care. However, Dr. Crowley has a very busy practice, and likes to be treated as a superior rather than a colleague, thus making the prospect of approaching him very daunting for the social worker.

Mary: Mr. Grantham and Mary's relationship has been a major issue in creating this dilemma. Had Mary been more understanding of Mr. Grantham's pain and drug use, he might have been more open about his meth use, and not requested the social worker's confidentiality. The social worker has also learned that a friend of Mary's had become addicted to prescription narcotics during cancer treatments and passed away recently, which may have contributed to Mary's reactions to Mr. Grantham.

Societal Values. There are three major issues in this dilemma which are strongly affected by societal values: life, privacy and confidentiality, and drug use.

Life is one of the most strongly held societal values, deeply ingrained in our culture. Mr. Grantham's diagnosis draws into question the natural order of life, as he is only 39, with a terminal cancer diagnosis. As a society, Americans have difficulties with death, especially the death of someone in their thirties. Society may view meth use as detrimental to life, but it is voluntary, whereas cancer may be viewed as an "uncontrollable attack from an enemy within" (Kastenbaum, 2007, p. 96).

The United States has a long history of valuing the privacy and confidentiality of medical professionals and their patients. The right to privacy was even a core component of the ancient Hippocratic Oath which states, "what I may see or hear in or outside the course of treatment which on no account must be spread abroad . . ." (Jonsen, Siegler, & Winslade, 2006, p. 171). As noted above, HIPAA was established by Congress to protect and ensure the safety of patient information.

Americans have negative perceptions of drug use, and the condemnation of methamphetamine use has grown exponentially as national drug campaigns focus on its detrimental effects (King, 2006, p. 3). Methamphetamine can cause adverse health effects, such as rapid heart rate and increased blood pressure, mood disturbances, and violent behavior, and increase the risk for HIV due to syringe use (NIDA). Since meth is considered highly addictive, and can have a negative impact, it is classified as a schedule II narcotic, and is illegal to use without a prescription.

Options for Action. The social worker involved in this case has developed four viable options to choose from. She could:

A. Go directly to Dr. Crowley and Mary and tell them about Mr. Grantham's past and current meth use and document in the medical record.

B. Document Mr. Grantham's meth use in the medical record and not directly inform Dr. Crowley or Mary.

C. Encourage Mr. Grantham to tell Dr. Crowley on his own and offer to be of support.

D. Honor her agreement with Mr. Grantham not to disclose his meth use to anyone.

Option A, *Risks*: If the social worker were to go directly to Dr. Crowley and Mary, it could jeopardize the relationship that she has built with Mr. Grantham. It would also be a breach of confidentiality, as Mr. Grantham disclosed this information and specifically asked that the social worker not tell Dr. Crowley and Mary. There is the risk that if Mr. Grantham is confronted by Dr. Crowley or Mary regarding his meth use, he may stop his chemotherapy treatments, which are controlling his cancer. Based on the current abusive relationship with his wife, it may also be possible that Mr. Grantham may react to confrontation in a volatile way, and hurt himself and others.

Benefits: The social worker would be upholding the professional relationship between herself and the medical team. Mr. Grantham's meth use may have interactions with his chemotherapy and may necessitate another type of chemotherapy. This may provide an opportunity for Mr. Grantham to enter a drug treatment facility, which would be beneficial both for his health and his relationship with his family. There is also the personal benefit to the social worker of not having to keep Mr. Grantham's secret, based on a promise given early in her internship.

Option B, *Risks:* By documenting Mr. Grantham's meth use in the chart, the social worker knows that Dr. Crowley and Mary could be made aware. This could result in the same risks as listed in Option A, with the additional risk that Dr. Crowley and Mary may be upset with the social worker for not disclosing this information to them directly, resulting in their distrust of the social worker.

Benefits: This is the least confrontational of all of the options for the social worker. While the information will be documented properly, she will not directly break her promise not to "tell" Dr. Crowley and Mary, as she would be "writing" and not "telling". Social work notes are often not read by the other medical staff, and essentially the social worker would not be lying, but rather shifting the blame onto Dr. Crowley and Mary for not being fully informed about Mr. Grantham.

Option C, Risks: There is the possibility that Mr. Grantham would become upset with the social worker for suggesting this, and would not trust her anymore. Mr. Grantham may also follow her suggestion, disclose his meth use to Dr. Crowley and Mary, who may become upset, refuse to give him more pain medication, and try to force him into treatment. This would then strain the relationship between Dr. Crowley and the patient. The relationship between the social worker and Dr. Crowley and Mary may also be impacted, if they feel the social worker should have disclosed earlier.

Benefits: The social worker would not be violating the confidentiality between herself and Mr. Grantham. Mr. Grantham may feel empowered with disclosing his drug use, and may opt to seek help. Mr. Grantham's drug use would no longer be a secret that the social worker must keep from the medical team, and Mr. Grantham would be able to get the support he needs throughout the rest of his treatment.

Option D, Risks: The major risk with this option is that Mr. Grantham's meth use may be more toxic in combination with the chemotherapy than if he were to be using meth alone. Also, the medical team might find out that the social worker knew about Mr. Grantham's meth use and had kept the information from them, thus leading to mistrust of the social worker by the medical team.

Benefits: The social worker would not be violating the relationship that she has established with Mr. Grantham. The social worker could continue to build trust with Mr. Grantham, and, through that therapeutic relationship, help Mr. Grantham to seek assistance with his drug addiction.

Critical Thinking

Practice Behavior Example: The social worker's dilemma is especially challenging because of the personalities of the colleagues involved in Mr. Grantham's care, and her concern about their reactions should she disclose Mr. Grantham's meth use.

Critical Thinking Question: The personalities and behavior of colleagues such as Dr. Crowley and Mary may influence professional ethical decisions. Would this be a consideration in your professional decision making? If so, is this a valid factor to consider in making professional decisions?

Course of Action. Option B, to document and not tell the doctors, appears to be the least confrontational of the options. However, Option C, to have Mr. Grantham tell the medical staff himself with support from the social worker is a better option. The social worker should assist Mr. Grantham to be willing to stop using meth, and then support him in being open and honest with his medical providers. If Mr. Grantham is unwilling to tell Dr. Crowley and Mary about his meth use, then the social worker should tell them herself. The social worker has kept Mr. Grantham's secret for enough time, and, if he is unwilling to change, she must disclose his meth use in his best interest. Also, the social worker is part of the medical team, and should disclose helpful information to the team about Mr. Grantham's health. At this point, a decision must be made that is within both personal and professional values boundaries.

Case Study Q (*Turnbull*)

Beauchamp, T. L., & Childress, J. (2009). *Principles of biomedical ethics.* New York: Columbia University Press.

Dolgoff, R., Harrington, D., & Loewenberg, F. (2009). *Ethical decisions for social work practice.* Belmont, CA: Brooks/Cole.

Health Insurance Portability and Accountability Act of 1996. (1996). Retrieved April 8, 2012 from Centers for Medicare and Medicaid Studies website: http://www.cms.gov/Regulations-and-Guidance/HIPAA-Administrative-Simplification/HIPAAGenInfo/index.html?redirect=/HIPAAGenInfo/

Individual Choice. Retrieved April 8, 2012, from the Office for Civil Rights website: http://www.hhs.gov/ocr/privacy/hipaa/understanding/special/healthit/individual-choice.pdf

Jonsen, A., Siegler, M., & Winslade, W. (2006). *Clinical ethics. A practical approach to ethical decision in clinical medicine* (6th ed.). New York, NY: McGraw Hill.

Kastenbaum, R. (2007). *Death, society, and human experience* (9th ed.). Boston, MA: Bacon and Allyn.

King, R. (2006). *The next big thing? Methamphetamine in the United States.* The Sentencing Project: Research and Advocacy for Reform.

National Association of Social Workers. (2008). *Code of ethics.* Retrieved from the NASW website, http://www.naswdc.org/pubs/code/code.asp?print=1& ____Policy Manual, 2012.

Richards, M. (2009). Electronic medical records: Confidentiality issues in the time of HIPAA. *Professional Psychology: Research and Practice, 40*(6), 550–556.

Rothman, J. (2009). *From the front lines: Student cases in social work ethics.* Boston: Allyn & Bacon.

CHAPTER SUMMARY

This chapter has addressed the responsibilities of social workers as professionals, and each case has presented a very personal and important issue that social workers might face. Responsibilities include professional comportment in areas such as preventing deception, fraud, and dishonesty. Preventing, and not engaging in, discrimination is an important part of professional function, and the most recent revision of the Code of Ethics has broadened "discrimination" groupings to include "gender identity and expression" as well as "immigration status."

One of the most challenging subsections of this standard is the section addressing appropriate conduct for a social worker outside of the professional setting. In addition to distinguishing between actions taken as a social worker and as a private

NASW Ethical Standard Four

individual, private conduct should also not compromise professional responsibilities. This would seem to imply that one should comport oneself in a professionally responsible manner at all times, in both professional and personal life.

In addition, it is the social worker's responsibility not to allow personal problems or challenges to affect professional functioning. This involves self-awareness and self-examination, and suggests that, should such conditions exist, it is the responsibility of the professional to ensure that they do not impact professional service to clients.

The painful challenge faced by the social worker in the first case, that of the two suicidal clients, is especially poignant, as it considers the role of personal values and assessment of quality of life, and the manner in which this impacts decisions made regarding clients. This case is particularly dramatic because it involves life and death, but it clearly addresses the important issue of consistency in decision making and some of the challenges this presents. Ultimately, the social worker determines that there is great value in treating each situation as unique, and assessing it within its own framework.

The second case presents a situation that is often encountered in host settings: the "host," in this case a physician, makes a determination regarding patient care and safety with which the family member, who has decisional responsibility, does not agree. Where does the social worker's responsibility lie? Should she always advocate for the client, or should she support the physician's judgment and work with the client toward accepting that? Where health and safety are the issues, who ultimately has the best understanding? What should be the priorities? The social worker arrives at a compromise decision, one that she believes will support both the client's wishes and the physician's judgment.

The ethical issue in the third case might be stated in a number of ways. Here, the social worker has chosen to consider confidentiality and promise-keeping from within the framework of professional behavior and functioning. Once a promise is made, is it ever ethical to break it? As a professional social worker, it is important to exercise thought and care in making difficult decisions. In this case, the worker must reconcile her professional responsibility to the patient, who might be risking further pain and shortened life; to colleagues, who are prescribing chemotherapy and other medications with no awareness of possible drug interactions which could complicate care; to her employing agency and to the Oncology Center, whose commitment to optimal patient care necessitates truth-telling. However, she hopes that she will be able to help the patient to understand the need to share this information, and to share it himself. If he refuses, her professional commitment will require her to share the information herself.

The following questions will test your knowledge of the content found within this chapter. For questions 1-6, please select the phrase that best completes each sentence. Question 7 is a brief essay question. For additional assessment, including licensing-exam type questions on applying chapter content to practice behaviors, visit **MySearchLab**.

1. Social workers practicing in rural areas:
   a. must often drive many miles
   b. have reduced caseloads
   c. may not be able to avoid dual relationships
   d. have additional responsibilities

2. In providing guidance for professionals, the Code of Ethics may also:
   a. hinder decision making
   b. foster professional dependency
   c. be detrimental to some clients' well-being
   d. limit options for action by professionals

3. There is a potential for harm and exploitation in:
   a. dual relationships with clients
   b. providing service to clients
   c. working in agency settings with clients
   d. following agency guildelines regarding client relationships

4. Professional responsibilities:
   a. are generally different for each profession
   b. have many similarities across professions
   c. apply to only licensed professionals
   d. are determined solely by the setting

5. A social worker's personal problems:
   a. unavoidably affect practice and service delivery
   b. must not be permitted to impact professional service
   c. should be shared with a supervisor
   d. are the social worker's personal business

6. Acknowledging the contributions of others:
   a. should only be done if it's helpful to clients
   b. invalidates the social worker's contributions
   c. is an ethical responsibility
   d. is generally a distraction to service provision

7. Social workers are responsible for conducting themselves in private in a manner that does not compromise professionalism. What are some examples of private behaviors that might *compromise* professionalism? Does this impact a social worker's basic freedoms?

10

NASW Ethical Standard Five

Social Workers' Ethical Responsibilities to the Social
Work Profession

CHAPTER OUTLINE

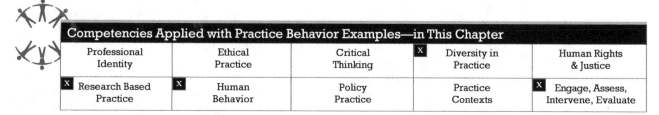

Competencies Applied with Practice Behavior Examples—in This Chapter				
Professional Identity	Ethical Practice	Critical Thinking	X Diversity in Practice	Human Rights & Justice
X Research Based Practice	X Human Behavior	Policy Practice	Practice Contexts	X Engage, Assess, Intervene, Evaluate

175

INTRODUCTION

Provisions of the Code

In making a commitment to the field of social work, workers also take on a commitment to the profession of which they are a part. Social workers, both individually and collectively, *represent* the profession, and the commitment to professional values and behavior and to a solid base of knowledge is vital. The two subsections of Standard five address the profession's integrity, the processes of evaluation, and the qualities of good social work research.

Subsection 5.01 addresses the integrity of the profession as a whole. It advocates the maintenance and promotion of high standards of practice on the part of all members (5.01a). Social workers are also obligated to support the values, ethics, knowledge base, and mission of the profession through research, discussion, and responsible criticism (5.01b).

Time and expertise should be contributed to support and enhance the profession, through activities such as teaching, research, consultation, legislative testimony, community presentations, and membership in professional organizations (5.01c). The next subsection encourages the contribution to the knowledge base of the profession specifically, and the sharing of knowledge with colleagues via literature, presentations, and conference participation (5.01d).

Licensure laws and state regulations have significantly decreased the instances of the use of unauthorized and unqualified persons using the title "social worker." However, despite these, abuses of the title continue.

Subsection 5.01d addresses what may be, at times, a challenging situation for social work professionals—the obligation to prevent the unauthorized and unqualified practice of social work. Workers have advocated for licensure laws in every state. These have been passed, and include specific qualifications, criteria, and levels of licensure. Social work agencies have, on the whole, respected such licensure. However, the title "social worker" may be assigned when an employee *functions* as a social worker. Social workers in host settings may especially find themselves confronted with unqualified and unauthorized (and unlicensed) "social workers" whose credentials do not include formal social work education. This may create problems for the worker on both a personal and an institutional level as he or she seeks to rectify this misuse of professional titles. However, there is a strong obligation to work toward the maintenance of high professional quality of service, which involves reserving the title "social worker" for members of the profession alone.

Subsection 5.02 addresses evaluation and research, asking that workers monitor and evaluate policies, programs, and practice interventions (5.02a); facilitate evaluation and research (5.02b); and critically use the results of such evaluation and research in practice, keeping current with new developments in the field (5.02c).

In terms of research in social work, workers must consider the consequences of such research and follow guidelines that protect participants (5.02d). These might include voluntary, written, and fully-informed consent for all participants (5.02e) or proxies if necessary (5.02f), informing participants of their rights to withdraw or refuse (5.02h), providing access to supportive services (5.02i), protection from harm (5.02j), assurance of anonymity and confidentiality (5.02l), protection of identifying information unless proper consent has been obtained (5.02m), and the avoidance of dual or multiple relationships or conflicts of interest (5.02o).

Social workers should not design or conduct research or evaluation that does not utilize informed consent procedures (5.02g), should discuss collected information only with professionals or with persons professionally concerned (5.02k), should report findings accurately, and should educate themselves and others about proper research practices (5.02p).

THE CASES

The cases included in this textbook are all grounded in students' experiences. However, many of the guidelines addressed by this standard are not in areas that students often encounter in their fieldwork placements. An effort has been made to relate the four cases included in this section to concerns students have experienced.

The first case places the worker's professional integrity, her responsibility to the value base of the profession, and her obligation to utilize her knowledge and skill against the rights of clients to self-determine. In an adoption agency setting, the worker is presented with parents who desire immediate placement for their 3-month-old baby girl. They are clearly in crisis, are anxious, and under a great deal of stress. They are unaware of, and uninterested in, any resources or information available to assist them in caring for their child, or in making decisions for her welfare as their primary consideration. They adamantly refuse any agency service other than immediate placement.

The worker is concerned that they are making a momentous decision without reflective thought and adequate information, both of which services she is professionally able and obligated to provide. Can she require that the parents accept counseling as a condition of placing their child for adoption when they clearly do not want this service? How can she meet her obligation to them, as well as to the profession?

In the second case, the worker in a rape crisis center is faced with difficult immediate decisions. Clients in crisis call for help and often ask the worker to decide for them whether their rape should be reported to the police. The worker has no in-person contact with them, and her relationship is based only on the clients' first telephone calls, when a decision regarding reporting must be made. She has little information regarding the individual client's values, vulnerabilities, strengths, and weaknesses.

The professional values of justice, honesty, integrity, concern for the welfare of society, and others suggest that the worker has an obligation to encourage the client to report the rape. The worker's agency, whose mission is to address issues of violence against women, encourages reporting.

However, statistics and studies about reporting rape force the worker to consider other issues as well. Research has repeatedly shown that very few reported cases reach the courts, and, of these, only a small fraction result in conviction. The process of reporting and prosecution is often humiliating, embarrassing, and painful for the victim. Is it justified to add to the victim's stress and vulnerability by encouraging reporting, when the chances of success in prosecution are so small? Is the worker not obligated, instead, to the protection of her vulnerable client and, therefore, to suggesting that the client not report?

The third case presents a conflict for the worker trying to support the values, ethics, and knowledge base of the profession. A medical social worker is assigned a patient with terminal cancer; both the patient and family want to continue treatment at the hospital. The physician feels that treatment is futile, and that the patient should be referred to hospice care, so that hospital resources could be utilized more appropriately. The patient and family associate hospice with death and refuse to consider this option.

The worker's primary obligation to her client, and that client's right to self-determination, would lead her to assist her client to remain in the hospital and to receive the care that she is requesting. However, she is working in a host setting: She also has an obligation to respect the expertise of other professionals and to follow written orders that are supported by hospital policy. She has a broader obligation to the optimal utilization of resources.

Case Study R   "My Clients Are in a Hurry!": Professional Integrity Versus Client Self-Determination

Abstracted from an unpublished paper by Shereen Rubenstein, MSW

Practice Context and Case Presentation

A private, nonprofit agency serves children in need of adoption services and their biological and adoptive parents. Located in a large urban center, the agency serves "hard-to-place" as well as "normal" children and has developed an excellent reputation for careful and thoughtful placement planning.

Mr. and Mrs. Smith desire to plan for adoption for their 3-month-old baby girl, Rachel. She has been diagnosed with cerebral palsy, possible blindness, and possible mild mental disability. The Smiths also have a 2-year-old son, whom they describe as "perfect."

The Smiths request immediate placement. They state that they have been considering adoption since the "nightmare" began at Rachel's birth, and they feel that they can no longer continue to care for her. They express concern about their future responsibilities in raising a disabled child—"changing her diaper at 10 years of age and still at 21," "routinely massaging her gums," "gliding a tube down her throat for feeding while having (their) morning coffee," and so on. They have waited these 3 months to ascertain that there was no error in diagnosis, but now they have been assured that Rachel's condition is permanent, and they wish to proceed immediately. They have adequate financial resources to provide for Rachel, but they do not wish to be responsible for the cost of raising a disabled child. They expressly state that they do not wish to become involved in receiving any counseling from the agency: Placement services were all that was required.

In assessing the Smiths' request, the worker feels that the Smiths are currently deep in crisis, mourning the loss of their "perfect" family, and unable to cope with the thought of a disabled child. They express a sense of failure and guilt, as well as confusion. In attempting to assess whether the Smiths have explored other avenues, she determines that they are unaware of the resources and support services available to assist parents of disabled children.

It seems unwise to the worker for the Smiths to make a hasty decision without adequate information and reflection, and without any counseling. Thus, the worker determines that it is not in their family's best interests to proceed with placement without utilizing the professional skills available to them to ensure the best decision for their future. Placing Rachel without these services would violate the worker's professional integrity, her obligation to serve her clients with skill and competence, and the standards of the profession that supports the professional social worker as having the knowledge and skill that would ensure that the best decisions are made and actions

---

Human Behavior

Practice Behavior Example: The worker notes that the Smiths are "mourning" the loss of their perfect family, and are expressing many characteristics of bereavement.

Critical Thinking Question: Feelings of bereavement and mourning such as these may be referred to as "non-finite grief," as opposed to feelings related to a "finite grief" that follows a loss such as death. How might you understand the differences between these two kinds of losses? How should this difference be considered in social work practice?

are taken by clients (Dolgoff, Loewenberg, & Harrington, 2009). Yet these clients are requesting placement immediately. The worker finds herself facing the dilemma of:

CLIENT SELF-DETERMINATION V. PROFESSIONAL INTEGRITY

Research and Related Literature

A study conducted in the intensive care unit with parents of neonatal/ill infants found common manifestations of extreme emotional stress (Dillard, Auerbach, & Showalter, 1980). In addition to displaying signs of depression, loss of appetite, and high anxiety, many were struggling with a great amount of guilt. Forty percent felt that they were responsible for their baby's illness. Yet, of the more than 250,000 children born each year with a mental or physical disability, the vast majority of parents do choose to parent them (Springen & Kantrowitz, 1990).

Feelings of guilt, failure, and helplessness are common among parents who have made an adoption plan for their disabled infants. They may feel that they are incapable of creating, or raising, a healthy baby. Financial stress and feeling emotionally "wiped out" are two common emotions, but parents also fear making an error by "giving away" a child who is not really disabled. Adoption experts seek to help these parents view their decision as one made out of love. They can be told that being honest and loving the child enough to know that others can give their baby what they fear they cannot is a good decision, and this thought can aid the grief process. A period of grief often occurs post placement. Practitioners feel that the adoptive home is the better home for the child, because adoptive parents do truly desire the child (Springen & Kantrowitz, 1990).

A strong support network may be critical in making such decisions. In the 1970s, Cassel, Cobb, and Kaplan conducted separate studies that all indicated a strong social support network can greatly help someone who is experiencing a crisis (Mor-Barak, 1988). The Smiths' network, except for Mrs. Smith's father, all support the adoption plan for Rachel.

The Smiths support their arguments with deontological reasoning. They feel that adoption for Rachel is in the baby's best interest: that another family would better be able to love her, support her, and care for her. A deontologist such as Kant would find this reasoning morally and ethically acceptable, for "to have moral worth, a person's motive for acting must come from a recognition that he or she intends what is morally required" (Beauchamp & Childress, 2009, p. 344).

Rights-based theory, such as liberal individualism, also supports the Smiths' decision, because "to have a right is to be in the position to determine, by one's choices, what others are to do or need to do" (Beauchamp & Childress, 2009, p. 351). The Smiths' right to choose also gives them the right to expect that the adoption agency will implement their choice.

However, the worker's ethical code suggests other obligations and responsibilities. The social worker has a responsibility to support the integrity of the profession, as stated in Section 5 of the Code of Ethics, which obligates workers to maintain a high standard of practice (5.01a) and to "uphold and advance the values, ethics, knowledge, and mission of the profession" (NASW, 2008, 5.01b). These support the worker's application of knowledge, skill, and competence to the client's problem. This would seem to preclude her acceptance of the Smiths' requests without provision of services to ensure that they are making the best possible decision for their family.

The worker recognizes that the Smiths are in crisis, based on their behavior and levels of stress and anxiety. A loss of something or someone close is oftentimes a precipitating event that causes a crisis for a person (Gilliland & James, 1993). The loss of the normal, healthy child that the Smiths expected represented such a precipitating event for them. Other common manifestations of persons in crisis include feelings of guilt, depression, lowered self-esteem, anxiety, lack of appetite, and difficulty in sleeping. The ability to rationalize, think logically, and make decisions may be impaired (Dixon, 1979). In speaking with the Smiths, the worker has become aware that most of these characteristics apply to them.

The Smiths also appear to lack information regarding resources to assist them with Rachel, and providing such information to them could be considered an extension of sub-sections 6.04a and b, which state that workers should act to ensure that all persons have access to the resources they need, as well as to expand the choices for all individuals. Early intervention services for the Smiths might include family training, counseling, home visits, case management, assessments, and respite care (Bishop, Rounds, & Weil, 1993).

A deontological approach to the dilemma suggests that it is important to properly assess a case and to offer the best possible services. Kant argues that morality is derived from reason rather than from intuition, emotions, conscience, or traditions (Beauchamp & Childress, 2009). This would direct the worker to thoughtfully consider the issues involved prior to acting upon the Smiths' request.

Author's Reflections, Reasoning Process, Resolution

The Smiths appear to be receiving contradictory messages from society. On the one hand, society asks that parents shield and protect their children from danger and harm. On the other, it sends clear messages that healthy, cute little babies are desirable. On the one hand, parents who adopt disabled children are praised; on the other, "society" in general still tends to discriminate against people with disabilities. The Smiths, and the worker herself, are caught in these contradictions.

To safeguard Rachel's interest and enable the Smiths to make a reflective decision unencumbered with her care, the worker determines that Rachel may be placed in a foster home temporarily. While this would mean an adjustment for the baby, the worker feels that the removal of Rachel from their care would allow the Smiths the time and the distance they need to consider all of the possibilities open to them. As a condition of accepting Rachel into care, the worker would ask the Smiths to come in for counseling and provide them with the information they need to make an informed decision. This would maximize their self-determination, relieve the pressure for immediate adoption placement, and enable the worker to provide the needed services to the family.

If, after counseling and the provision of information, the Smiths continue to desire adoption for Rachel, the worker would accept her for placement.

Postscript. Before presenting the above plan to the family at their next appointment, the worker received a call from the Smiths. Unable to keep Rachel a moment longer, they have placed her for immediate adoption with another agency, one who was willing to accept her without providing services to the family.

Case Study R (Rubenstein)

Beauchamp, T., & Childress, J. (2009). *Principles of biomedical ethics* (6th ed.). New York: Oxford University Press.

Bishop, K., Rounds, K., & Weil, M. (1993). P. L. 99–457: Preparation for social work practice with infants and toddlers with disabilities and their families. *Journal of Social Work Education, 29*(1), 36–45.

Dillard, R., Auerbach, K., & Showalter, A. (1980). A parents' program in the intensive care nursery: Its relationship to maternal attitudes and expectations. *Social Work in Health Care, 5*(3), 245–251.

Dixon, S. (1979). *Working with people in crisis: Theory and practice.* St. Louis, MO: C. V. Mosby.

Dolgoff, R., Loewenberg, F. M., & Harrington, D. (2009). *Ethical decisions for social work practice* (6th ed.). Itasca, IL: F.E. Peacock.

Gilliland, B., & James, R. (1993). *Crisis intervention strategies.* Pacific Grove, CA: Brooks/Cole.

Mor-Barak, M. (1988). Support systems intervention in crisis situations: Theory, strategies, and a case illustration. *International Social Work, 31,* 285–304.

National Association of Social Workers. (2008). *NASW code of ethics.* Washington, DC: Author.

Springen, K., & Kantrowitz, B. (1990, October 22). The long goodbye: When parents give a disabled child up for adoption, the pain often lingers. *Newsweek, 16,* 77–80.

Case Study S Rape: When Professional Values Place Vulnerable Clients at Risk

Abstracted from an unpublished paper by Eileen A. Dombo, MSW

Practice Context and Case Presentation

An urban rape crisis center is a private, community-based organization dedicated to ending all forms of violence against women through counseling and advocacy services to sexual assault survivors, through community education, coalition work with other local and national community organizations, legislative monitoring, and advocacy on relevant issues. The center maintains a 24-hour hotline staffed by social workers. Advocacy services include assistance in reporting to the police and/or pursuance of legal action and a companion program where workers accompany clients to hospitals, police encounters, and court appointments.

Hotline callers, like other survivors of sexual assault, often feel a loss of power, which may manifest as an inability to be assertive. Some clients decide that it would be empowering to report the rape to the police and/or take some legal action against the perpetrator. Others do not wish to pursue this course of action. Still others are uncertain what course of action to pursue and ask the hotline worker's advice.

As a social work professional, the worker is strongly committed to the ethical principle of social justice, which is a core value and a mission of the profession, as stated in the Preamble of the NASW Code of Ethics (NASW, 2008). Thus, it would appear that the worker's obligation is to encourage the caller to report the incident. This would raise public awareness and support accurate statistics. The perpetrator could be caught, face charges, and go to jail, thus protecting other women.

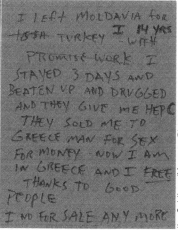

However, the worker's previous experiences in the companion program has also enabled her to have an understanding of the difficulties victims encounter in the process of reporting. This process can be traumatic for many rape survivors who are not prepared for the insensitive and harsh treatment they receive from the police, hospitals, and the legal system. Providing full and honest information about the process can dissuade a victim from reporting. Hotline workers who face this question during a single telephone contact know very little about the caller and are often uncertain of whether strong encouragement to report is in the best interest of the rape survivor.

Professional social workers have a responsibility to address the needs of vulnerable populations, such as this 14-year-old trafficked girl in a shelter in Greece, through both advocacy and direct service.

Jim Goldberg/Magnum Photos

The dilemma can be stated as follows:

PROFESSIONAL COMMITMENT TO SOCIAL JUSTICE v. OBLIGATION TO CLIENT'S BEST INTEREST

Research and Related Literature

Estrich (1987) states that rape is the most underreported crime in our society. She states that underreporting affects how society perceives the crime: People assume that rape does not happen that often because of the low statistics. Estrich's findings support the decision to urge the caller to report because it will raise awareness and statistics. The more survivors report, the more attention the issue of rape will get from the police, courts, and society.

Koss (1985) found that only 10–50 percent of rapes are reported to the police. In an effort to increase reporting, Adams and Abarbanel (1988) have reported that, workers at a rape treatment center in California, wrote a manual for colleges and universities to help them handle the issue of sexual assault. In the manual, they encourage administrators to adopt policies that encourage victim reporting of sexual assaults. They assert that reporting will help prevent assaults from happening to others and facilitate the provision of services to survivors. Clearly, the information presented by Estrich, Koss, and Adams and Abarbanel shows the need for survivors to report rape because it will increase the awareness of the crime. The police department's Sex Offenses Branch stated that they would encourage all victims of rape to report immediately because this allows more evidence to be collected and increases the chances of successful prosecution.

> **Recently, there has been increased attention given to underage rape victims, particularly young children. Increased reporting of underage rape will be reflected in statistics in the near future.**

However, 98 percent of the survivors who do press charges will never see their attacker caught, tried, and imprisoned; more than one half of the cases brought to prosecution will be dismissed; and one half of convicted rapists serve less than 1 year in prison (Senate Judiciary Committee, 1993).

When a survivor decides to report, the police are contacted, and the survivor is taken to the hospital and is given an examination, which includes an evidence-collection procedure that is very detailed and sometimes painful. Interaction with the police and hospital staff can be traumatic: The rape survivor must often wait for the police to respond to the call, then wait again in the hospital emergency room because a rape situation is not deemed to be a priority unless there is also a critical injury. Often, officers and hospital staff are not trained to deal with survivors of sexual assault, and frequently their own personal biases about rape and rape victims are revealed through their contact with the survivor.

After hospital procedures are completed, the survivor must fill out a report and may be taken back to the scene of the crime. A police investigation will follow and, depending on the amount of evidence the police are able to collect, there will either be an arrest or the case will be referred to the United States or the respective State's Attorney's Office for further investigation. If it is then determined that there is enough evidence to pursue, the survivor may have to appear in court and testify. In court, the survivor is often made to answer questions that suggest that it is the survivor who is to blame for the rape. This is also quite traumatic (Rape Crisis Center, 1995).

Diversity in Practice

Practice Behavior Example: Age, gender, and sexual orientation may also affect the way in which rape victims are treated by medical and justice personnel.

Critical Thinking Question: How might these rape victims be treated differently? Should hotline social workers consider these potential differences in treatment in making recommendations for reporting?

Estrich (1987) notes that many reported rape cases do not go much further than the police report due to lack of evidence. She states that, in many cases, authorities do not see the case as fitting the definition of rape and that they are "not treated as criminal by the criminal justice system" (Estrich, 1987, p. 8). Bachman (1993) found that women did not report their rape because they felt it was too personal or they feared they would not be believed. Koss (1985) found that some victims are in such denial about the rape that they cannot bring themselves to report it or feel that if they do report it they will not be believed. Professionals at the center agree in perceiving that reporting is often traumatic for the survivor and that the perpetrator is rarely brought to justice.

Author's Reflections, Reasoning Process, and Resolution

In the United States, people are presumed to be innocent until proven guilty. Until someone is found guilty by a court of law, the accused is only the "alleged rapist." The burden of proof is on the victim. Since she must prove that the man accused of raping her actually did so, in effect, she is the one to be put on trial. Our society also values independence and individual privacy. "Proving" rape generally involves a loss of privacy: One's sexual history, and the experience itself, must be revealed in court, often an extremely traumatic experience for the victim.

The Code of Ethics provides guidance in resolving this dilemma. Section 1.01 addresses commitment to clients' well-being as a *primary* responsibility. The very next sentence in that section, however, suggests that the worker's responsibility to society may, at times, supersede this commitment. Section 1.03a explicates the obligation to informed consent. Section 1.06a addresses conflicts of interest. Is an obligation on the part of the worker to both social justice and best interest of client such a conflict? If so, should the worker inform the client of this conflict? Section 5.01b states the professional obligation to advance the mission, values, and ethics of the profession. This would seem to support the social justice side at least as strongly as the client's best interests side of the dilemma. Section 4.04 requires that social workers be truthful with clients. Being truthful supports giving complete information about the problems and difficulties that the survivor may experience if she elects to report. It is often difficult to assess client values based on a crisis telephone call, and the worker may not be able to utilize such a call as a resource in decision making.

The worker values autonomy and independence and believes that empowerment can be a positive tool. Justice is power; thus, reporting can be very empowering. However, the worker's experience has demonstrated to her that the criminal justice system is not sensitive to the needs of rape victims, and that the likelihood of actually bringing the rapist to justice is slim. Thus, concern for the protection of the client from the sometimes harsh and insensitive process, combined with the small likelihood of success, leads the worker to believe that the risks associated with reporting may not be worthwhile if the client is herself reluctant to initiate the process.

Ultimately, however, this worker believes that it is her obligation to provide full and complete information to clients who ask about reporting and, indeed, to all clients. Such information supports and enhances empowerment for all clients, for it enables each person to make the decision about reporting in accordance with her own values and understanding of herself. Where a client asks the worker's advice, provision of information can be supplemented with an exploration of client values and beliefs, thus ensuring that the decision made is truly that of the client's.

While social justice would support reporting rapes, it is not legally mandated that the social worker herself engage in such reporting. Social justice, in the sense of reporting crimes, can only be demanded by the survivor. Providing full information enables the survivor to be treated with consideration, respect, and justice.

Case Study S (*Dombo*)

Adams, A., & Abarbanel, G. (1988). *Sexual assault on campus: What colleges can do.* Santa Monica, CA: Santa Monica Hospital Medical Center.

Bachman, R. (1993). Predicting the reporting of rape victimizations: Have rape reforms made a difference? *Criminal Justice and Behavior, 20*(3), 254–270.

Estrich, S. (1987). *Real rape: How the legal system victimizes women who say no.* Cambridge, MA: Harvard University Press.

Koss, M. P. (1985). The hidden rape victim: Personality, attitudinal and situational characteristics. *Psychology of Women Quarterly, 9*, 193–212.

National Association of Social Workers. (2008). *NASW code of ethics.* Washington, DC: Author.

Rape Crisis Center. (1995). *Rape crisis center training manual.* Washington, DC: Author.

Senate Judiciary Committee. (1993). *The response to rape: Detours on the road to equal justice.* Washington, DC: Author.

Case Study T   "Discharge Her to a Hospice Now!"—A Conflict of Professional Loyalties

Abstracted from an unpublished paper by Josephine K. Bulkley, J.D., MSW

Practice Context and Case Presentation

On an oncology service at a major university hospital, the worker has been assigned a terminal cancer patient—a mother of three young children, with a devoted and supportive husband and family. The physician has determined that further efforts are futile, thus making the patient's continued hospital stay an improper utilization of resources. She orders the social worker to refer the patient for hospice care.

The worker has attempted to present the hospice concept to the patient and family, and it has been adamantly refused. Both patient and family associate hospice care with death. They do not accept the patient's poor prognosis and request continued care and treatment in the hospital. Due to financial considerations, palliative care is not an alternative for this family at this time.

Many patients receiving cancer treatment at this hospital are admitted to the oncology unit a number of times. Although some patients accept hospice services or palliative care services, many do not accept these and wish to continue to receive all medical treatment, including palliative care aimed toward the relief of pain, as hospital inpatients. Some return to the hospital's outpatient clinic routinely for appointments with their primary attending physician, and they are admitted if a complication arises. Some patients choose to die in the hospital.

The central ethical dilemma involves a conflict between the social worker's ethical responsibility to abide by the policies, regulations, and recommendations of the employing organization (the hospital and medical staff) and her responsibility to advocate or protect the interest of the patient and family. The above case may be considered an example of conflicts in the duty of fidelity, "divided loyalties" (Beauchamp & Childress, 2009; Reamer, 1990, p. 87), or loyalties to multiple parties (Proctor, Morrow-Howell, & Lott, 1993). Kugelman (1992) suggests that social workers may be called upon to make decisions in cases where the hospital's interests favor discharge, while patients' interests would support continued in-hospital care.

It is also incumbent upon the social worker to consider her own responsibility to the hospital in which she is serving her internship. The functioning and maintenance of the hospital as a whole depends on appropriate utilization of its resources, which may, at times, conflict with clients' rights to self-determine. Organizations develop protocols and priorities, which support their mission and purpose.

The dilemma may be stated as follows:

RESPONSIBILITY TO CLIENT ADVOCACY V. RESPONSIBILITY TO EMPLOYING ORGANIZATION

Research and Related Literature

Responsibility to Client Advocacy. In hospitals, the primary focus of most social workers' intervention is an adequate and appropriate discharge planning (Proctor et al., 1993). A social worker who believes that a particular discharge plan is best for the client when the

A major difference between hospice care and palliative care involves treatment. While hospice care generally precludes aggressive treatment, and is often viewed as "end-of-life care," palliative care enables patients, families, and physicians to determine appropriate care, and its time frame tends to be open-ended. Hospice care is covered by Medicare and other health plans, while palliative care is often not a covered service. However, the physician has ordered hospice care in this case, and palliative care is not an option in every area of the country.

client is requesting something different is faced with a conflict between what he or she believes is in the client's best interest and supporting self-determination on the client's part. A study of ethical dilemmas experienced by 16 hospital social workers revealed that the most common conflict involved the social worker's dual obligations: to her or his perception of client's best interests and to supporting and fostering the client's self-determination (Proctor et al., 1993). The study also found that this ethical conflict frequently arose where there was disagreement concerning discharge destination.

A fundamental ethical principle of social work practice in Standard 1.01 of the Code of Ethics is the social worker's primary responsibility to the client. There is little doubt that a social worker should consider his or her client's interests as paramount. Beauchamp and Childress suggest that the principles of respect for autonomy, justice, and utility justify the obligation to act in good faith to keep vows and promises, fulfill agreements, and maintain relationships and fiduciary responsibilities. In a hospital setting, social workers may have conflicts with medical staff because "a psychosocial understanding of client needs often leads social workers to disagree with physicians about treatment and discharge" (Proctor et al., 1993).

A client's right to self-determination is considered a fundamental precept of social work and is a basic obligation of the worker. This obligation is accorded the utmost esteem by the profession (Hepworth, Rooney, Dewberry Rooney, Strom-Gottfried, & Larsen, 2010; Rothman, 1989).

According to Abramson (1985, p. 387), self-determination "refers to that condition in which personal behavior emanates from a person's own wishes, choices and decisions." The extent to which self-determination has priority over other values and principles "is a historical and continuing struggle" (Proctor et al., 1993). Moreover, Proctor et al. (1993, p. 171) note that self-determination "has been recognized as a primary aspect of ethical issues arising in health care settings; patient bills of rights in many hospitals explicate the importance of self-determination."

The duty to promote a client's self-determination arises out of a basic moral principle regarding respect for autonomy. Autonomy may be defined as "a form of personal liberty of action where the individual determines his or her own course of action, in accordance with a plan chosen by himself or herself" (Abramson, 1985). Beauchamp and Childress (2009, p. 100) state that all theories of autonomy "view two conditions as essential . . .: *liberty* (independence from controlling influences) and *agency* (capacity for intentional action)." Drawing from the work of Alan Gewirth, Reamer (1990) states that a basic ethical guideline in resolving a conflict between values or principles is that "an individual's right to freedom takes precedence over his or her own right to basic well-being" (p. 63). Thus, a social worker should respect an individual's right to choose to engage in self-destructive behavior, with two caveats. The client's decision must be voluntary and informed, and the consequences must not threaten the well-being of others (Reamer, 1990). According to Reamer (1990, p. 62), as drawn from Gewirth, another person's well-being takes precedence over a person's right to freedom.

Responsibility to Employing Organization. Reamer notes that social workers generally must respect the rules and regulations of employers. This is not a matter of blind and rigid loyalty without regard for consequences, but a contracted obligation in the sense that if the social worker works for an agency, he or she works for and not against it. Second, the social worker does what the agency employs him or her to do in fulfilling the agency's declared purpose and service function, not something else.

Practice Contexts

Practice Behavior Example: This case takes place in a host setting—a hospital. Host settings may include medical settings, criminal justice settings, educational settings, private sector settings, and many others.

Critical Thinking Question: How might the role of the social worker in host settings differ from social agency settings? What are the special issues/considerations of which the social worker must be aware in host settings?

A social worker who is employed by a hospital, therefore, has an ethical obligation to support the recommendations of the medical staff concerning patients. Under the current financial healthcare crisis, the hospital and medical staff have an economic interest in the "efficient use of acute care beds for financial solvency" (Proctor et al., 1993), thereby encouraging rapid discharge of patients and avoidance of multiple or repeated hospitalizations.

A hospital's need to consider the most efficient use of scarce resources to ensure its survival (Kugelman, 1992) is a legitimate interest on the part of doctors and hospitals, one justified by the principle in biomedical ethics called distributive justice (Beauchamp & Childress, 2009). Under utilitarian theory, which considers the greatest good for the greatest number to be its guiding principle, only the end or consequences are important, not the means. Stopping aggressive treatment with one patient is appropriate if more patients who have a greater chance of survival benefit.

Reamer (1990) raises the question of when a doctor should shift treating a dying patient aggressively to using less-expensive efforts of making the patient comfortable and free of pain, as hospice care provides, and rather divert funds for the care of patients who have a greater chance of survival. A related concept is that of *medical utility* or the way in which scarce medical resources are allocated. Beauchamp and Childress (2009) suggest that consideration of medical utility is morally imperative in health care, and that both patients' needs and the potential for successful treatment are important considerations.

Moreover, Rothman (1989) suggests that there are "external restrictions on choice," which compete with the primacy and efficacy of the principle of self-determination. "Restrictions" can include laws and policies, agency and program structures, limits to professional intervention, and the client's unique situation, such as economic and family circumstances, as well as other factors. Because of these constraints, he suggests that social workers' interventions need to be grounded in "reality" and in an understanding of constraints in order not to frustrate and defeat clients' unrealistic expectations.

He also suggests that client self-determination may have to be limited due to "competing professional considerations" that are especially relevant for hospital social workers, who are functioning in a host environment. Social workers are often part of a team in hospitals, courts, penal institutions, and other settings. In these host settings, the primary goals, the pace of services, and the role of client self-determination are generally controlled by the hosts—doctors, lawyers, penal institution professionals, and others—whose understanding of the situation may differ markedly from that of the social worker. The social worker may be considered "soft," or "permissive" (Rothman, 1989).

Social workers in hospitals often make choices that support the hospital's or doctor's recommendations. Several studies illustrate this point. Kugelman (1992) conducted a qualitative study regarding 20 hospital social workers' responses to a fictional ethical dilemma, involving obligation to a medical center versus an obligation to promote the patient's right to self-determination in refusing surgery for metastatic cancer. Half the participants were unable to maintain support for their client's wishes at the expense of the doctor's recommendations. Several workers noted issues concerning the doctor's or hospital's "power" in deciding to limit the extent of their advocacy role. Workers described fear of losing their jobs and feeling that it is the doctor's decision, lack of respect for clients' rights, futility of supporting the patient, and need to persuade the client of the doctor's decision (Kugelman, 1992).

Walden, Wolock, and Demone (1990) also found that when presented with a vignette involving an elderly patient whose family wanted continued hospital care while the hospital was pressuring for discharge, most social workers did not choose the client-oriented response of advocating for the family. Interestingly, however, the study found that MSW students in hospital settings were more likely to advocate for the patient and less likely to demonstrate loyalty to the hospital or doctors.

The tendency of social workers in a hospital to support the hospital may be a reflection of their status in this host setting. There are significant pressures placed on social workers to rubber stamp or effectuate the recommendations of medical staff and a strong feeling of powerlessness to advocate a different position or one supporting the patient. One respondent in the Kugelman (1992) study stated: "I think what happens in the system is that people tend to say, this shouldn't be but I know it would be an exercise in futility." Another worker stated: "I tend to think that in hospitals when you [the social worker] start increasing, upping the ante, you usually lose" (p. 72).

Author's Reflections, Reasoning Process, and Resolution

Ethical Theories. Teleological or utilitarian theories justify the social worker's obligation to the hospital, professional colleagues, and society based on the need for rapid discharge, prevention of multiple hospitalizations, and the maximization of limited medical resources (Beauchamp & Childress, 2009; Reamer, 1990). These theories hold that certain actions are considered good because of their consequences in terms of promoting the "maximum good for everyone" and are less concerned about the individual (Dolgoff et al., 2009). Moreover, utilitarian theories also justify persuading the client to accept hospice, as hospice would be generally likely to produce the best consequences or results for the patient and the family. Thus, utilization of hospice care would benefit the patient and the patient's family, as well as the hospital, hospital staff, and other patients. According to Reamer, most ethical decisions by social workers are based on utilitarian or teleological principles.

Deontological theories state that certain actions are intrinsically right. These would justify respect for patient autonomy and freedom, promoting self-determination, and accepting the client and her uniqueness and individuality. In addition, the Ethics of Care theory (Beauchamp & Childress, 2009) also justifies respect for the client's autonomy, and it values empathy, sympathy, and knowledge of the particular client's needs. According to Beauchamp and Childress, Ethics of Care theory places

> emphasis on traits valued in intimate personal relationships, such as sympathy, compassion, fidelity, discernment, and love. Caring in these accounts refers to care for, emotional commitment to, and willingness to act on behalf of persons with whom one has a significant relationship. Noticeably downplayed are Kantian universal rules, impartial utilitarian principles, and individual rights. (2009, pp. 36–38)

The NASW Code of Ethics. In the Ethical Standards section of the Code of Ethics, more specific guidelines are provided for all social workers. Section 5 states that workers should maintain and promote high standards of practice and that they should uphold the "values, ethics, knowledge, and mission of the profession" (NASW, 2008, 5.01a–b).

Relevant guidance is provided in several other sections as well. Section 1.01, the first ethical standard written into the Code, attests to the social worker's primary commitment to clients, and Standard 1.02 develops this as an obligation to respect and support client self-determination. Section 2.03 asks that workers contribute to multidisciplinary discussion and try to resolve differences with other disciplines. Section 3 of the Code addresses responsibilities to practice settings, and Standard 3.09 specifies commitment to employers, obligating workers to adhere to such commitments as well as to making employers aware of the worker's commitments to the NASW Code of Ethics. Subsection 3.09d states specifically, however:

> Social workers should not allow an employing organization's policies, procedures, regulations, or administrative orders to interfere with their ethical practice of social work. Social workers should take reasonable steps to ensure that their employing organizations' practices are consistent with the *NASW Code of Ethics.* (NASW, 2008)

Thus the Code would seem to support and justify the worker's obligation to advocate and serve the best interests of the client and to support client self-determination as primary.

Client and Worker Values. Client and worker values also impact on decision making and must be considered when attempting to reach a resolution. The client and family seem to share a strong commitment to their values, which include (1) caring, (2) privacy, (3) self-determination, (4) well-being, and (5) loyalty to each family member.

The worker's personal values include (1) loyalty and fidelity; (2) caring; (3) freedom, self-determination, and respect for autonomy; (4) justice; and (5) fairness.

Rationale for a Compromise Position. There are several options for action that would support one or the other side of the dilemma. However, the worker chooses to attempt to reach a compromise between the doctor's position and the client's desires. According to the associate director of the social work department, "ethical consults" are available when ethical dilemmas or conflicts arise needing immediate attention. Consults via the hospital's ethics committee may be convened within 24 hours and directly address issues facing the hospital and patients. The consult involves a team that includes a doctor, nurse, clergy member, lawyer, social worker, and usually the patient and the family.

This worker clearly supports the client's right to self-determination and believes that she has an ethical obligation to advocacy on behalf of her client. Both her personal values, and those of her client and family, would support her advocacy for the right of her client to continue to receive care in the hospital. In addition, the NASW Code of Ethics would appear to support the primacy of client interest in this conflict between client desires and hospital policies.

Nevertheless, because of the many factors noted earlier (i.e., the social worker's peripheral role in the hospital, the worker's duty to the hospital, and the very real issues of resource allocation), the option of seeking an ethical consult to attempt a compromise through a meeting of all the parties appears to be the optimal position in this situation. Taking a stand in complete opposition to an attending physician would likely result in numerous negative consequences, as well as prove to be futile.

Case Study T (*Bulkley*)

Abramson, M. A. (1981). Ethical dilemmas for social workers in discharge planning. *Social Work in Health Care, 6*(4), 33–41.

Abramson, M. A. (1985, September). The autonomy-paternalism dilemma in social work practice. *Social Casework, 66*(7), 387–393.

Beauchamp, T. L., & Childress, J. F. (2009). *Principles of biomedical ethics* (6th ed.). New York: Oxford University Press.

Hepworth, D., Rooney, R., Dewberry Rooney, G., Strom-Gottfried, K., & Larsen, J. (2010). *Direct social work practice: Theory and skills* (8th ed.). Pacific Grove, CA: Brooks/Cole.

Kugelman, W. (1992). Social work ethics in the practice arena: A qualitative study. *Social Work in Health Care, 17*(4), 59–77.

National Association of Social Workers. (2008). *NASW code of ethics*. Washington, DC: Author.

Proctor, E. K., Morrow-Howell, N., & Lott, C. L. (1993). Classification and correlates of ethical dilemmas in hospital social work. *Social Work, 38*(2), 166–177.

Reamer, F. G. (1990). *Ethical dilemmas in social service* (2nd ed.). New York: Columbia University Press.

Rothman, J. (1989). Client self-determination: Untangling the knot. *Social Service Review, 63*(4), 598–612.

Walden, T., Wolock, I., & Demone, H. W. (1990). Ethical decision-making in human services: A comparative study. *Families in Society: The Journal of Contemporary Human Services, 71*(2), 67–75.

CHAPTER SUMMARY

This chapter has addressed the responsibility of an individual professional to the profession as a whole. One of the major underlying concepts is that every social worker's attitudes, behavior, and performance as a social worker impacts the profession as a whole. The responsibilities this entails include supporting the ethical values and practice standards of the profession as a whole, and contributing to the profession in terms of teaching, evaluation, and research.

Each of the three cases presented in this chapter have ethical concerns related to this area. In the first case, "My Clients Are in a Hurry!", the writer is concerned about professional integrity: her responsibility as a social worker to provide services to clients who come to her agency. When clients refuse services, the social worker is unable, in effect, to perform her professional function, which she considers an ethical obligation. She arrives at a compromise decision, which she believes respects her client's wishes as well as her own professional integrity. However, in the meantime, her clients have found another agency which is willing to provide the adoption services they are requesting without the professional counseling she believes necessary, and one is left to wonder about the ethics and professionalism of *that* agency!

The second case addresses the challenges often faced by social workers offering hotline services: how to determine the best interests of the client based on limited, often incomplete knowledge, grounded in information provided by clients in immediate crises. In the case of rape and reporting, already fraught with ethical and procedural complexities, addressing client needs and societal responsibilities on a hotline is especially complex. The social worker arrives at a determination that professionalism creates a responsibility to informed consent, which, in the case of rape, involves sharing information about issues involved in reporting and proceeding with criminal action.

The third case, involving the physician's request for hospice placement for a client whose family is adamantly opposed to hospice's image, values, and goals, suggests an ethical conflict for the social worker in regard to responsibilities to the client and to her employer. The employer focuses on utilization of resources—in this case inpatient hospital care, while the family is unprepared to face the patient's demise. Ultimately, torn between these two obligations, the social worker determines that her professional responsibility in this case may best be met through seeking a consultation with an ethics committee.

In each case, the writers were aware of their professional responsibilities, and of the ways in which their own actions ultimately affected the profession as a whole. Each utilized research in exploring options and in gaining a clearer view of the issues.

The following questions will test your knowledge of the content found within this chapter. For questions 1-6, please select the phrase that best completes each sentence. Question 7 is a brief essay question. For additional assessment, including licensing-exam type questions on applying chapter content to practice behaviors, visit **MySearchLab**.

1. Responsibilities to the social work profession include all except:
   a. research
   b. responsible criticism
   c. volunteer work
   d. discussion

2. The major difference between hospice care and palliative care involves:
   a. treatment options available in each program
   b. the patients' diagnoses
   c. the location of services
   d. the type of referral

3. When participating in research, it is important to ensure:
   a. anonymity of researchers
   b. informed consent of participants
   c. consent of all family members
   d. publication of research studies

4. In addition to women, who are the traditional victims, rape victims include all except:
   a. children
   b. men
   c. gays and lesbians
   d. animals

5. The conflicting obligation to the client and to society-at-large is:
   a. rarely encountered in social work
   b. Is best addressed by individual social workers
   c. Is definitively resolved in the Code of Ethics
   d. Often requires consultation and deliberation in the practice setting

6. Limiting client self-determination:
   a. should only be considered when it is clearly in the interest of the client
   b. is never permissible
   c. can only be done with client consent
   d. must be first determined by an ethics committee

7. This ethical standard addresses the "integrity of the social work profession." How would you define "integrity" in terms of professional responsibilities?

John Vink/Magnum Photos

11

NASW Ethical Standard Six

Social Workers' Ethical Responsibilities to the Broader Society

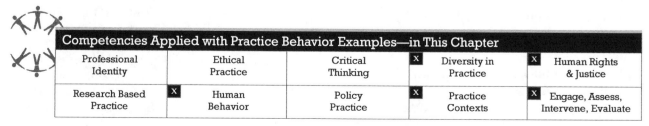

Competencies Applied with Practice Behavior Examples—in This Chapter									
	Professional Identity		Ethical Practice		Critical Thinking	x	Diversity in Practice	x	Human Rights & Justice
	Research Based Practice	x	Human Behavior		Policy Practice	x	Practice Contexts	x	Engage, Assess, Intervene, Evaluate

INTRODUCTION

All professions have a special relationship to the society in which they are embedded. There is a contract, implicit in some areas and explicit in others, that exists between the profession and the society. Licensure, laws affecting professional conduct and privilege, malpractice laws, and other "official" mechanisms may be used to delineate and define the role of the profession in society.

In common with members of other professions, social workers have an ethical responsibility to the promotion of the "general welfare" of society. Because of the specific roles and functions that the social work profession assumes, and is granted, within the society, this obligation to the "general welfare" carries ethical responsibilities that affect the diurnal functioning of each professional. Social workers often act as the "agents" of society, performing such functions as administering its social programs; caring for those who are weak, young, old, disabled, or otherwise unable to care for themselves; working to improve the individual and collective position of the disadvantaged members of society; helping to ensure social justice for all; and preserving for all of society the safety and the basic freedoms that are inherent in its structure.

Provisions of the Code

The Preamble of the Code of Ethics outlines social work's commitment to social justice and advocacy as follows:

> Social workers promote social justice and social change with and on behalf of clients...are sensitive to cultural and ethnic diversity and strive to end discrimination, poverty, and other forms of social injustice. These activities may be in the form of...advocacy, social and political action, policy development and implementation. (NASW, 2008)

Social justice is a core value of the profession. This translates into the ethical principle "Social workers challenge social injustice":

> Social workers pursue social change, particularly with and on behalf of vulnerable and oppressed individuals and groups of people.... [C]hange efforts are focused on issues of poverty, unemployment, discrimination, and other forms of social injustice...to promote sensitivity to and knowledge about oppression and cultural and ethnic diversity. (NASW, 2008)

The social work commitment to the "general welfare" of society on a global level includes support for U.S. government policies which address basic human needs in a culturally sensitive manner.

Section 6 of the Ethical Standards of the Code of Ethics provides more specific guidance for social workers in fulfilling these obligations.

Subsection 6.01 asks social workers to promote the "general welfare of society," from local to global, and to advocate for conditions that allow the fulfillment of basic human needs for all. Social justice may be promoted through "social, economic, political, and cultural values and institutions" (NASW, 2008).

The commitment to respect for diversity, both social and cultural, is extended from the United States to a global level. Social workers "should promote policies and practices that demonstrate respect for difference," expand cultural knowledge, advocate for culturally competent programs and institutions, and safeguard the rights and equity of all (6.04c). As in other sections of the Code that address discrimination, Section 6.04 has been revised in 2008 by the NASW Delegate Assembly to include *gender identity or expression* and *immigration status* (NASW, 2008).

Social workers also have a commitment to help educate the public about these issues, to encourage participation (6.02), to provide services in public emergencies (6.03), and to act to prevent exploitation and discrimination (6.04d).

THE CASES

The majority of ethical dilemmas encountered by professionals in relation to society concern the dual obligation to clients and to the broader society. Others relate to issues such as meeting the needs of present members of society versus ensuring the welfare of future members, and conflicting obligations to society and the employing agency. Often, ethical issues that involve the "general welfare" imply an understanding of the general values of a society—a necessary precondition for the promotion of its welfare. The task of defining these values in a way that is clear to all can be difficult in a diverse, multicultural country such as the United States. Society defines and regulates itself through the enactment of laws and policies that support its foundational values. As agents of society, as well as members, social workers are responsible for administering and upholding the laws that the society has made. This responsibility assumes even more challenging dimensions when a worker has responsibility for the members of society who cannot advocate for themselves: children, the elderly, the mentally disabled or incompetent, and others.

The Rocinha Favela in Rio de Janeiro, Brazil, the largest slum in the world, represents an urgent global social justice concern.

Christopher Kolaczan/Shutterstock

These obligations also contain the possibility of ethical dilemmas, especially when the laws are in conflict with workers' own values, their perception of their clients' best interests, or the values of the profession as a whole. The case examples included in this chapter illustrate some of these areas of ethical conflict for professionals.

The first case presents a major confidentiality issue in the context of a hospital trauma center. A patient has been brought to the center following an automobile collision. In the process of assessment, hospital tests reveal that the patient was driving under the influence of both drugs and alcohol. Her right to privacy is supported by federal and state laws, the hospital's policies, and the NASW Code of Ethics. A clear mandate for confidentiality? Yes—but the patient is a school bus driver at a local elementary school.

The worker in the second case is confronted with an adolescent who informs her that he is planning to resume dealing marijuana. He has been in treatment for 8 months and has made significant progress in school performance, behavior at home, and sociability. She must consider whether her primary obligation is to report his plan to the authorities, when there is no legal obligation for her to do so, or to maintain confidentiality and continue to attempt to work with him, addressing this problem in treatment.

A particularly dilemma-laden conflict is presented in the third case in this chapter, which addresses society's obligation to protect the well-being and rights of its chronically mentally disabled homeless members. Must these two concepts, "rights" and "well-being," remain always in conflict? Who decides how "well-being" is to be defined—the client or the policy maker? The author, working in an advocacy program, must try to determine the best interests of this special population in order to support the policies that best serve their interests.

The social worker in the fourth case is called to address the challenges faced by an elderly lady who was found lying on her apartment floor by the police during a well-being check, unable to get up or call for help because of the extreme degree of clutter in her apartment. She quickly notices that both the heater and the stove, which the client uses on a regular basis, are surrounded by clothing and other flammable items. Wanting to support her client's self-determined choice of lifestyle, she is faced with the very real possibility of imminent harm to the other residents of her apartment building by the potential for fire. However, as an Adult Protective Services (APS) worker, her client is clearly the elder, and not the other residents of the building. She must balance her sense of responsibility to both her client and the other residents while remaining within the scope of APS practice.

The fifth case in this chapter revisits child welfare and adoption concerns, addressing an issue that has arisen out of recent changes in policy at both the federal and state levels. A social worker in a government child welfare agency that functions in support of current state laws finds herself confronted with a major ethical concern: State-mandated guidelines, which are designed to support the best interests of children, stipulate brief time frames for parents to work on reunification plans. If these are not met, parental rights are terminated and children are placed in adoptive homes. These time frames do not seem to take into account some of the complex and intractable problems that parents face. Believing that it is in the child's best interest to remain with the birth family and culture if at all possible, the worker finds state guidelines to be overly limiting. In exploring the issue, she arrives at a conclusion that surprises even her.

The final case involves an issue that is often in the news, widely discussed, but not easily resolved: the conflict between religious practice and secular laws and policies. As *parens patriae*, the state attempts to institute laws that protect the rights and well-being of all people, especially its most vulnerable members. These rights include the freedom of religion—the right to practice one's faith and follow one's beliefs. However, there is an important caveat: this right may be limited when there is a potential for harm. In this case, parents of a child with a serious illness which has become terminal due to lack of medical care are continuing to refuse medical intervention to extend the child's life, in favor of religious practices and rituals. It then becomes necessary to explore the church and state relationship in relation to a specific 2-year-old, who is unable to participate meaningfully in decision making.

| Case Study U | A Journey to Moral Action: Balancing Personal, Professional, and Legal Obligations |

Abstracted from an unpublished paper by Penelope Nabakov, MSW

Practice Context and Case Presentation

A large urban medical center serves as a major health facility, and also as a trauma center for the surrounding area of the city, which includes a number of residential communities. During an internship in the trauma center, this social worker has participated in many discussions about the ethical dilemmas that the trauma center social workers encountered. One case in particular, however, was often cited as especially challenging: that of a woman who arrived at the trauma center one morning, having been in an accident involving a head-on collision between two motor vehicles. The other driver was not hurt; however, the woman was injured and was admitted to the hospital for treatment. The following day, in completing the trauma assessment, one of the social workers discovered that the patient had a positive toxicity screen for both alcohol and methamphetamines. The patient had shared with the social worker that she was a school bus driver for elementary school children, and had been scheduled to work the previous afternoon. It became apparent to the social worker that the patient, who had arrived at the hospital intoxicated in the morning, would presumably have gone to work with alcohol and drugs in her system had the accident not occurred.

The social worker was confronted with a major ethical dilemma. Confidentiality policies clearly stated that information regarding the toxicity screen was private and could not be shared. However, it was apparent that the children who rode this driver's bus were at grave risk. What should the social worker do in this situation?

The dilemma can be stated as follows:

RESPONSIBILITY TO CLIENT'S CONFIDENTIALITY V. RESPONSIBILITY TO PREVENT HARM
TO THE LARGER SOCIETY

Research and Related Literature

To arrive at a resolution, it is necessary to explore various sources of guidance and information. First, the NASW Code of Ethics can be consulted for guidance, followed by ethical theories and principles that can provide a framework for decision making. Government laws and policies, including DUI laws, as well as the relevant policies of the hospital in which this ethical dilemma has occurred must be understood and considered as well.

NASW Code of Ethics. The NASW Code of Ethics identifies several ethical responsibilities that serve as guidelines for the profession. These can be viewed as elements that both impact our daily practice as social workers and contribute to the profession's legitimacy. The Code offers a set of principles to guide the behavior of individual social workers as a means of creating cohesion within the larger ethos of the profession as a whole. These principles form the core of the social worker's identity and are essential in defining the basis and scope of daily practice. In addition, the Code also seeks to provide guidance when ethical dilemmas occur. The Code covers topics that include responsibility to clients, to colleagues, to the profession, as professionals, and to the larger society. The first section, Social Workers' Ethical Responsibility to Clients, of the Code of Ethics outlines specific obligations, which include informed consent, privacy, and confidentiality.

The segment of the Code that pertains to privacy and confidentiality is the largest and contains the most specificity. Most social workers would agree that privacy and confidentiality are essential to gaining trust, which could arguably be the most important prerequisite in being of service to our clients. With regard to privacy, social workers are urged to respect it, and not to solicit information unless it is essential to the provision of services (NASW, 2008). Information from clients is to be kept private, and there exist only limited instances in which a social worker can share the contents of client–social worker interactions: upon a client's request; if abuse is suspected; if a threat is made against a specific person; in instances included under state or federal laws; and according to the policies of each agency (which cannot conflict with state or federal laws). Before beginning work with a new client, the social worker should obtain informed consent, a process that entails explaining confidentiality and the aforementioned exceptions to it (SAMHSA/CSAT Treatment Improvement Protocol, 2008a, Appendix B, Legal and Ethical Concerns).

While the Code was formulated to provide guidance in complex situations, it cannot always achieve this goal. The Code itself recognizes its limitations:

> [The Code] does not provide a set of rules that prescribe how social workers should act in all situations.... Further, the NASW Code of Ethics does not specify which values, principles, and standards are most important and ought to outweigh others in instances where they conflict. (NASW, 2008: 1)

In relation to the current ethical dilemma, the Code states that clients' interests are always of primary importance, except on the limited occasions when the social worker's loyalty to the larger society supersedes that due to the client. From this statement, it is difficult to ascertain whether the Code would consider the situation described here as one that warranted a confidentiality breach to potentially minimize harm against others. Driving intoxicated does not *necessarily* imply imminent harm. The bus driver could drive one time, or a thousand times, while under the influence, without causing an auto accident. However, if she did get behind the wheel and cause injury to others as a result of driving intoxicated, the social worker would know that this could have been preventable. So, the question remains: Does the harm of revealing the patient's drug use (legal issues, job loss) justify the potential benefit to the larger society (preventable loss of life or injury)?

The Code of Ethics by itself simply does not suffice as a means of solving this ethical dilemma, which seems to require further consultation and exploration. The Code foresaw the possibility of such instances occurring, and states:

> A Code of Ethics cannot guarantee ethical behavior. Moreover, a Code of Ethics cannot resolve all ethical issues or disputes or capture the richness and complexity involved in striving to make responsible choices within a moral community.... For additional guidance social workers should consult the relevant literature on professional ethics and ethical decision making and seek appropriate consultation when faced with ethical dilemmas. (NASW, 2008: 2)

Ethical Theories and Principles. By analyzing "commitment to clients" and "prevention of harm," as they are presented in the Code of Ethics alone, the social worker assigned to this case would not be able to find a clear solution to this ethical dilemma. This is primarily because, in this situation, the two principles appear to be in a competing position: by honoring one ethical standard, the other one would be violated. When this type of situation occurs, it can be helpful to consult with an appropriate hierarchy of ethical values.

In *Ethical Decisions for Social Work Practice* (2008), authors Dolgoff, Loewenberg, and Harrington have attempted to develop an ethical principles screen that can be used when ethical principles, such as "commitment to clients" and "prevention of harm," seem to provide conflicting guidance. They state:

> More specific guides are needed whenever two or more of these criteria point toward different alternatives...we believe that the preferred way of solving such conflicts among ethical principles is a lexical ordering of these principles—that is, rank ordering them from the most important to the least important. (64)

However, they also note, "A lexical ordering of ethical principles can provide social workers with a guide, but such a guide is not meant to be a magic formula that can be applied blindly" (64).

The Ethical Principles Screen aligns principles in a hierarchy. Starting with the most important, these are (1) protection of life, (2) equality and inequality (treating equal situations equally, and unequal ones unequally), (3) autonomy and freedom, (4) least harm, (5) quality of life, (6) privacy and confidentiality, (7) truthfulness, and (8) full disclosure (Dolgoff et al., 2008). Using the Ethical Principles Screen, it becomes clear that protection of life is the most important principle in the hierarchy. Applying this ethical tool to the current dilemma would place the client's interests lower in the hierarchical order than that of the children she might harm. However, as the authors state, this hierarchy cannot be applied blindly. And, while it is helpful to have principles and screens to guide social workers through these types of situations, it is ultimately up to the social worker to analyze each situation, be aware of relevant laws and policies, and apply the principles of ethical standards on an individual basis.

Government Laws and Policies. Social workers who practice in a medical setting are also subject to the laws of the Health Insurance Portability and Accountability Act (HIPAA). As federal legislation, HIPAA confidentiality laws would supersede any conflicting state laws or agency policy. HIPAA was created to increase the availability and coverage of health insurance for individuals (DHHS, n.d.). Its purpose was to limit discrimination and loss of coverage for those people who either are already ill or have high-risk factors by protecting their health information. HIPAA limits the instances in which a patient's medical information can be shared or disclosed with others, and states that confidential information can only be shared with the consent of the patient and when providing information to ensure continuity of care, such as sharing the results of a test with another provider (DHHS, n.d.).

States vary tremendously when defining doctor–patient privilege, and thus laws are affecting this particular dilemma. In California, where the dilemma occurred, residents have an inalienable right to privacy as set forth by the state's constitution; this has resulted in extensive protections for medical and mental health information (SAMHSA/CSAT Treatment Improvement Protocol, 2008). California considers the content discussed between a social worker (licensed or not—even trainees are covered) and her or his client to be privileged, even in the presence of a third party, which would apply to the situation in the case study as emergency rooms are busy and privacy is not always an option (SAMHSA/CSAT Treatment Improvement Protocol, 2008a). This is further evidenced by *United States* v. *Eide*, where the court ruled that emergency department records were protected and could not be used against the patient for purposes of prosecution or criminal investigation (875 F.2d 1429 9th Cir. 1989).

Many of the laws that govern confidentiality allow for the sharing of limited information for continuity of care, or with insurance companies for the sake of reimbursement. While all of these regulations appear to provide solid personal protection, even this limited sharing arrangement has led to discrimination against individuals with issues of substance use or abuse. As a result, the federal government expanded the regulation covering confidentiality, with new laws specifically governing the confidentiality of alcohol and drug abuse patient records (SAMHSA/CSAT Treatment Improvement Protocol, 2008a). These regulations require written consent for information to be shared with others, even within the system of continuing care. Later court determination found that they did not always apply in general medical or trauma settings, depending upon the context in which the information regarding alcohol and drug use was acquired. For example, if the attending doctor asks about alcoholism during emergency liver failure, the information is considered to be general and medical, and therefore not subject to the specialized regulations that prohibit the sharing of patient records between partnering healthcare providers.

Critical Thinking

Practice Behavior Example: The author here has selected Loewenberg, Dolgoff, and Harrington's Ethical Principles Screen as the preferred theoretical framework. These authors place protection of biological life at the top of their hierarchy.

Critical Thinking Question: As we have seen in the Introduction of this text, different choices of ethical frameworks can engender different results. On what basis might a social worker determine the preferred ethical framework to use?

Almost all of the privacy laws, rules, and Codes of Ethics make an exception to the right of confidentiality when the safety of others, or of the patient or client, is at stake. Social workers who fall under the category of "mental health professionals" are subject to a ruling in 1974 by the Supreme Court of California that such professionals have a duty to protect members of society from imminent harm. This ruling requires social workers to notify individuals in the community (and local authorities) if someone is being threatened with imminent danger by one of his or her clients. Commonly referred to as the "duty to warn," this ruling was the result of a landmark legal case, *Tarasoff* v. *Regents of the University of California*, in which a patient admitted to his psychologist that he wanted to kill a girl who had rejected him (Corey, 2007). Bound by confidentiality, the psychologist did nothing, and the girl was subsequently murdered by the client.

Brought before the Supreme Court, this case created the grounds for the first exception to confidentiality, and tasked mental health professionals with the obligation of protecting members of society from the actions of their clients. Most states have adopted this caveat in some form. As summarized in the majority opinion, "The protective privilege ends where the public peril begins" (*Tarasoff* v. *Regents of the University of California*, 1976).

In California, social workers are also *Mandated Reporters*. This is a legal term applied to members of various professions, such as doctors, police, teachers, and emergency services staff, who have frequent contact with vulnerable populations (children, elders, people with disabilities) and are obligated to report risk or suspicion of abuse, neglect, and/or harm to the appropriate government agency. In California, child abuse is defined as a physical injury by other than accidental means (California Department of Social Services).

DUI Laws. Drunk driving laws in California are found in Vehicle Code Section 2352, which states that it is unlawful to drive under the influence of drugs or alcohol. Private vehicle drivers who drink break this law with 0.8 percent alcohol in the blood, but commercial vehicles, which would include a school bus, require lower than 0.04 percent blood alcohol levels (www.dmv.ca.gov/pubs/vctop/d11). The client's alcohol and drug level upon admission clearly is in violation of these laws. In addition, "increased penalties are imposed where there is a minor passenger in the vehicle at the time of drunk driving. In California, this is defined as an individual under the age of 14" (www.californiadrunkdriving.org).

In support of offering protection for vulnerable populations, in this case children, "enhanced penalties" are provided for drunk drivers with minor passengers (www.caduilaw.com/drunk_driving_laws/enhancements/minor_passenger.html).

Driving under the influence can also become a felony if there is any injury:

> Any person who, while under the influence of intoxicating liquor, or under the combined influence of intoxicating liquor and any drug, drives a vehicle and when so driving does any act forbidden by law or neglects any duty imposed by law in the driving of such vehicle, which act or neglect proximately causes bodily injury to any person other than himself, is guilty of a felony. (California Vehicle Code Section 23153)

Hospital Policies and Procedures. As a setting where there are often legal and ethical concerns, the hospital has guidelines that catalog the correct action steps to be taken to reduce unlawful or unethical circumstances. While state and federal regulations protect patient confidentiality, it is the corresponding hospital policy and procedures that dictate how the law will be implemented within the daily routine of the hospital (Hospital Policies and Practices, 2008). These policies and procedures are a hybrid of federal regulations, state laws, and the agency's stated mission.

According to hospital policy, all employees must honor both HIPAA and California state laws covering confidentiality. The hospital will not release any protected health information without separate patient authorization, except under very limited circumstances (Hospital Policies and Practices, 2008). These include public health activities, judicial proceedings, law enforcement, coroner, and some research purposes. The hospital can also disclose private information when reporting suspicion of abuse, neglect, endangerment, domestic violence, or other crimes to prevent or control disease, injury or disability, and to avert a serious threat to health or safety. Under this last listing, the policy states,

> We may use and disclose your medical information when necessary to prevent a serious threat to your health and safety or the health and safety of the public or another person. Any disclosure, however, would only be to someone able to help prevent the threat. (Hospital Policies and Practices, 2008)

Author's Reflection, Reasoning Process, and Resolution

I do not believe that ethical decisions can be made absolutely or subjectively. Instead, I subscribe to being a relativist. While relativists may have no absolute, consistent rules, they have the freedom to judge every situation or moral action within the constraints that invariably shape and influence every decision. The notion of equilibrium applies to my thoughts on the role of an individual within society and vice versa. While it may not be purely possible, I believe that much of creating a good society is in finding the right balance between respecting individual autonomy while protecting the right not have your beliefs and actions infringed upon by another.

Much of what I have attempted to describe earlier has been carefully considered by ethicists both past and present. Of the core ethical theories that currently exist, I believe that my values most closely align with some of the principles prevalent in deontological theories. Namely, I believe that motive is incredibly important when assessing action, and that the outcome of a situation cannot be the sole defining criterion of whether an action was good or bad. In addition, I am in agreement with two of Kant's principles: that human beings may not have free will but that they should act as though they do, and that human beings should always be treated as ends, never as means.

I also find that some of the deontologist W. D. Ross' values match those of my own personal value list: nonmaleficence, beneficence, justice, self-improvement, and gratitude. However, several values that are not listed by Ross but crucial to my personal value stance include autonomy, well-being, right to basic goods, and respect for life. Of all of these, I consider respect for life and autonomy to be the most important in my personal values. While these are very broad terms, I do believe that they can be described with some degree of specificity.

I would define autonomy as the right to make choices about your own life, free from the constraints of others and their ideals, while respect for life includes a consideration of the value and worth of both one's own life and that of others. I believe that the value of justice encompasses many other smaller values: fairness, the right to basic goods (food, housing, human relationships, education), and both participating in and respecting the social contract. For me, the value of generosity contains beneficence, respect (both for life and for others), competence, and a degree of social awareness. While many values form my personal ethical stance, I find that many of them fall under the three broader categories of autonomy, justice, and generosity.

Beauchamp and Childress' model (2009), with its four clear decision-making principles of respect for autonomy, nonmaleficence, beneficence, and justice, supports my personal ethical values. However, it is not only its simplicity and congruence with my values that appeal to me: It is also the fact that these values are not ranked. I believe that this model fits well with my belief in the autonomy of the social worker to make responsible decisions,

It is important to be aware that the conditions under which patients are routinely informed of, and consent to, HIPAA regulations might not, in many cases, fulfill the criteria for valid informed consent.

in that it allows the greatest flexibility in applying the principles based on each individual circumstance. As a relativist, I believe it is important for the social worker to be able to consider each situation, rather than following a one-size-fits-all set of rules.

While I believe that most of my professional and personal values align nicely, there is one area where I can foresee possible conflict. Personally, I cherish the right to individual autonomy and thoroughly believe in the right of each person to make her or his own choices, even "bad" ones. However, in my professional work, I believe that there will be times when I cannot honor the decision or choice of a client, especially if it hurts another or seriously jeopardizes her or his own life and well-being. This is one instance where I can clearly see my personal ethics coming into conflict with my professional ones.

In a professional situation, when confronted with an ethical problem, I believe that I, with Dolgoff et al. (2008), would place the protection of life first, then and only then followed by my client's interests, and then by those of society. And, by "society," I include society's laws as an expression of the societal will. I believe that one should subscribe to the social contract, and while I may not agree with every law, I understand the value of laws in protecting us and creating a cohesive whole. Beyond the protection of life, if I were forced to choose, I believe that I would place the rights of the individual above those of society.

As I reread my last sentence, I must recognize, however, that it clearly calls into question the core of what I believe to be my ethical stance: that attempting to define ethics in the abstract divorces the dilemma from the very real specifics that make up each situation. This is why I believe that a relativist guideline that allows for individual beliefs, societal norms, and situation specifics to be weighed equally is the best option for resolving ethical dilemmas.

We construct our personal value system largely influenced by the societal values of our time. In the United States, we place a huge value on privacy and confidentiality, as well as on autonomy. Our support of these values actually creates the current dilemma: In another culture, such a debate might not even exist, for the safety of other members of society would always be considered primary. Our society values both privacy and autonomy, and the safety of members, especially those, such as children, who are considered to be most vulnerable.

Several options can be considered that support the social worker's responsibility to the wider society. These include the following:

- Notify the police of a patient's toxicity screen at the time of initial accident, hoping for a DUI charge that would result in loss of license and hence her job driving a school bus.
- Notify the driver's employer, hoping for loss of employment.
- Notify the school, hoping for loss of employment.

In support of the client's right to privacy and confidentiality, I could:

- Explain my duty to report her behavior from a personal and professional ethical stance. Attempt to convince patient that she has a problem and what she is doing is not safe.
- Recommend treatment as a means of keeping her job.
- Do nothing—always an option!

In determining a course of action, I believe that my primary responsibility must be to the protection of life. While I do not know if, or when, the driver might jeopardize the lives of the children in her care on the bus, I must consider the very real possibility that an incident might occur. Therefore, I must consider my responsibility to larger society, and particularly to vulnerable members, as primary in this instance. California drunk driving laws support my concerns by enhancing penalties to drivers operating a vehicle under the influence with passengers under 14 years of age.

However, as I do not like the idea of reporting her behavior without giving her an option of removing the potential threat, I would explain my duty to warn to my client as necessary to the ethical, professional, and legal principles to which I am responsible. If the client expresses a willingness to prevent the harmful situation from reoccurring, I would make a report to CPS and refer her for substance abuse treatment. I believe that this outcome is the best option available and attempts to honor all of the values and principles discussed throughout this case.

Case Study U (*Nabakov*)

Beauchamp, T., & Childress, J. (2009). *Principles of biomedical ethics.* New York: Oxford University Press.

California Department of Social Services. (n.d.). *Department of Social Services.* Retrieved June 3, 2009, from Child Protective Services website: www.dss.cahwnet.gov/cdssweb/PG93.htm

CA DUI laws were located at: California Vehicle Code Section 231532 and 23153, www.dmv.ca.gov/pubs/vctop/d11, www.californiadrunkdriving.org, www.caduilaw.com/drunk_driving_laws/enhancements/minor_passenger.html

Corey, C. (2007). *Issues and ethics in the helping professions.* Pacific Grove, CA: Brooks Cole Publishing.

DHHS, D. O. (n.d.). *HIPAA general overview.* Retrieved April 27, 2009, from Department of Health and Human Services Web site: www.cms.hhs.gov/HIPAAGenInfo/01_Overview.asp

_____ Hospital Policies and Practices. (2008).

National Association of Social Workers. (2008). *NASW Code of ethics* (pp. 1–32). Washington, DC: Author.

SAMHSA/CSAT Treatment Improvement Protocol. (2008a). Appendix B: Legal and ethical issues. *Tip 24: A Guide to Substance Abuse Services for Primary Care Clinicians,* 1–42.

SAMHSA/CSAT Treatment Improvement Protocol. (2008b). Chapter 6: Legal and ethical concerns. *Tip 16: Alcohol and Other Drug Screening of Hospitalized Trauma Patients,* 1–63.

Tarasoff v. *Regents of the University of California,* 551 P.2d 334 (Supreme Court of California 1976).

Case Study V   Dealing Drugs: Can Confidentiality Ever Be Justified?

Abstracted from an unpublished paper by Julie B. Goodale, MSW

Practice Context and Case Presentation

An adolescent in a suburban high school with a personal history of violence had been heavily involved with dealing marijuana. Through court intervention, he was transferred to a different high school and was asked to meet with a Youth Services social worker.

The social worker has been seeing the client for approximately eight months on a weekly basis. During this time, a relationship of trust has developed that has enabled the client to discuss his problems and ask for help from the worker. The client has remained in school, passed his courses, and functioned outside of school without recourse to any violence. He regularly keeps appointments. The worker is encouraged by his progress and feels that his continued trust and the therapeutic relationship could be pivotal for the client's future.

Although the client at first refrained from selling drugs, he has recently been contacted by his former supplier, who convinced him that he should go "back into the business." He has confided to the social worker that he plans to resume selling drugs in the immediate future. The worker has been unable to dissuade him from his intention to resume selling marijuana. He does not consider this a "serious drug" and says, "If I don't do it, someone else will. I might as well be the one getting the money!" The worker is concerned that harm to society will result from the client's resumption of drug dealing.

On the other hand, the client has made solid gains during the time she has worked with him. He trusts her and has been able to work well with her, sharing information, accepting support, and sustaining the gains he has made. If the worker reports his intention to authorities, she places at risk her continued work with this client, his trust of her, and the maintenance of his gains. While she is distressed with his intention to deal drugs, she wonders whether it would be more helpful, both to him as an individual and to society as a whole, if she continues to work with him and attempts to address his drug dealing in the course of her contacts with him.

The dilemma may be stated as follows:

CONFIDENTIALITY V. OBLIGATION TO SOCIETY

Research and Related Literature

Confidentiality is the right of the client and is clearly stated in the Code of Ethics, Section 1, which states:

> Social workers should respect clients' right to privacy.... Once private information is shared, standards of confidentiality apply [1.07a]. Social workers should protect the confidentiality of all information obtained in the course of professional service, except for compelling professional reasons. The general expectation...does not apply when disclosure is necessary to prevent serious, foreseeable, and imminent harm to a client or other identifiable person or when laws or regulations require disclosure without a client's consent. (NASW, 2008, 1.07c)

The underlying belief is that mutual trust is essential to the maintenance of a therapeutic relationship between a client and a worker (Seelig, 1990). This relationship enables changes in the client's attitude, behavior, and functioning.

The Code of Ethics also obligates social workers to the primacy of client interests and to trustworthiness. These suggest that, professionally, the worker should act so as to retain the client in treatment and should continue to provide services to him.

However, Section 6 of the Code also obligates the worker to support the best interests of society and the general welfare. In Section 6.01, social workers are obligated to "promote the general welfare of society" (NASW, 2008). Among social workers, it is commonly accepted that it is unethical to disclose information shared in confidence. Such information should not be shared with third parties (Reamer, 1990). Also, according to Moore (1994), "Implied in the issue of confidentiality is the notion of the individual's right to privacy" (p. 165).

There are a few exceptions to the obligation of workers to preserve confidentiality. These are (1) if the client is in danger of harming self or other, (2) if the client and social worker mutually agree to tell a third party, and (3) if the social worker is subpoenaed to testify in court.

It is unclear whether selling marijuana constitutes harm as intended in the first exception to the obligation to confidentiality. A person is under no legal obligation to inform the authorities of illegal activities. Failing to be a good Samaritan is not a crime (Forer, 1986).

The policy of the agency does not clearly and unequivocally mandate reporting of drug dealing. Rather, situations are addressed as they occur on a case-by-case basis, and a course of action is determined that seems appropriate to the individual client. Colleagues at the agency, when consulted, stated that they did not feel that dealing marijuana constituted harm as intended in the exceptions to the obligation to confidentiality.

Although there may be no legal responsibility, there are other reasons for people to act on behalf of others. According to Senator Orrin Hatch (1992), "Individual responsibility...is *the* first principle of limited government" (p. 959). The United States was founded on a principle of individual freedom without interference from large governing bodies. However, a limited government can only be feasible if the people in that society are able to govern themselves, both socially and individually (Hatch, 1992). Individual responsibility is a necessary precondition for a civilized legal order (Calabresi & Lawson, 1992).

The courts and the entire justice system depend on citizens' actions (Forer, 1986). Calabresi and Lawson (1992) state that "without a sense of personal honor—and, more importantly, a sense of shame—any form of social organization is doomed" (p. 957). There have been documented cases where the public interest supersedes the client's right to privacy (Moore, 1994), the most notable being *Tarasoff* v. *The Board of Regents of the University of California*, the landmark precedent in duty-to-warn cases.

In the current dilemma, one can presume that society at large is the "intended victim." The client may sell drugs to someone who overdoses or drives while under the influence and kills or injures an innocent bystander. Dealing drugs possesses potential for harm to others, both users and the general public.

In attempting to protect members of society from the harms of drugs, federal laws make drug use and dealing a crime. While the worker is not mandated to report illegal actions, as noted above, there are ethical issues involved as well in protecting knowledge of criminal activity.

Author's Reflections, Reasoning Process, and Resolution

An ethical theory that is applicable to this dilemma appears to be utilitarianism. Utilitarianism derives from a consequentialist, or teleological, perspective in that the major thrust and concern are the consequences of a course of action. Utilitarians seek "the greatest good for the largest number of people" (Dolgoff et al., 2008). In determining a course of action, utilitarians consider the needs of everyone affected, and the ultimate course chosen should be the one that produces the "maximal balance of positive value over disvalue" (Beauchamp & Childress, 2009).

Act utilitarianism asks, "What good and bad consequences will result from *this* action in *this* circumstance?" (Beauchamp & Childress, 2009, p. 339). In considering the dilemma in question, one might note that a bad consequence, clearly, is that the client's trust will be broken and the client, who is in need of treatment, will likely leave therapy. A good consequence might be that one less person is dealing drugs, reducing the exposure for the potential harm to drug use. However, it is unclear in this particular situation whether another person would be recruited to take the client's place, as he contends, thus negating any potential positive effect.

If one considers simply the greatest good for the largest number of people, the interests of society in preventing additional exposure and access of its members to drugs clearly provides the utilitarian answer. Our society clearly values autonomy and personal freedom. Applying these to this situation would seem to support the right of the client to make money in any way that he chooses. If he chooses to violate the law, he has the freedom to do so, unless caught. Members of society may also exercise personal freedom and autonomy in choosing whether to risk the potential harms of using marijuana. Another societal value, safety, conflicts with freedom and autonomy in this instance, however. Drugs endanger users as well as others, and this knowledge creates the laws that currently exist against using and selling drugs.

The client values money, power, and status. According to him, he was the "best" marijuana dealer in the area. He is not concerned about responsibility to others or to society as a whole, nor does the illegality of his actions trouble him.

The worker values honesty, truth, justice, education, and job training. These values have led the worker to cooperate with authorities in the past in ensuring justice and protecting society. She does not agree with the position of taking an "easy out"—selling drugs, rather than staying in school and learning a skill.

Parents' rights to information regarding minors who are adolescents varies by state law. It is important to be informed about parental rights and rights of minors in the state in which services are rendered.

On the other hand, the worker values trustworthiness very highly. She is concerned with trying to maintain her relationship with this client, and she feels that breaching confidentiality and reporting his drug dealing would cause the client to terminate much-needed treatment. Also, she feels that breaching confidentiality would reflect negatively on her own professional self-concept.

Five potential options for action are suggested in examining this dilemma. First, the worker can choose to maintain complete confidentiality, telling no one what the client has confided in her. Second, the worker may inform her supervisor, with the request that confidentiality be maintained by the supervisor as well. Third, the worker may elect to inform the police or drug enforcement agency. Fourth, she may choose to inform the school authorities and cede to them the responsibility for future action. Fifth, as the client is a minor, she may inform the client's parents and attempt to enlist their assistance in discouraging the client from pursuing his stated intentions.

The social worker feels that confidentiality is the right of the client. The client assumed that the information shared would not be divulged, and the Code of Ethics does not seem to provide clear and specific guidance in this area. The worker's respect for autonomy and personal freedom lead her to the conclusion that the client has the right to determine his own course of action, just as the potential users of his services have the right to determine theirs. Her strong commitment to trustworthiness causes her to feel that the best service that she can render to the client—and, by extension, to society as a whole—is to keep the client in treatment and to try to assist him to reflect on, and perhaps to reconsider, his decision.

The worker would share information about her client with her supervisor, asking the supervisor to maintain the client's confidentiality. As the policy of the youth service agency does not require the reporting of drug use or dealing, this position would not be a violation of commitments made but, rather, a support for future growth and change for this client.

Case Study V (*Goodale*)

Beauchamp, T. L., & Childress, J. F. (2009). *Principles of biomedical ethics.* New York: Oxford University Press.

Calabresi, S., & Lawson, G. (1992). Foreword: The Constitution of responsibility. *Cornell Law Review, 77*(5), 955–958.

Dolgoff, R., Loewenberg, F. M., & Harrington, D. (2008). *Ethical decisions for social work practice.* Itasca, IL: F.E. Peacock.

Forer, L. (1986). Autonomy and responsibility: A search for new bases of legal rights and obligations. *Utah Law Review, 1986*(4), 665–693.

Hatch, O. G. (1992). A departure on the people. *Cornell Law Review, 77*(5), 959–963.

Moore, S. E. (1994). Confidentiality of child and adolescent treatment records. *Child and Adolescent Social Work Journal, 11*(2), 165–175.

National Association of Social Workers. (2008). *NASW code of ethics.* Washington, DC: Author.

Reamer, F. (1990). *Ethical dilemmas in social service.* New York: Columbia University Press.

Seelig, J. M. (1990). Privileged communication. *Journal of Independent Social Work, 4*(4), 75–80.

Case Study W   Outpatient Commitment: Must Mental Disability Preclude Civil Liberty?

Abstracted from an unpublished paper by Kimberly Platt Haywood, MSW

Practice Context and Case Presentation

Program development and social policy implementation and analysis can pose unique ethical questions, affecting the whole of the population being served. Legal advocacy for homeless persons with mental disabilities poses a particular kind of ethical challenge, one undertaken by the Advocacy Center.

A study estimates that on any given day in the United States, there are 600,000 homeless people (Kassebaum, 1995). Another study shows that between one-fourth and one-third of this homeless population is severely mentally disabled (Cohen & Thompson, 1992). Kanter (1989) believes that psychiatric problems may result in homelessness, although homelessness may also induce or prompt the symptoms of mental disability. The number of chronically mentally disabled homeless people has increased over the years, largely due to policies of deinstitutionalization, where the patients have moved from institutions to inadequate community-based mental health services (Cohen & Thompson, 1992). As a result, a whole population of homeless people could theoretically benefit from mental health services, whether inpatient or outpatient, voluntary or mandatory. *Outpatient commitment* is a procedure in which an individual deemed harmful to himself or herself or others is court-ordered to receive treatment in the community (Kanter, 1989).

In July 1995, Nancy Kassebaum (R-KS), chair of the Senate Committee on Labor and Human Resources, proposed a bill that would have required outpatient commitment of mentally disabled homeless persons who are gravely disabled (Kassebaum, 1995). The bill defines "gravely mentally disabled" as individuals "who are at risk of death, harm, or illness because they are too mentally ill to secure food, clothing, shelter or medical care" (Kassebaum, 1995, p. 2). Senator Kassebaum believes that this population remains homeless because they lack mental health services and adequate housing (Kassebaum, 1995). If they were required to receive treatment, Senator Kassebaum believes that their number would be drastically reduced. She feels that legislation is needed to require outpatient commitment because a current lack of treatment facilities hinders this commitment.

While a large number of the chronically mentally disabled people are homeless and do require services that are often not available, some advocacy groups believe that outpatient commitment is not the answer. The Advocacy Center also feels that the commitment laws violate the constitutional right of equality by discriminating against people with disabilities (Goldman, 1995).

Torrey and Kaplan's national survey of the use of outpatient commitment, published in 1995, found that this type of commitment was frequently used with homeless, mentally disabled individuals in 12 states and the District of Columbia. States where outpatient commitment was not commonly used cited concerns about civil liberties, liability, fiscal burdens, and others. Although the authors felt that outpatient commitment's potential for reducing rehospitalization was good, they found that the service was underutilized (Torrey & Kaplan, 1995).

The ethical dilemma faced in this case may be stated as follows:

**SOCIETY'S OBLIGATION TO ENSURE OPTIMAL CARE
FOR MEMBERS v. INDIVIDUAL RIGHTS TO FREEDOM
AND WELL-BEING FOR ALL**

Research and Related Literature

Scheid-Cook (1987) believes that outpatient commitment is a compromise between the individual's right to freedom and the need for society to care for its mentally disabled population. Because of outpatient commitment, patients may live in the community rather than in hospitals. Scheid-Cook (1987) defends outpatient commitment on the grounds that people who are mentally ill have "no insight into their mental illness; they would not voluntarily comply with treatment" (p. 174). The author advocates laws that not only protect society from the individual and the patient from himself or herself, but also represent a lesser deprivation of liberty. Scheid-Cook (1987) studied court-ordered outpatient commitment and its effectiveness, finding that most individuals in outpatient commitment were chronically mentally disabled, usually schizophrenic males in their mid-thirties with a history of frequent hospital admissions and medication refusal. Mental health professionals successfully used involuntary commitment as leverage to enable community mental health centers (CMHC) to keep patients on medication and in programs (Scheid-Cook, 1987).

Wilk (1988) calls involuntary outpatient commitment "the legal and psychosocial process whereby an allegedly mentally disordered and dangerous person is forced to undergo mental health treatment or care in an outpatient setting" (p. 133). The dangerous person can be a danger to himself or herself, not just a danger to society. Citing the American Psychological Association, the author considers whether mental health professionals should hold liberty and privacy issues in higher regard than all other interests.

Wilk also analyzes various studies that test the effectiveness of involuntary outpatient treatment and raises many related issues. One is the worker's personal safety and the safety of the patient. In an inpatient setting, dangerous patients may be restricted and more closely supervised than in an outpatient setting, where the therapist will often see the patient alone in an office (Wilk, 1988).

Social workers' potential liability is another issue: Questions of responsibility if a client is harmed or harms another person, the duty of the worker to warn a potential victim, and potential worker responsibility if the patient is not taking medication or complying with a treatment plan need to be addressed before the worker treats an involuntary outpatient (Wilk, 1988).

The forced nature of the treatment also raises issues: The fear here is that social workers will be nothing more than monitors of medication (Wilk, 1988). "Forced treatment" is another phrase for *involuntary commitment*. With all that we have learned about starting where the client is, how effective would the social worker be with a client who is court-ordered to be there and is not only noncompliant but also frequently misses appointments?

Wilk (1988) states in summation that involuntary commitment requires more time from judges and other professionals, more resources, and more monitoring of commitment practices. Even after these are considered, involuntary commitment may only be beneficial to a small number of patients (Wilk, 1988).

Engage, Assess, Intervene, Evaluate

Practice Behavior Example: Potential for harm to self or others and safety for the broader society are issues affecting the rationale for several positions regarding outpatient commitment.

Critical Thinking Question: While acknowledging that it is impossible to be completely accurate in assessment, should potential for harm be a limitation to the intervention option of outpatient commitment for people who are chronically mentally ill?

Belcher (1988) believes that social workers face a dilemma when trying to meet the needs of clients without violating their rights. The author notes that the profession relies heavily on liberty and dignity of clients, and to stay true to those values and provide appropriate care to the individual, the worker may have to supersede other rights. Belcher (1988) cites Judge Bazelon, who believed that commitment should "be interpreted more narrowly to refer to treatment that is in the best interest of the individual" (p. 398). When considering involuntary commitment, the possibility that the person's quality of life will ultimately be improved through treatment must be considered (Belcher, 1988). Belcher (1988) also argues that although mentally disabled homeless people may be exercising their rights, they "are able to determine little for themselves and are unable to self-direct their lives" (p. 398). Committing people may be a violation of their right to self-determination, but failing to commit people who are homeless and also mentally disabled may eventually lead to their deaths. While advocating for the right to self-determination, one must also advocate for physical well-being (Belcher, 1988).

McGough and Carmichael (1977) believe that involuntary commitment is a deprivation of liberty, justified if an individual is a harm to others, but not without due process and equal protection under the law. Beyond liberty there is the person's right to "self-determination and bodily integrity" (p. 316). However, mental illness may preclude the ability to exercise these rights in one's own best interest (McGough & Carmichael, 1977).

Kanter (1989) states that most states legally allow involuntary commitment if people are considered at risk for harming themselves or others. The author cites the American Psychiatric Association's (APA) stance that states should "reject the" danger to themselves and others "criterion" and replace it by saying that the person is "likely to suffer substantial mental or physical deterioration" (p. 93). This new criterion shifts the focus from harm to others to harm/neglect of self. It also shifts the decision for commitment from the legal to the medical community (Kanter, 1989). The APA defends its position of commitment without consent, saying that "patients have the right to treatment that is the most appropriate and therapeutic available" (Kanter, 1989, p. 93). Overall, the author believes that involuntary commitment does not address the needs for housing, treatment, and other services for the homeless population (Kanter, 1989).

Author's Reflections, Reasoning Process, and Resolution

Freedom and well-being are two concepts valued by our society. The Supreme Court has stated that liberty is not an absolute right, but "freedom from restraint" should be equally enjoyed by everyone (McGough & Carmichael, 1977, p. 309). McGough and Carmichael (1977) quote John Stuart Mill's *On Liberty*, which says that "freedom is pursuing our own good in our own way, so long as we do not attempt to deprive others of theirs" (p. 309). Mill also writes that "each is the proper guardian of his own health, whether bodily, or mental, or spiritual" (p. 309).

Dolgoff, Loewenberg, and Harrington(2008 state, "Coercive intervention may be justified when (1) there is grave threat to basic social values or to fundamental social institutions or (2) when there is a clear and present danger that very great or irreversible harm will be done or will occur unless preventative action is taken" (p. 99).

Gewirth (Reamer, 1990) believes that freedom and well-being are the two basic fundamental rights of human beings, but at times these two rights conflict with one other. In *Reason and Morality*, Gewirth writes that people must develop a hierarchy of values in times of conflict (Reamer, 1990). He offers guidelines for making ethical decisions: (1) Basic goods come first; (2) an individual's right to well-being takes precedence over another person's right to freedom; (3) an individual's right to freedom takes precedence over his or her right to well-being; (4) the obligation to obey laws, rules, and regulations to which we have freely and voluntarily agreed takes precedence over our freedom; (5) an individual's right to well-being may override laws, and regulations; and (6) the obligation to prevent basic harm and protect basic goods overrides the right to retain one's property (Reamer, 1990).

In summary, Gewirth believes that an individual's right to self-determination and freedom takes precedence over all, even the person's own well-being, except when one person's freedom hinders another person's' well-being. This position is in consonance with this author's personal values, which strongly support freedom and liberty.

The Code of Ethics addresses the present population and dilemma issues in several sections. First of all, there is a commitment on the part of the social worker to the client's interests as primary (section 1.01). However, in this case the application of this guideline is unclear: Is the primary obligation to freedom or to (society's and/or the worker's conception of) well-being?

Immediately after the primacy of client interest, the Code addresses self-determination and the obligation of the worker to support client self-determination, except in cases of "serious, foreseeable, and imminent risk to themselves or others" (1.02). It would seem that if a worker wanted to follow this obligation, he or she would need to consider each client on a case-by-case basis: There may not *always* be such risk involved for the client. One issue with the population of mentally disabled homeless involves decisional capacity: "When social workers act on behalf of clients who lack the capacity to make informed decisions, social workers should take reasonable steps to safeguard the interests and rights of those clients" (1.14).

Should it be assumed that mental disability de facto makes one incompetent, and that, therefore, the worker, or "society," is justified in making decisions for such clients? Are there variations in the degree of mental disability, in the type of mental disability, in the client's particular circumstances, that can justly affect decisional capacity, or must one rule hold for all? Social workers are obligated to "promote the general welfare of society" and to "advocate for living conditions conducive to the fulfillment of basic human needs" (6.01). They should:

> Engage in social and political action that seeks to ensure that all people have equal access to the resources, employment, services, and opportunities they require to meet their basic human needs and to develop fully. (6.04a)
>
> Act to expand choice and opportunity for all people, with special regard for vulnerable, disadvantaged, oppressed, and exploited people and groups. (6.04b)
>
> Act to prevent and eliminate domination, exploitation, and discrimination. (NASW, 2008, 6.04d)

From these sections, it seems clear that the social worker has a responsibility to support and advocate for people who are mentally disabled, as a vulnerable and disadvantaged population. Freedom, civil liberty, and well-being seem to be supported by the Code's positions.

Court-ordered outpatient treatment makes the recipients involuntary clients. Subsection 1.03d addresses these clients specifically, obligating social workers to "provide information about the nature and extent of services and about the extent of clients' right to refuse service." This would seem to "expand choice and opportunity" (NASW, 2008, 6.04b) but might be compromised by the client's mental disability, which can affect decisional capacity, thus returning the primary obligation for ensuring client rights and well-being to the worker.

The worker in this case believes that people have both the right to freedom and self-determination and the right to well-being. However, individuals cannot make decisions and exercise self-determination when they are trapped inside a mental illness. To be able to exercise the right of self-determination, a person must be competent to make decisions. If the mentally disabled homeless person is initially forced into treatment and becomes stable, then refuses treatment, the right to self-determination should override society's obligation to well-being. However, treatment may be required in order to ensure the validity of such decision making. Involuntary commitment might thus be a necessary step in the process of ensuring optimal self-determination.

Case Study W (*Platt Haywood*)

Belcher, J. R. (1988). Rights versus needs of homeless mentally ill persons. *Social Work, 33*(5), 398–402.

Cohen, C. I., & Thompson, K. S. (1992). Homeless mentally ill or mentally ill homeless? *American Journal of Psychiatry, 149*(6), 816–823.

Dolgoff, R., Loewenberg, F. M., & Harrington, D. (2008). *Ethical decisions for social work practice.* Itasca, IL: F.E. Peacock.

Goldman, H. H. (1995, July). Testimony on behalf of the Judge David L. Bazelon Center for Mental Health Law before the Committee on Labor and Human Resources: United States Senate on the Reauthorization of the Substance Abuse and Mental Health Services Administration. Washington, DC.

Kanter, A. S. (1989). Homeless but not helpless: Legal issues in the care of homeless people with mental illness. *Journal of Social Issues, 45*(3), 91–104.

Kassebaum, N. L. (Senator). (1995, June). *Homeless mentally ill in the SAMHSA Reauthorization, Flexibility Enhancement, and Consolidation Act of 1995.* Testimony given to the Senate Committee on Labor and Human Resources. Washington, DC.

McGough, L. S., & Carmichael, W. C. (1977). The right to treatment and the right to refuse treatment. *American Journal of Orthopsychiatry, 47*(2), 307–320.

National Association of Social Workers. (2008). *NASW code of ethics.* Washington, DC: Author.

Reamer, F. G. (1990). *Ethical dilemmas in social service.* New York: Columbia University Press.

Scheid-Cook, T. L. (1987). Commitment of the mentally ill to outpatient treatment. *Community Mental Health Journal, 23*(3), 173–182.

Torrey, E. F., & Kaplan, R. J. (1995, August) A National Survey of the Use of Outpatient Commitment. *Psychiatric Sources, 46*(8), pp. 778–784.

Wilk, R. J. (1988). Involuntary outpatient commitment of the mentally ill. *Social* Work, 33(2), 133–136.

Case Study X   Hoarding: Drawing the Line Between Personal and Public Rights

Abstracted from an unpublished paper by Kari Kientzy, MSW

Practice Context and Case Presentation

Adult Protective Services (APS) was established to help address elder abuse and neglect in the United States. The primary role of protective service workers is to investigate alleged abuse and neglect, and to provide short-term crisis case management when needed. In California, APS addresses reports of abuse to seniors (aged 65 and above) and dependent adults where there have been allegations of physical, financial, and sexual abuse, as well as abandonment, isolation, abduction, and self-neglect. Reports of abuse must be investigated within 10 days of the initial referral.

As an APS intern, this worker received a police well-being-check incident report for Miss Raymond, who lived in a multiple-unit apartment complex, and who had been found on the floor, unable to pick herself up, buried under clothing and debris. It was apparent that Miss Raymond was a hoarder/clutterer, and that this was the main reason she had been unable to pull herself up. When the worker visited, the client was found sitting outside her apartment door. There was nowhere to sit inside, due to the large amount of clutter, predominantly stacked books and clothes, throughout her one-bedroom, third story apartment. Although assessing her safety in her home environment was the purpose of this visit, the worker quickly realized that she had to be concerned about the safety of those around Miss Raymond as well. Miss Raymond stated that she used her oven for cooking and an old-fashioned radiator for heat, but both had papers, boxes, and other flammable items stacked in front, on top, and all around them, all creating a danger of fire.

APS interventions and services are voluntary, as long as clients are competent to make their own decisions and are not a danger to themselves or others. The agency recognizes a client's right to self-determination, and works with the client to reduce or eliminate the abuse and/or neglect before attempting involuntary interventions. Miss Raymond had not been determined to be incompetent. While she had the right to live the lifestyle of her choice, her choices were placing those around her at imminent risk. What should be the role of the social worker in these circumstances? While clients with hoarding behaviors pose several ethical dilemmas for social workers, the one that seemed the most pressing to address was this:

CLIENT'S RIGHT TO SELF-DETERMINATION V. WORKER'S RESPONSIBILITY TO LARGER SOCIETY

Research and Related Literature

In the United States, key ethical issues for human service professionals include autonomy, privacy, beneficence, justice, and nonmaleficence (Johnson, 1999). APS was created with three primary goals: (1) to provide services to elders and dependent adults who are unable to protect their own interests or to care for themselves, (2) to prevent and remedy the abuse, neglect, or exploitation of elders and dependent adults who have been harmed or are at risk of harm, and (3) to seek maintenance for the elder or dependent adult safely in their home environment, when appropriate (CDSS, 2002). Clients are often involuntarily referred to APS, yet must be interviewed and investigated regarding abuse and neglect allegations.

Self-determination plays a central role in APS policies and procedure manuals in that "an elder or dependent adult who has been abused may refuse or withdraw consent at any time to preventive and remedial services offered by an adult protective services agency unless they are incapacitated and unable to give consent" (CDSS, 2002). Thus, services are voluntary, and the agency respects a client's right to self-determination, working to reduce or eliminate the abuse and/or neglect by developing and implementing a service plan. Agency policies and procedures state that APS "is not intended to interfere with the lifestyle choices of elders or dependent adults, nor to protect those individuals from all the consequences of such choices" (CDSS, 2002). Workers respect clients' rights to make bad decisions and try to provide due diligence by informing clients about the consequences of their actions or choices.

In investigating decision-making factors, Lynn Bergeron found that "APS workers are held accountable for their decisions, either to intervene in cases of elder abuse to prevent further harm, or not to intervene to preserve the individual's autonomy and self-determination. Workers are constantly in a double bind: a decision to intervene against the elder's wishes may violate the elder's right of self-determination. Yet, to withhold treatment when abuse has been substantiated with the high probability that it will occur again may violate the elder's right to protection" (Bergeron, 1999). Because of the paternalistic role that APS is designed to play in society, workers often encounter ethical issues regarding self-determination.

An adult's right to choose danger over safety is acknowledged as long as the client is competent. But what if, in the worker's judgment, clients are unable to understand the options available, or the inherent consequences of their decisions for themselves and others, and are thus unable to formulate an informed decision due to an inability

Legally, people are considered "competent" unless they have been judged incompetent in a court of law. Thus, many people who are in effect incompetent or have intermittent competence are still considered legally competent, with all of the decision-making rights accorded to competent members of society. This can create challenging situations for social workers attempting to provide services and to ensure safety.

to understand how the relevant information applies to their circumstances? Joy Duke (1997) states that "when confronted with an adult who lacks the ability to make an informed choice, whose need for help is urgent, and whose suffering will continue unless there is intervention, the role of the APS social worker is to decide whether the provision of protective services is justified in the absence of the adult's expressed consent to receive the essential services." In discussing general issues APS workers encounter, Atkinson and Nelson (1995) state that "clients have the right to assume risks in how they live their lives...the worker's professional obligation is to provide information to clients or their families about potential risks and to help identify alternatives to the present course of action and behavior" (Atkinson and Nelson, 1995, p. 220).

Together with self-determination, beneficence and the prevention of harm are considered to be responsibilities of the social work profession. The utilitarian John Stuart Mill considered beneficence fundamental in producing the greatest good for the greatest number, believing that society should allow individuals to live according to their own convictions, as long as they do not interfere with the freedom of others, or unjustifiably harm others (Beauchamp & Childress, 2009, p. 103). Immanuel Kant reasoned that individuals have a choice about beneficent acts, but that it was wrong to inflict harm on another. According to Beauchamp and Childress (2009), "Respect for autonomy has only *prima facie* standing, and competing moral considerations sometimes can override this principle. Examples include...endanger the public health, potentially harming innocent others." Can hoarding items in one's apartment endanger the public's health and meet the definition for causing unjust harm to others?

While APS has policies and procedures to ensure the safety of others if there is a possibility of threats of violence or imminent harm as defined by the *Tarasoff* v. *Regents of University of California* (1976) case, there is no written procedure for how to handle situations that endanger the public health and safety. According to Duke (1997), while adults are entitled to have their choices respected, when these jeopardize the safety and well-being of others, best practice requires social workers to consider the best interest of others. Duke recognizes the need to consider society's best interest, but does not define "best practice" nor specify circumstances in which social workers are required to not solely respect a client's autonomy.

Recent research on the effects of hoarding behavior on society includes San Francisco's Mental Health Task Force on Hoarding and Cluttering study findings that "the two biggest financial burdens were unquestionably evictions and fires. One hoarding-related fire caused $500,000 in damage...an eviction typically costs a landlord more than $22,750, and...about 400 to 800 hoarders are evicted (in San/Francisco – au) every year" (Harrell, 2009). Research on hoarding as a public health concern has found that substantial clutter can lead to health code violations, fire hazards, evictions, and substantial costs to the family and the community, and that community agencies must intervene to protect the individual and those living nearby (Frost, Steketee, & Williams, 2000). Frost et al. (2000) looked at public health complaints against hoarders in Massachusetts, and found that 19 percent of reports were from social service agencies. This seems to indicate that other social workers have put society's safety above a client's right to self-determination if the matter is a public health violation.

Author's Reflection, Reasoning Process, and Resolution

Section 1.01 of the NASW Code of Ethics addresses a social worker's commitment to clients. "Social workers' primary responsibility is to promote the well-being of clients. In general, clients' interests are primary. However, social workers' responsibility to the larger society or specific legal obligations may on limited occasions supersede the loyalty owed clients, and the clients should be so advised" (NASW, 2008). Miss

Raymond is willing to work with the worker to reduce her clutter, but she does not appear to be able to understand the threat that her behavior and lifestyle pose for her neighbors.

Section 1.02 states that "social workers respect and promote the right of clients to self-determination and assist clients in their efforts to identify and clarify their goals. Social workers can limit clients' right to self-determination when clients' actions pose a serious, foreseeable, and imminent risk to themselves or others" (NASW, 2008). Miss Raymond's hoarding does pose a serious, foreseeable, and imminent risk of fire hazard, with items stacked on and around her radiator and oven. The Code of Ethics does give the worker authorization to consider interventions that may be against what the client would want to do.

Anetzberger (1999) developed a hierarchy of principles specifically for APS workers to utilize when ethical issues are encountered. Her model is applicable to this case, as it was developed for those investigating elder abuse and delivering protective services. Key principles from most to least important considerations for intervention are

1. *Freedom over safety:* The client has the right to choose to live at risk of harm, providing he or she is capable of making that choice, harms no one, and commits no crime.

2. *Self-determination:* The client has a right to choose to live at risk of harm, providing he or she is capable of making that choice.

3. *Participation in decision making:* The client has a right to receive information to make informed decisions and to participate in all decision making affecting his or her circumstances to the extent that he or she is able.

4. *Least restrictive alternative:* The client has a right to service alternatives that maximize choice and minimize lifestyle disruption.

5. *Primacy of the adult:* The worker has a responsibility to serve the client, not the community concerned about safety.

6. *Confidentiality:* The client has a right to privacy and secrecy.

7. *Benefit of doubt:* If there is evidence that the client is making a reasoned choice, the worker has a responsibility to see that the benefit of doubt is his or her favor.

8. *Do no harm:* The worker has a responsibility to take no action that places the client at greater risk of harm.

9. *Avoidance of blame:* The worker has a responsibility to understand the origins of any maltreatment and commit no action that will antagonize the perpetrator and so reduce the chances of terminating the maltreatment.

10. *Maintenance of family:* The worker has a responsibility to deal with the maltreatment, a family problem, if the perpetrator is a family member, and give the family the necessary services to resolve the problem.

According to this model, the worker has a responsibility to respect Miss Raymond's choices and decisions (principle 2) and has a responsibility to the client, not to the community who may be concerned about safety (principle 5). This hierarchy would be in effect only if her actions do not harm others (principle 1) and she was provided information to make an informed decision (principle 3). Utilizing Anetzberger's principles, as Miss Raymond's actions do put others at risk of harm, and thus the worker can limit the client's choice of personal lifestyle.

In considering personal values and principles, this worker finds it hard to come up with a better guide than the old proverb of the Golden Rule, "Do unto others as you would have them do unto you." It is a means to achieve reciprocity, and there is comfort in the Golden Rule because it addresses all people with equal consideration and respect. Since the worker does not believe in determinism, applying the Golden Rule to the notion of free will helps to create a basic sense of order and an underlying moral code that can aid in ensuring human rights. Treating others as you would like to be treated provides a means for society to support each individual's basic goods by assuming that others would want the same basic goods. This rule is difficult to apply to Miss Raymond because while she knows that her behavior is harmful to herself, she is not able to see how it can harm others. She would not look negatively upon hoarding behavior done by others around her.

Traditionally, when this worker is faced with reasoning through ethical issues, she tends to examine the different sides of the issue, using a careful process of information gathering and reasoning. The worker tends to fluctuate between being a relativist and a subjectivist, believing that situation, place, and context have an important role in making a decision, and also believing that subjectivism takes into account a sense of self-determination in that individuals have their own understanding of right and wrong. These stances do not appear to be mutually exclusive; the interplay between individual beliefs and the context of the situation are at the forefront of most ethical dilemmas. If Miss Raymond owned her own home, in a rural, remote area, would there be the same sense of responsibility to protect society from her actions? Her location and proximity to others in a three-story apartment building in a dense urban center play a central role because her behavior places others at risk.

Miss Raymond has lived in her current one-bedroom apartment on the third floor of her building for the last 40 years. Clearly, she values staying in her apartment highly. She has severe arthritis and has to go up several flights of stairs to reach her third-floor apartment. Although she has a history of falls, she refuses a ground unit, stating that she "would rather be dead than have to move." She values both her privacy and freedom.

She has family and friends, but does not want to burden them with her problems, though they have offered to help her with cleaning. Although she values her relationships, she would rather "take care of things herself." She values her independence and feels that her lifestyle choice does not affect others. Her charitable nature wants to ensure that if she does give away some of her possessions, they go to someone she knows would benefit from them. She is open to assistance from professionals and nonfamily members, as long as they are nonjudgmental and agree to assist her on her terms.

In some ways, Miss Raymond's values are enigmatic and contradictory to each other. She values charity and assisting others, but does not see how her behavior and actions affect others. She holds her personal relationships in high standing but values her independence more in not wanting to ask those closest to her for assistance. She responds well to professionals who are nonjudgmental and are there to assist her with her goals of maximizing independence and remaining in her apartment. Miss Raymond does not seem to understand the potential harm she is causing to others, so she does not see the ethical problem that the social worker is facing. Respecting her values, the worker should encourage the client to declutter her apartment to maximize her independence, and try to locate charitable organizations to donate her items so that she knows they are going to a good cause.

On a broader societal level, residents of a nation, state, county, and city enter into a social contract to abide by certain rules, and give up certain rights to a government in order to maintain social order. By living in a city, Miss Raymond is subject to certain rules and regulations that support safety for herself and other apartment dwellers. American society also values independence and autonomy, when these do not harm others. A majority of the time, there are penalties, both criminal and civil, when an individual puts independence and autonomy above doing no harm to another.

The mission statement of the Department of Aging and Adult Services, to which APS belongs, is to "…coordinate services to older adults, adults with disabilities and their families to maximize self-sufficiency, safety, health and independence so that they can remain living in the community for as long as possible and maintain the highest quality of life" (SFGOV, 2009). The policies, procedures, and goals for APS reinforce this mission statement by providing services to those who are unable to protect their own interests or care for themselves and need assistance to mitigate abuse and neglect to remain independent and safe in the community.

If acting in support of Miss Raymond's right to self-determination, the worker would attempt to educate her about the importance of decluttering her apartment for her own safety and that of those around her, and to avoid potential eviction. She would encourage and assist her in the cleaning and decluttering process. It has been shown that approaches dealing with hoarding behavior that do not have the client's consent and are involuntary can be very traumatic to the client (Mental Health Association of San Francisco, 2009). People struggling with compulsive hoarding may experience ambivalence about making changes, and researchers recommend that the client be directly involved with, and supported in, making decisions to let possessions go. Working one-on-one with Miss Raymond and setting a modest goal to clear one bag of possessions a day, increasing this amount over time, would be a way to empower her to achieve the goal of decluttering her apartment herself.

If she was not willing to declutter her apartment, a harm reduction model to help clear space by removing items from around the heater and oven to minimize the risk of her apartment being a fire hazard would be suggested. If Miss Raymond still did not agree, and was able to demonstrate competence, the social worker would withdraw, leaving her business card for possible future service. These possible actions would be solely honoring Miss Raymond's right to self-determination and would not be addressing the potential harm to others.

However, if Miss Raymond did not agree with the harm reduction model and immediately move the items from around her oven and heater, then it is this writer's opinion that she is unable to recognize the potential harm to others, thus necessitating actions against her wishes. APS is part of a large city government, which includes the Department of Public Health, Environmental Health Division, which responds to reports of unsanitary or dangerous conditions or activities that may be a public health concern in the city. It is within an APS social worker's scope of practice to coordinate services with other agencies to maximize self-sufficiency, safety, health, and independence. While social workers have a responsibility to society's safety, specifically addressing conditions that may be a public health concern is not within their scope of expertise. It is the worker's responsibility to refer this client's situation to the appropriate government agency.

In support of informed consent, the worker would advise the client of the referral to Department of Public Health and of their procedures, and give her the chance to decide how she wants to proceed. If the client receives a citation as a result of the referral, and is then willing to access services, the social worker could continue to work with the client through the decluttering process. If the client does not want services at that time, she would be provided with contact information for future service.

The worker believes that Miss Raymond does not appear to understand the potential harm that she imposes upon her neighbors although she is aware of the worker's concerns for her safety and the safety of those around her. Based on this, the worker has told Miss Raymond that she will refer her to the Department of Health for inspection, and has explained the process to her carefully. If, as a result of the inspection, the client is cited for a health code violation and is then willing to address her clutter, the worker will continue to work with her to establish decluttering goals. With this resolution, it is hoped that the safety issues of society are addressed, while the worker–client therapeutic relationship and rapport are maintained.

In determining this course of action, the worker recognizes that the obligation to prevent harm must be primary, and thus supersedes the client's right to self-determination in this situation. The worker will serve the client with maximum professionalism and competence and assist the client in obtaining the services needed. This resolution does not try to change Miss Raymond's lifestyle and force her to involuntarily get rid of her possessions, but it is a means to help her understand, from another source, that she is putting others at risk, and to outline what needs to be done to reduce this risk.

This resolution supports the worker's, profession's, agency's, society's, and some of the client's values in reducing the imminent risk the client imposes upon her neighbors, while maximizing her independence and right to self-determination. While she has the right to remain in her home environment and to self-determination regarding her own health and safety, her actions should not put others in harm's way. By working with Miss Raymond through the Department of Public Health inspection, the worker is able to assist the client within her own scope of practice. This resolution ensures that the client is abiding by the Department of Public Health standards, does not put her at risk, and gives her the opportunity to be the catalyst for change, therefore honoring her independence and right to self-determination.

Case Study X (*Kientzy*)

Anetzberger, G. (1999). Ethical issues in personal safety. In T. F. Johnson (Ed.), *Handbook on ethical issues in aging* (pp. 187–205). Westport, CT: Greenwood Press.

Atkinson, V. L., & Nelson, G. M. (1995). Adult protective services. In G. M. Nelson, A. C. Eller, D. W. Streets, & M. L. Morse (Eds.), *The field of adult services: Social work practice and administration* (pp. 215–230). Washington, DC: NASW Press.

Bergeron, L. R. (1999). Decision-making and adult protective services workers: Identifying critical factors. *Journal of Elder Abuse & Neglect, 10*(3), 87–113.

California Department of Social Services. (2002). *Manuals of policies and procedures: Adult Protective Services Program.* Retrieved April 22, 2009, from www.dss.cahwnet.gov/ord/entres/getinfo/pdf/apsman.pdf

Duke, J. (1997). A national study of involuntary protective services to adult protective service clients. *Journal of Elder Abuse & Neglect, 9*(1), 51–68.

Frost, R. O., Steketee, G., & Williams, L. (2000). Hoarding: A community health problem. *Health and Social Care in the Community, 8,* 229–234.

Harrell, A. (2009, March 24). Gathering Storm. *SF Weekly News.* Retrieved April 20, 2009, from www.sfweekly.com/2009-03-25/news/gathering-storm/1

Johnson, T. F. (1999). *Handbook on ethical issues in aging.* Westport, CT: Greenwood Press.

Mental Health Association of San Francisco. (2009). *Beyond overwhelmed: The impact of compulsive hoarding and cluttering in San Francisco and recommendations to reduce negative impacts and improve care.* Retrieved May 1, 2009, from www.mha-sf.org/documentSharing/BeyondOverwhelmed.pdf

National Association of Social Workers. (2008). *NASW Code of ethics.* Washington, DC: Author.

SFGOV. (2009). *Human Service Agency: Seniors & adults with disabilities.* Retrieved May 9, 2009, from www.sfgov.org/site/frame.asp?u=http://www.sfhsa.org/DAAS.htm

Tarasoff v. *Regents of the University of California.* (1976).

Case Study Y	Permanency Planning For Young Children: Are Brief Time Frames *Always* In The Child's Best Interest?

Abstracted from an unpublished paper by Maria Melendez, MSW

Note: This case study is a policy companion to case study G in Chapter 1, entitled "Permanency Planning for Very Young Children: What Happens to Family Preservation?" In that case, specific clients with specific personal characteristics are presented, in contrast to the policy-focused discussion of the issue here. It is recommended that these two cases be read together to enable a consideration of the difference between abstract and concrete policy considerations.

Practice Context and Case Presentation

National and state policies reflect society's understanding of the best interests of its members, especially those that are most vulnerable: children, the elderly, people with disabilities, and those unable to make decisions for themselves. Policies set and uphold standards that seek to enhance the well-being and quality of life of all people. The policies are grounded in societal values and principles, and are meant to be utilized and applied equally to everyone who meets set criteria for needs and services. This case will consider a state policy, grounded in societal perceptions of a child's well-being and best interests, which mandates that children be placed in permanent homes if reunification with biological families cannot be achieved in a timely manner.

The Children and Family Services Agency serves children of all ages from a broad range of ethnicities, cultures, and socioeconomic backgrounds. The agency is composed of a number of smaller units, which serve family needs by providing the "reasonable services" that a parent might need in order to reunify with their child within the time frame that the court establishes. "Reasonable services" vary according to the function of a particular unit, but should be provided in the parent's language of preference and be culturally sensitive to parents' needs and concerns.

Statewide guidelines presumed to serve the child's best interests dictate the amount of time that a parent has to reunify with his or her child. If the parent fails to comply with the reunification plan within the state-determined time frame, parental rights are terminated, and the child is placed for adoption. Placing the child for adoption within these time frames, though, may have negative as well as positive effects. On the positive side, the child is placed in a permanent, stable home, with loving parents who can provide support and nurturing within a relatively short period of time. On the negative side, adoption severs the child's relationships not only with parents, but also with siblings and other family members and caregivers, and, often, with the culture of his or her community. These separations can have a strong impact on the child psychologically.

The agency strives to promote the best interest of the child while serving birth families in a sensitive manner, one that recognizes the macro challenges that can negatively affect parents' ability to care for their children. Although the best interest of the child is the primary consideration, the statewide time frames, which allow between six and twelve months maximum for reunification, create a tension in the professional relationship which is palpable to both parents and social workers. Are time frames such as these, with little or no flexibility to account for special circumstances, truly in the best interests of the children? This social worker is concerned that factors and issues other than time frames should be taken into account when considering severing the parental ties to their children.

The ethical dilemma can be stated as follows:

SOCIAL WORKER'S PERCEPTION OF BEST INTEREST OF THE CHILD V. SOCIETY'S PERCEPTION OF BEST INTEREST OF THE CHILD AS DEFINED BY STATEWIDE REUNIFICATION GUIDELINES

Research and Related Literature

Definitions of "best interest of the child" include laws and policies that protect vulnerable children from abusive situations. As agents of the society, the social work profession has witnessed and worked within many interpretations of "best interest" over time.

Laws and Policies. The Social Security Act of 1935 formally recognized that aid need-ed to be provided for dependent children who were in need, so that they could remain in their homes. This was a change from earlier policies, which removed children from homes that were determined to be harmful to them (Schene, 1998). The Child Abuse Prevention and Treatment Act (CAPTA, 1974) provided funding to states to protect chil-dren from abusive homes by developing methods of identifying abuse and standards for responding to child maltreatment. These supported both a concern for child safety and a belief that children's needs were best met in their own homes through programs of family preservation (Schene, 1998).

The Indian Child Welfare Act of 1978 requires that children with Indian ancestry be placed within their family or tribe. It is the role of the social worker to notify all of the state's tribes in writing to see whether a tribe will recognize a child as a member. If a tribe affirms the child's membership status, that tribe then takes jurisdiction over the child (Schene, 1998). This law also implicitly demonstrates that the government considers that it is in the best interests of the child to remain with his or her own family or tribe.

The Adoption and Safe Families Act (ASFA) of 1997, signed into law by President Bill Clinton, clarified and amplified the policies of the earlier CAPTA of 1974, and was a response to children's prolonged stay in the foster care system: It was felt that fam-ily preservation had been prioritized for too long, and adoption should be given priority (Bartholet, 1999). Family preservation services had been prioritized with no limitations or conditions; the act changed priorities by stating that "the child's health and safety shall be the paramount concern" (Smith, 2003).

Under ASFA, child welfare services to parents are not required if the child has been subjected to "aggravated circumstances" (Smith, 2003). These include, but are not limited to, abandonment, torture, chronic abuse, and cases in which the parent has been involved in committing murder or voluntary manslaughter of another child. If pa-rental rights have been terminated for one child, the agency bypasses services for the next child and places him or her in an adoptive home. ASFA specifically states that when a child is removed due to any of the above-mentioned circumstances, the court may determine that reunification efforts should not be made, and that adoption services should be provided to ensure the child's well-being (Bartholet, 1999).

ASFA also established clear statewide reunification time frames, giving parents of children up to 3 years of age 6 months to reunify, with the possibility of extending this to 12 months. Parents of children older than 3 years may receive 12 months of services, which can be extended to 18 months. In the case of sibling groups, the time frame for the group is that applicable to the youngest sibling (Bartholet, 1999). While this regulation has made it challenging for parents to reunify with their children, it has also provided permanent and nurturing homes quickly for children whose parents were unable to meet the time guidelines.

A social work concern with ASFA (1997) regulations is the challenge of keeping sib-lings together. Siblings who are placed separately then lose contact with each other, as well as with other family members. It is especially important to note that many of the children who come into protective custody are members of families who rely in other family members, friends, and neighbors for childcare and have had significant daily in-teractions with them. Therefore, ties to siblings, family members, and friends are often exceptionally strong. Infants and young children may have been cared for primarily by older siblings, and be closely bonded to them (Mary Draizen, personal communication, 2009).

State laws regarding concurrent planning attempt to mitigate the effects of possible delays in permanency planning. Concurrent planning is initiated when a child is re-moved from home. Permanency planning is developed along two tracks simultaneously:

the family reunification track, to prepare to return the child home with parents, and the adoption track, as a backup plan in case reunification fails. Typically children who enter foster care are placed either with an approved relative or with a foster home; however, the county also has "fost-adopt" homes, in which the foster parents are willing to adopt the child if he or she cannot reunify with their birth parent.

Agency Mission and Procedures. Social workers in the Family Reunification and Family Maintenance Units are trained to incorporate the county's mission statement to their work:

> To promote the social and economic well-being of individuals and families through a responsive, accessible, and flexible service delivery system that recognizes the importance of family, cultural and ethnic diversity, and the increased vulnerability of populations at risk. (County Social Services Agency Policy Manual, 1998)

However, challenges can occur when other factors that the social worker believes should be considered conflict with the state-determined guidelines for time frames. Although there is a general recognition of the possible impact of these factors, this has not translated into support for services to maintain and enhance family functioning within a more flexible time scheme and plan. Instead, child welfare agencies have focused on providing substitute child-rearing environments for children whose parents are unable or unwilling to parent their child (Costin, 1998).

Agency social workers working with the 0- to 3-year-old age group feel powerless when confronted with making a recommendation and a difficult decision when there is evidence that other issues, such as culture, language, economic circumstances, mental illness, and substance abuse have made it impossible for parents to comply with reunification plans within the state's guidelines. The evidence required by the court leaves little room for consideration of these issues. However, prior to 1997, the child welfare system offered the parent an unlimited period of time for receiving family reunification services without severing parental ties. This writer's colleagues were aware of parents who received reunification services for 10 years or more. Services for parents terminated only when the child was emancipated from the system. Children's foster care placements could be prolonged, as an example, by their parents' "inability" to free themselves from substance abuse in order to effectively demonstrate their capacity to care for their children (personal communications with colleagues, 2009).

In addition, these social workers believe that in cases where no parents are available to care for the child, and adoption is the only option, children should be given the opportunity to remain connected with their siblings and extended family members. They believe that family ties should be preserved, and that a child should be placed with their birth family if at all possible. If such a placement is not possible, they should have the opportunity to remain connected to them (personal communications with colleagues, 2009).

Child Development Considerations. Research studies have shown that a child needs to have a primary attachment to a caregiver and identify the age of 6 months to 4 years as a particularly vulnerable time for separation from caregivers (Orfirer, 2004). This is the period when models or templates of attachment relationships and expectations of the world are formed. According to John Bowlby's attachment theory (1988), loss and trauma during this time can have long-term consequences for the child, including depression and anxiety. This challenges the popular belief that young infants are not aware of, and not affected by, changes in primary caregiver or home.

Children who become County Agency clients were generally abused or neglected. These children often have higher levels of mood and behavioral problems than the general population (Knorr, 2007). Sleep disturbance, temper tantrums, and uncontrolled crying are often experienced by children in foster care due to previous abusive environments. It is in the best interest of foster children to be in a nurturing and loving home, and to be helped to overcome their traumatic experiences and to create strong attachments with their new primary caregiver (Knorr, 2007). Multiple foster home placements are harmful to the child's psychological development in denying a child family roots, a place to call home, and a feeling of being wanted and loved (Knorr, 2007). Creating a stable and nurturing permanent home is in the best interest of a child.

While the reunification of children in foster care with parents is the primary goal of the child welfare system, the passage of ASFA in 1997 has impacted reunification rates. In the past eight years, reunification takes longer periods of time, while adoption seems to be rising at a rapid rate (Wulezyn, 2004). Limited timelines, race, and the social worker's restriction to "reasonable" efforts in assisting with family preservation have had an impact on reunification. Currently, infants and adolescents are less likely to reunify with their parents due to age. Infants have briefer, stricter time frames, concurrent planning, and are often placed in "fost-adopt" homes (Wulezyn, 2004). Adolescents typically age out of the system as it is harder to find adoptive families for them, and mental health and substance abuse problems make it difficult to locate suitable permanent placements. Adolescents also often run away or are "absent without leave" (AWOL) (Wulezyn, 2004).

Social workers also often face tough decisions around concurrent planning, which involves assessing which children are less likely to reunify with their parents and therefore would most likely need a permanent home that is willing to adopt them. For many social workers with whom this writer spoke, concurrent planning poses additional ethical dilemmas (Mary Draizen, personal communication, 2009). Assessing reunification can be a subjective process, in which the social worker's personal and professional values are often being challenged, while still influencing his or her decision.

It is also difficult to engage parents, and to develop a working relationship with them, when the social worker must reveal that the child could be adopted if reunification fails (Wulezyn, 2004). It could also be argued that when a social worker finds a "good" concurrent home for a child, there may be less effort to reunify. To date, there are no detailed evaluations of the impact of concurrent planning and family reunification, but these concerns are certainly worthy of consideration and further research. The literature also suggests that a social worker's training and communication and engagement skills can alleviate some of the birth parents' and the foster parents' concerns (Wulezyn, 2004).

If parents have multiple problems, family reunification can become more challenging as well (Wulezyn, 2004). Problems can include substance abuse, mental illness, housing problems, financial and economic issues, and the special challenges of being a single parent. These may make it almost impossible to successfully reunify within such a short time period. Research also suggests that one of the primary determinants of successful reunification is the provision of post-reunification services. However, providing these services poses a challenge as maintaining contact between parents and social workers in the context of parents' perceptions of the child welfare system may feel threatening and coercive (Wulezyn, 2004).

At worst, parental rights may be terminated and an adoptive home may not be found, thus leaving the children to face multiple foster homes, schools, and social challenges. Studies suggest that instability has a huge effect on a child's mental health. In fact, many children who enter foster care with no known behavioral problems often leave the system with both behavioral and emotional problems due both to separation from birth parent and poor transitions between placements. Although social workers would like to transition children in the least harmful way, strict time frames sometimes cause the child's emotional well-being to be forgotten (Wulezyn, 2004).

Recidivism. In concluding this section, it is important to state that although reunification is still common, the recidivism rate is very high. Typically, children who reunify and re-enter the foster care system do so within a year. About 70 percent of children who were reunified returned to foster care within a year. Fifty-seven percent returned within three months, and almost 40 percent were back in protective custody within 90 days (Wulezyn, 2004). Over the past 20 years, very little effort has gone into the establishment of meaningful family reunification programs, while over that same period of time adoption incentives have been strengthened (Wulezyn, 2004). This suggests that awareness of the value and importance of family reunification may have to be increased.

Author's Reflection, Reasoning Process, and Resolution

The County Child Welfare Agency's programs support four core values: responsibility, integrity, initiative, and respect. As the agency's policy manual does not define these clearly, this writer asked a few social workers on the staff to help define them. A common response was, simply that they all relate to the provision of services to clients and families (personal communication with colleagues, 2009). The agency reflects a major societal value of family preservation and dignity and worth of a person. The *agency's* mission is to promote well-being and make efforts to keep families intact. However, because of the agency's need to adhere to statewide regulations in various areas, the *community's* perception is that the agency's function and goal are to move children away from birth parents. This may impact consumers of services.

The child welfare system can be difficult to navigate at times, due to agency policies and a bureaucracy that seems to create barriers for clients. Social workers in this setting work closely with families and children to support family preservation. Because the social worker is presumed to have the greatest knowledge of the family's circumstances, parenting abilities, and relationships, it is his or her role to make "objective" recommendations to the court regarding actions on behalf of the child's welfare. However, in spite of the social worker's best efforts, it is almost impossible for her or his personal values and perceptions of the child's best interest not to have a role in the recommendations. This creates the possibility that recommendations to the court may be influenced, to some extent, by individual social workers, and by their perception of the strengths and needs of the parents, as well as by the social, economic, cultural, and other circumstances that may be affecting their meeting reunification plans within the time frame specified by the courts.

This writer's personal values include family, stability for children, self-determination, and respect for family and cultural connections, including language. These values guide both personal life and professional services to clients. It is also recognized that the personal values of birth parents, foster parents, and adoptive parents should be considered highly in planning.

The NASW Code of Ethics (2008) has defined six core values to guide social workers in addressing ethical dilemmas in practice. These are service, social justice, dignity and worth of person, importance of human relationships, integrity, and competence.

In addressing dignity and worth of a person, the Code requires that a social worker should always attempt to resolve tensions between societal values and clients' best interest. The social worker tries to support her perception of the best interest of the child, which may mean additional time for reunification, while agency and societal perceptions of children's best interests support limited time frame guidelines. A clear resolution is not provided, however. One of the complicating factors is the understanding that the worker's perceptions of the child's best interest are also affected by subjective, personal values.

The Code's definition of the importance of human relationships is conveyed in the agency's mission statement, which supports the centrality of family relationships to the child's well-being and the agency's responsibility to the preservation of the child's family. Many families get "lost" in the bureaucratic child welfare system; the social worker's responsibility to competence, also a core value, requires that professional skills be utilized to support family preservation, as the mission statement requires.

Another core value is to provide services in a manner that supports social justice. This means understanding the population that is being served in terms of culture, values, language, and, most importantly, their ties to one another. As part of the effort to serve families in a just manner, social workers' perception of the best interest of the child considers his or her specific context, while statewide guidelines apply equally to everyone.

Alan Gewirth's (1978) statement that human beings have a fundamental right to freedom and well-being seems to address the issues in this dilemma. His hierarchy of personal needs includes the following: (1) basic goods—health, food, shelter, and mental equilibrium; (2) nonsubtractive goods—goods that will not limit a person's ability to achieve their goals, such as acceptable living conditions and reasonable labor; (3) additive goods—such as knowledge, self-esteem, material wealth, education, and recreation, which clearly support a child's right to permanency planning through either family reunification or adoption.

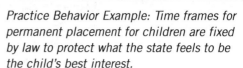

Diversity in Practice

Practice Behavior Example: Time frames for permanent placement for children are fixed by law to protect what the state feels to be the child's best interest.

Critical Thinking Question: Legal time frames ensure consistency and equal treatment, and support the goal of accelerated permanency placement for all children. However, as the author notes, legal time frames do not allow for special circumstances or needs, or account for cultural issues and concerns. Do you believe that variable time frames should be considered in certain circumstances? Can a system be both fair and consistent, allowing for special accommodations as needed, or are the two mutually exclusive?

Options for action may support either side of the dilemma. In support of workers' perception of the best interests of the client, one possible course of action is for social workers to continue to reunify families when possible, as they are currently doing. Although the social worker can influence decision making in regard to a specific case, statewide regulations regarding time frames may supersede her or his recommendations. In such a case, the social worker can advocate for maintenance of a connection with the birth family or siblings. Although it is difficult to return a child to the home environment when the parent is not able to care for him or her, or the social worker encounters policies that make a child's return impossible, a worker could advocate for a placement with extended family, so that the child will be connected to his or her cultural roots and birth family. If the plan is adoption, the worker can first advocate for placement with siblings, if there are any. If this is not possible, the social worker can assist the child and adoptive family to maintain contact with them. Ultimately, in support of state time frames and guidelines, the social worker can support severing all previous ties and a full commitment to the centrality of the adoptive family to the child's best interest.

Although the primary mission of the child welfare system is to support and reunify families and help them thrive in society, strict statewide guidelines can impede reunification, and/or have an influence on recidivism rates. Research on recidivism and programs to assist reunified families has noted a lack of such programs, especially in family situations that involve mental illness or substance abuse. In support of current time-frame guidelines, social workers can advocate for funding and assist in the development of such programs. The fairness and social justice values of the profession also support funding further research studies to determine what services are being offered, and whether these are effective. This is a crucial first step to the success of families reunifying within short time frames.

While it is important to have adoption incentives, it is imperative to emphasize family reunification if the child welfare system is to create a more consistent and coherent approach to supporting family preservation. In addition, advocating at the policy level for more flexible time frames for birth parents in special circumstances would encourage both social workers and parents to work on reunification.

Current state guidelines in regard to time frames were developed in support of society's perception of the child's best interest. Previously, children remained in foster care for indefinite periods, often until they aged out of the system. Children placed in a series of foster homes encountered long-term difficulties, and it was felt that all children had a right to a stable and nurturing home environment. A child cannot be maintained in foster care until the parent is ready to care for him or her. In many cases, parents are never ready, and these children become "legal orphans," which poses other problems for both the state and the children.

Although this writer entered the ethical decision-making process believing that the child's best interest was reunification, and that family preservation was essential, research and deliberation has caused her to reconsider and to support society's determinations of best interest, as these are developed in state time frame guidelines. This writer understands that a child needs a stable home where she or he can create roots and feel grounded. The challenges that many of our families face are at the macro level of practice, and it is often difficult to treat substance abuse or mental illness within a short period of time. Unfortunately, many families this writer's agency currently serves have one or both of these problems. Children need stability and consistency, and they should not be forced to move from one foster home to the next until their parent is ready to care for them. This writer would also advocate that, when possible, the maintenance of sibling and extended family relationships be supported.

Case Study Y *(Melendez)*

Adoption Assistance and Child Welfare Act. (1980). Retrieved from www.laws.adoption.com/statutes/adoption-assistance-and-child-welfare-act-of-1980.htm

Adoption and Safe Families Act. (1997). Retrieved from www.acf.hhs.gov/programs/cb/laws_policies/cblaws/public_law/pl105_89/pl105_89.htm

Bartholet, R. P. (1999). *From child abuse to permanency planning: Child welfare services, pathways, and placements.* New York: Aldine de Gruyter.

Belsky, J. (2003). Etiology of child maltreatment: A developmental-ecological analysis. *Psychological Bulletin, 3,* 413–434.

Bowlby, J. (1988). *A secure base.* New York: Basic Books.

Child Abuse Prevention and Treatment Act. (1974). Retrieved from www.childwelfare.gov/pubs/factshetts/about.cfm

Costin, L. B. (1998). The historical context of child welfare. In J. Laird & A. Hartman (Eds.), *A handbook of child welfare* (pp. 34–60). New York: Free Press.

_____ County Social Services Policy Manual. (1998).

Gewirth, A. (1978). *Reason and morality.* Chicago: University of Chicago Press.

Indian Child Welfare Act. (1978). Retrieved from www.Tribal_institute.org/Lists/Chapter21_icwa.htm

Knorr, K. (2007). The impact of trauma: A developmental framework for infancy and early childhood. *Psychiatric Annals, 37*(6), 108–110.

NASW Code of Ethics. (2008). Retrieved from http://www.socialworkers.org/pubs/code/code.asp

Orfirer, K. (2004). Creating threads of continuity: Helping infants and toddlers through transitions in foster care, *The Source, 13*(2), 1–23.

Schene, P. (1998). *Accountability in nonprofit organizations: A framework for addressing the public interest.* Ann Arbor, MI: UMI Dissertation Information Service.

Smith, C. (2003). Children and welfare reform: Analysis and recommendations. *The Future of Children, 12*(1): 5–25.

Wulezyn, F. (2004). Family reunification. *The future of children,* 14(1).

Case Study Z Preparing a Child for Death: Medical and Religious Considerations

Colette Hottinger, MSW

Practice Context and Case Presentation

Agency Setting. The County Child Welfare Services' Emergency Response Unit, my internship placement, assists individuals and families to achieve economic self-sufficiency, promotes community and family strength, and works to ensure child safety and well-being. I investigate and evaluate cases of reported abuse and neglect of children in order to determine appropriate child welfare service needs for the family. I assess for safety or risk factors that could cause harm to children, including alcohol and drug use, domestic violence, discipline techniques that may result in physical or emotional harm, and sexual abuse, and investigate whether the family's basic needs are being met.

Ethical Problem Encountered. I received a referral for a young family with two sons, aged 2 and 5. The husband is a high school graduate, while the mother dropped out of school when she became pregnant with her first child. The family has been receiving assistance through Child Protective Services, as they were reported by the county hospital for medical neglect of their 2-year-old son, diagnosed with late-stage neuroblastoma of the eye.

Neuroblastoma is a solid cancer that manifests outside of the cranium, and occurs most commonly in childhood and infancy. The hospital states that early symptoms are obvious and should have been noticed by the parents. However, they did not seek care and, by the time the child was admitted to the hospital, the cancer was so advanced that it was identified as fatal. As the hospital had never had a case of neuroblastoma so far advanced, they called experts in the field from the East Coast to help determine the course of care. The family was requested to take the child to numerous time-consuming appointments to try a series of treatments. They committed to the appointments, but, with time, increasingly failed to attend.

The family advocate, the social work supervisor, and I noticed that the family had begun dressing the child in solid white at all times. During home visits, it was also noticed that the family was praying over the 2-year-old, and conducting a series of traditional rituals. The family held strong religious and cultural beliefs, and stated that they would rather have their child at home during his last days than going back and forth to the hospital. They also told me that they wanted to prepare their son for his journey to his afterlife.

The case moved on through a series of court hearings, which considered whether the child should be placed in a foster home that would address his medical needs for care, and take him to his treatment appointments, or whether the investigation should be dropped so that the child could remain at home to spend his remaining time with his family. The hospital believed the treatment could extend the child's life for a time, although the neuroblastoma would eventually be fatal. They advocated for placing the child in a foster home, where such treatment would be enabled and ongoing medical care be provided.

The Central Ethical Issue. According to the NASW Code of Ethics, social workers must respect and promote the right of clients to self-determination and assist clients in their efforts to identify and clarify their goals. However, *parens patriae*, Latin for "the nation as parent" refers to the public policy power of the state to intervene against an abusive or negligent parent, legal guardian, or informal caretaker, and to act as the parent of any child or vulnerable individual who is in need of protection to ensure safety and well-being.

Practice Contexts

Practice Behavior Example: Several agencies may be simultaneously involved in working with the same clients.

Critical Thinking Question: Both Child Protective Services and the hospital are involved with this client and his family. However, the social and ethical responsibilities and mandates of these two agencies might differ. What are some of the differences? What do you view as the potential ethical ramifications of these differences, if any? Do you believe that each agency should work independently out of its own ethical framework and prepare its own recommendation, or do you believe that the social workers of the two agencies should work together to present one joint recommendation to the judge?

The ethical dilemma may be stated as follows:

PARENTAL RIGHTS TO SELF-DETERMINATION V. *PARENS PATRIAE* OBLIGATION OF THE
STATE TO THE CHILD

Research and Related Literature

Literature Review. Neuroblastoma is "a disease in which malignant (cancer) cells form in the nerve tissue of the adrenal gland, neck, chest, or spinal cord," with a potential for spreading elsewhere. It "often begins during early childhood," and, by the time it is diagnosed, has usually spread to the lymph nodes, the bones, bone marrow, liver, and skin (Medicinet.com).

Symptoms of neuroblastoma include lumps, bulging eyes, dark circles around the eyes, bone pain, swollen stomach, weakness, and lumps under the skin (Medicinet.com). These are the signs that the child's physicians believe should have been observed and acted upon by his parents.

The child's age, and the stage of the cancer, affects prognosis, and, according to the Medicinet website, "children with neuroblastoma should have their treatment planned by a team of doctors with expertise in treating childhood CA." Treatments include surgery, radiation therapy, chemotherapy, and, possibly, some of the newly developed therapies (Medicinet.com). It is important to note that, while the child's condition did not appear to be reversible, treatments could treat the pain and prolong life.

Parental Refusal of Treatment. A 1998 study evaluating deaths of children from families in which faith healing was practiced in lieu of medical care, in order to determine if such deaths were preventable, reviewed cases of child fatality in faith-healing sects, and studied the probability of survival for each child, estimated based on the expected survival rates for children with similar disorders who receive medical care (Swan, 1998, pp. 625–629). The sample size, 172 children who died between 1975 and 1995, was identified by referral or record search. The criteria for inclusion was evidence that parents withheld medical care due to their reliance on religious rituals, and sufficient documentation to determine the cause of death (1998, pp. 625–629).

The results revealed that 140 fatalities were from conditions for which survival rates with medical care would have exceeded 90 percent. Eighteen more had expected survival rates of less than 50 percent (1998, pp. 625–629). All but three of the remainder would likely have had some benefit from clinical help. This study concluded that when faith healing is used to the exclusion of medical treatment, the number of preventable child fatalities, and the associated suffering, are substantial and warrant public concern (1998, pp. 625–629). The study suggested that existing laws might be inadequate to protect children from this form of medical neglect.

Legal Status. According to the California *Children's Welfare and Institutions Code*, "severe neglect" occurs when there is negligent failure of a person having the care or custody of a child to protect the child from severe malnutrition or medically diagnosed nonorganic failure to thrive ("California children's welfare," 2012). "Severe neglect" includes those situations of neglect where any person having the care or custody of a child willfully causes or permits the person or health of the child to be placed in a situation such that his or her person or health is endangered, as proscribed by Section 11165.3, including the intentional failure to provide adequate food, clothing, shelter, or medical care ("California Children's Welfare," 2012).

However, it is also documented that a child receiving treatment by spiritual means as provided in Section 16509.1 of the Welfare and Institutions Code, or not receiving specified medical treatment for religious reasons, shall not *for that reason alone* be considered a neglected child ("California Children's Welfare," 2012; emphasis added).

An informed and appropriate medical decision made by parent or guardian after consultation with a physician or physicians who have examined the minor does not constitute neglect. Section 16509.1 states, "No child who in good faith is under treatment solely by spiritual means through prayer in accordance with the tenets and practices of a recognized church or religious denomination by a duly accredited practitioner thereof shall, for that reason alone, be considered to have been neglected within the purview of this chapter" ("California Children's Welfare," 2012).

A study published in the *Journal of American Academy of Pediatrics* argues that "medical neglect" evaluations should focus on the child's needs rather than the caregiver's motivations or justifications. The article further argues that religious objections should not be granted fundamentally different status from other types of objections (Carole, 2007, p. 857). It is asserted that although adults can refuse medical care for themselves, the U.S. Supreme Court has stated that parents do not have the right to deny their children necessary medical care (2007, p. 857). The article cited the case of *Prince* v. *Massachusetts*, which states, "The right to practice religion freely does not include the liberty to expose the community or child to communicable disease, or the latter to ill health or death.... Parents may be free to become martyrs themselves. But it does not follow they are free, in identical circumstances, to make martyrs of their children...." (2007, p. 857).

Patsner notes that while there is legal precedent for a state to intervene where nonintervention would place others at risk, cases where there is no risk to others are less clear (2009, pp. 1–2). He also notes that there have been only few cases where parents have been charged, or threatened to be charged, for "refusing to treat a *potentially* life-threatening condition in their child, and the issue is unclear" (2009, p. 2; emphasis added). He also notes that family law is not federal, and so differs from one state to another, but that no state has developed clear guidelines based on "child's age, level of understanding, type of disease as well as curability by the withheld therapy" (2009, p. 3).

Patsner states that "parents are generally not allowed to sacrifice the lives of their children whose health interests they are supposed to protect..." and notes that this issue is a "classic confrontation" between religion and medical ethics (2009, p. 3).

In Defense of Prayer-Based Care. A study conducted at a palliative care center interviewed 160 terminally ill patients who were diagnosed with 3 months life expectancy. The study's measuring instruments were the spiritual well-being scale, the Hamilton depression rating scale, the Beck hopelessness scale, and the schedule of attitudes toward hastened death (Guy, 2007, pp. 299–306). The results suggested a high correlation between depression and patients who had low spiritual well-being. The study also suggests that spiritual well-being offers some protection against end-of-life despair in those for whom death is imminent (2007, pp. 299–306).

Additional research has asserted that terminally ill children are best cared for in their respective homes. In an article entitled "Improving Care of Dying Children," the author argues that parental attachment and nurturing must not be put aside because a child is dying (Martinson, 1995, pp. 258–262). The greatest importance should be given to making the most out of the limited time left with the child. The author argues for in-home hospice care as well as bereavement counselors that can visit in the home (1995, pp. 258–262).

An article from the University of Rochester Medical Center in the Health Encyclopedia clearly addresses the current issue. It states that "The child and family have the right to refuse treatment. Often, options for treatment are offered which may extend the child's life, but not provide a cure. The quality of life should be considered as well as the possibility of extending it" (University of Rochester Medical Center, p. 1). It is also suggested that "Many families want their loved ones to die at home in their natural and most comfortable setting," and that "Time for anticipatory grieving should be provided when the child is diagnosed with a terminal illness" (p. 1).

Consultation with NASW Code of Ethics. The Preamble of the National Association of Social Workers' Code of Ethics states the profession's primary values, and those that seem most related to this ethical dilemma are dignity and worth of the person and social justice (NASW, Preamble, 2008). The Ethical Principles that build on these two values are "Social workers respect the inherent dignity and worth of person," and "Social workers challenge social injustice." These concepts are quite broad, and clearer direction may be found in exploring the Ethical Standards of the Code, which are more specific.

Social workers should do their best to ensure that their clients have the information about services and resources that they need for decision making. Ethical Standard One addresses social workers' commitment to clients (NASW, 2008). These include: "The social worker has a primary responsibility to promote wellbeing of clients. In general, clients' interests are primary. However, social workers' responsibility to the larger society or specific legal obligations may on limited occasions supersede the loyalty owed clients, and clients should be so advised" (NASW, 1.01, 2008), and "Social workers may limit clients' right to self-determination when, in the social workers' professional judgment, clients' actions or potential actions pose a serious, foreseeable, and imminent risk to themselves or others" (NASW, 1.02, 2008).

Also relevant is a consideration of Section 1.05 of the Code, which addresses cultural competence and social diversity, and states that "Social workers should understand culture and its function in human behavior and society, recognizing the strengths that exist in all cultures" (NASW, 1.05a, 2008). It also states that "Social workers should have a knowledge base of their clients' cultures and be able to demonstrate competence in the provision of services that are sensitive to clients' cultures and to differences among people and cultural groups" (NASW, 1.05b, 2008). Social workers should also "obtain education about and seek to understand the nature of social diversity and oppression with respect to race, ethnicity, and national origin" (NASW, 1.05c., 2008).

The sixth ethical standard also provides some guidance, although remaining fairly general. It suggests that workers must "promote the general welfare of society" and "advocate for living conditions conducive to the fulfillment of basic human needs" (6.01) as well as ensuring that both cultural values and institutions are "compatible with the realization of social justice" (NASW, 2008, 6.01). These would suggest that the worker has a responsibility to assist clients to meet basic human needs, which would include health care and pain relief. This standard also suggests an obligation to find a way to merge "cultural values and institutions" with "social justice"(NASW, 2008, 6.01). In this case, "cultural values" (the family's religious values) and "institutions" (the hospital) do not agree, and "social justice" might involve finding a way to reconcile the two such that the client's "basic human needs" might be met.

Section 6.04b (NASW, 2008, 6.04b) states that social workers should "act to expand choice and opportunity" with a special regard for vulnerable people. Children are considered to be a vulnerable population—even more so when suffering and in pain. The child's parents might not be acting in his best interests as determined by broader society, especially in terms of pain relief. In this case, the judge represents society's interests and the social worker must determine whether it is in the child's best interest to intervene to ensure access to health care and pain relief. This complex theoretical issue—of parental rights to follow their religion when it affects children's well-being—becomes a social work issue when specific recommendations must be made.

Theories and Principles. Of the ethical guidelines for decision making based on theories and principles, I feel that Alan Gewirth's principles are the most suitable for addressing legal and ethical issues in practice. He recognizes that the individual's principles may at times conflict with the principles of others, and that choices are sometimes necessary among ethical principles. I believe that a person has the right to intervene if another person's rights or well-being are being violated. Gewirth grounds the basis of the intervention on the person's ability to act in the future, should present rights and well-being be violated. I also agree with Gewirth that a client's right to privacy can be overridden if there is a risk of danger to the client or others. Gewirth's rankings of values and goods addresses the needs of vulnerable people generally and also of medically fragile and terminally ill children.

However, the general ethical theory that I believe most applicable to the current ethical dilemma is Carol Gilligan's Ethics of Care, which suggests that individuals are interdependent. I believe that relationships influence actions and provide a contextual background for both making and understanding decisions. In this case, the parents have a strong belief in their religion, and place faith above the physicians' perception of his medical needs. The Ethics of Care would support empathy and understanding in working with these parents.

Agency and Hospital's Mission and Principles. My agency's programs and units work to achieve and maintain the highest standards of quality by supporting community-based and client-focused collaborations and partnerships, and value learning practices throughout the organization, including continuous quality improvement, development, and innovation. Thus, the agency would support learning to understand the client's belief system and attempting to work within it to meet the needs of the child.

Agency values also include respecting and honoring the diversity, rights, and dignity of staff as well as clients, with the health and well-being of children as the top priority. This is supported through a wide range of programs designed to protect or prevent child neglect and abuse. The agency and its staff members use a set of practice protocols to guide their decision-making and to develop appropriate interventions. These practice protocols are consonant with the agency's mission and values. Although the agency respects the diversity and integrity of its clients, the top priority is child safety and well-being. Religious protocol respects a family's right to religious practice unless it impedes the child's imminent safety. Usually detention petitions are filed with the courts in cases of medical neglect (_____ Policy Manual, 2009).

The goal of the hospital caring for the child is to provide state-of-the-art care in a warm and supportive environment that includes ongoing direct communication with a primary care physician. The hospital places treatment and communication with patients and families along with medical progress in treatment as its top priority, which naturally conflicts with the parent's refusal to accept treatment (_____ Hospital Policy and Procedure Manual, 2012).

Author's Reflection, Reasoning Process, and Resolution

In addition to the above information, it is essential to consider the specific values and beliefs which influence this ethical decision, as well as the available options and resources for addressing the issues involved before arriving at a resolution of the dilemma.

Personal Value Base. I was raised in an Evangelical Christian home, with the philosophy that human beings by nature were evil and born with sin, and that it was not until a person was saved, born again, or forgiven for all their sins that they truly were a person who had a life deemed acceptable both in eyes of God and of the Christian congregation. Because I grew up in a religiously affiliated home, I can empathize with the family's need to conduct religious ceremonies to get the child right with God before his death. I see the difficulty the family may have in viewing the world through the lenses of science-based evolutionary theory.

I believe that people do not want to cause harm to others, or cause others to experience pain. I believe that human beings value their own lives, as well as the lives of others. I do, however, believe that when a person's well-being is threatened, it can override concern for others, manifesting in changes in emotional, financial, physical, and mental states. In this case, the parents feel a need for the preservation of the beliefs and rituals that are an integral part of themselves, thus placing themselves in opposition to the medical establishment.

I believe that the goal human life is to pass ethical and moral values to offspring. The last and most important act the parents can do, in this case, is instill their moral and religious beliefs in their dying child.

I have a difficult time believing in "the good" for an overall majority, as I don't feel that individuals' needs can always best be met through a "majority rules" society. I believe that the needs of all people are equally important. Individuals contribute to the overall good of society, and in return society contributes to the overall good of individuals. I consider myself a subjectivist, because I believe each individual has a different view of what constitutes right and wrong, and has the ability to mold their lives through free will.

When I am confronted with a professional ethical dilemma, I turn first to my own value system, then to my agency's policies, the NASW Code of Ethics, and law. If there is a conflict between my personal value system and the agency's or the profession's codes, I would seek consultation with my supervisor, always placing the needs of the child first and advocating for changes in policies which are detrimental to my clients.

Values of the Affected System. I feel that the child who is my client would choose to remain with his mother and father, in a comfortable and familiar environment. At 2 years of age, his concept of death is not well-developed, and he would certainly choose to remain with his parents rather than being placed in a foster home with medical treatments. From an attachment viewpoint, the child feels most safe and secure in the care of his mother.

The family's support network shares religious and cultural beliefs, and prayer and unity with others appears to be their best option at this time. The parents were told the child is terminally ill, and they wish him to be comfortable surrounded by loved ones. The parents feel overwhelmed and ashamed in the medical institution, and would rather let the child live out the remainder of his life in peace.

Societal Values. I believe society values their perception of the best interest of the child above cultural or religious factors. Life preservation, no matter how temporary, seems to take precedence over quality of life. I think this may be because the general population fears death. Individuals also tend to be valued above families and groups. Through this review of research and policies related to this case study, I have understood that society has determined that neglecting medical attention is a form of abuse, even when the child is terminally ill. Legally, therefore, a family bereavement process which takes place in lieu of the child being medically cared for is deemed maltreatment in this society.

Options/Choices for Action. An option that might collapse the dilemma would seek to locate resources that would allow for the child to stay at home with his family while receiving treatment, perhaps involving a hospice or palliative care nurse, home care, or home-based medical treatment.

Another option is to work to educate the family about neuroblastoma and its treatments. The family could very well not understand the reasons for the physician's recommendations for their son's treatment. Medical personnel using advanced terminology may not be clearly understood by the parents, and a clearer and more concrete approach to medical information might assist them to have a better understanding of the goals of the medical team. Conversely, the healthcare staff can benefit from a better understanding of the family's cultural and religious beliefs. I could attempt to facilitate understanding and communication between family and healthcare establishment, grounded in their common interest in care for the child.

As another option, I could attempt to advocate for the child to remain in the home utilizing the recommendation portion of the detention report, and submit this to court. Because the child's fatal diagnosis is due to a medical condition that was not directly caused by the parents, family unity and familiar surroundings for the child could be preserved until his death.

However, one could also argue that the parents medically neglected the child by not bringing him in for his regular medical exams, prior to the development of his neuroblastoma. Had the parents provided for regular healthcare visits, the early onset symptoms could have been caught, and treatment begun at a point where there could have been success in preserving the child's life. Placement in a foster home would ensure medical attention and relief of pain.

Resolution of Dilemma. Because I believe that the child's feelings and life experiences should be the primary consideration, I would seek to resolve the dilemma in a way that best meets his needs. Family love and support appear to be paramount in the child's needs hierarchy. Sensitive to religious and cultural values, I would seek to ensure the best possible quality of life for the child in the time he has left by attempting to support both child and family in their efforts to prepare for his death. Child Protective Services' claim that the child was being medically neglected did not take into account religious treatments that were being followed as alternatives to western medical practices. However, I would monitor the child to observe for imminent danger, in which case further interventions would be necessary. Therefore, I would argue against the child entering foster care at this time.

I would implement this decision by collaborating with other professionals involved, and write my recommendation letter to the judge, advocating for the family's wishes to keep the child in his home. I would also identify resources for the family regarding in-home medical treatment and have this alternative plan included in my recommendation letter to the court.

Case Study Z (*Hottinger*)

California Children's Welfare and Institutions Code. (2012). Retrieved from http://www.aroundthecapitol.com/code/Welfare_and_Institutions_Code.html

Carole, J. (2007). Recognizing and responding to medical neglect. *Pediatrics, 127*(3), 857.

Guy, M. (2007). The desire for death in the setting of terminal illness: A case discussion. *Physicians Post Graduate Press, 8*(5), 299–306.

_____ Hospital Policy and Procedure Manual. (2011).

Martinson, I. M. (1995). Improving care of dying children (In Caring for Patients at the End of Life [Special Issue]). *Western Journal of Medicine, 163*, 258–262.

Medicinet, www.medicinet.com, downloaded May 9, 2012.

Patsner, B. (2009, June). *Faith versus medicine: When a parent refuses a child's medical care.* Health and Law Perspectives, Health and Law Policy Institute, University of Houston Law Center, http://www.law.uh.edu/healthlaw/perspectives/

_____ Policy Manual. (2011).

Swan, R. (1998). Child fatalities from religion-motivated medical neglect. *Pediatrics, 101*(4), 625–629.

University of Rochester Medical Center. *For parents: Important decisions to be made in the dying process.* Health Encyclopedia, http://www.urmc.rochester.edu/encyclopedia/content/asx? downloaded May 9, 2012.

CHAPTER SUMMARY

Ethical Standard Six addresses the responsibilities of social workers to the broader society. Unlike the commitment to a specific client, where the ethical responsibilities may be conflicted, but are generally quite clear and specific, the social worker's responsibilities to broader society are more abstract, more general, and thus much more subject to interpretation by all involved: social work professionals, agencies, governmental bodies, and "society," however one might define it. Defined narrowly in terms of a specific community, responsibilities to society may be easier to determine, and can be grounded in ethical principles and also in cultural norms and relationship patterns, traditions, preferences, and belief systems. Defined more broadly, society becomes a more abstract mixture of groups with varying interests, values, traditions, and relationships with each other, and must include a consideration of the dominance of certain groups, inequality of access to goods and services, power differentials, and differences in priorities. On a global level, the responsibility to ensure the ability to meet basic human needs for all people has proven to be a very challenging task.

Standard Six is the briefest of the standards included in the Code of Ethics, having only four subsections, each stating ethical responsibilities in broad and abstract terms. Subsection 6.01, social welfare, includes a responsibility to "the general welfare of society, from local to global levels..." and advocates for basic human needs and social justice for all people. Subsection 6.02 states a commitment to "the facilitation of informed participation" by all members of society in developing social policies and designing institutions.

Unlike the other three sections, subsection 6.03 provides clear and concrete direction, stating that social workers are responsible for providing professional services in public emergencies. The profession's commitment to this has been clearly evident both nationally during natural disasters, such as hurricanes and floods, terrorism, and other emergencies, and internationally, as social workers have been active participants in missions to other countries suffering from wars, famines, natural disasters, and civil unrest.

The final subsection, 6.04, includes ethical principles that have been noted in previous standards of the Code, and applies them here on a societal, rather than an individual, level. Thus, social workers should advocate for social and political action to enhance all people's ability to access basic goods and services and to develop fully, with a special consideration for those members of society who are vulnerable, oppressed, and exploited, and with respect for both social and cultural diversity. This responsibility includes preventing discrimination, and includes pursuing activities in the political area as well.

Each of the cases included in this chapter is framed to include a responsibility to the broader society. The first and second cases have been placed together so that the reader can consider commonalities and differences: both involve the responsibility to confidentiality and the potential for harm to the broader society. However, the two social workers ultimately have chosen opposite courses of action, and it is important to follow their reasoning and to determine one's own potential course of action should this kind of dilemma arise.

In "A Journey to Moral Action," the author has taken us on a journey that has been shared by many workers in her field placement, who consider this a "classic case" of competing ethical obligations. The ethical dilemma occurs in a host setting—a hospital—thus involving not only social–work related principles and concerns, but also laws and regulations of the host setting. Ultimately, the course of action selected affects the reputation and position of the hospital and all of the professions functioning within it. In considering the dilemma of potential for injury and death to third parties in society, and patient rights to confidentiality, this writer has determined that her greater obligation is to the protection of life.

The teenager who told his social worker that he plans to resume dealing drugs constitutes another potential for harm to society. Here again, the social worker must balance her obligation to confidentiality for the client with the possible harm his actions might cause in his school and community. One of her considerations was the almost certain fact that should this teen agree not to deal drugs, he would most probably simply be replaced with another, so that the "harm" to society would occur in either case. Ultimately, the social worker determined that her responsibility to client confidentiality, and to keeping the client in treatment, supersedes her obligation to society.

Outpatient Commitment for mentally ill people is the subject of the next case, with a consideration of the possible limitations on freedom that this entails, as well as the potential for harm to self or others in society as people become involuntary clients. As a "forced treatment," outpatient commitment limits freedom and requires medication management and accountability on the part of patients. Yet the alternative, inpatient commitment, further restricts freedoms, although it offers protection for society from potential harms. The author believed that self-determination must be predicated upon competence. If a mentally ill person complies with medication, becomes stable, and *then* decides to refuse treatment, his right to refuse should be respected. Thus, she has determined that involuntary commitment and treatment may be necessary steps toward "ensuring optimal self-determination."

The right to self-determination was also the central issue when the subject of hoarding in the context of multi-unit housing for elders was addressed, but there was also the underlying issue of safety and the prevention of harm to the client living in extreme clutter. The well-being of "society" in this instance referred to the other elderly residents in the housing complex, who may be exposed to the danger of fire should the client's hoarding be permitted to continue unchecked. If the client has the right to choose self-determination over personal safety, how should this impact the rights of other residents? Ultimately, the social worker has determined that the client does not seem to be able to comprehend the potential dangers to herself and to her neighbors should her cluttering continue. Her professional obligation to prevent harm was primary, and she referred the client for evaluation to the Department of Health.

In restructuring time frames for permanency planning for young children, societal laws reflect both values and knowledge. The integrity and primacy of the family is a deeply held societal value. Children, our society believes, are nurtured best in a stable, consistent, loving home, and it is the responsibility to society, in its role as ultimate *parens patriae*, to support the well-being of families. While priority is clearly given to the biological bond, and thus to assisting families whose children have been removed due to abuse or neglect to reunify with them, strong consideration is given to the well-being of the child. This well-being consists of having a stable placement as early in life as possible, in order to form strong and positive attachments to parents and other family members. Permanency planning policies have shortened time frames to support the best interest of the child. Because the biological parents may be working with serious issues, which take a longer time to resolve, they may lose the opportunity to reunify. Should time frames remain the same, ensuring equal treatment and equal opportunities for all parents, or should they be adjusted individually dependent on parental needs and goals? Ultimately, the author found that society's responsibility was primarily to the well-being of the child, and therefore that briefer time frames for permanency placements were in the best interest of the child, who was the primary client.

The last case has addressed an issue that recurs dramatically with a certain frequency. It explored the limits of parental rights in our society. The specific case presented addressed the parents' wish to withhold medical treatment for their dying child, believing that religion, ritual, and the presence of community members was more effective in addressing this 2-year old's needs. They had not taken their child for treatment when symptoms developed, and his condition was now fatal.

The social worker, whose role under *parens patriae* was to investigate cases of possible abuse or neglect, and to make recommendations to the court, had to determine the role of the state, and her own role as the state's representative. She eventually determined that the two-year old's best interest was to remain with his parents, especially since treatments would only prolong life, not cure his illness.

Each of these cases include an interesting paradox in addressing the ethical responsibilities of social workers to society: the client, rather than standing apart from society, is herself or himself a *member* of the society as well. The "rights" of members of the society apply to herself or himself also. This requires careful consideration on the part of the social worker: limiting client rights in a particular instance potentially supports limiting those rights for all members of the society. The way in which "harms" are defined must apply to the client as well as to the society. Rather than standing in opposition to each other, "client" and "society" are inextricably interwoven.

The following questions will test your knowledge of the content found within this chapter. For questions 1-6, please select the phrase that best completes each sentence. Question 7 is a brief essay question. For additional assessment, including licensing-exam type questions on applying chapter content to practice behaviors, visit **MySearchLab**.

1. Standard 6.01 states that social workers have a global responsibility to work toward:
   a. addressing basic human needs
   b. gathering input from others
   c. the United States taking a leadership role
   d. fulfilling professional needs

2. "Public" emergencies might include all except:
   a. major floods
   b. epidemics
   c. domestic violence
   d. severe hurricanes

3. The Code of Ethics states that participation in social and political action:
   a. is strongly encouraged
   b. must remain a personal choice
   c. is dependent upon agency policy
   d. is a professional responsibility

4. Loewenberg, Dolgoff, and Harrington's Ethical Principles Screen ranks _____ as the highest obligation.
   a. protection of biological life
   b. self-determination
   c. client confidentiality
   d. least harm

5. Beauchamp and Childress' four principles for ethical decision making:
   a. rank autonomy as the highest principle
   b. rank social justice last
   c. do not rank the principles
   d. suggest that each person should rank the principles according to personal values

6. Social workers' responsibilities to society:
   a. come before responsibilities to any one individual
   b. are embedded in law
   c. should be determined by the society itself
   d. should maximize goods and minimize harms

7. Subsection 6.04 of the Ethical Standard states that social workers should engage in political and social actions addressing basic human needs, opportunities, and social justice. However, no particular party, platform, or group is suggested as representing these social work ethical principles. Several political groups address these issues very differently, so that a social worker presumably could act to promote their individual perception of social work goals through widely divergent approaches. Might this mean that social workers can take opposing positions on ways to meet the same goals? What might be the impact on the profession of such divergent political and social actions?

Index